ID0787880

Nobody's Burden

Nobody's Burden

Lessons from the Great Depression on the Struggle for Old-Age Security

Edited by Ruth E. Ray and Toni Calasanti

LEXINGTON BOOKS
Lanham • Boulder • New York • Toronto • Plymouth, UK

Published by Lexington Books
A wholly owned subsidiary of The Rowman & Littlefield Publishing Group, Inc.
4501 Forbes Boulevard, Suite 200, Lanham, Maryland 20706
http://www.lexingtonbooks.com

Estover Road, Plymouth PL6 7PY, United Kingdom

Copyright © 2011 by Lexington Books

All rights reserved. No part of this book may be reproduced in any form or by any
electronic or mechanical means, including information storage and retrieval systems,
without written permission from the publisher, except by a reviewer who may quote
passages in a review.

British Library Cataloguing in Publication Information Available

Library of Congress Cataloging-in-Publication Data

Nobody's burden : lessons from the Great Depression on the struggle for old-age security
/ edited by Ruth E. Ray and Toni Calasanti.
    p. cm.
  Includes index.
  ISBN 978-0-7391-6531-7 (cloth : alk. paper)
  1. Old age assistance—United States—Case studies. 2. Older people—Services for—
United States—History—20th century. 3. Older people—United States—Social
conditions—20th century. 4. Older people—United States—Economic conditions—20th
century. 5. Depressions—1929—United States. 6. United States—Social conditions—
1918-1932. I. Ray, Ruth E., 1954- II. Calasanti, Toni M.
  HV1461.N63 2011
  362.6'3097309043—dc23
                                2011018910

♾™ The paper used in this publication meets the minimum requirements of American
National Standard for Information Sciences—Permanence of Paper for Printed Library
Materials, ANSI/NISO Z39.48-1992.

Printed in the United States of America

Contents

Acknowledgments

The editors and authors wish to thank the following for their assistance in the research and writing of this book:

Jo Johnson, chair of the Westland (Michigan) Historical Commission and the Friends of Eloise and head of the Eloise Museum, for her assistance in obtaining historical source material on Eloise.

Susan Connelly Murphy, former student in the Master's of Library and Information Science program at Wayne State University and current owner and principal consultant of Connelly Information LLC, for her assistance in conducting archival research and identifying historical source material on Eloise and the Detroit Department of Public Welfare.

Susan Marie Potter, former student in the Master's of Library and Information Science program at Wayne State University for her assistance in finding historical sources on private charities during the Great Depression.

Tim Wintermute, Executive Director of the Luella Hannan Memorial Foundation, for supplying newspaper articles on the formation of the LHMH and the first annual report of the LHMH, along with access to the employment files of LHMH staff and the minutes of the Board of Trustees meetings during the Great Depression. Tim has expressed interest and provided encouragement and support for this project all along.

Mike Smith, Director of the Walter Reuther Library of Labor and Urban Affairs, for permission to use images from the case files and a photograph from the historical collection. Thanks to Mike, too, for opening the archives on a Friday in September just for Toni Calasanti, even though the library was closed for staff development. We also thank all of the staff in the reading room of the Reuther Library for the many hours they spent bringing boxes of case files to us.

The Wayne State University Humanities Center for a small grant in 2008 to support the Hannan Archival Research Group.

The Wayne State University College of Liberal Arts and Sciences and the Department of English for financial assistance to create the index for this book.

The Institute for Society, Culture, and Environment and The Center for Gerontology at Virginia Tech for financial support to explore the archives.

Chapter 1

Studying the "Burden" of Age: The Work of the Hannan Archival Research Group

Ruth E. Ray

"Life has a burden for everyone's shoulder.
None can escape from its trouble snare.
Miss it in youth, it will come when you're older
And fit you as close as the garment you wear."

This verse represents a common attitude toward life during the Great Depression and toward old age in general. It was included in a letter sent in June, 1930, from a retired minister to his social worker, reminding her of the "kind promise to get the doctor for me" and expressing concern that, "I am not too great a burden to you" (Luella Hannan Memorial Foundation Collection, Case #122). This was a time before New Deal safety nets were established by the Franklin D. Roosevelt administration in 1935, including unemployment insurance, disability benefits, and old-age insurance. Older people (anyone over the age of forty) were discriminated against in the job market, and few employers offered pensions. The working and middle-classes were expected to make money for as long as possible, eking out a living as best they could in sales, sewing, or housekeeping when manual labor, trade and professional positions were no longer available to them. Many older people rented out rooms in their homes and apartments for income. There was no national health insurance, and people paid for whatever health care they received out of pocket, unless they were poor enough to be taken in by city clinics and

1

hospitals as charity cases. When they could no longer support themselves, old people were expected to live with their children, who were legally obligated to support their parents, or to rely on extended family or friends. If "self-supporting" is the measure of a good old age, old people *were* a burden to themselves (they worried constantly about becoming and being a burden), their families, and society. In 1955, Eleanor Roosevelt, writing a foreword on the subject of "Social Responsibility for Individual Welfare," declared the social insurance policies of her husband's administration to have been a great relief to American society as a whole in relieving this burden: "I can remember when we started old age pensions. Now the idea is not very shocking to us—a mutual contribution towards this security in old age. We started care for the blind and the crippled. Many said that it was simply a humanitarian gesture, but it was more than that. It is a real insurance so that they will not remain a burden on society" (xxxv-xxxvi).

One of the great American fears then, as now, was the loss of independence. As feminist theorist Eva Kittay points out, a founding premise of democratic liberal ideology is that all people should be "free and independent equals." Yet this notion is "belied by empirical reality" and ignores the fact that dependencies and "asymmetries" (differing aptitudes and abilities) are inherent in the human condition. It also ignores the experiences of most women, who play the primary role in tending to dependent people and who, because they have internalized this role, are more likely than men to be concerned about "burdening" others with their own care when they are old (Kittay 1999, 4). To deny the fact of dependency and dependent people of all ages, at all periods in life, and to deny the dependency work of those who care for them, is to deny what it means to be human. Kittay's argument, which reflects the beliefs of most feminists who study the ethics of care, is that a social justice agenda must acknowledge, respect and fully support dependent people, dependency work, and all those who do such work.

In this book, we pursue various aspects of this agenda in terms of theory and practice, taking an historical approach to put a human face on old age and to advocate for social change in elder care. We draw evidence from case files kept by a private organization, the Luella Hannan Memorial Home (LHMH) in Detroit, Michigan, which granted pensions to a select group of old people just before and during the Great Depression. It is only coincidental that the LHMH began to assist the elderly poor in the year that the Great Depression struck. In 1925, when Luella

Hannan established the trust that supported this effort, Detroit was enjoying a period of intense growth and prosperity. Historian Kevin Boyle describes 1925 Detroit as "America's great boomtown, an industrial juggernaut of unprecedented power" that "coursed with cash." That year, Detroit's leading retailer, J. L. Hudson, built a twenty-one-story high department store, the tallest in the world, and the city was flooded with immigrants and other new residents seeking greater opportunities for employment and entertainment (Boyle 2004, 3). The main appeal of the city, of course, was the prosperity created by a thriving auto industry, which Boyle describes as "the industrial version of the gold rush." Not only did Henry Ford perfect the assembly line in Detroit, which allowed for the mass production of affordable Model Ts, but other auto makers converged on the city as well; the Dodge brothers and Walter Chrysler created sprawling plants to rival Ford's, and smaller machine shops and parts plants were developed to support them. Boyle concludes that this industrial "frenzy transformed Detroit itself into a great machine. By 1925, its grand boulevards were shadowed by stark factory walls and canopied by tangles of telephone lines and streetcar cables" (Boyle 2004, 14). The population at the time was 1.25 million, and the city seemed, to residents and outsiders alike, to be electric with possibilities. Indeed, Boyle quotes a magazine reporter who wrote at the time, "Detroit is Eldorado. It is staccato American. It is shockingly dynamic" (Boyle, 14).

Yet many of Detroit's elders, left widowed and penniless, beset by health problems and unable to work, or unsuccessful in their efforts to compete with the thousands of younger people flooding the job market, struggled to get by with little or no income. In 1925, Luella Hannan, widow of wealthy real estate investor William W. Hannan, established a trust to support older people who found themselves in just these circumstances. The fund was specifically developed "for the purpose of founding, building, and maintaining a home for aged or infirm persons of the City of Detroit, Wayne County, Michigan, who have been accustomed to enjoying the comforts of life, but who, through change of fortune, have come to reduced circumstances." Luella Hannan had seen many of her own friends and associates fall on hard times in old age and wished to provide a better alternative to the dreaded county poor house. In accordance with her wishes, between 1925 and 1928, the LHMH Board of Trustees attempted to buy property in a prominent suburb of Detroit but met resistance from local residents who protested that an old-age home would diminish their property values. Therefore, shortly before her death

in 1928, Mrs. Hannan abandoned the idea of building a home and requested that the trustees support older people in their own homes.

This effort began in January of 1929, and the first client was funded
in March of that year. Additionally, that spring the LHMH began to administer money from another fund, the John Scudder Trust for Old
People, established in 1925 by humanitarian John Scudder, a friend of
Luella Hannan's, "to aid, in the broadest manner, in the care of elderly
people without means of support" and to do so "without regard to race,
creed, sex or color." The Scudder Trust shared the same trustees, social
work staff, and application process as the LHMH, but the funds were
initially kept separate and the money dispensed on the basis of different
criteria. The Luella Hannan Memorial Foundation Collection (LHMFC),
which is now located in the Walter Reuther Library of Labor and Urban
Affairs on the campus of Wayne State University, includes all the applications and documents related to the administration of both funds. We
examine what it was like to live into old age during the Great Depression, as represented in these case files.

Age and Gender Issues

For the LHMH, "old" meant sixty years of age or older for women and
65 years of age or older for men.[1] These earlier understandings of old
age, though historically accurate, are contested today, when the average
retirement age of sixty-five is considered closer to midlife than old age
(or at least the "youth" of old age). However, in 1929, when the first
LHMH pension was granted, white women (the majority of LHMH
clients) who had reached the age of twenty had an average life expectancy of sixty-nine; for white men, it was sixty-six; for black women (one
client) it was fifty-seven; and for black men (one client) it was fifty-six
(U.S. Department of Health and Human Services 2007).

As we will see, despite being culturally constructed as "old" at the
age of sixty or sixty-five, in 1929, as now, there was considerable diversity among the population of elders in terms of health, ability, and overall
attitude toward aging. Some clients were truly frail and dependent, even
at the age of sixty. Others appeared "much younger than their years" to
the social workers that investigated their cases, and these clients tried to
stay independent for as long as possible. Consider, for example, the case
of a woman who applied for a pension in May 1930, at the age of ninety-

two. She had been selling expensive lingerie on a commission basis in an exclusive area of the city, sometimes making as much as $200 a month, until she fell at the age of eighty-eight and was unable to continue this work. At the time of her application, she was still actively working in sales, trying to make a living by selling greeting cards from home. Other clients were made anxious by their longevity. In the case of one seventy-seven year old woman, the social worker notes that "she cannot understand how anyone her age can possibly continue to be in such good health as she is enjoying. . . . [S]he states that all members of her family have lived to an old age, and she supposes she will do the same. However, she dreads thinking of living to be a burden to anyone" (LHMFC, Case #92).

Some older people themselves challenged the definition of "old age" established by the LHMH for its applicants. One eighty year-old woman who wrote to the organization after reading in the *Detroit Free Press* about its newly established fund for "aged people" of sixty or sixty-five, begs to differ: "I do not call that *aged*—only for those that are broken down in ill health or financially at that age" (LHMFC, Case #72, emphasis added). In another case, a woman's obsessive need to appear younger endangered her prospects for receiving a pension. Because of certain evasions during her 1929 intake interview, the LHMH requested that the woman undergo a psychiatric evaluation as part of the investigation of her case. The woman explained to the psychiatrist that, when she was a child, her paternal grandmother had been so bad tempered that the woman had become afraid of her and "dreaded the thought of . . . ever becoming old and cross like her." From that time on, the woman had never told her age to anyone and would not allow family members to talk about their ages. By 1929, she had kept her age a secret for so long that she no longer knew it herself. The psychiatrist noted in his letter to the LHMH that he could not get an accurate history of the woman because "she pleads ignorance of the date of almost any incident in the life of others of her family as well as herself," which he describes as a "peculiar blindspot which she has acquired in relation to age and time relations." He concludes that, at this stage in her life, the "distortion must be accepted as part of her mental pattern" and could not be changed (LHMFC, Case #197). This latter case, especially, reflects the negative connotations that many associated with the word "old" and the experience of aging in early twentieth century America.[2] Haber and Gratton confirm that during the industrial era, the medical model of aging became predominant and, in conjunction with a culture that valued youth, vitality, and productivity, life after age sixty, indeed, life after forty, was expected to bring increasing weakness, frailty and dependence. According to popular advice literature of the time, "in order not to look 'out of date,' old-fashioned, or unemployable, the public was advised to avoid any hint of oncoming senescence" through hair dye, corsets, face creams or other measures that would mask the signs of aging (Haber and Gratton 1994, 165).

The fact that few people "retired" before the onset of Social Security meant that men were expected to support themselves and their families indefinitely. This is why the LHMH had fewer single male applicants (20 percent) and couples (18 percent) than female applicants (62 percent) during this period. Even men in great financial distress were ashamed to apply for assistance. They would first rely on informal personal sources, including friends, neighbors, and landlords, for as long as possible before seeking help from charitable organizations. One seventy-one year-old man who applied for a pension in December of 1929 said he had been living "on the kindness of others" for several months. Once a real estate agent who had also sold stocks and bonds, he had recently been employed as a salesman for a concrete products company on a commission basis. Although still employed, his income had gradually decreased until he was earning nothing at all. He owed four weeks back rent for his seven dollars a week room and forty-four dollars to a boarding house for fifty-five meals he had eaten on credit. He stated that he was reluctant to ask for financial assistance, as he had never done so before, but the landlady and boarding house mother were "pressing him for money, but in a nice way." When he finally came into the LHMH office to apply for a pension, he had three cents in his pocket. After investigation, the man was granted a fifty dollar monthly pension, with the stipulation that his association with the concrete company be "continued as before if it is satisfactory with [the owner of the company] so that the man will still feel that he is of some use in the world" (LHMFC, Case #334). In other cases, the LHMH granted men temporary relief until such time as they could support themselves, as in Case #44, a sixty-eight year-old former mineralogist who was given seven dollars a week for a short time, plus a twenty dollar advance to "establish himself in the peanut business."

Several other cases that were not funded illustrate the emotional challenges that old men, in particular, faced when seeking assistance from a charitable organization. A seventy-three year-old man who had formerly owned a painting and wallpaper-hanging business was living with his daughter-in-law and granddaughter in 1930, his son having died suddenly the previous year, leaving his wife in debt. The daughter-in-law could not pay the back taxes on her home and wanted to move to Texas to live with her son from a previous marriage. She was desperate to find a home in Detroit for the old man so that she could leave the state. When the social worker called to interview him, she found "at times his voice would choke and tears come into his eyes and he would shake his head to think he had been reduced to where he had to seek charity or be a burden upon the Community Fund" (LHMFC, Case #367). Investigation of the case continued for a while and then was dropped when the man disappeared, presumably having moved in with friends.

Men in general were also more reluctant than women to sign over their remaining assets in exchange for care, which was required by most old-age homes, including the LHMH. They were also more likely to resent the oversight of social workers and the attempts of charitable organizations to exert control over their affairs. One man, age seventy-six, once a prominent real estate investor who claimed to have known William W. Hannan himself, was ailing and nearly destitute by the time he applied for an LHMH pension in October, 1929. The man walked with two canes due to a badly dislocated hip; his right arm was "useless" and his memory poor due to a stroke suffered three years earlier; he had a "bad rupture on his left side caused by abscesses, spread from his hip"; his glasses no longer fit, and he needed dental care. However, he withdrew his application when the LHMH required that he either sell (at a considerable loss) or sign over three rental properties which, though they generated little income, were the only remaining assets he had to bequeath to his widowed daughter and her children. Another sixty-nine year-old man who applied for assistance in March, 1929, was granted five dollars per week but declined the help, having secured some work playing the violin and wanting to remain self-supporting for as long as possible. This decision cost him dearly; when he applied again in November of that year, his temporary employment having ended, the LHMH had exhausted its funds, and his application was denied.

The Hannan Archival Research Group

In the following pages, we draw evidence from a body of 508 applications for pensions submitted to the LHMH between 1927 and 1934, along with extensive case notes on those who were granted pensions, to explore a number of questions that concern gerontologists and the general public today. Old age is still a "social problem" in the sense that feminist historian Linda Gordon uses the phrase: "An issue that is of concern even to those who do not directly experience it, one which creates an experienced threat to the social order and is deemed to require collective action in response" (1988, 314). As twenty-first century baby boomers ride what Ken Dychtwald calls an "age wave" to the year 2035, when 70 million Americans will be age sixty-five or older, they are increasingly concerned with how they will live in their old age, given the fraying of New Deal safety nets and the "great risk shift" in American policy-making back toward private responsibility for old-age insurance (Hacker 2006). These concerns are not uniquely American; the looming prospects of an aging population and its attendant needs reflect a global trend. According to Dychtwald, the United Nations expects that by 2050, there will be nearly two billion people in the world who are sixty years of age or older, a ratio of one in every five people (1999, 3). How will they support themselves? How will they meet the rising costs of health care? To what extent can they rely on family? How will they cope with increasing disability and loss? Underlying these very practical concerns are deeper, existential and moral issues: What is the value of human life beyond the years of "productivity"? Who will care about, and for, old people in the twenty-first century?

For two years, the Hannan Archival Research Group (HARG), which consists of faculty and graduate students from six disciplines (anthropology, communications, English studies, political science, social work and sociology), studied the LHMH archives. A majority of us (nine out of fourteen) are also gerontologists. Although some of us identify as feminists and some do not, this volume reflects the strong feminist perspective of its editors, one of whom (Ruth Ray) developed and facilitated the group with funding from a forty thousand dollar Research Enhancement Program grant in women's studies from Wayne State University. As editors, we consider the book a major contribution to feminist gerontology, which focuses on diversity and social justice in old age. Co-editor Toni Calasanti has argued that feminist approaches are uniquely situated to help gerontologists understand the diverse experiences of all older adults, as well as diversity in the aging process itself. Feminism also makes us more attuned to ageism, as well as sexism, in arguments that homogenize "the old," privilege "successful" or "productive" aging, and create a binary between the "successful" aged and those who are a "burden" (Calasanti 1999, 51; see also Chapleski, this volume). In the last half of the twentieth century, feminists also successfully challenged the binary between "public" and "private" in their efforts to bring value, respect and greater compensation for women's work inside and outside the home. This same argument should be applied to old-age care; it is not a private matter, but a broadly public concern, because everyone stands to benefit when elders are supported and valued. While some members of our group identify as feminist change-agents, others do not, and this diversity is reflected in the types of contributions to the book: some chapters focus on historical description or case analysis, while others draw implications from these analyses to argue for change in old-age policies and practices today. But we all support the primary goal of feminist gerontology: to illustrate the complexity, diversity and inherent value of old people's lives and to "make being old, in all its diversity, acceptable" (Calasanti 1999, 53).

Members of HARG worked individually and in small groups in the archives and met monthly to share cases, discuss findings, and respond to each other's work-in-progress. Initially, we chose cases, not because they were representative of the elderly population at the time, but because they included rich details that raised interesting issues that provoked strong reactions in us as researchers. We chose cases that complicated and advanced our understandings of "burden" and "care" and that invited comparative readings. We agree with historian Linda Gordon, who, in conducting her own qualitative research on social work case files, came to the conclusion that "what is revealing of deeper patterns is more significant than what is representative" (1988, 306). In the tradition of much women's studies scholarship, our knowledge building has been collaborative and generative, as we have shifted between case study and theory. Originally, each of us brought specific theories to bear on our readings of the files; over time, however, our multi-disciplinary analyses and group discussions forced us to challenge those theories and look for alternative perspectives. At one point, we read Michel de Certeau's *The Practice of Everyday Life* (1984), searching for new ways to interpret the negotiations we were seeing in the case files between old people and their social workers. De Certeau provided no methodology for the work we were doing, but he did confirm the importance of studying everyday tactics used by ordinary people to meet their needs in a culture that is often indifferent to them.

Whenever possible, we brought in experts who could extend and comment on our collective work. From the beginning, sociologist Toni Calasanti served as visiting consultant to the group, speaking to us about the gender, race and class dimensions of "social security" as a cultural construct and Social Security as a system of planned benefits (Calasanti and Slevin 2001). She and Jill Harrison, who was then a PhD student at Virginia Tech, visited Detroit periodically to work in the archives and develop their own analyses, focusing specifically on issues that arose in the cases of the two African-American clients, as compared to white clients with similar backgrounds. With funds from a WSU Humanities Center grant, we also sponsored a two-day visit from old-age historian W. Andrew Achenbaum, who urged us, as historiographers, to dig deep into the case studies while simultaneously thinking broadly in our analysis, considering the larger socio-historical context of Detroit and the nation during the time of the Great Depression. Informed by his own research on old-age assistance (Achenbaum 1978, 1986, 2005), he encouraged us to examine the lives of old people in the context of their families, since familial alliances and discords have always been central to the quality of older people's lives. Achenbaum reminded us that old-age assistance programs help young and midlife people, too, in relieving some of the responsibility on younger generations for supporting their elders.

As there is no other interdisciplinary group of our kind studying the experiences of old age as reflected in historical case files, we each developed our own approach to examining and interpreting the cases. Early in our work, certain themes emerged from our readings, most prominently the concept of burden and the negotiations between social workers and clients around the construction of burdenhood. In December 2008, a special double issue of the *Journal of Aging, Humanities and the Arts* devoted to "accommodation and resistance" in old age featured some of our initial case study analyses. Since that time, we have added cases to complicate and elaborate on this early work and have continued to read in several literatures that bear directly on our study, including the history of Detroit; the history of the Great Depression; New Deal policies and the people behind them; and the history of social work. Since we do not have a trained historian in our group, we have tried to fill this gap by reading widely, broadening our understandings of the Progressive Era and the Great Depression. We found encouragement in the words of sociologist and historian Gaye Tuchman, who invites us to approach history as daily experience that anyone, historian or not, can (and should) observe and interpret: "Most simply, we all live history, and not merely in the grand sense of wars, recessions, and political transformations. Rather, we live out the assumptions of our *époque* in the most mundane aspects of our lives . . . . [H]istory is a living story that speaks both the tensions between past and present and an era's structure of feelings" (1994, 313). In the end, ours is a book about old people and the everyday experiences of old age, rather than a history of the Great Depression or even a history of old age. While of interest to historians, this book is written primarily for social gerontologists, women's studies scholars, social work professionals, and students drawn to stories of people living through hard times. If we have done our job, readers will come to see the Great Depression as a "living story," understanding not only what it felt like to be old during this time, but also what it feels like to be old today, when, despite the safety nets of Social Security, Medicare and Medicaid, older Americans still fear becoming a burden to themselves, their families and society. Such an understanding is especially crucial now, in 2010, as the United States slowly emerges from a two-year recession that devastated the working and middle-class. Currently, entitlement programs are increasingly targeted for "reforms" that could strip them of their ability to provide old people and their families some modicum of protection against financial and physical dependence.

The Hannan Archives

What makes this book unique is the data on which it is based. The poignant stories we tell and the conclusions we draw are inspired by cases that, to our knowledge, make up the only intact social work archives of its kind in the United States. The Luella Hannan Memorial Foundation Collection (LHMFC) consists of nineteen boxes containing 822 files of men and women in metro Detroit who applied for old-age pensions between 1927 and 1971, at which time the Foundation began to provide "indoor relief" in the form of an old-age home built especially for its clients, replacing the "outdoor relief" (assistance to elders in their own homes) that it had provided for the previous forty-two years.

The files contain face sheets and detailed case narratives prepared by the social workers, who were then called "Visitors"; applications containing demographic information and supporting references; correspondence between staff, clients and others; and additional material pertinent to the case, including lists of items purchased for clients, doctors' reports, newspaper clippings and other artifacts. There is also a separate file containing photographs of some clients. To access this collection, we were each required to sign a restricted use statement protecting client confidentiality. No names or other information that would identify the clients or their relatives can appear in print; therefore, we gave each client a pseudonym, although we have used their actual case numbers. We have used the real names of LHMH trustees and staff, as these are matters of public record. To supplement the case materials, we consulted other primary sources from the period, including staff employment records and the corporate minutes of the LHMH Board of Trustees; the first annual report of the LHMH, published in March, 1930; and Detroit newspaper stories published in the late 1920s about the formation of the LHMH.

For our own research purposes, we developed a finding aid that allowed us to track clients who applied for pensions by their initials; date of application; source of referral; age, gender, race, marital and health status; disposition of case, whether funded or not; and length of case until termination. Based on this finding aid, we can generally characterize the people who applied for pensions between 1927 and 1934 as follows:

- They ranged in age from forty-eight to one-hundred.[3]
- The majority (62 percent) were single women (never married, divorced, separated, widowed or deserted), while 20 percent were single men, and 18 percent were couples applying jointly.
- They were predominantly white, including some Canadian, English, Irish, German, Polish, and Danish immigrants, with five applicants listing themselves as "colored" or "Negro."
- Most were residents of the city of Detroit, although some lived in nearby communities.[4]
- Most applicants had at least a "common school" education through the eighth grade, although some had graduated from high school, and a few were college educated.
- The longest-supported client received a pension for thirty-four years, from age sixty-three to ninety-seven (see Bailey-Fakhoury and Dillaway, this volume, for details on this case).

Social class is a highly significant category in terms of understanding these case files and therefore requires some discussion. Selection of

LHMH clients was in large part determined by social class, which was closely interrelated with ethnicity and race, as interpreted by the staff in terms of the assumptions and values of Luella Hannan and the Board of Trustees. Because the LHMH trust supported persons who had "been accustomed to enjoying the comforts of life but who, through change of fortune, [had] come to reduced circumstances," several clients had made social and economic contributions to the city through their professional and/or philanthropic work in earlier years. Luella Hannan herself was a wealthy white woman nearing the end of her life when she donated the largest part of her estate to the LHMH. She appointed a Board of Trustees (for life) made up of three prominent white, middle-aged men in the city: Julius C. Peter, who served as treasurer, was a banker with the Detroit Trust Company; Ferris D. Stone, secretary, was a partner in the law firm of Miller, Canfield, Paddock and Stone; and Dr. Joseph A. Vance, board chairman, was a Presbyterian minister. One other board member, Otis A. Brown, was a close friend of Mrs. Hannan's who resigned shortly after her death. Luella Hannan served as chair of the Board until her death in 1928, at which time Rev. Vance became chair. In February 1929 the Board hired a part-time executive secretary, Leon W. Frost, a professional social worker, who also served as Executive Director of the Children's Aid Society. Mr. Frost, age thirty-nine, hired a part-time staff of female Visitors also in their thirties to investigate cases and make recommendations for grants from both the LHMH and Scudder funds. All staff members were white and middle-class.

The two trusts were distinct in the minds of the LHMH staff and trustees. Based on case notes and other available sources, most Hannan clients were considered "high types" (a common term of the day) who showed "refinement" and "culture," whether or not they had come from socially prominent backgrounds. Leon Frost offered a description of the typical Hannan client in an interview that appeared as part of a *Detroit Free Press* article in 1930: "There is, of course, a long waiting list from which we must select the highest type of person with the greatest need. We must judge by cultural background and economic difficulty. For this reason, a majority of our people are those with a record of training and experience in the professions" (Bower 1930).

We can look to the first annual report of the LHMH, published in early 1930, for examples of the prototypical Hannan client, a few of whom were featured in and photographed for this report. One example is Mr. W, age seventy-nine, described as a "modest, intelligent bachelor" who had graduated from Rensselaer Polytechnic Institute. Mr. W had worked all his life as an engineer and inventor and had written a pamphlet called, "The Engineer and the Intellectual Life," which is included in the case file. He had spent all the money he had made in his life on inventions and had nothing to live on in old age. In describing his character, the annual report refers in brief to an incident that is drawn in detail in his file. The Visitor's case notes describe an afternoon on May 28, 1929, when she introduced Mr. W to another man, Mr. C, and they all went out to lunch at a nice restaurant. According to the Visitor, while Mr. C was "fairly well dressed," Mr. W was not, having grown so thin that his only suit no longer fit. Also, "his coats were held together with a rubber band, his vest with a safety pin, and his watch held in place by a shoe string in place of a watch chain." Yet the Visitor enthusiastically reports that Mr. W's "breeding [was] shown in the way he carried off the situation of entering Westwood Inn with his watch chain, cuff links, and loose suit. He was magnificent in his absolute lack of embarrassment in this situation. He seemed entirely unconscious of the fact that he was not properly dressed" (LHMFC, Case #77). For Mr. W's profile in the annual report, written by Leon Frost, this incident is summarized as follows: "He is slightly stooped, walks carefully with a cane, and can amble into a fashionable restaurant in his faded, baggy suit and too large collar, with a magnificent unconsciousness of his appearance and a quiet dignity that will bring him instant courtesy from the most snobbish of head waiters." Both the Visitor and Mr. Frost conveyed their impression of Mr. W as cultured and refined, despite his poverty.

In contrast to Hannan clients, Scudder clients were usually described in the case files as "laborers" or "typical middle-class" people who had been "hardworking" and "thrifty" all their lives. Illiterates and immigrants who did not speak English were not considered for pensions.[5] Within the first five months of their availability in 1929, the Scudder funds were exhausted, and most subsequent applications were denied. Of the total 508 applications received between 1927 and 1934, 254 were funded: 83 percent of those funded (210) were Hannan clients, and 17 percent of those funded (44) were Scudder clients.[6]

The following excerpt from a Visitor's notes illustrates the distinctions made between Hannan and Scudder clients by LHMH staff. The applicant, a woman of sixty-three, came to the LHMH office on November 8, 1929, having been referred by the Serviceman's Bureau, to which she had also applied for assistance:

W [oman] was dressed rather well, and upon first appearance, believed to be a Luella Hannan case; therefore, took face sheet information. . . . Further conversation with her disclosed that she was a woman of little education, having attended common school only until 11 years of age; that she used very poor grammar and English and her attitude was one that showed very little contact with refined people. She talked quite defiantly and spoke in such a way as to impress V[isitor] that we, or someone, owed to her the future maintenance of her home (LHMFC, Case #280).

In her summary of this brief file, the Visitor concludes, "an interview disclosed she was a Scudder case, consequently we could not take her [because Scudder funds were exhausted], nor was it likely that the DPW [Department of Public Welfare] would help her, as she receives a Spanish-American War pension."

The fact that a majority of LHMH clients represented the middle class or upper-middle class, with a few from the upper class, distinguishes the LHMH case files from those kept by other charitable organizations during this period, such as the Children's Aid Society, or various family welfare agencies on which most historical studies of social work are based. In the 1920s and 1930s, these organizations assisted the chronically poor and destitute,[7] focusing on problems of physical neglect. As such, many middle-class Visitors wrote from a superior position of "othering" clients who were different from them in terms of background, needs and values (Brush 1997). This discursive othering may invite a corresponding response in readers of such case files. In contrast, many LHMH Visitors, aside from their differences in age and life stage, shared socio-economic backgrounds that were similar to those of many clients. By extension, middle-class researchers (like us) who now read their files and write about them, share some of the clients' experiences, as well. The fact that, in 2010, we can relate so closely to the problems of many LHMH clients and their families confirms that the archives have broader implications beyond the Great Depression. In 2010, as the result of a deep recession that has affected Detroit even more profoundly than the rest of the United States,[8] members of the Hannan Archival Research Group have become especially sensitive to the fact that economic insecurity affects all socio-economic classes, including a large portion of the American middle class and even the educated, upper-middle class. As Hacker notes, "insecurity today reaches across the income spectrum, across the racial divide, across lines of geography and gender. It speaks to the common 'us' rather than the insular, marginalized 'them'" (2006, 6).

A Narrative Compass

We have followed a narrative approach in researching and writing this book. Consistent with standard narrative practice, we first read for common themes and looked for patterns across cases (Polkinghorne 1988). In analyzing the content of case narratives, we looked for the consequences of choices made, vulnerabilities, gaps, and a multiplicity of experiences across files (Webster and Mertova 2007) that would generate further discussion about the ethics of elder care, social justice and policy reform. In writing our chapters, we have oriented ourselves around the particulars of elders' lives as represented in the case files, relying on Visitors' notes and, in cases where correspondence is available, the words of the clients themselves. We have tried to avoid the trap of othering, as defined by feminist psychologist Michelle Fine: "inscribing individuals or groups in such a way that mutes their voices and perspectives, interprets their concerns out of context, 'structures' their experience in such way that garners approval from elite audiences while distancing us further from the subjects of our writing" (1994, 75). We acknowledge, however, the challenges of writing about old people from another era without projecting our own "existential and aesthetic anxieties" onto their lives and stories (Fine, 75). We have therefore taken direction from Robert Stake, who has written extensively on the method of case study. He reminds us that, since qualitative researchers are "guests in the private spaces of the world," our "manners should be good and [our] code of ethics strict" (1994, 244). Over time, we developed a code of ethics specific to the archives: treat clients, Visitors and case material with respect, working to identify and eliminate personal biases (ageism, racism, sexism, classism) in our readings and interpretations; develop an understanding of the case in its entirety, rather than reading selectively to support pre-formed ideas; supplement case material with additional historical and theoretical sources to increase depth of understanding; show respect for each other's work and the collective enterprise of the group by writing with a knowledge of all other chapters; and show respect for readers by making interesting, coherent and persuasive arguments.

The case files themselves, our primary source of data, were written in a narrative style that we found compelling, with entries organized chronologically around visits between the client and the social worker. One Visitor in particular, Anna Wentink, demonstrates a flair for evocative, ethnographic writing, and her clients often come alive on the page. Indeed, Visitors in the 1920s were taught to write in great detail, and their case notes were used to train new social workers and generate professional guidelines for the field. Such case notes were also used as evidence in legal cases and to support social reform movements. Karen Tice, author of *Tales of Wayward Girls and Immoral Women: Case Records and the Professionalization of Social Work*, explains the relative value of case notes in the early twentieth century. Social workers

> delved deep into the everyday lives of clients and had protracted interactions with those individuals. They provided accounts of these relationships and approached the construction of knowledge in ways that sharply contrasted with typical practices in male-dominated professions such as psychiatry . . . [S]ocial workers saw more of life—and saw it differently. . . . As routine visitors to living rooms and kitchens of impoverished clients, they witnessed the ups and downs of family fortunes and the ways in which clients tried to stay afloat . . . (1998, 190).

Understanding the significance of case notes, Mary Richmond, considered to be the "mother" of social work, along with her contemporary Jane Addams (Mann 1942), devoted a large section of her classic textbook, *Social Diagnosis* (1917) to evidence gathering and note taking. Richmond initially trained visitors (who in the early 1930s came to be called "social workers") to write detailed notes by developing their observational powers and reading fiction and biography. Richmond believed that case records should be comprehensive and coherent, demonstrating a "depth of understanding" and "historical feeling" that approached the style of good literature (Agnew, 196). According to one of Richmond's biographers, "she mined works of modern literature for insights into social casework, finding in Willa Cather's *My Antonia*, for instance, a 'sane and liberal' novel that could be an inspiration for caseworkers' record writing" (Agnew 2004, 195). Richmond was not alone in turning to literature as a model for case writing. Other social workers of her day, including Clare Tously of the New York Charity Organization Society and Frank Bruno of the Minneapolis Family Welfare Association, urged Visitors in the late 1920s to "imitate the art of dramatic writing and highlight the conflict, tension, pathos and tragedy found within case histories" (Tice, 54).

Thanks to LHMH Visitors' detailed and sometimes dramatic case notes, especially those of Anna Wentink, the primary worker during the Great Depression, HARG members have vicariously shared some of the experiences of old men and women living during this time. In reading these notes, we have become more empathetic toward, as well as more knowledgeable about, the experiences of old people in the past and present. In writing with and through these notes, if we have done our job well, readers, too, "will come to know some things told, as if [they] had experienced them" (Stake, 240). Consistent with the professional values of Mary Richmond, we intend for our case analyses to "illuminate both individual lives and the broader social context," revealing the crucial connections between individual need and social reform (Agnew, 197).

Finally, we intend the stories of LHMH clients to be a "narrative compass" for readers, just as they have been for us. In their collection, *A Narrative Compass: Stories that Guide Women's Lives*, editors Betsy Hearne and Roberta Seelinger bring together women's studies scholars to write about the stories, fictional and non-fictional, that have guided their intellectual work. In *Nobody's Burden*, we write about the stories that have challenged, and in many cases changed, our own understandings of aging and old age. Indeed, we have come to understand that historical writing itself is a kind of storytelling that links us to our communal past. When done well, it creates a dialectic relationship between past and present. Archival research, especially, helps us "begin to recognize patterns that resonate through the years to our current practice[s] and institutional dilemmas," making us more keenly aware of "the pervasive and continuous influence of individual, social and cultural pressures" over time (Welsh 1998, 121).

The Trouble with Case Notes

Our reliance on case notes written by social workers in the 1920s and 1930s is both a strength and limitation of this project. Although we consulted the writings of clients themselves whenever possible, we have relied heavily on the narrative authority of Visitors in constructing our biographical sketches of clients and analyzing the issues and concerns they faced. This approach is valuable in that few studies make use of historical case notes, which, if they have not been destroyed, are often difficult to access due to confidentiality issues (Hayes and Devaney 2004). Case files of public and private charitable organizations that have been made available to researchers, such as records from the Massachusetts Society for Prevention of Cruelty to Children (est. 1878); various Children's Aid Societies, Associated Charities, and Family Welfare Organizations dating from the late nineteenth and early twentieth centuries; and the Salvation Army archives[9] are a unique source of first-hand observational data and a grounded approach to knowledge-building. As historian Karen Tice notes, such case files can be "gold mines for scholars interested in social welfare history and the lives of stigmatized others" (1998, 3). Additionally, the practice of writing detailed notes on each visit with a client, as reflected in these case records, may soon be obsolete. Many social workers now rely on computer technologies for tracking and managing clients, a practice that, although efficient, involves the "potential loss of client individuality and social workers' creativity and insight" (Tice, 193).

However, like all observational data, case notes reflect the biases, blind spots and professional agenda of the caseworkers and "may reveal more about authors than subjects" (Tice, 3). Historian Linda Gordon confirms this assessment, concluding that, "with few exceptions, the case records represent the case workers' opinions, even when they were trying to represent the clients' point of view" (1988, 13). The power differential between caseworkers and clients, too, is reflected in the fact that some clients were uncooperative and withheld information. As Gordon explains, "from the clients' point of view, even well-meaning caseworkers could do a good deal of damage through misunderstandings and the structural inflexibilities of the system" (16). Further, because case records were evaluated by the social worker's superiors, she needed to justify her actions by showing that they were appropriate to the client. Therefore, a worker "sometimes had to disguise both her inadequacies and her excellence; the case record could be allowed to show neither too little nor too much action for clients" (Gordon, 17).

Tice's approach to the dilemma of relying on such incomplete and biased information, however "scientific" and "objective" the caseworker tried to be, is to focus on the records as texts that reflect the politics of case workers attempting to gain entrance into an emerging field. "As professional constructions," writes Tice, "case writings created clients, authorities, problems, and solutions. Caseworkers transformed clients' biographies into professional representations shaped by emerging professional interests" (3). Such records, when "read through the professional agendas that directed them . . . not only tell a great deal about what caseworkers actually did and thought but also reveal insights into the subjectivities of social work's clients" (3-4).

From the standpoint of textual politics, it would be easy to critique the professional, disciplining gaze that structured the LHMH case files and turned old men and women into "file persons" (Brush 1997). Although an important critical contribution, this would not serve our current agenda, which is to better understand social concepts of elder care, old-age policy and the early practice of geriatric social work. We therefore use data from the LHMH case files to illustrate themes, articulate social issues, and generate ideas for reform. A critical study of the discursive practices of LHMH social workers, reflective of the politics of scientific charity in the Progressive Era, as well as the age, race, class and gender politics of the period, is the interesting subject of another study.

Overview of Chapters

Unlike most edited books, which are loose collections of chapters written around a central theme, *Nobody's Burden* draws its strength from the cumulative effect of chapters that work together to make an argument. We take our inspiration from Roland Barthes, who challenges interdisciplinary collaborators to meet a higher standard: "To do something interdisciplinary, it's not enough to choose a 'subject' (a theme) and gather around it two or three sciences. Interdisciplinarity consists of creating a new object that belongs to no one" (qtd. in Clifford 1986, 1). This is especially true of interdisciplinary scholarship that follows a narrative methodology. Narrative inquiry itself is interdisciplinary, crossing the boundaries of many fields, and research on individual narratives, including case histories, is also interdisciplinary, requiring an understanding that all stories are interconnected in complex ways, situated within other individual narratives, as well as social, cultural and institutional discourses (Riessman 1993; Tice 1998; Webster and Mertova 2007). Even a single case file entails competing and overlapping narratives: notes and letters from the client; the Visitors' (often more than one over a period of years) summaries of the client's narratives; Visitors' summaries of their interactions with the client and his or her friends, neighbors, landlords, and caregivers; Leon Frost's summaries of his interactions with the client, his presentation of issues and questions regarding the case to the Board of Trustees, and the Board's decisions; and narratives from people outside the organization, including those who wrote letters of recommendation on the client's behalf and, in a few cases, those who wrote newspaper stories about the client. As scholars, we are caught in this narrative web, and our writing must reflect at least some of its many interwoven strands. This has proven a challenge for us, as well as an opportunity to expand our knowledge and our ways of knowing.

In structuring the book, we have tried to show connections across narratives. The book follows fairly closely the definition of feminist qualitative research proposed by Virginia Olesen (1994): Parts II and III place at the center and make "problematic" old men and women's "diverse situations and the institutions and frames that influence those situations," while Part IV addresses that problematic through "theoretical, policy, and action frameworks in the interest of realizing social justice" (158) for both men and women. Part I provides historical context for understanding the diverse experiences and situations discussed in Parts II and III.

In Part I, Tom Jankowski and I describe the old-age assistance programs in the State of Michigan and particularly the city of Detroit, once hailed by Mayor Frank Murphy as the "great city of plenty," after it fell on hard times during the Great Depression. Jankowski describes the system of public support available to old people, including job assistance, public welfare, and housing in the county poor house. I describe the network of charities operating in the city, with particular attention to the LHMH, its staff and Visitors, explaining how its methods and clientele compared to those of other charitable organizations at the time.

In Part II, we provide short life narratives of the clients whose files we have studied closely. Our intention is to create more rounded characters than those that appear in the case-study chapters, with an emphasis on personality, family situation, and distinguishing characteristics. Taken together, these narratives show how diverse the population of older adults was in the 1920s, even within the small and selective group of LHMH clients.

In Part III, research teams provide close readings of cases, showing how specific clients negotiated their needs with the Visitors and raising issues of relevance today, including quality of care and quality of life; the desire for autonomy and independence; how identity or personhood is maintained in old age, despite individual and social losses; the question

of who "deserves" assistance and how much; and the role of social workers in mediating individual, institutional and societal needs. In the final
chapter of this section, Janet Langlois and Mary Durocher offer a haunting image to reinforce the significance of this book for today's readers.
They explain that the fears and anxieties individual elders felt during the
Great Depression were expressions of the broader cultural fear of becoming dependent on others who could not or would not provide for them.
Old people were rightly afraid of becoming "ghosts"—invisible, marginalized, avoided and forgotten members of society. Langlois and Durocher suggest that all the contributors to this book are telling "ghost stories" in resurrecting the details of lives that have been forgotten,
discarded or repressed. Through these tellings, we jog the social memory
and identify the "ghosts in the machine" of old-age care and social policy. The pressing need to reform old-age policy and promote greater social responsibility for elder care today and in the future is the "haunting
burden" of our time.

Finally, contributors to Part IV take a retrospective and prospective
approach, looking back at the cases analyzed in Part III through a wider
lens by considering the impact of ageism, racism, sexism, and classism
on the distribution of social, economic and personal assistance to older
people during the Great Depression and today. We draw on critical gerontology, feminist theory and feminist ethics to rethink elder care and
old-age policies so that people now and in the future might experience a
better old age.

Notes

1. Neither the language of the trust nor the corporate minutes of the Board
of Trustees explains why the organization chose the ages of sixty and sixty-five
or made the gender distinction in terms of age qualifications, but they were
probably just following the standards of the day. According to Beal (2008), the
Benjamin Rose Institute of Cleveland, another foundation that provided private
pensions to older people during this period, used these same age criteria for
women and men and also capped their pensions at fifty dollars per month, as did
the LHMH.

2. Such cases of age aversion surely reflect gender relations, as well as age
relations at the time. An informal survey of the cases suggests that female applicants were far more likely to express a fear of "old age" itself than male applicants.

3. The forty-eight year-old applicant was unusual. She lived with a handicap and therefore qualified for a pension under the Hannan trust because she was "in-firm," though not old.

4. The Board of Trustees decided early on that they would use the words "city of Detroit" in their "geographical rather than political sense and that they should be deemed to include the suburbs of Detroit" (Corporate Minutes, LHMH, April 2, 1929).

5. A fuller discussion of the LHMH staff and clients, compared to other charitable organizations and elder recipients of relief during this period, along with the amounts and provisions of the LHMH pensions, is provided in Chapter 3.

6. As the Depression wore on, and in later years of the LHMH, distinctions between Hannan and Scudder clients became increasingly blurred: case records show that clients were shuffled back and forth between funds, depending on which one had money available, but occasionally on the basis of a "decline" in the client's status with the organization. More details on these two trusts are provided in Chapter 3.

7. For our purposes, Linda Gordon's "imprecise categories" for determining social work clients' standard of living provide a useful guide for determining the social class of LHMH applicants. Destitute means "lacking necessities for health, e.g. shoes, fuel, food"; poor means "maintaining life and health at a minimal standard and with chronic insecurity and uncertainty"; working class means "competence, living without chronic insecurity or uncertainty about ability to keep family members adequately housed, warmed, clothed, and fed, and with at least some items defined as non-necessary, e.g., a watch"; middle class means "those with standards, aspirations, or employment that set them above manual laborers"; and upper or prosperous class refers to "those who [can] afford substantial luxuries" (1988, p. 307).

8. For a popular media account of Detroit's current social and economic troubles, see the October 5, 2009 *Time* magazine cover story, "The tragedy of Detroit: How a great city fell—and how it can rise again."

9. See historical works based on these archives by Kunzel (1993), Tice (1998) and Gordon (1988).

References

Achenbaum, W. Andrew. 1978. *Old Age in the New Land.* Baltimore: Johns Hopkins University Press.

Achenbaum, W. Andrew. 2005. *Older Americans, Vital Communitie*s. Baltimore: Johns Hopkins University Press.

Achenbaum, W. Andrew. 1986. *Social Security.* Cambridge, UK: Cambridge University Press.

Agnew, Elizabeth. N. 2004. *From Charity to Social Work: Mary E. Richmond and the Creation of an American Profession.* Urbana, IL: University of Illinois Press.

Barthes, Roland. 1984. *Le Bruissement de la Langue.* Paris: Le Seuil.

Beal, Eileen. 2008. *The First 100 Years.* Cleveland, OH: Benjamin Rose Institute.

Bower, Helen. 1930. "239 Live in Comfort Under Hannan Will: Clients are Those Who Have Been Accustomed to Higher Standards." *Detroit Free Press*, June 25, Sunday section.

Boyle, Kevin. 2004. *Arc of Justice: A Saga of Race, Civil Rights, and Murder in the Jazz Age.* New York: Henry Holt.

Brush, Linda. 1997. "Worthy Widows, Welfare Cheats: Proper Womanhood in Expert Needs Talk about Single Mothers in the United States, 1900-1988." *Gender and Society* 11: 720-746.

Calasanti, Toni. 1999. "Feminism and Gerontology: Not Just for Women." *Hallym International Journal of Aging* 1: 44-55.

Calasanti, Toni, and Kathleen Slevin. 2001. *Gender, Social Inequalities and Aging.* Lanham, MD: AltaMira.

Clifford, James. 1986. "Partial truths." Pp. 1-26 in *Writing Culture: The Poetics and Politics of Ethnography,* edited by James Clifford and George E. Marcus. Berkeley, CA: University of California Press.

DeCerteau, Michele. 1984. *The Practice of Everyday Life.* Trans. Steven Rendall. Berkeley, CA: University of California Press.

Dychtwald, Ken. 1999. *Age Power: How the 21st Century will be Ruled by the New Old.* New York: Tarcher/Putnam.

Fine, Michelle. 1994. "Working the Hyphens: Reinventing Self and Other in Qualitative Research." Pp. 70-82 in *Handbook of Qualitative Research,* edited Norman K. Denzin and Yvonne Lincoln. Thousand Oaks, CA: Sage.

Gordon, Linda. 1988. *Heroes of Their Own Lives: The Politics and History of Family Violence.* Urbana, IL: University of Illinois Press.

Haber, Carole and Brian Gratton. 1994. *Old Age and the Search for Security: an American Social History.* Bloomington, IN: Indiana University Press.

Hacker, Jacob S. 2006. *The Great Risk Shift.* New York: Oxford University Press.

Hayes, David and John Devaney. 2004. "Accessing Social Work Case Files for Research Purposes: Some Issues and Problems." *Qualitative Social Work* 3: 313-333.

Hearne, Betsy, and Roberta Seelinger, eds. 2009. *A Narrative Compass: Stories that Guide Women's Lives.* Urbana, IL: University of Illinois Press.

Kittay, Eva Feder. 1999. *Love's Labor: Essays on Women, Equality and Dependency.* New York: Routledge.

Kunzel, Regina G. 1993. *Fallen Women, Problem Girls: Unmarried Mothers and the Professionalization of Social Work, 1890-1945.* New Haven: Yale University Press.

Luella Hannan Memorial Foundation Collection. Walter Reuther Library of Labor and Urban Affairs. Wayne State University, Detroit, Michigan.

Mann, Ruth Z. 1942. "Jane Addams -- Mary Richmond: The Impact of Two Personalities on the Development of Social Work." *Alumni Newsletter* (New York School of Social Work), January: 1-2, 6-8.

Olesen, Virginia. 1994. "Feminisms and Models of Qualitative Research." Pp. 158-74 in *Handbook of Qualitative Research,* edited Norman K. Denzin and Yvonne Lincoln. Thousand Oaks, CA: Sage.

Polkinghorne, Donald. 1988. *Narrative Knowing and the Human Sciences.* New York: State University of New York Press.

Riessman, Catherine K. 1993. *Narrative Analysis.* Newbury Park, CA: Sage.

Roosevelt, Eleanor. 1955. "Social Responsibility for Individual Welfare." Pp. Xxxv-Xxxvii in *National Policies for Educational Health and Social Services,* edited by James E. Russell. New York: Doubleday.

Stake, Robert. 1994. "Case Studies." Pp. 236-47 in *Handbook of Qualitative Research,* edited by Norman K. Denzin and Yvonne Lincoln. Thousand Oaks, CA: Sage.

Tice, Karen. 1998. *Tales of Wayward Girls and Immoral Women: Case Records and the Professionalization of Social Work.* Urbana, IL: University of Illinois Press.

Tuchman, Gaye. 1994. "Historical Social Science: Methodologies, Methods and Meanings." Pp. 306-23 in *Handbook of Qualitative Research*, edited by Norman K. Denzin and Yvonne Lincoln. Thousand Oaks, CA: Sage.

U.S. Department of Health and Human Services, Center for Disease Control and Prevention. 2007. *National Vital Statistics Reports,* vol. 56, no. 9.

Webster, Leonard and Patricie Mertova. 2007. *Using Narrative Inquiry as a Research Method.* London: Routledge.

Welsh, Kathleen. 1998. "History as Complex Storytelling." *College Composition and Communication* 50: 116-122.

Part 1

e Wayne County Asylum and Poorhouse, known locally as Eloise, "the finest
»rhouse in the world," circa 1926.

Part One

The Burden of Age in the Great Depression

In this section, Thomas Jankowski and Ruth Ray explain what was happening in the city of Detroit, the State of Michigan, and the nation in regards to old-age support during the Great Depression. Other social historians have argued that Detroit is a good case study for the analysis of structural forces that underlie inequality and poverty in the United States. The city, for example, is at the heart of Thomas Sugrue's prize-winning book, *The Origins of the Urban Crisis* (1996). Jankowski and Ray explain why Detroit is also a good lens for observing the specific effects of industrial capitalism on old people and their families.

Although most clients of the Luella Hannan Memorial Home (LHMH) had been middle class in terms of their income and values and a few had even lived upper-class lifestyles, they had lost the assets (property, savings and in some cases stocks and bonds) that would have supported them in old age. While a few female clients had never worked for pay, most still wanted to work but could not do so because of illness and the ageism of employers. As a result, they had no choice but to rely on family and friends or to seek assistance from charitable organizations. As historians Carole Haber and Brian Gratton explain in *Old Age and the Search for Security* (1994)(cite, chapter 3), the fewer children one had, the more likely he or she was to live with a child; more children meant more sources of income and a higher chance that an elder could live alone. Independent living was most people's preference in 1929, as it is today. Elders who had no children or who were estranged from their families inevitably had to seek assistance from public agencies or private

31

charities, an embarrassing and guilt-inducing option but still preferable to the county poorhouse.

Both the City of Detroit and the LHMH were "progressive" for their time in terms of the level of support they provided to old people and their families. Yet without a national plan for public pensions or medical insurance in place and with very few elders receiving private pensions, these local forms of support, however progressive, fell far short of providing for a good old age.

Chapter 2

Public Response to the Needs
of Old People

Thomas B. Jankowski

I am confident that here in Detroit, we will do our part bravely and courageously and perhaps wage the battle just a little bit better than it is being waged elsewhere. We should, because we have been tempered to the struggle longer than our more fortunate neighbors. Our fibre has been toughened.
— Frank Murphy, Mayor of Detroit, 1933[1]

Boom and Bust Cycles in the Great City of Plenty

To better understand the issues facing Hannan clients discussed in the succeeding chapters, we must first understand the time and place in which those clients lived. We are, in large part, a product of our environment, and our attitudes and behavior are strongly shaped by social context. The period of the late 1920s and early 1930s in the United States marked the culmination of decades of growth in its population, economy, and infrastructure, followed by a crash and then a prolonged depression. The place in which the Hannan clients lived during this period, Detroit, Michigan, was an exaggerated microcosm of the nation, in which the growth was extraordinarily steep, the crash was particularly sharp, and the depression was unusually deep. The dramatic social and economic upheaval created as the Roaring 20s collapsed into the Great Depression provided the context in which the Hannan clients struggled against poverty in old age, and was a major contributor to the fear that already marked the struggle—fear of loss of independence and autonomy, fear of

33

being a burden to one's family, and fear of being sent to Eloise, as the county poorhouse was known. Even before the crash, many elders faced that fearful struggle, and even before the crash, the conditions in this industrial city considered to be signs of progress—the crowding, construction, and noise that came from rapid economic development—must have been unsettling to those who were accustomed to the quieter, less chaotic Detroit of an earlier era.

The Detroit of 1929 bristled with energy. The preceding three decades of growth had propelled it from a typical large city of about 286,000 residents to a booming metropolis of nearly 1.6 million, the fourth largest city in the U. S. (Gavrilovich and McGraw 2006, 289). Detroit automakers produced over 5.3 million cars in 1929, most of them in the city and a few surrounding suburbs, and Detroit workers were the most productive and highest paid in the nation. Between 1927 and 1929 alone, the city saw the opening of an astonishing array of its major cultural institutions, including the Ambassador Bridge to Canada, the Detroit Institute of Arts, the Detroit Zoo, Greenfield Village and the Henry Ford Museum, the Fisher Building, the General Motors Building, Olympia Stadium, and the University of Detroit main campus. Detroit was home to many of the wealthiest American industrialists, but also boasted the highest rate of homeownership among the working classes and the most extensive streetcar system of any city in the U. S. Explosive growth, plentiful high-paying jobs, long shady streets lined with affordable single-family homes, a bustling downtown, extensive public transportation, and ample amenities seemed to make the Detroit of the late 1920s a worker's paradise. No wonder Frank Murphy, in his inaugural address after being elected mayor in 1930, referred to Detroit as "this great city of plenty" (Fine 1975, 258).

There was a less celebrated and much less pleasant underside to the urban economy of Detroit's boom years. Streams of migrants from the Southern US followed a huge influx of immigrants from Poland, Italy, the Middle East, and elsewhere, all seeking jobs in Detroit's factories. Most of these newcomers entered the city at the economic and social margins, and some had great difficulty working their way toward the center even in the best of times. When times were bad, "[t]hese more recent arrivals, coming to Detroit in response to the extraordinary demand for labor, [were] hardest hit," an injury that left lasting scars (Johnson 1922, 48). Despite having roared ahead at breakneck speed for the better part of three decades, Detroit's economy remained a seasonal and cyclical roller coaster of hirings and firings, overtime and layoffs, booms and busts, especially for line workers and laborers. The seasonal dips and turns in employment caused widespread, painful, but mostly temporary turmoil in the lives of working families. Some of those whose lives were most severely disrupted by extended cyclical recessions and depressions, on the other hand, were never able to recover. Yet even the worst economic disruptions during Detroit's economic heyday, such as the downturns in 1894 and 1907 and the depressions of 1914-1915 and 1920-1921, were merely a portent of much worse things to come when the Great Depression hit the city at the end of 1929.

Detroit's industrial juggernaut carried hundreds of thousands of workers into the relatively comfortable ranks of the middle class over the first part of the twentieth century, but it also crushed others beneath its wheels. Older workers, in particular, suffered disproportionately from periodic economic downturns because they were considered to be less suited for the physicality of factory work, less adaptable to new methods of manufacturing, and because there was no law to protect them against age discrimination. "Even in good times, old people were among the last hired and first fired; a majority of them were poor" (Patterson 1986, 40). Age discrimination at the time was hardly hidden; many companies were quite clear about their "policy of not hiring anyone over some stated maximum age, the limit being placed sometimes as low as forty-five years or even lower" (Durand 1968, 114-5). Statistics from 1935 show that Michigan workers age sixty to sixty-four suffered from an unemployment rate about 65 percent higher than that of their counterparts age forty-five to forty-nine (U. S. Department of Labor 1936, 1158-9).

The Structural Dependencies of Old Age

Employer-sponsored pensions were just beginning to become more common, especially after pension trust income was exempted from Federal taxation in 1926, but it was a rare older worker at the dawn of the Great Depression who was vested in a pension. Michigan had no public pension program until 1933, and the federal Social Security Act would not be signed into law until 1935 and would not pay its first monthly benefit check until 1940. Workers were commonly unable to accumulate enough savings during their working years to sustain themselves adequately in old age when they were unable to work or find employment. Older women in particular were more likely to have had little or no history in the paid labor force, or to have had lower status and lower paid jobs during their working lives. They were also more likely to outlive their spouses, upon whom many of them depended for financial support, and were therefore especially vulnerable in old age. For both women and men, old age was commonly tarnished by economic struggle and poverty, even in times of otherwise widespread prosperity.

When an older Detroiter was unable to work for whatever reason—a downturn in the economy, age discrimination, lack of marketable skills, poor health, disability—and received no financial support from a spouse, to whom did he or she turn for sustenance? The first line of support, of course, was the family, primarily adult children. Adult children helped to support elders in their own homes or, as was commonly the case, in the elders' homes when they were no longer able to care for themselves. It was adult children, chiefly daughters or daughters-in-law, who assumed the task of personal caregiving when elders became sick or infirm. It was therefore the adult children to whom elders were most afraid of becoming a burden.

Despite the thoroughly modern nature of industrial Detroit society, the traditional agrarian norm of filial obligation remained a strong cultural imperative. The shift away from farming to a wage labor economy, and away from rural multi-generational households to urban nuclear families, was marked by growing geographical mobility and the loosening of extended family ties. These gradual changes in economic and social circumstances in the nineteenth century were accompanied by gradual changes in cultural norms in the twentieth, but only after a significant "cultural lag" (Ogburn 1922, 200). The manner in which urban working families lived in industrial society, particularly during times of financial struggle, did not equip adult children to meet the traditional cultural expectation of care for elder parents, yet that expectation persisted.[2] The tension created by this cultural lag was a source of significant stress in many families faced with providing such care during the 1920s and 30s.

Cultural lag, as one might expect, is accompanied by what Matilda White Riley and colleagues called a "structural lag" that is reflected in the "institutional and organizational arrangements" existing in the public sphere and enshrined in the law of the day (Riley, Kahn, and Foner 1994, 17). Michigan's poor law in effect at the dawn of the Great Depression had been last amended in 1925, but its origins could be traced to the poor laws of Pennsylvania and the Northwest Territory Poor Relief Act of 1795 (Bruce and Eickhoff 1936, 7), and beyond that to the Elizabethan poor laws of sixteenth and seventeenth century England (Matson 1933, 5-7). Structural lag was the product of these "[o]ld methods copied from England by the original states [being] adopted by Michigan with little or no attempt to adapt them to the changed circumstances of a new country" or a new economic system (Bruce and Eickhoff 1936, 14). The foundation of Michigan's poor law was a traditional, and arguably outmoded, concept of familism. Its hallmark was the requirement that adult children of means were required to support elderly parents who were unable to provide for themselves. This law came with sharp teeth:

> Whoever, being an adult resident of the state and possessed of or able to earn means sufficient to provide food, shelter, care, and clothing, for a parent within this state who is destitute of means of subsistence and unable either by reason of age, infirmity, or illness to support himself, neglects or refuses to supply such parents with necessary shelter, food, care, and clothing, shall be, upon conviction thereof, imprisoned in the county jail or workhouse at hard labor for not less than three months nor more than one year. (State of Michigan 1925, 192)

Few if any were prosecuted under this law; more often their parents were denied any form of public relief instead. Many adult children readily accepted the customary responsibility to provide for their indigent elders, and did so without complaint, albeit not without struggle. Others, however, had to be socially or legally coerced to provide care for their elderly parents, creating stress and frustration that was harmful for everyone involved. Plenty of dependent elders were cared for under this cloud of duress, and they and their progeny paid a price not only financially but also in the destructive emotions of guilt, shame, anxiety, and resentment.

There was another major drawback to the traditional kinship-based approach to old age relief: not every older person had adult children who were present and able to provide even grudging support. Those who were unable to depend upon an adult child for support were instead forced to rely on a web of extended family, friends, landlords, tenants and neighbors to help them get by. Sometimes the recipient of informal care and support was able to reciprocate by performing services such as childcare and laundry. More often, care and support were provided without compensation, out of a sense of moral obligation, compassion, or pity.

When social networks such as these did not exist or were simply not able to provide the resources for survival, there were few other options available. In most areas of Michigan there were few private charities apart from statewide organizations such as the Salvation Army, St. Vincent de Paul Society, and the American Red Cross (Stein-Roggenbuck 2008, 41-2). In big cities, there were a much wider array of private charitable organizations, frequently run by religious institutions, that older people could petition for help. The Luella Hannan Memorial Home (LHMH), which was non-sectarian, was one such organization. Although unique to Detroit, the LHMH was similar to charitable organizations in other urban areas, such as the Benjamin Rose Institute in Cleveland. (Further discussion of the private charity network in regards to old-age assistance can be found in Chapter 3.) In most cities across the US, the private charities were the primary backup against destitution in old age when the support of family and friends was unavailable. Other cities, including Detroit, also had municipal systems of public welfare that, to varying degrees, helped the poor to subsist.

In both private and public cases, there were strong elements of moralism and paternalism, of tailoring support—or denying it—based on the worthiness of the recipient, his or her ability to work, and the concern over fostering dependency. Those who had the potential to support themselves through work were sometimes given aid, but the aid was contingent on their efforts at rehabilitation. Those whose poverty was seen primarily as the result of old age were lumped in with the other "impotent poor"—people who could not work, were not responsible for their own impoverishment, and who were considered naturally dependent and therefore not subject to having their independence corrupted by charity. The impotent poor—the old, the sick, the disabled, children, and widowed and abandoned mothers—were granted the status of being deserving of charitable or public relief almost by default. However, especially in the case of poor elders, their deservingness still rested upon the assumption that their dependency was not a result of laziness, profligacy, intemperance, or some other personal moral failure, but rather through circumstances entirely beyond their control. Evidence to the contrary could be legitimately cited as justification for denying assistance, and often was.

A Progressive Approach to Public Welfare

Residents of the City of Detroit were protected by a safety net, perhaps thin by today's standards, but one that was not available to most other Americans. Detroit had developed an unusually robust municipal welfare system that provided outdoor assistance to poverty-stricken residents, including older adults, to help them remain in their homes (Johnson 1929, 33). It was a generous system for its time; Detroit Department of Public Welfare (DDPW) client families could count on receiving vouchers for groceries, heating fuel, rent subsidies, and medical care worth on the order of about thirty to forty dollars per month, which was nearly twice what most other cities with welfare programs provided (Stillman 1931, 9).

An indicator of the dark shadow cast by Detroit's precipitous economic growth, the DDPW's caseload slowly crept up through the last several years of the 1920s, reaching an average of about four thousand families in 1929. This was a historically heavy caseload that strained the department's resources, but it managed to maintain this level of support without faltering, and its caseworkers were quite proud in doing so. The DDPW officially boasted, with a viewpoint that was remarkably progressive for its time, that it "stands beside Detroit families when trouble overtakes them anywhere from the cradle to the grave." In particular, "When disaster comes in the last years of life, the Old Age Support Fund makes it possible for the dependent aged to receive relief and care in their own homes" (City of Detroit 1930, 8). The Old Age Support Fund was not large, supporting forty-six cases in 1930, made up of eighty-three individuals, which suggests that nearly all of the cases were couples. Many more old people were being supported by the general relief fund; one source identifies the "principal problem" of 585 of the cases under care by the DDPW in May of 1930 to be "old age" (Stillman 1931, 20).

For those in the rest of Michigan—and nearly all of the rest of the United States—no such public system of outdoor relief existed. Michigan's poor law assigned ultimate responsibility for the care of the indigent who had no family able to care for them to the Superintendents of the Poor in their respective counties (State of Michigan 1925, 194). The poor law allowed county governments to levy a tax to house and feed the poor, and to bill local township or city governments for the cost of providing that care to their indigent residents. Nearly all of the counties in the state, to the extent that they supplied much relief to speak of, relied upon indoor relief, and had only a county infirmary to keep old and sick poor people alive. Michigan's county infirmaries were the absolute last line of defense against death from exposure to the elements and malnutrition. Even Detroit, with its generous municipal welfare system, relied on the county infirmary to house its indigent and homeless population, particularly those who were also sick and old. A typical county infirmary was located on a farm and staffed by a farmer and his wife as keeper and matron, some of whom were awarded the position because they were the lowest bidder for it. The able-bodied poor were expected to work on the infirmary farm as compensation for the cost of their care. The quality of Michigan's infirmary facilities varied a great deal; some were "modern, well equipped, and designed to afford the care needed by the persons who must live out their remaining years dependent upon strangers," while "others afford shelter but little more" (Matson 1933, 25-6). The Wayne County Infirmary, in whose coverage area Detroit was located, was one of the former. Indeed, it was an institution so huge and so unique that it warrants special attention.

In Wayne County, the vehicle through which the county Superintendents of the Poor met their statutory obligation was an institution known as the Wayne County House, the Wayne County Asylum and Poorhouse, or, during the 1920s and 30s, the Wayne County General Hospital and Infirmary at Eloise. To local residents of Detroit and the surrounding area, it was known simply as Eloise. When all other options for support and care were exhausted, Eloise was the last resort. For older Detroiters who were unable to house or care for themselves, and had no family or friends to help them, the prospect of going to Eloise was a constant source of worry. First built on the outskirts of Detroit five years before Michigan attained statehood, the County House was re-established in the "awful wilderness" about fifteen miles west of the city in 1839 (Keenan 1913, 55). There it remained for nearly 150 years. In 1894 a U. S. Post Office was established on the grounds and given the name Eloise, after the young daughter of the Detroit Postmaster, and the moniker soon became associated with the entire institution. As the population of Detroit exploded, Eloise grew at a rapid pace to keep up with the concomitant growth of its indigent and mentally ill population (Clark 1982, 18). Although it was a county institution, members of the Detroit Public Welfare Commission held a majority of the seats on the Wayne County Board of Superintendents of the Poor, and therefore Eloise was largely under the control of the city of Detroit.

By the dawn of the Great Depression, the Eloise complex had become a city in its own right. It encompassed more than 900 acres and had its own water treatment, sewage, and power plants, fire and police departments, and railroad and streetcar stations. It had extensive farms, barns, and greenhouses, food processing facilities such as a cannery and bakery, shop buildings and laundry houses, and dozens of structures that housed both residents and employees. Its facilities included an insane asylum (later referred to as the psychiatric hospital), a general hospital, a tuberculosis sanitarium, and of course, the poor house, which was renamed the infirmary in 1913. As with the other social and institutional systems of Detroit, it was severely strained by the Great Depression.

Overwhelmed by the Great Depression

The effect of the Great Depression on the city and its residents, charities, public welfare system, and institutions was profound. The stock market crash in late October of 1929 that marked the end of the Roaring 20s sent Detroit's economy into a tailspin. Thousands, and then hundreds of thousands of factory workers were thrown out of work within months. By October of 1930, more than half of workers in Detroit's manufacturing sector were out of a job (Fine 1975, 201). Automobile production nosedived, falling more than 75 percent within two years. Even those who kept their jobs saw their income fall precipitously. Autoworkers, the best paid of the manufacturing employees, experienced a more than 40 percent cut in wages even when they managed to avoid unemployment.

The level of un- and under-employment spawned by the stock market crash in October of 1929 was staggering both in the speed of its climb and the height of its peak, and the poverty it created quickly led to a crushing burden on the DDPW. The "new poor," as the long-term structurally unemployed were called, began to crowd out the "old poor," the temporarily idled workers and the widows, orphans, disabled, and elderly who had formerly made up the bulk of the welfare caseload. It is difficult to overestimate the chaos that the Depression caused in Detroit's municipal welfare system. A study undertaken by Professor Charles C. Stillman in July of 1930 found that within the first six months of the beginning of the Depression, DDPW caseloads skyrocketed to six and a half times their former number, and spending grew to unsustainable levels, from less than $104,000 in September of 1929 to over $762,000 in March of 1930. At that time, DDPW was handling over twenty-three thousand cases, compared to a caseload of about 3,500 only six months earlier (Stillman 1931, 5-6; City of Detroit 1930, 11).

The DDPW expanded as quickly as it could to keep up with the growing need for its services, opening several new district offices and more than doubling the number of social workers and supervisors between October of 1929 and May of 1930, from forty-one to ninety (Stillman 1931, 17). However, supply simply could not keep up with demand, and case-loads increased from an already high average of 76 to "an absurd ratio" of 209 families under care per social worker, a level that encapsulated "the utter inadequacy of the staff to compete with the tremendous problem presented" (Stillman 1931, 19) and represented an "unreasonable and almost inhuman...burden put upon the individual case worker" (Stillman 1931, 27). One poignant indicator of the chaos at DDPW occurred when its founding superintendent, Thomas Dolan, a "man of great sensitivity and compassion" who had worked in the field of public welfare for nearly forty years and served as DDPW superintendent since it was established in 1918, suffered what was described as "a complete nervous collapse" in the spring of 1930 and was unable to return to work for two months (Fine 1975, 260). As Stillman grimly described it, "The Department gave and gave, and kept right on giving. It was itself in a pathological condition. It reflected and re-enacted the hysteria of its clients" (1931, 51).

By the end of 1930, the DDPW was serving about forty-five thousand client families, thirteen times as many as it had just before the Depression hit. The Department spent a total of about $1.5 million on general relief in 1929, and over $8 million in 1930 (City of Detroit 1931, 8). At the same time, the sharp drop in economic activity led to an equally steep decline in tax revenue, putting the city on a direct path to bankruptcy. The public welfare commission attempted to deal with this budgetary nightmare by cutting allowances and caseloads to the bone, again and again, which spurred many protests and accusations that such cuts were "tantamount either to a confession of unwarranted relief" before they were made "or a ruthless abandonment of needy families" afterward (Stillman 1931, 26). The DDPW, squeezed by dire need on one side and limited budgets on the other, swung wildly through the next couple of years between expanding caseloads and brutal culling.

By February of 1931 the DDPW's caseload had again climbed to a high of almost 51,000 families, approximately 229,000 people, and it spent nearly $1.8 million in that month alone, more than the entire year of 1929. By March, the social work staff had grown to 257 to handle the overwhelming caseload (Fine 1975, 303). To try to get a handle on its budget, the DDPW had been reducing grocery allowances to its clients, and when that didn't sufficiently stem the bleeding, it began taking the "drastic and brutal" step of dropping whole groups of people from its rolls: "all single persons, all healthy married couples without children, couples with one child, families with anti-social records, and the like" (Norton 1933, 5). In June the Pence Committee, appointed by Mayor Frank Murphy to audit the DDPW, reported that the department had "completely broken down" and recommended new leadership to help "bring order out of the chaos" (Fine 1975, 304). The 1930-1931 fiscal year ended with about $12.5 million having been spent on relief at the same time the city experienced "an alarming increase in tax delinquencies" (Norton 1933, 5).

In response to the budget crisis, the city council set a DDPW budget of $7 million for the 1931-1932 fiscal year and "reversed its old policy of permitting the department to spend first and seek appropriations after-wards" (Norton 1933, 4-5). Within several months the department was in such dire financial condition that aid to those still remaining on its rolls, including the elderly poor, was reduced to a subsistence ration, a so-called "survival food allowance" (Fine 1975, 333). The public welfare commission had succeeded in forcing the DDPW to stop paying clients' rent in May of 1932, and by July 150 client families were being evicted from their homes each day. The public welfare commission voted to drop nearly eighteen thousand structurally unemployed families—the new poor—from its rolls in June of 1932, despite its recognition that "chaos and violence" may result. Mayor Frank Murphy rushed home to Detroit from Chicago, where he was attending the Democratic national conven-tion, to veto the decision. The commission still managed to force 2,300 cases off the rolls by August, when the city's grocers stopped honoring DDPW grocery vouchers because of the city's mounting debt. By then, the city had completely exhausted its resources (Fine 1975, 338-9). The Detroit Department of Public Welfare, once deemed "outstanding...for the volume and quality of its public social welfare work" had barely "creaked and staggered through to the close of its fiscal year" ("The De-partment of Public Welfare" 1927, 1; Norton 1933, 6). The conditions for severe social unrest were ripe, and broad agreement that "The city re-quired assistance from outside if it were to avert the disaster that seemed to be impending" began to take hold (Fine 1975, 339).

The City of Detroit could no longer afford to operate its municipal relief system without the external support that came later in 1932 in the form of loans from the federal Emergency Relief and Construction Act, and still later as grants through the Federal Emergency Relief Adminis-tration (FERA). By mid-1933, about two-thirds of the relief funds spent in the State of Michigan came from FERA (Haber and Stanchfield 1936, 27). DDPW caseloads were also significantly reduced when its structu-rally unemployed clients were moved off the rolls into the work-relief programs of the federal Civil Works Administration (CWA) and Works Progress Administration (WPA).

When Frank Murphy took office as mayor in 1930, one of his first acts was to establish the Mayor's Unemployment Committee (MUC) to address critical issues in the public welfare system: the strain on re-sources caused by the surging numbers of new poor, the bureaucratic hurdles faced by the DDPW, the lack of public awareness of and com-munity involvement in addressing poverty at the local level, and the dire need for redoubled relief efforts in the City. A large part of the MUC's mission was to fill the gaps left by the DDPW, which primarily served families and offered little to the many single men who had come to Detroit in search of work and were left with no jobs and no family to turn to. Murphy was in many ways ahead of his time; he made extra efforts to include the city's immigrant and Black population in the MUC and other governmental bodies, he recognized the structural causes of unemployment when others persisted in blaming the victims, and he argued that relief should be provided "not as a matter of charity, and not paternally, but as a matter of right" (Fine 1975, 257).

The MUC raised money from private sources (about a quarter million dollars overall), conducted a census of the unemployed, distributed donated food and clothing, fed indigent children in the schools, provided legal aid to those at risk of eviction, and ran a Free Employment Bureau that placed nearly sixty thousand people in jobs (Fine 1975, 270). One significant task undertaken by the MUC was to attempt to provide housing for the thousands of unemployed and homeless single men in Detroit, in partnership with the private sector. With the assistance of private charities such as the McGregor Institute, the American Red Cross, Volunteers of America, and the Salvation Army, and using idled factory buildings donated by the General Motors and Studebaker corporations, the MUC opened two large "lodges" that at their peak housed and fed over ten thousand men daily (Fine 1975, 274). The MUC disbanded in 1933, but in its short existence it had developed many innovative approaches to addressing unemployment and poverty, and some of its relief programs were transferred to more permanent organizations, such as the DDPW and the Legal Aid Bureau.

Clearly, the municipal effort to relieve the poverty created by the Depression was unusually vigorous in the City of Detroit. Stillman found that from September to December of 1929, Detroit's total public and private expenditures on outdoor poverty relief accelerated very quickly compared to other cities. Relief expenditures in Detroit nearly tripled, rising 182% compared to increases of 63 percent in Minneapolis, 62 percent in Buffalo, 59 percent in St. Louis, 25 percent in Cleveland, and 21 percent in Chicago. The only relative increase comparable to Detroit's was in Toledo, which spent 140 percent more in December than in September, but that city's outdoor relief expenditures in December totaled only $35,000 compared to $552,000 in Detroit. The scale of Detroit's relief effort dwarfed all other cities, including the larger city of Chicago, which spent only $219,550 on total outdoor relief in December, a mere 40 percent of Detroit's expenditures (1931, 1-4). In fact, expenditures on public relief in Detroit "accounted for more than 25 percent of *all* the public general relief dispensed in the United States in 1930" (Fine 1975, 307; italics in original).

Too Little Too Late

Public awareness of elder poverty had been growing long before the Depression began, and public pension solutions advocated by organizations such as the Fraternal Order of the Eagles in the early 1920s, followed by the American Association for Social Security and then the broader Townsend movement were gaining popular currency. These ideas initially met with little success at the federal level, but some success in the states, ten of which had established some kind of public pension plan by 1930 (Stein-Roggenbuck 2008, 72). By the time an old-age pension program was adopted in Michigan, late in 1933, there were already twenty-eight states with old-age pension laws. Michigan's establishment of a statewide pension system was not only late, it was also too little—its function seemed to be more to provide "symbolic reassurance" than to actually provide and fund an adequate mechanism for the support of elder Michiganians (Powell, Williamson, and Branco 1996, 15). Eligibility requirements were stringent: potential recipients were required to be age 70 or older, far beyond the average life expectancy at the time, and to have been U. S. citizens for at least fifteen years and continuous Michigan residents for at least ten years (Stein-Roggenbuck 2008, 72). The average pension paid under this program was less than ten dollars per month (Stevenson 1936, 240).

The pension program was funded by the state but administered by the counties. Successful applicants who owned a home were required to deed their property to the county before drawing their pension. Pensioners who surrendered their property received a lifetime lease to remain in their homes. Less than a third of those who were technically eligible applied, and few of those who applied received a pension. Over 42,000 applications were submitted from an estimated eligible population of almost 150,000 in the state, but by the end of 1934, only about 15,000 of those applications had been evaluated at all, and only 2,660 awarded (Armstrong 1935, Exhibit C). The statewide pension system therefore barely scratched the surface of poverty among the old in Michigan. Eligible applicants who lived in poverty but owned a home were understandably reluctant to relinquish their property in exchange for such paltry benefits. The system required the counties to evaluate the pension applications, but they were not equipped to handle the task of investigating so many applicants. At the state level, the system was severely underfunded due to Michigan's precarious fiscal condition in the throes of the Depression and to the law's poor provisions for collecting a designated head tax. Sufficient resources were not available to provide for Michigan's struggling elders until the state received grants under the federal Old Age Assistance program, which was implemented in 1935. Until then, the vast majority of old men and women faced with poverty in the midst of the Depression were simply unable to rely upon even a meager pension from the State of Michigan.

Growth of the County Poor House

The Great Depression not only severely strained Detroit's families, the Detroit Department of Public Welfare, and the State of Michigan, but also put Wayne County and its infirmary at Eloise to the test. The absolute bottom of the safety net, the last place older destitute Detroiters could go to escape death from homelessness and starvation, Eloise weathered the storm remarkably well and better than most local institutions. Indeed, even after four years of dealing with the fallout of the Depression, one contemporary commentator labeled Eloise "the Finest Poorhouse in the World" (Robbins 1934, 9). The DDPW had always referred clients who were unable to live independently to Eloise, but when the Depression hit, that trickle became a flood. In 1930 alone, the DDPW referred nearly five thousand people to Eloise (City of Detroit 1931, 9).

In order to house the onslaught of indigents entering the institution, the infirmary was continuously expanded during this period. In 1930 its largest dormitory, N Building, was constructed, and within the next few years had been renovated to house more than seven thousand residents. N Building was huge, occupying nearly a quarter-mile strip of land and housing dozens of wards for a total floor area of over ten acres. In order to feed such a throng, its sprawling cafeteria was served by what was claimed to be the largest institutional kitchen in the world, including rows of stainless steel appliances and six huge coffee urns that piped hot coffee to a 200-gallon reservoir in the cafeteria (Clark 1982, 25; Ibbotson 2002, 52).

At the depths of the Depression in 1933, the Eloise infirmary provided warm beds and hot food to over fourteen thousand people over the course of that year alone (Superintendents of the Poor 1933, 35). Although existing records are too incomplete to pinpoint the exact age distribution of its residents, it is certain that most of those living in the infirmary were elderly. Haber and Gratton note that, on a national level, the proportion of poorhouse residents age sixty or older increased through the early twentieth century, reaching two-thirds by 1923 (1994, 123). There is no reason to expect the age profile of the Eloise infirmary population to be very different. The typical infirmary resident at Eloise was an older man; in fact, the staff referred to infirmary residents in general as "pogies," an acronym that stood for "poor old guys in Eloise" (Ibbotson 2002, 49). Even so, during its population peak in 1933, about two thousand of those residing in the infirmary were women (Superintendents of the Poor 1933, 35).

Despite tremendous expansion, the infirmary buildings were generally over their rated capacity throughout the Depression, and the sleeping areas were over crowded. Photographs taken during this era depict N Building wards crammed with long rows of double bunk beds, and the floor of the women's infirmary building lined with mattresses. The huge and crowded wards of the Eloise infirmary must have been frightening to those who were not only accustomed to living on their own, but also living comfortable middle-class lifestyles, such as the clients discussed in the following chapters. The idea of compulsory labor must have been frightening as well, particularly to those older women who had done little paid labor and had depended on their fathers and husbands for support throughout their lives; yet at Eloise, all able-bodied residents were expected to devote a minimum of four hours per day working to help run and maintain the facility. In 1933 there were 3,266 residents (called "patients" by the staff) who were "employed throughout the entire Eloise Hospital and Infirmary, in the kitchens, dining rooms, wards, shops, farms, dairy, and general maintenance" (Gruber 1934).

Little is known about the experiences of the residents who lived in the Eloise infirmary during the Great Depression. Nearly all of the official resident records have been lost, and no writings by those who resided there at the time have been found. A few contemporary published and unpublished works describe the institution itself, but all were written by employees rather than residents, and they tend to focus on the facility and its administration rather than the lives of the people who lived, and sometimes died, there. A cemetery was established on the grounds of Eloise in 1910, and about 7,100 deceased infirmary residents were buried there in the thirty-eight years it was used (Ibbotson 2002, 94). The graves are either unmarked or marked only with numbered stones, and the records for most of those have been lost. Stephen Pimpare observed that historians frequently neglect "the lived experience of the poor and marginalized," and the paucity of source material on the poor and marginalized residents of Eloise bolsters that view (2007, 247).

The only known Depression-era history of Eloise was completed in 1933 but never published. Written by a long-time member of the Eloise management, Stanislas Keenan, it was intended to be the second edition of one originally published in 1913, but was not published due to Wayne County's financial struggles at the time. Only a single short chapter of the book, out of a total of forty-five chapters, deals with the "Inhabitants of Eloise" (Keenan 1933, 644-8). The remainder of the book provides great detail on the buildings, facilities, programs, and managers of the institution, but conspicuously neglects its residents, further confirming Pimpare's point. The small amount of Keenan's work devoted to the old and poor Eloise residents was suffused with sympathy toward them, although it was primarily couched in the language of paternalism and moralism commonly used in that era when discussing poverty and its victims. In fact, the concepts of worthiness, blamelessness, filial obligation, and social class frequently employed to describe the old poor in the early twentieth century in general, and used in many of the Visitors' accounts and public descriptions of the Hannan clients in particular, provide the foundation for Keenan's description of the Eloise infirmary residents:

> Many of our inmates, many even of the unfortunate class addicted to the use of alcoholics, have not lost the breeding and training of their youth. Beneath their rough vesture beat hearts still susceptible to "the slings and arrows of outrageous fortune," and the ever-present thought of what they were, and what they are, smites them cruelly. We have men and women who have known the good things of life, who asked no odds of any man until the hand of fate smote them down. We have men of education and refinement who filled an honorable sphere of life before the clouds of misfortune darkened their existence. To the Infirmary they come when relatives and friends have grown tired of them, and wish they were dead. Poor old men and women bowed down beneath the weight of years seek rest in our institution where the cruel world can buffet them no more, where heartless sons and daughters no more can make the evening of their lives a bitter sorrow. If you would learn what sorrow is, if you would know what unfeeling children are ofttimes, mingle with our poor . . . What a blessing for those aged sufferers there is such a place as the big Wayne County Infirmary, with a big-hearted county behind it . . . Shut out from the rest of the world those destitute creatures with snow-white locks, and faces deeply seamed with sadness and sorrow, find at Eloise a release from contemptuous shrugs and withering scorn. (Keenan 1933, 646-7)

Keenan describes Eloise as a safe and deserved refuge for innocent victims of circumstance, a place of respite from poverty and the harsh judgment of society for those who have landed there through no fault of their own. It also casts the county as the kind and understanding paternal figure on whom the victims of poverty can rely. This contrasts with the popular notion of Eloise as a place to be feared and scrupulously avoided, an awful dumping ground for life's losers. In the words of a local amateur historian of Eloise, "[p]arents used to drive their kids past in cars and tell them that if they weren't good they'd drop them off at Eloise" (Cauffiel 2001, 62). Despite the fact that the indigent residents of the infirmary and the mentally ill residents of the asylum lived in entirely different buildings on the grounds of Eloise, there was little distinction in the popular imagination. The horror of insanity and the shame of poverty combined to stain Eloise as a terrible place in the public mind. Generations of Detroiters "grew up believing that it wasn't a haven, but a place to be dreaded" (Cauffiel 2001, 62). Those generations included the Hannan clients who spoke of their fear of being compelled to live out the remainder of their lives behind the iron gates of Eloise (see Langlois and Durocher's description of one such client in chapter 9). Eloise was able to avoid the dysfunction and financial ruin experienced by the DDPW, but it was not able to escape its reputation as a place of fear and failure.

Fear, Dignity, Control, and the Failure of Local Public Welfare

As the following chapters will show, the Hannan cases reflect the lives of people whose struggles against poverty involved a good measure of fear in their efforts to maintain dignity and control over their own lives. They feared being unable to support themselves, becoming a burden to their families, and losing control of their lives to adult children, relief workers, and institutions. Applicants and clients especially feared being sent to Eloise, a reflection of the general fear of the poorhouse that had plagued old age for generations. As an early advocate for a nationwide public pension system noted, "The poorhouse stands as a threatening symbol of the deepest humiliation and degradation before all wage-earners after the prime of life" (Haber and Gratton 1994, 134). It also stands as a symbol of the ultimate loss of autonomy, privacy, and agency, a brick-and-mortar monument to the loss of control. The fear of the poorhouse, therefore, was not unique to those who faced the prospect of going to Eloise in Depression-era Detroit, but it was greatly augmented by fear arising from the economic crisis that led to widespread unemployment and poverty, social unrest, and the collapse of the municipal welfare system that had served those in need so well in the past.

What broader lessons can be learned from Detroit's experience in the 1920s and 1930s? If any city's public welfare system were going to survive the Great Depression intact, it should have been Detroit's. The DDPW ran the largest, best-funded, most professionalized public welfare system in the United States, and even it could not stand up to the overwhelming rush of need unleashed by the economic collapse that began in October 1929. Despite the department's best efforts, it had ceased to function effectively by the fall of 1932, when as many as 1,700 unemployed and homeless men were sleeping on the streets (Fine 1975, 280). The DDPW was finally revived, not through increased local funding, but by massive external assistance from the Federal government.

This revival was not without controversy, for a significant political faction in Detroit saw the involvement of the Federal government as a threat to local control, what Stein-Roggenbuck calls "home rule" and "fiscal localism." Wrapped up in these concepts, besides an obvious aversion to increased taxes on any level and the resistance to outside influence, particularly from the Federal government, are the local approaches to social welfare that emphasize prevention, deterrence, and rehabilitation of those in poverty (Berkowitz 1991, 8). Home rule and fiscal localism were also associated with "a hostility to professional social work" and a preference for welfare administration by "business professionals" who could assure efficiency and the minimization of waste. It seems that the greatest fear of some was not widespread poverty and the social unrest that might arise from it, which were the concerns that motivated people such as Frank Murphy, but rather the "fear of creating dependence and a reliance on the private sector for solutions to the economic downturn" (Stein-Roggenbuck 2008, 3). However, the investigative and rehabilitative functions of the DDPW were the first to be cast aside as caseloads grew to unmanageable heights. At that point, the department focused on merely preventing immediate homelessness and starvation rather than the longer-term goals, steeped in moralism, of keeping malingerers off the rolls and providing poor families with the training and middle-class values that would convert them into productive members of society.

Of course, moralistic concerns about rewarding laziness and reinforcing bad values and behavior with "easy assistance" persisted long beyond the acceptance of Federal funds by local welfare systems. As

Stein-Roggenbuck points out, Federal relief programs such as those run by CWA and WPA were geared toward "employables," those people who had the ability to work and just needed rehabilitation or the opportunity to do so. As such, enrollment in these programs was adjudicated by investigative social workers who made decisions based on the moral worthiness of the applicants and their families. *"Unemployable* individuals, unable to work because of age, health, disability, or family responsibilities, were confined to the local relief programs," such as those run by DDPW and funded by Federal grants (2008, 79; italics in original). The unemployables were not considered to be at risk for welfare-created dependency because their physical or social conditions made them naturally dependent, and they were not candidates for rehabilitation for the same reason. However, whether it applied to candidates for rehabilitation or not, some measure of moralism, concern over dependency, and deterrence persisted in the local relief programs of the DDPW.

These same moral values have persisted as guiding principles of welfare policy to the present day, becoming particularly apparent during discussions of welfare reform such as those that occurred during the 1980s and 1990s. In the case of old people, although it is no longer reflected in the law and public policy, the impulse sometimes remains to retrospectively judge them in the conduct of their working lives against the standards of industry, frugality, and temperance, and therefore to assign moral culpability for their poverty in old age. Some element of moralism is likely to persist in future debates over the public policy of welfare and social insurance in America.

Another guiding principle of welfare policy, familism, also persisted through the Depression era and beyond, but has not fared as well in more recent years. As was clear in the 1930s, familism as a basis for the distribution of relief, particularly old-age relief, has its limits. Some people do not marry, some do not have children, and some have poor families or do not get along with their families. The people who have no families upon which to rely in times of hardship are ill served by a system built on familism. As society has developed, so has the notion of individuality and autonomy, so that filial obligation faces intense competition from the desire of family members to live independently and to be free of the expectations of care. As society has evolved, so have new alliances that cannot be easily reconciled with the traditional nuclear or three-generation family (children, parents, and grandparent), such as single-parent families, families headed by unmarried and same-sex partners, grandparents raising grandchildren without the presence of the middle generation, and fictive kin—groups of friends who are not related but who function like a kinship network. The superiority of the nuclear family as the primary moral and economic unit is still strongly propounded in many circles, but practical concerns over the definition of the family and the rights of individuals should preclude a return to familism. Such a policy concentrates the potentially costly risk of old age within families, or within individuals without families, leaving them vulnerable to catastrophe. The great value of a social insurance program such as Social Security is that it distributes that risk widely across the population, minimizing the impact of an aging-related crisis on individuals and families. In chapter 11, Toni Calasanti provides an extended argument for such risk-management through social insurance programs. She uses specific Hannan cases as graphic examples of what the lives of old people and their families were like before Social Security was available and argues that today, Social Security supports the family system, not just its elder members, and is therefore crucial to the general public welfare.

Moralism and familism in the administration of public welfare certainly created problems for applicants to the DDPW, but they had little to do with the downfall of the Department. What created the conditions for municipal welfare failure was the severe economic crisis, combined with the inherent limits of fiscal localism. The cost of retaining local control over funding of public welfare was the total inability of the system to handle the demands imposed by the Depression. When a significant segment of the economy fails, as did manufacturing during the Depression, and when that segment of the economy is concentrated in certain geographical areas, as manufacturing was in Detroit, local funding solutions will inevitably fall short as tax revenues decline. Geographic concentration of certain industries also concentrates the risk of bankruptcy when those industries fail, unless that risk is pooled with other areas susceptible to different failures.

The logic of risk pooling on a national basis is that it prevents failures such as those experienced by older Detroiters during the Depression. Sharing the risk widely across a large *geographical area*, in contravention to the principles of fiscal localism, minimizes the risk to particular states and cities. Likewise, sharing the risk widely across a large *population*, in contravention to the principles of familism, minimizes the risk to particular families and individuals. Certainly personal responsibility takes an important place in the panoply of American values, but if the Depression taught us anything, it should have been that the systemic failures and structural collapses inherent in capitalism engulf plenty of good hardworking people in their wreckage, people who cannot be blamed for their economic losses. Developing a sense of shared responsibility and instituting some measure of protection against the risks posed by the structure of our economic system is essential to individual security, and hence to collective well being. Re-familizing and re-localizing our approach to old-age support would only re-concentrate that risk and place us in the same vulnerable position occupied by elders during the Great Depression.

While I have made a socio-historical argument here for national safety nets that distribute economic and social risks, contributors to part 3 of this volume provide case histories that illustrate the risks specific old people and their families endured during the Great Depression. Collectively, these chapters provide concrete micro-level evidence for the macro-level arguments I have made here, and they inform the concluding chapters in which Toni Calasanti and Ruth Ray explain the ethics of social responsibility and interdependence from which these safety nets must be woven if they are to endure. In the next chapter, Ruth Ray provides more evidence against the over-reliance on familism and fiscal localism. She describes how local charity networks were also overwhelmed by the Great Depression and in no position to fill the gaps created by limitations in the public welfare system. Many fell through those gaps, and even old people and their families who were supported by charities, including the Luella Hannan Memorial Home, struggled and often suffered.

Notes

1. From a radio address delivered by Frank Murphy on March 6, 1933, quoted in Lunt (1965, 77).
2. This historical perspective is not without controversy. Historians of aging have argued about modernization theory and whether and when advancing industrialization and changes in economic conditions led to changes in the status of families and their elders. Is it true that "on the basis of existing data, . . .a solid and for the first time thorough modernization of the elderly has occurred . . . during the interwar years" (Achenbaum and Stearns 1978, 310)? Or is it rather that the "transition in age relations began in America before urbanization [and] industrialization" and that "[w]e must, therefore, reject 'modernization'" as an explanation for these transitions (Fischer 1978, 102)? Or perhaps the truth is to be gained by "relinquishing the quest for universal patterns of development" entirely (Hendricks 1982, 339). Whatever the case, elder poverty was a significant problem during this era (Patterson 1986, 40) and the expectation that adult children would house and care for their parents was a significant source of "intergenerational tensions" (Gratton and Haber 1993, 147).

References

Achenbaum, W. Andrew. 1978. *Old Age in the New Land.* Baltimore, MD: Johns Hopkins University Press.

Achenbaum, W. Andrew and Peter N. Stearns. 1978. "Old Age and Modernization." *The Gerontologist* 18: 307-312.

Armstrong, Barbara Nachtried. 1935. *Old Age Security Staff Report.* Washington, DC: Bureau of Labor Statistics Committee on Old Age Security. http://www.ssa.gov/history/reports/ces/ces2armstaff.html.

Berkowitz, Edward D. 1991. *America's Welfare State: From Roosevelt to Reagan.* Baltimore, MD: The Johns Hopkins University Press.

Bruce, Isabel Campbell and Edith Eickhoff. 1936. *The Michigan Poor Law.* Chicago, IL: The University of Chicago Press.

Cauffiel, Lowell. 2001. "A World Apart." *Hour Detroit Magazine,* April.

Clark, Alvin C. 1982. *A History of the Wayne County Infirmary, Psychiatric, and General Hospital Complex at Eloise, Michigan 1832-1982.* Detroit, MI: Wayne County Board of Institutions.

City of Detroit. 1930. *Detroit Department of Public Welfare Annual Report for the Calendar Year of 1929.* Detroit, MI: Department of Public Welfare.

City of Detroit. 1931. *Detroit Department of Public Welfare Annual Report for the Calendar Year of 1930.* Detroit, MI: Department of Public Welfare.

Durand, John D. 1968. *The Labor Force in the United States, 1890-1960.* New York, NY: Social Science Research Council.

Fine, Sidney. 1975. *Frank Murphy: The Detroit Years.* Ann Arbor, MI: University of Michigan Press.

Fischer, David Hackett. 1978. *Growing Old in America.* New York, NY: Oxford University Press.

Gavrilovich, Peter and Bill McGraw. 2006. *The Detroit Almanac.* Detroit, MI: Detroit Free Press.

Gratton, Brian and Carole Haber. 1993. "Rethinking Industrialization: Old Age and the Family Economy." Pp. 134-59 in *Voices and Visions of Aging: Toward a Critical Gerontology,* edited by Thomas R. Cole, W. Andrew Achenbaum, Patricia L. Jakobi, and Robert Kastenbaum. New York, NY: Springer.

Gruber, Thomas. K. 1934. *Report Given on January 10, 1934 to the Wayne County Superintendents of the Poor by T. K. Gruber on Employment of Patients.* Eloise, MI: Author.

Haber, Carole. 1993. "'And the Fear of the Poorhouse'": Perceptions of Old Age Impoverishment in Early Twentieth-Century America." *Generations* 17, no. 2: 46-51.

Haber, Carole and Brian Gratton. 1994. *Old Age and The Search for Security: An American Social History.* Bloomington, IN: Indiana University Press.

Haber, William and Paul L. Stanchfield. 1936. *Unemployment, Relief and Economic Security.* Lansing, MI: State Emergency Welfare Relief Commission.

Hendricks, Jon. 1982. "The Elderly in Society: Beyond Modernization." *Social Science History* 6, no. 3: 321-45.

Ibbotson, Patricia. 2002. *Eloise: Poorhouse, Farm, Asylum, and Hospital 1839-1984.* Chicago, IL: Arcadia Publishing.

Johnson, Fred R. 1922. "Public Relief of Unemployment." *The Survey* 48, no. 2: 47-8.

Johnson, Fred R. 1929. "The Field of Public Welfare." *Annals of the American Academy of Political and Social Science* 145, no. 1: 31-6.

Katz, Stephen. 1996. *Disciplining Old Age.* Charlottesville, VA: University of Virginia Press.

Keenan, Stanislaus M. 1913. *History of Eloise: Wayne County House, Wayne County Asylum.* Detroit, MI: Thos. Smith Press.

Keenan, Stanislaus M. 1933. *History of Eloise: Wayne County House, Wayne County Asylum* (2nd ed.). Unpublished manuscript.

Lunt, Richard D. 1965. *The High Ministry of Government: The Political Career Of Frank Murphy.* Detroit, MI: Wayne State University Press.

Matson, Opal. V. 1933. *Local Relief to Dependents.* Detroit, MI: Michigan Commission of Inquiry into County, Township, and School District Government.

Norton, William J. 1933. "The Relief Crisis in Detroit." *The Social Service Review* 7, no. 1: 1-10.

Ogburn, William Fielding. 1922. *Social Change.* New York, NY: B.W. Huebsch.

Patterson, James T. 1986. *America's Struggle Against Poverty, 1900-1985.* Cambridge, MA: Harvard University Press.

Pimpare, Stephen. 2007. "Toward a New Welfare History." *The Journal of Policy History* 19, no. 2: 234-52.

Powell, Lawrence Alfred, Williamson, John B., and Branco, Kenneth J. 1996. *The Senior Rights Movement: Framing the Policy Debate in America.* New York: Twayne Publishers.

Riley, Matilda White, Kahn, Robert L., and Foner, Anne. 1994. *Age and Structural Lag.* New York, NY: John Wiley & Sons.

Robbins, Daniel M. 1934. "Eloise, the Finest Poorhouse in the World." *Michigan Christian Advocate*, February 15, 9.

State of Michigan. 1925. "Public Act 146." In *Public Acts of the Legislature of the State of Michigan Passed at the Regular Session of 1925*, 188-212. Lansing, MI: Robert Smith Co.

Stein-Roggenbuck, Susan. 2008. *Negotiating Relief: The Development of Social Welfare Programs in Depression-Era Michigan, 1930–1940.* Columbus, OH: The Ohio State University Press.

Stevenson, Marietta. 1936. "Old-Age Assistance." *Law and Contemporary Problems* 3, no. 2: 236-45.

Stillman, Charles C. 1931. *Outdoor Relief as Administered by the Detroit Department of Public Welfare* (Report 119), February. Detroit, MI: Detroit Bureau of Governmental Research.

Superintendents of the Poor. 1933. *One Hundredth Annual Report of the Super-intendents of the Poor, Wayne County Michigan.* Detroit, MI: The Inland Press.

The Department of Public Welfare. 1927. *Community Fund News of Metropolitan Detroit*, June.

U. S. Department of Labor. 1936. "Michigan Population and Unemployment Census, 1935." *Monthly Labor Review* 43: 1157-64.

Chapter 3

Private Response to the
Needs of Old People

Ruth E. Ray

"Charity begins at home, and justice begins next door."
—Charles Dickens, 1844

On September 8, 1933, four years into the Great Depression, President Franklin D. Roosevelt spoke to the Conference on Mobilization for Human Needs, reinforcing the common belief that charity begins at home:

> When we came to the problems of meeting the emergency of human needs, we did not rush blindly in and say, "the Government will take care of it." We approached it from the other angle first. We said to the people of this country, "When you come to the problem of relief, you face the individual family, the individual man, woman and child who lives in a particular locality, and the first objective and the first necessity are that the citizens of that community, through the community chest, the social and charitable organizations of the community, are going to be expected to do their share to the utmost extent first" (Roosevelt 1933, n.p.).

In speaking to charity workers from around the country, President Roosevelt made clear that the federal government would step in to provide "emergency relief" only after all other sources of support had been exhausted—first familial, then communal (through churches and other charitable organizations), then local and state governments, which he admonished to stop "thinking in political and not in human terms." Many historians have documented the prevailing attitude at the time among both politicians and charity workers as "grounded in a traditional welfare philosophy of local self help" and founded on the belief that "we are our brother's keeper" (Jones 1990, 14-15).

The spirit of Roosevelt's National Recovery Administration (NRA) was, in the President's words, one of "cooperation" in which many levels of society would work together to meet human needs and "build from the bottom up." Roosevelt spoke directly against the tendency at each level "to put the burden on somebody else with the general thought in the back of our heads, 'If we don't do it somebody else will, and, in the last analysis, the kindness of Uncle Sam will see to it that we do not fail'" (1933, n.p.). Prior to Roosevelt's New Deal policies, the state carried little of the burden for economic relief, and the federal government considered it "entirely outside the scope of its functions to participate in 'paternalistic legislation,'" including aid for dependent women, children and elders (Mueller 1936). President Herbert Hoover's stance in 1930 was that private charity and local government, not the federal government, were the best means of support for those struggling in the early years of the Depression.

In fact, city governments carried much of the responsibility for relief in those early years. Surveys from the Great Depression indicate that in 1931, about 70 percent of the relief in U.S. cities was provided by public welfare departments and 30 percent by private agencies (Benjamin 1932). Assistance from public welfare typically consisted of "home relief"—a grocery order, fuel, clothing, and in some cases money for rent—and when possible "work relief"— a job for one or more family members. A 1931 study of thirty cities in the state of New York by the Joint Committee on Unemployment Relief found that relief for a family of four ranged widely, depending on the city, from three dollars every other week to six to seven dollars every week (Benjamin 1932).

However, city governments alone could not meet the rise of human need during the Great Depression, as Thomas Jankowski (chapter 2) made clear in his description of Detroit's public welfare system. The Department of Statistics of the Russell Sage Foundation, which began collecting data in 1929, reported that nationwide, amounts spent on relief by charities increased steadily between 1929 and 1930 and jumped dramatically in 1931, at which point many reached or exceeded their capacity (Benjamin 1932). The Executive Director of the Federation of Jewish Charities in Philadelphia wrote in 1931, "as a social worker, I have no hesitation in saying that although we are spending in the United States hundreds of millions of dollars a year in the maintenance of our private philanthropies, we are bankrupt when it comes to tackling the situation before us" (Billikopf, 69). This was the case even though the number of philanthropic organizations had increased dramatically in the 1920s at the national level, as well as in the city of Detroit.[1] Public and private charities together could not respond adequately to the "clamoring for relief" caused by widespread unemployment, poverty, homelessness, and hunger (Benjamin 1932, 135).

Just as public and private charities found themselves overwhelmed, so did families, friends, and neighbors. Over time, there was considerable decline in the "informal personal relief" (Mueller 1936) that had once kept people off "the dole"—loans from family members and friends, corner grocers who sold on credit, and landlords who allowed a few missed payments. As LeRoy Bowman explains in a 1932 article, the economic Depression "sapped the community in America," and by 1931, "in vast numbers of cases, resources of friends, neighbors and relatives [had been] exhausted" (925).

The result was a significant drop in the general standard of living, as well as a corresponding drop in relief standards and a curtailment of social services. According to a November 20, 1935, editorial in *The Nation*, a publication of the National Relief Administration, relief standards in New York city were by then 40 percent below those of private welfare agencies, with no allowance for household expenses or carfare to look for work; inadequate allowance for clothing; and "so little for rent that families frequently had to use part of their food money of about eight cents a meal per person to make up their rent deficit" ("This Business of Relief," n.p.). Community organizations, including parents' and teachers' associations, service clubs, urban leagues and settlement houses, tried to help fill the gap, and more pressure was brought to bear on individuals to contribute to the humanitarian effort (Bowman 1932). Yet with all of these efforts combined, communities were unable to meet even the most basic needs of many residents. Homelessness rose to levels never before seen in America's industrial cities. In Detroit, when Frank Murphy was inaugurated as mayor in 1930, he pledged to assist the "great city of destitute folks living within a city" who needed immediate assistance (Fine 1975, 258). Murphy immediately established the Mayor's Committee on Unemployment, whose first job was to document the number of unemployed people living in Detroit. Based on its first informal census in October 1930, the Committee concluded that 110,000 people were without jobs, and many were sleeping in city parks. In July 1932, when the Department of Public Welfare announced that, contrary to previous reports, it would not be able to reimburse landlords for months of unpaid rent, hundreds of families were evicted, and a city park in southwest Detroit was set up as an emergency camp, with private citizens and the National Guard donating tents ("How the Depression Changed Detroit"). By February 1933, 210,000 Detroit residents had registered as unemployed with the mayor's committee (Fine 1975, 265).

The plight of the old man and woman during this time was especially severe, given that public relief focused on finding work for young and middle-aged men and assisting families with children. Elders who had no families were destined for charity-sponsored old-age homes or the county poorhouse. In Detroit, men and women over sixty, most of whom had no pensions from their former employers, pieced together support from many sources, both public and private: the Detroit Department of Public Welfare, lodges and fraternal organizations, the Wayne County Soldiers' and Sailors' Relief Committee, the Detroit League for the Handicapped, the Goodfellows, the Detroit Newsboys' Association, the Detroit Police Relief Fund, churches and religious organizations, neighborhood clubs, landlords, family, and friends. They also did odd jobs to provide an occasional income, such as sewing, piecework and day work. A great many took roomers into their houses and apartments, an arrangement that provided their only regular source of income.

Charity and the Family System

"The burden is quite heavy for the daughter, Mrs. W, who now is caring for her mother, her aunt, her three minor children, and part of the support of a married daughter" (LHMFC, Case #456).

Against this socio-economic backdrop, the pensions provided by the Luella Hannan Memorial Home (LHMH) were comparatively generous for the small and select group of people to receive them. The LHMH made it clear, however, that its assistance was "not intended and [would] not be used to relieve relatives of their just financial responsibilities" (LHMH Board of Trustees 1930). It also made clear that its pensions were to cover the expenses of elder clients only and "not be used as a family income" (LHMFC, Case #354), although the lines between old-age and family support soon blurred in actual practice. The LHMH social workers (then called "friendly visitors" in the field of social work and "Visitors" in the case files) interviewed siblings, children, grandchildren, and occasionally nieces and nephews of applicants to determine their ability to support the elder family member. Many applications were denied when Visitors decided that family members could provide support.

In other cases, a pension was granted with the stipulation that a certain amount go directly to a family member, usually the one with whom the elder resided, in exchange for room and board. In one case, for example, a man, age eighty-four, and his wife, age seventy-eight, were living with their daughter and son-in-law in a five-room house that the younger couple was buying. When the elder couple was granted a pension in 1929, this amount helped pay the mortgage and other household bills. However, when the elder woman became mentally incapacitated and was committed to Eloise, their pension was reduced by half, and the younger couple struggled with the decline in family income, eventually losing their home.

The LHMH case files vividly illustrate the long-term effects of the "business depression," as it was referred to in the files, on families of all types, regardless of socio-economic class. Even formerly wealthy people struggled when they were old. Widows who had been comfortably supported by their prominent banker and businessmen sons found their source of income greatly diminished when the men suffered "reversals" that left them struggling to support their own wives and children.

One Family Among Many

One case of a working class family is especially revealing in terms of the financial stresses particular to the city of Detroit, which had depended on the automobile and related industries for its booming economy in the 1920s. By 1927, Ford's River Rouge plant had become the largest industrial complex in the world, with a multiplex of ninety-three buildings and its own railroad tracks, police and fire stations, hospital, and bus lines. At its peak, the Rouge plant employed over 100,000 and was producing one new car every forty-nine seconds ("History of the Rouge" 2009). Detroit attracted thousands to work in the automobile industry, but during the Depression, when the demand for cars plummeted, workers sometimes got only three or four months of employment out of the year (Romer 1933) and then were laid off indefinitely. Detroit historian Frank Rashid (2009) describes the Rouge Plant as "the epitome of American industry in the 1920s and 1930s," evident in its own promotional materials, as well and its place in the cultural imaginary. In 1937, for example, Upton Sinclair's novel, *The Flivver King*, "deliver[ed] perhaps the most intense criticism of Henry Ford as an American prototype and the Rouge as the centerpiece of industrial capitalism" (Rashid n.p.). More than 50 years later, the Rouge Plant was featured in "A Job at Ford's," Part 1 of the

1993 PBS documentary *The Great Depression*, as "the centerpiece of its examination of the period from the apparent prosperity of the mid-twenties to the 1932 Ford hunger march, in which four demonstrators were killed by security forces employed by Henry Ford" (Rashid n.p.). During the time of the hunger march, the overall unemployment rate in Detroit was reportedly 30 percent and considerably higher in the auto industry.

These are the historical facts. The LHMH case files reveal something of what it *felt* like to be old and dependent on family members who were unemployed during this time. The Visitor's notes in the case of Mrs. Train, a Scudder client, help us see how she and her son, a Ford worker, who already had a conflicted relationship, responded to the added stress of illness and unemployment during the Great Depression.

Mrs. Train was seventy-one years old when she applied for a pension in June 1929. At that time, she lived in a "nicely furnished duplex" in a "fairly good residential district" with her son Harvey and his wife Hazel. Mrs. Train had been sickly for many years. The doctor said she suffered from neuritis (inflammation of the nerves), and her prognosis was doubtful. The Visitor describes Mrs. Train as having "faded brown eyes with deep dark circles beneath"; her feet and ankles were swollen, and she had difficulty walking. Even more striking to the Visitor, however, was the woman's negative attitude. She reports that Mrs. Train was "inclined to whine. She sees very little to hope for in life and feels very much hurt at her son's treatment of her, is entirely out of sympathy with her daughter-in-law and all her friends and family. She is pathetic in her fear of life and death, and begs childishly to be taken care of" (LHMFC, Case #75). Mrs. Train was clearly worn out from the oppressions of hard labor and single motherhood. She had done "day work" (general housekeeping) and raised five children alone after her husband died in 1900, leaving her with no income. By 1929, Harvey was her only surviving child. Mrs. Train had been hospitalized in 1925 for "psychopathic inferiority and anterior sclerosis" and had also spent some time in Eloise until Harvey came and got her. The Visitor describes Harvey as a man who "seems to resent [his mother] being in his home, but when she goes away he always comes and gets her, and is very angry when she asks [others] for help" (LMHFC, Case #75). Earlier Mrs. Train had sought old-age assistance at the probate court, and the judge had ordered Harvey to pay his mother fifteen dollars a week for her care, but the Visitor notes that Mrs. Train felt this was "a little hard on Harvey, and nothing more has been done about it."

When the Visitor approached Harvey for an interview, she found an angry, worried man trying to juggle the responsibilities of supporting both his wife and mother. He told the Visitor that he was financially strapped but willing to care for Mrs. Train in his home, even though the situation was "terrible" and he felt "constantly torn between the two women," as well as "humiliated beyond measure by these [charity] organizations investigating him" (LHMFC, Case #75). The LHMH granted Mrs. Train five dollars per week as a supplement to Harvey's support, which Mrs. Train had requested "so that she would not be obliged to ask Harvey for every nickel that she needs." In this case, however, the pension did not relieve the family burden, and the following month, the Visitor found the family situation "acute," with Mrs. Train in a "bad frame of mind," constant quarreling, and Harvey responding with violent temper tantrums. Harvey told the Visitor he felt a duty to his mother and wanted to provide a good home, but he was emotionally spent and "on the verge of shooting the whole family from desperation." The situation seemed to improve temporarily with the Visitor's mediation but quickly deteriorated again in her absence. Over the next few months, Mrs. Train grew more and more depressed and agitated, worrying incessantly about her chronic ailments and what would become of her.

Over time, the Trains experienced increasing financial difficulties. Harvey was getting fewer hours at the Ford Plant, and the family moved twice, seeking cheaper housing. In March, 1930, the Visitor found Mrs. Train in a "crying fit," saying that Hazel's mother had died and the couple wanted to take in Hazel's younger sister and "get rid of her." Mrs. Train told the Visitor that she wanted "to die immediately" and that she could "not understand why she [was] permitted to live since life [was] such a burden to her." By August 1930, Harvey was working only three days a week and had begun drinking more frequently. In March 1931, he hit a man while driving his automobile and was arrested for drunken driving. Hazel's arm was broken in the accident, and Harvey had to pay a $100 court fine, give up his car, and agree to pay $500 restitution to the man whom he had injured. After the accident, Harvey and his wife fought constantly, and Harvey had even more difficulty supporting the family. Hazel, who was working only part-time herself, told Mrs. Train that she should go to Eloise. All were miserable. In June of that year, Mrs. Train repeated to the Visitor "over and over again that she hoped she could die in the near future."

By the spring of 1932, Harvey and Hazel had moved again, looking for a larger home so they could take in Hazel's sister and her elderly father. Meanwhile, Mrs. Train was trying to gain admittance to the old-age home run by the Little Sisters of the Poor. In June of that year, Hazel was laid off from her job for a month's "vacation" with no pay. Harvey was temporarily working five days a week but still making monthly payments to the accident victim. The following month, Hazel was laid off indefinitely, and Harvey was back down to three days a week at Ford's. That September, Harvey came into the LHMH office to report that he had found his mother "sitting on the floor beside an open gas jet." Three days later, Harvey was laid off indefinitely from the Ford Plant. He stayed home to care for Mrs. Train, whose health had declined to the point where she could no longer control her bladder and could barely walk, while his wife worked part-time at another job. A year later, the Visitor reports that Harvey was still unemployed and had "taken to drink."

This family story ends sadly. Mrs. Train's health continued to decline; in September 1933, she was transferred to Eloise, where she died five months later. Harvey told the Visitor that he could not "bear to think of [his mother] being 'dumped into a hole' by the Eloise authorities" and offered to repay the LHMH in monthly installments if they would bury his mother. The LHMH agreed, and Mrs. Train was buried in February 1934 in a "wooden ruff box." Harvey requested specifically that the LHMH accept money from him only in the repayment of this debt, because he did not want to be "placed in the position of having [his wife] say she [had] helped pay for his mother's funeral arrangements." Harvey's sense of filial responsibility continued long after his mother's death. Ten years later, on July 31, 1944, he came into the LHMH office, having bought four plots in a local cemetery for his brother, his mother, his wife and himself, and asked for permission to remove Mrs. Train's body to the family plot.

The story of the Trains illustrates the cumulative effects on an entire family of prolonged unemployment and its attendant miseries, combined with a lack of social benefits for its elder members. While this family was better off than many, certainly those living in tent cities during this period, they still struggled mightily, and not just financially, but emotionally as well. Clearly, this family system needed more social support than one charitable organization could provide, even though the small LHMH pension to Mrs. Train was twice what the State of Michigan would provide in 1934 under its newly established pension law. As Haber and Gratton (1994) explain, for the poor and working class, the economic crisis of the Great Depression "challenged the ability of the family fund to meet basic needs. For the middle class, it proved the incapacity of the private market to guarantee autonomy in old age" (180). Because the Depression affected all socioeconomic classes, it "forged a coalition that demanded that the government ensure a respectable old age—without a continued reliance on the sacrifices of family members" (180). Eighty years later, the time for coalition building has come around again; despite the federal entitlement programs now in place, many Americans need more support—financial, social, and familial—to ensure a respectable old age in the twenty-first century.

LHMH within the Charity Network

In other cases, especially after LHMH resources diminished as a result of the Depression, the Visitors tried to adjust family members' thinking and priorities so that elders could continue living at home. In one case, for example, by the time the applicant, a sixty-two year-old widow, applied for a pension, the LHMH funds were severely taxed. In her investigation, the Visitor found the woman living with her bachelor son and a grand-daughter who belonged to another son whose whereabouts were unknown. The girl was a sophomore in high school and was "not domestically inclined" but was instead "a bookworm and a student," having recently published two stories in her high school literary magazine. The LHMH granted temporary aid to the woman until her son was again employed full time. Part of the Visitor's plan for the family was to ascertain "whether the grand-daughter cannot take a business course at school in preference to merely a literary one with the end view of becoming self-supporting as soon as possible" (LHMFC, Case #248).

Most clients accepted the Visitors' initial plans, because the level of support provided by the LHMH could not be found anywhere else in the city or even the country. A 1930 survey of facilities for the care of old people in Detroit, probably conducted by Executive Secretary Leon Frost and reported in an unsigned memorandum to the Board of Trustees, lists nine private institutions that provided "indoor relief" (institutional care) to people age sixty and over, and most of them were full to capacity. The total number of people provided for in these homes was 581, but the need was far greater: four had waiting lists, and two planned to build new homes to accommodate more residents. All but two were religiously affiliated, and Blacks were accepted at only one place, the Phyllis Wheatley Home, which was designated "for colored only." In addition to these private homes for the aged, the Department of Public Welfare provided about eighty-five old-age pensions or "outdoor relief" (in-home support), according to the survey, and the Eloise Infirmary at that time housed 2,576 old people.[2] The memorandum concludes by reinforcing the need for further research on elder care in the city. Specifically, it mentions the need for a "detailed analysis of the types of care available" across these institutions; an estimate of the number of elders whose needs were not currently being met, including a study of the Eloise population to determine how many clients might be better housed in private institutions; recommendations for "filling the need cooperatively with other agencies"; and suggestions for "better integration of all agencies dealing with old people." The LHMH policy was to deny applicants who were already living in one of these institutions and to drop pensioners who became senile or insane, transferring them to Eloise, where they became wards of the State.

The LHMH decision to support older people in their own homes, as opposed to a facility called the Luella Hannan Memorial Home, had come about gradually. Between 1926 and 1928, the LHMH met resistance to its plan to build a home and was unable to find a suitable location in the Detroit neighborhoods it had investigated. Therefore, late in 1927, the Board began to discuss "the advisability and possibility of immediately starting the work of the Home in assisting certain worthy old people by paying their board and lodging in existing institutions" (LHMH Corporate Minutes, December 11, 1927). At its January 8, 1928, meeting, the Board once again considered the advisability of expending funds in caring for "certain old people," and Mr. Stone, the secretary, was instructed to bring to the next meeting the letters he had received in response to Detroit newspaper articles about the formation of the LHMH. At this meeting, Mr. Norton, an official from the Detroit Community Union was present for an informal discussion "as to the best way in which the Home might for the present disburse certain moneys to worthy applicants who might eventually become guests of the Home" (LHMH Corporate Minutes, January 28, 1928). Mr. Norton was of the opinion that investigations made by the Children's Aid Society (CAS) were comparable to those to be made by the LHMH and suggested that the trustees make arrangements for the part-time use of CAS staff. The following year, in February 1929, an arrangement was made for Leon Frost, Executive Secretary of CAS, to serve as part-time executive secretary for the LHMH. Mr. Frost proposed to do the work for $1000 during the remainder of 1929, with assistance from an investigator and home placer (at $1800 per year) and a stenographer (at $1500 per year), following the salary schedule of the Detroit Community Union,[3] along with $1400 for use of a car. It was the Board's intention, still, to build a home sometime in the future, as evident in its discussions during 1929 and 1930. During these first years, worthy applicants had to agree to live in the home when built. Through the early years of the Depression, the Board and staff continued to refer to itself as the "Home" or the Luella Hannan Memorial Home, although it did not actually build an old-age home until 1971.

We have surmised from the case files that the cost of admission to Detroit's homes for the aged varied considerably. One could be admitted to the Little Sisters of the Poor home for no payment, while admission to the exclusive Thompson Home for Old Ladies required a considerable sum. Most of the homes also charged monthly fees. Moderately priced facilities, such as the Arnold Home and the Kings' Daughters and Sons Home for the Aged, averaged thirty-five to forty dollars per month in 1930 and forty-five to fifty dollars a month in 1935-36. Most of these homes, however, did not accept married couples. The only alternative to an old-age home was a small pension (a maximum of twenty dollars per month, according to case records) from the Department of Public Welfare or emergency assistance in the form of car fare, food, or clothing from the Detroit Associated Charities. In contrast to these sources, most of the pensions provided by the LHMH were sufficient to support a modest but independent lifestyle. The average pension was thirty to fifty dollars a month, which in 1929 was enough to cover room and board in a rooming house or food and rent in a "light housekeeping" apartment or hotel, with five to ten dollars remaining for incidentals. In addition, the LHMH paid for doctor and dental care, bought clothing that could not be purchased with the incidental money, and covered burial costs when necessary.[4]

Given this comparatively generous assistance, along with the stated mission of the LHMH (to assist those "who have been accustomed to enjoying the comforts of life") and its self-representation among Detroit charities, the LHMH developed a reputation among Detroit social workers as the "Cadillac" of charities (Kayrod 2006). Among members of the general public, too, the LHMH was considered (rightly or wrongly) a "rich concern" with "lots of money" (LHMFC, Case #142) that preferred clients with "aristocratic background" (LHMFC, Case #492). When the LHMH also began to administer funds from the more inclusive Scudder Trust, other agencies heard about this (probably through word of mouth, because the LHMH sent no formal written notice) and began to refer clients. In December 1929, for example, an LHMH Visitor got a call from a county social worker with a case she hoped the organization would accept. The worker described her client as industrious, conservative and respectable and, according to the Visitor's notes, "stated that she realized that W[oman] was from plain working people with no educational or cultural background, but understood that the requirements for

the Luella Hannan Memorial Home had been greatly lowered recently"
(LHMFC, Case #302).

In other cases, social workers from various agencies in the city tried
to cast their descriptions of clients in terms that would make them more
acceptable to the LHMH. In November 1930, for example, the newly
established Subcommittee on Relief, part of the Mayor's Committee on
Unemployment, referred a couple, ages 88 and 100, who had requested
aid in the form of food and clothing. According to the letter sent to the
LHMH, the Committee's Visitor found that the couple were living with
an adopted son, age forty-one, who was employed as a laborer and earning fifty dollars a month; his wife, age twenty-nine; their four children,
one of whom was "mentally retarded"; the older couple's widowed
daughter, age fifty-two, employed and earning forty-five dollars a month;
and the widowed daughter's son, age twenty-four, unemployed and also
probably "mentally defective." This family of ten was living on ninety-
five dollars a month and had been assisted by the Department of Public
Welfare the previous summer when the adopted son was not working.
The Committee's Visitor described the elder couple in a way that might
at least merit an initial visit from an LHMH Visitor:

> Mr. C is a very alert old gentleman for a centenarian. He does not wear
> glasses; takes a keen and active interest in the affairs of the day, regis-
> ters and votes regularly. He is convinced that he could qualify for a po-
> sition, and nothing can discourage this idea. The only reason he has not
> registered at the Unemployment Bureau is that he could find no one to
> bring him down town. He begged that he and his wife should not be se-
> parated . . . . The investigator felt that they were of higher type than
> their children and had seen "better days" (LHMFC, Case #469).

Although Mr. C appeared intelligent and ambitious, had "seen better
days" (he and his wife had operated a small grocery business), and was
of a "higher type" than his working-class children, the LHMH Visitor
who later called on the couple concluded that "this case was so plainly
not Hannan that V[isitor] did not bother to make out a face sheet." She
based this conclusion on the fact that the man and woman "had very little
schooling, M[an]a few years in common school and W[oman] just three
months" and they were "living in a little old ramshackle house which
their daughter-in-law. . . is buying on contract" (LHMFC, Case #469).
The Visitor concluded that "the old folks need coal and food; otherwise
they could manage to get along" and referred the case to the Department
of Public Welfare.

On occasion, however, applicants referred by other agencies, including the Department of Public Welfare, did receive pensions from the LHMH. An example is Case #130, a seventy-one year-old woman referred by a DPW worker in June 1929. In a letter to the LHMH, the worker describes the woman as a "high type woman, who has always been in comfortable circumstances." However, she had spent a lot of money on the children of her second husband, and her remaining assets were tied up in theater stock, which was paying very small dividends and which she could not sell. Upon investigation, the LHMH Visitor found that, although born into a working class family (the woman's father had been a foreman in a machine shop), and although the woman had left school at age fifteen to assist her mother, she had married men who had increased her financial status and left her property. This woman was granted a pension.

The Worthy Client[5]

The LHMH Visitors, under the guidance of Leon W. Frost, followed the tenets of the Detroit Associated Charities (DAC), of which the Children's Aid Society, also directed by Frost, was a member. Founded in 1879, the DAC, like other charity organization societies around the country, functioned as a clearinghouse for many private and public charities in the city. It was established on the assumption that the job of charity workers was to address immediate problems and assist the poor in adapting to their environment; this work was best achieved through cooperation among all charitable organizations, following a standardized method of investigating and documenting cases (Zunz 1983; Agnew, 2004). From the inception of the DAC, private charity workers in Detroit had cooperated with public workers from the Board of Poor Commissioners, sharing "the same vision of the poor and work[ing] from the same premises," although serving different clientele (Zunz, 262).[6] According to social historian Olivier Zunz, in Detroit, Blacks and the Anglo-Protestant groups were more disposed to "accept the practice of a thorough investigation" from the DAC, while Catholics, Jews and non-English speaking groups "were more suspicious and avoided the private charities altogether if they could" (270). These religious and cultural divisions are, in fact, reflected in the LHMH case files: a majority of the 508 applicants between 1927 and 1934 were white and Protestant, mainly Episcopalian, Presbyterian, and Methodist. Fifteen percent of the applicants identified themselves as Catholic, and none identified as Jewish, at least in their intake interviews. Only five applicants were identified as "colored" or "negro," indicating that most Blacks neither self-selected nor were referred to the LHMH by local agencies. The 508 applicants were referred by a variety of sources, about 25 percent of which were charitable organizations. Another twenty-three percent referred themselves, and 18 percent were referred by friends or acquaintances. The remainder were referred by doctors, hospitals or convalescent homes, church and business associates, or family members. Occasionally (in twenty-three cases), members of the LHMH Board of Trustees referred clients.

Most people who applied for pensions were responding to the organization's self-promotional efforts, including stories that appeared in the Detroit press between 1927 and 1929 describing qualified applicants under the Hannan Trust as "cultured" and "refined" people. Additionally, Leon Frost circulated a letter in early 1929 to educators, businessmen, lawyers and doctors in the city requesting referrals and using the same language of culture and refinement. A doctor who wrote a letter of referral in May, 1929, in response to Frost's request, summarized his understanding of the intent of the LHMH as giving aid and security to a "carefully selected class of women who have seen 'better' days and have suffered financial loss through the death of a husband or otherwise" (LHMFC, Case #173). The fact that twenty-three percent of the applicants referred themselves, often by letter, suggests a higher level of literacy than one would likely find among the rolls of the DAC.[7]

The difference between Hannan and Scudder clients was primarily one of socio-economic status, as determined by the Visitors and Mr. Frost. The Scudder Trust cast a wider net, providing "aid, in the broadest manner, in the care of elderly people without means of support" and to do so "without regard to race, creed, sex or color." Practically speaking, the Visitors interpreted the language of the two trusts in terms of education, background, and personal bearing. The working and middle-class applicants (carpenters, mechanics, waitresses, housekeepers, seamstresses, laundresses) without education beyond common school and who had not acquired some measure of "refinement" through reading, travel or personal associations were typically given Scudder grants, when funded. Although the LHMH reputation for assisting "high types" under the Hannan Trust was well known, some people who did not fit this definition also applied. One woman, in desperation, applied in November 1929 but withdrew her application when she discovered all the "red tape" required for an investigation. She told the Visitor that she probably wouldn't have been granted a pension anyway, because "this fund was never intended to help working people" (LHMFC, Case #301). A week later, the woman, who was Catholic, applied for assistance from the Society of St. Vincent de Paul.

Indeed, the minutes of the LHMH Board of Trustees reflect some ambivalence toward the Scudder trust in those early years. This is evident in the first (and only) annual report of the LHMH, published in 1930, which makes merely passing reference to the Scudder fund, the Board having decided that "while the John Scudder Fund for Old People should be mentioned in the booklet, a conspicuous place should not be given" (LHMH Corporate Minutes, January 31, 1930). Although the two trusts had both been established in the same year (1925), the Hannan fund was immediately put under the directorship of the LHMH Board of Trustees. The Scudder fund was placed under the guardianship of the Detroit Security and Trust, which had made no immediate plans for distributing the funds.[8] Because of its similar purpose, and because the LHMH had already established a process for administering its own funds, at the suggestion of the Detroit Security and Trust Co., the LHMH assumed responsibility for the Scudder Fund in early 1929. At this time, the Scudder fund amounted to approximately $200,000. Both trusts had been established in perpetuity, meaning that the principles of the trusts could not be spent; only the interest income was available to support clients. Throughout the Depression and thereafter, the LHMH Visitors, Mr. Frost and the Board grappled with the practical issues involved in administering the trusts jointly.

From the beginning, the process of granting pensions to Scudder clients was complicated by financial and legal issues. Scudder applicants were investigated and temporarily funded through the Hannan trust until the Scudder fund was properly established for relief-giving purposes and the cases could be transferred. Clearly, the LHMH Board meant for this to be a temporary arrangement for the first few clients only. The following month, however, the Board discussed the fact that court authority was necessary to administer the Scudder trust in the same way as the Hannan Trust. It therefore decided to continue supporting Scudder cases until the legal issues could be resolved (Corporate minutes, May 20, 1929). Thus began a long practice of shifting clients back and forth between the two trusts, depending on which had available funds. For the purposes of case management, however, clients were still designated as "Hannan" or "Scudder" in the files; when they were moved to another fund, the first case was formally closed, and the client received a new case number under the second fund.

The Scudder fund was nearly exhausted within the first six months of its availability. By September, 1929, qualified Scudder applicants were being denied support on the basis of insufficient funds, and Mr. Frost was instructed to review all Scudder cases "to see if any could be legitimately transferred to the Home" (Corporate minutes, September 6, 1929). Following Mr. Frost's review, nine Scudder clients were transferred at the same allowance, but the Board decided to deny all new applicants (Corporate minutes, September 20, 1929). Mr. Frost was instructed thereafter to investigate only Hannan cases, although two exceptions were made in 1933 and 1934, the latter being the mother-in-law of the late John Scudder himself.

The definition of "worthiness" under both trusts became more stringent over time. By early 1930, the worthy client, for all practical purposes, was a strictly Hannan type who was in dire straits, with no prospects for support from any other source. A funded client who had appeared both worthy and needy in March of 1929 may well have been rejected for the same pension in the fall of that year due to insufficient funds. Indeed, it is questionable whether the very first Hannan clients accepted in March and April of 1929 would have passed muster a year later.

Consider the cases of Jennie McGinnis (Case #1), Sadie James (Case #2) and Elsie Strong (Case #3), all of whom referred themselves by letter in 1927. Miss McGinnis, sixty-four, was born of Scottish farmers and received a public school education. She was single and had supported herself throughout the years as a seamstress. The Visitor found her apartment clean but plain and described the kitchen as "disorderly," the cupboards seeming to "reflect an unsettled mind—nothing has a place. The house generally has very few feminine touches, giving a general atmosphere of austerity" (LHMFC, Case #1). However, Miss McGinnis had worked for prominent women in Detroit who reported that she was respectable and worthy of assistance, and people from her church also wrote letters of recommendation, describing her as an industrious and conscientious worker. Miss McGinnis also had $700 in savings, which for several months she resisted signing over to the LHMH after she was accepted as a client.

Sadie James, age sixty-two, had very little formal schooling due to chronic health problems and had never married. She had lived with a married sister for the fifteen years prior to applying for a pension. Miss James had no means of support other than this sister, and she had no social connections. She offered only to "pray for you and Mrs. Hannan as long as I live" in exchange for support from the LHMH. After her March, 1929 visit to Miss James's home, the Visitor described the woman as neurotic and hypochondriac, yet she was granted five dollars a week, direct to her sister, to offset the costs of her room and board, with the LHMH also providing clothing and medical care.

Elsie Strong, age sixty-six and a widow, had been living in the Old Soldiers' Home in Grand Rapids, Michigan, since 1926, her husband having been a veteran of the Civil War. A former practical nurse, Mrs. Strong had broken a hip and walked with the aid of two crutches. She had lived in Detroit for forty-four years and wished to return so that she could be near friends and pursue litigation on some property she owned. There was also a legal problem surrounding her rights to a veteran's pension, which the LHMH Visitor later helped her resolve. Despite early evidence that Mrs. Strong would be "troublesome and hard to please," she was granted a pension of twelve dollars per week and brought to Detroit via train to live in a boarding home.

All three of these women would likely have been Scudder clients had the fund been available at the time of their application.[9] Miss James was definitely a "Scudder type," while Miss McGinnis might later have been called a "high-type Scudder" because she had cash and social capital (ties to prominent women) that she was able to leverage on her behalf. Mrs. Strong had been a middle-class working woman, and although she had some assets, they were tied up in litigation and government bureaucracy, and she was unable to access them herself, much less sign them over to the LHMH.

Different Clientele

How did the Visitors and Mr. Frost relate to the Scudder clients? It is difficult to say, given that staff opinions are not explicitly stated in the case files. In reading the case notes, however, it appears that the first two Visitors brought over from the Children's Aid Society were perhaps less accepting of Scudder applicants, as suggested by their evaluative language. In one case, for example, the Visitor described the applicant as "only a Scudder client," and in another, the Visitor noted that the applicant was "not even a Scudder case, not to mention a Luella Hannan case." In their descriptions of applicants, the Visitors clearly distinguished between Hannan and Scudder clients. Words and phrases used to describe Hannan types were approving: "come[s] within the class for whom our institution has been established," "from one of the oldest Detroit families," "friends have been among the best of people," "a more worthy woman could not be found," "a lady in every respect," "native refinement and poise," "of good breeding," "used to nice things of life," "good moral character," "educated," "traveled," and "cultured." Scudder clients and their homes were described in more matter-of-fact terms— "ordinary middle-class working family," "a middle class residence, scantily furnished"—or in terms of personal characteristics that reflected sound habits of mind and body: "gentle but strength of will and determination," "respectable looking, hard working type," "optimistic," "appreciative," "gracious," "thrifty," "neat and clean." Scudder clients were hard-working people who had seen better days but who had not necessarily been used to the better things in life. The Scudder pensions were generally ten to twenty dollars per month lower than the Hannan pensions, presumably because Scudder clients were used to living on less, while Hannan clients expected (and were granted) a higher standard of living.

A review of the 508 applications for Hannan and Scudder pensions taken between 1927 and 1934 indicates that by far the largest number of applicants (343) were investigated in 1929, the first year funds became available, including 210 (61 percent) single women (never married, widowed, divorced or deserted); 77 (23 percent) single men; and 56 (16 percent) couples applying jointly. Of these, 196 (57 percent) were funded, 159 under the Hannan trust and 37 under the Scudder trust. Funded Hannan clients included 98 women, 35 men and 26 couples; funded Scudder clients included 10 men, 21 women, and 6 couples. Between 1930 and 1934, fifty-eight more pensions were granted, most of them to Hannan clients. After that time, due to the financial stresses of the Depression on the LHMH itself, no applications were taken again until 1946. The average length of pensions was eight years, with the shortest lasting two weeks (after which the client was dropped for "noncompliance") and the longest lasting thirty-four years (Case #131, described by Bailey-Fakhoury and Dillaway in chapter 6).

Leon Frost, who took seriously his role as a social worker, does not seem to have shared the Board's ambivalence and advocated for at least some of the Scudder clients. He tried to keep the human element in front of the Board, which was increasingly preoccupied by legal and financial matters as the Depression worsened. In July of 1931, for example, after the LHMH had initiated the first of two reductions in Scudder pensions, one Scudder client, Mr. Baker, wrote a letter of thanks to the LHMH for a birthday card, noting that he had "enjoyed it more than all the money you could have sent in its place." On the very day he received it, Mr. Frost sent a copy of the letter to each Trustee, along with the following note, which appears in the file of Mr. Baker:

My dear Mr. Stone:

I am again taking the liberty of sending on to you a copy of a letter I have just received today. The old gentleman is seventy-one years of age. Of course, you are denied a part in not seeing this letter as he wrote it, as the poor wavering hand shake with which it was written only brings closer to one the need which this man has for strong support. Incidentally, he is one of our Scudder family.

I sincerely trust that I am not appearing overly sentimental in passing on this type of material to you as well as the other Board members, but there is such an overwhelming temptation to do it in these days of dire stress.

I know that personally I get a very deep satisfaction from feeling that our organization is lightening the burden, and I am, of course, sure that you fully see this point of view; so it is with this explanation rather than with one of apology that I am passing on to you the copy.

> Very sincerely yours,
> Leon W. Frost
> Executive Secretary

P.S. Since the last meeting we have succeeded in reducing pensions sixty-three dollars per month without causing any injustice or depriving any clients of what they really need. No ill feeling has been evident in this, which was made strictly on a consultation basis with each individual involved (LHMFC, Case #171).

However paternalistic in tone, the letter reflects the challenges Mr. Frost faced in administering the organization's funds during a time of tremendous need and diminishing resources. He had to meet the requirements of the Board—sober, business-minded, men who, in trying to maintain the solvency of the trusts, were becoming more and more parsimonious—while still supporting clients, practicing "good social work" (a reference he made several times in notes on different cases), and maintaining positive relationships with the clients and their families, not to mention the beleaguered Visitors.

With the first sign of decline in its own finances, in January 1930, the Board began to limit the type of clients it would consider even for Hannan pensions. By then, the Hannan fund had been almost completely allocated for pensioned cases. Throughout 1930, the requirements of the Board became increasingly stringent, and in April of that year, Mr. Frost was instructed to use "utmost caution" and to bring to the Board only "the most urgent" cases that "fell in the Hannan classification without question" (LHMH Corporate minutes, April 8, 1930). At this meeting, Mr. Frost was also instructed to survey all local institutions and organiza-

tions that cared of old people for the purposes of "designating two Detroit institutions which [could] be best helped by appropriations from the
estate of John Scudder" (LHMH Corporate minutes, April 8, 1930). Perhaps the Board was attempting to relieve itself of the responsibilities for
providing outdoor relief to Scudder clients by allocating the remaining
Scudder funds to existing institutions. Mr. Frost apparently conducted
the survey, but subsequent Board minutes throughout the 1930s make no
further reference to the proposed re-allocation of Scudder funds, and the
LHMH continued to administer them in the same manner.

Making a Case: The Work of the LHMH Visitor

The LHMH clients' case files look very much like the files kept by other
charitable organizations in the early twentieth century. Consistent with
standards established by the Charity Organization Society movement,[10]
each file contains a face sheet, which includes a case number; the date of
application; the client's name, address, date and place of birth, date of
marriage, and date of partner's death or divorce (if applicable); years
residing in the city; former occupations, names of employers, and length
of service and salary; a list of assets, including property and life insurance policies; memberships in lodges or fraternal organizations; and a list
of children, grandchildren and other possible sources of support, along
with their ages, addresses and occupations. The face sheet appears first in
the file, followed by an account of the intake interview, which usually
took place in the applicant's home within a week of the referral. The intake sheet includes a notation on how the applicant was referred and
when, followed by the Visitor's assessment of the applicant and his/her
environment in terms of type of home and family, physical description,
health and personality, church and recreational preferences, and the
client's cultural background. This section is followed by several narrative
paragraphs that provide a personal history of the applicant, including early family life, education, marriage and occupations, children, and current
situation. Following the life narrative is a section on income that includes
the amount of money the applicant needed to meet monthly expenses,
acquired debt, and the applicant's total income. At the end of the document, the Visitor concludes with a statement of the "problem" and a
"plan" for addressing it, followed by a recommendation that the applicant be funded, that further investigation was needed, or that the case be
closed. Cases recommended for funding were referred to Mr. Frost, who
presented them to the Board of Trustees for a final decision. Mr. Frost

himself recorded the Board's decision in the case file and wrote letters to all applicants reporting the decision of the Board. If an applicant was not funded, the case was closed.[11] In the case of funded applicants, the Visitors then began a chronological log in which they described all subsequent interactions with and about each client. Typically, clients received visits at one-month intervals. Any changes in the client's status in regards to health, finances, living situation, or attitude were recorded, along with arising legal or economic issues, followed by a new plan to address the changes in situation. When the case was transferred from one Visitor to another, the first Visitor provided a summary of the case-to-date. The case was closed when the client died, was transferred to another fund, or was dropped from the rolls. After closing the case, the Visitor provided a final summary. Sometimes the log was extended after the final summary in situations where the organization continued to be involved in familial, legal or financial issues regarding the client's estate. Photographs were taken of some clients, usually in or around their homes or in front of the LHMH office, and these were also placed in the case file.[12]

Case files often included one or more folders in addition to the main folder containing the face sheet, intake interview, and case log. These additional folders include correspondence from the client, letters of recommendation, copies of correspondence to the client from the LHMH, signed agreements between the LHMH and the client, transfer sheets detailing moves from one place to another, change-of-term forms recording an increase or decrease in pension, medical records and letters from physicians, a list of clothing purchased over the years, and other information pertinent to the case. Files range in length from a single page, in the case of applicants not investigated, to several hundred pages, in the case of long-term clients. Maintaining these detailed files was extremely time-consuming for the Visitors, even with the help of a stenographer.

There were five main Visitors who investigated applicants and wrote these case notes: the two original investigators transferred from the Children's Aid Society (CAS) and three former teachers, two with bachelor's degrees and one with a master's degree in biology.[13] The two CAS visitors each stayed for about a year. Another visitor was hired in the middle of 1929, and these three investigated the first rush of cases with the help of a few temporary volunteers in late 1929.

The second group of workers—the third visitor and two others hired in early 1930—followed through on these cases, visiting clients monthly and documenting their situations. Anna Wentink was one of the new hires in 1930 and became the only Visitor employed by the LHMH after

March 1933, working with all clients throughout the Great Depression and WWII. Mrs. Wentink was apparently well suited to geriatric social work, despite its many pressures and demands, and in 1948 assumed Mr. Frost's position as Executive Secretary. Ellen Kayrod, who worked as an LHMH visitor under Anna Wentink in the 1950s and assumed her position as Executive Secretary when she retired in 1965, describes Wentink as a "very caring and loving person" who "instilled in us to be always mindful of the client" (Kayrod 2006). Kayrod and the other visitors apparently learned a great deal about caring for old people from Anna Wentink.

The LHMH Visitors were paid according to the scale of the Detroit Community Union, starting at $100 a month. The more experienced CAS workers made $150-$165 a month. Their caseload was heavy, and the job was extremely demanding: the LHMH visitors, along with their counterparts in other organizations in Detroit and around the country, functioned as the "shock troops" of the Depression (Benjamin 1932). According to the first LHMH annual report, between March 1, 1929, and January 1, 1930, the original three visitors made 1,305 calls, conducted 646 office interviews, and made 1,056 supervisions on pensioners. They investigated 171 boarding homes, traveled 16,597 miles, and made 59 shopping trips for clients (LHMH Board of Trustees, 1930). Yet these statistics, though staggering, do not come close to documenting the physical, social and emotional labor required of the Visitors during this time.

In *Friendly Visiting Among the Poor* (1906), author Mary Richmond, who was then General Secretary of the Charity Organization Society (COS) of Baltimore, names "tact" and "good will," either "instinctive or acquired" as the two main qualities needed to be a good Visitor. She considered the best training for the job to be "life itself," along with study and experience. Richmond describes the work of the Visitor as "intensely personal," since "friendly visiting means intimate and continuous knowledge of and sympathy with a poor family's joys, sorrows, opinions, feelings, and entire outlook on life" (180). Later, in her book *Social Diagnosis* (1917), Richmond, by then Director of the Charity Organization Department of the Russell Sage Foundation, wrote that Visitors needed to become "accustomed to spend themselves unsparingly" and accept that their lives would be "filled with demands." The whole premise underlying social casework, for Richard and the COS movement, for which she was spokesperson, was "sympathetic study of the individual in his [sic] social environment" (32), the ideal outcome being social justice.[14]

The first task for the LHMH Visitors was to determine whether an applicant qualified for a Hannan or Scudder pension and, if so, how much and under what conditions. If the applicant was granted a pension, the Visitor then oversaw the case until closed. What distinguished LHMH Visitors from social workers in other charitable organizations, such as family welfare agencies, was their exclusive focus on people over sixty (they were among the first geriatric social workers in the U.S.) and the fact that most of their clients had never before applied for charitable assistance.[15] The very characteristics that originally qualified applicants for pensions under the Hannan trust (educated, cultured, refined, socially connected) also made them more likely, when funded, to challenge and negotiate the terms of their pensions. Given the active role that many Hannan clients assumed in the management of their pensions, we cannot adopt, as Karen Tice argues on the basis of her historical study of case files, "simple social control explanations of harsh workers administering to placid clients." Instead, we need "a more kaleidoscopic understanding. . . to account for the mutuality and accommodation between clients and case workers" (Tice 1998, 113). The chapters in part 3 of this volume illustrate the various types and levels of negotiations that occurred between the LHMH Visitors and their clients. My purpose here is merely to sketch out how Visitors made their initial decisions based on the first interview, explaining in more detail how they made the case differently for Hannan and Scudder clients.

Besides family background, occupation, and education, the Visitors followed other class-based indicators, such as physical appearance, affiliations, and the way applicants expressed themselves. If a person looked like she had once had nice clothing, however faded and worn her garments were at the time of application; if her home and personal interests displayed a taste for "better things"; if she enjoyed travel, literature, music, art, and the theater; if she had become accustomed to associating with a "better class" of people; and if she was an intelligent and interesting conversationalist, she was a "Hannan type." If the applicant was of sound moral character, thrifty, conscientious, trustworthy, and hard working but had an "ordinary" background and a common school education, she was a "Scudder type."

Occasionally, the Visitors described "high type" Scudder clients who might legitimately be transferred to the Hannan fund when Scudder monies were exhausted. One example is Case #399, a sixty-five year-old woman who in 1930 had both property and an insurance policy that she was willing to sign over and whom the Visitor determined might still find work selling her homemade furniture polish when the Depression ended. This client was accepted under the Scudder fund, even though few applications were being considered during this period. Some other

Scudder clients were given special consideration at the height of the Depression. For example, in the spring of 1933, Mr. Frost was instructed to move "certain Scudder cases," provided they were "of high enough type," along with several Hannan clients, to the Madison-Lennox Hotel, which the LHMH had acquired through the Hannan estate and which was suffering serious business losses[16] (Corporate minutes, April 6, 1933). One such client, a seventy-five year-old former businessman, had been homeless for several days when he applied for a pension in October 1929, spending his nights "on the streets or resting or sleeping in a cheap all-night theater" (LHMFC, Case #244).

Hard Times for Charities

The case files in late 1929 and early 1930 reveal the early signs of financial stress on the Luella Hannan Memorial Home itself. A closer examination of the minutes of the Board of Trustees meetings helps explain the extent of the problems and their effect on the heavily burdened staff, as well as the clients.

Luella Hannan had established the Hannan Trust in 1925 with $5000, and the LHMH was authorized to commence business as a corporation in October 1925. Mrs. Hannan's check was converted to an interest-bearing certificate of deposit, and the corporation was to be financed further through "donations, bequests and devises and endowment." It appears that, of the three trustees Mrs. Hannan appointed for life, the Rev. Joseph Vance donated his time and so did Ferris Stone, although later he may have charged for some of his legal services, while Julius C. Peter, an official with the Detroit Trust Company, charged for his services as manager of the Hannan Trust.

The Trustees spent the years between 1926 and 1928 trying to acquire a site for the Home. Also during that time, Mrs. Hannan devoted the residue of the estate of her late husband, William W. Hannan to the Women's Hospital and Infants' Home of Detroit and to the LHMH, which received a sum of one million dollars in cash, real estate, stocks, bonds and securities, to be paid in installments as required by the Home to carry out its purpose. The cash from this estate, deposited in July of 1927, amounted to $50,000. The Trustees scouted sites in Palmer Woods, Grosse Pointe, Highland Park, Indian Village, Bloomfield Hills and the neighborhoods surrounding the Detroit civic and art centers—the most wealthy and prominent areas of the city. They also investigated operating costs of established homes to which they considered themselves comparable: St. Luke's Home in Highland Park, the Hollenbeck Home in Los Angeles, and a Presbyterian institution in Evanston, Illinois. The Trustees purchased a property in Grosse Pointe, a suburb in which Mrs. Hannan herself had once resided and where her nephew still lived, but encountered strong opposition to the construction of an old-age home from residents of that city (including her nephew). Given these problems, Mrs. Hannan directed the Board shortly before her death in 1928 to use the income from the Hannan Trust to support elderly people in their own homes. This plan had been first discussed at the December 11, 1927, meeting as an alternative until the property inherited from the Hannan estate could be placed in a more liquid state. The Board discussed the plan again in 1928 and began to enact it in February 1929.

At the April 2, 1929, Board meeting, Julius Peter reported that the estimated annual income of the Home was $143,000, an amount that he felt was more than sufficient to provide pensions for worthy clients. At that meeting, the terms of the Hannan pensions were discussed, with the recommendation that clients turn over all funds in their possession at the time of acceptance, that they be paid a percentage of earnings from these funds until their death, and that the remainder be used for burial and reimbursement to the Home for its assistance. The Board expected that its pensioners would contribute at least some resources in support of the Home's operations. But the year 1929 proved to be an overwhelming period for both the LHMH and its clients. The organization was immediately swamped with applications, and two more investigators had to be hired within the first six months of dispensing aid.

Despite the high number of applications and the growing demands on Mr. Frost and the Visitors, the Hannan Trust remained healthy through 1929. In October 1929, Mr. Peter reported that the income in the Hannan Trust had accumulated in excess of $100,000, and the Board authorized him to invest part of this income in short-term municipal bonds. In December of that year, all clients received $5 Christmas checks, Frost received a $250 Christmas bonus, and the Visitors and stenographer each received a $50 bonus. Additionally, Frost's salary for 1930 was boosted to a fixed rate of $275 a month, a very comfortable middle-class wage.

Despite this outward prosperity, the minutes of the Board meetings in 1930 reflect a growing concern (and conservatism) regarding finances. On January 14, Mr. Peter's financial reports showed that the remaining income (after investments) from the Home was "just about currently expended for pensioned cases." The Board's language in regard to future client selection became increasingly cautious over the next few months, and in April 1930, the Board began to scrutinize pensioners' expenditures more closely, dropping some clients for non-compliance. The Board decided that in the future the LHMH would notify accepted clients that "a grant had been *temporarily* made, rather than to word the notification so that it might be construed that a permanent pension had been granted" (Corporate minutes, June 20, 1930, emphasis added). This was a significant change in both attitude and policy, as previously the LHMH and its clients had behaved as if a pension, once awarded, represented a long-term commitment—what we would today call "life care." In October, Frost was instructed to "accept only absolute emergency cases" and the following month he was told not to prepare an annual report for the year 1930 "on account of economic conditions." That year, the staff's Christmas bonuses were half what they had been the previous year.

More cost-saving measures ensued over the next two years, some of which actually benefited a few clients. For example, The LHMH began to allow clients to live in the homes they had turned over to the organization; since it was unable to sell the houses for profit, Julius Peter had determined that the LHMH could at least receive a tax exemption if the properties were used for charitable purposes.[17]

The LHMH continuously engaged in negotiations with clients and their families to limit expenses. A letter written by Ferris Stone to a probate court judge on July 13, 1931, reveals the extent to which the LHMH was attempting to control expenditures. Stone wrote the letter in response to a legal guardian's appeal to the court that the LHMH pay for an additional month that a pensioner had stayed in the Noble Sanitarium prior to being committed to Eloise as a result of senile dementia. Stone, a lawyer, acknowledged that the LHMH had a "technical liability" for the bill, which amounted to $1.10 per day for a total of $42.90, but appealed to the judge on the grounds of insufficient funds. He provided a short narrative of the LHMH and then explained its current financial situation:

> In our enthusiasm we took on a large number of cases—in fact, we obligated ourselves to the full amount of the income of the trust at that time. Since that time our income has been very much depleted but the obligations to these old people have gone on, except as they have been terminated by death. In the year of 1930 we spent some $17,000.00 more than our current income and made that inroad upon a comparatively small accumulation of income from previous years. This year we are now running at a rate of deficit of approximately $20,000.00 (LHMFC, Case #282).

Stone concludes that the woman and her guardian might have a legal claim against the LHMH, but they did not have a "just" claim, since no injustice was done the woman by terminating her case and sending her to Eloise, as she was senile and did not know where she was living. Further, an injustice would be done to other LHMH clients by diverting scarce monies to support her case. Stone ends the letter with an appeal to the greater good: "If a strictly legal claim is to be made, it will be at the ultimate expense of the pensioners of the Home" (LHMFC, Case #282). Stone was unsuccessful in this appeal, and the LHMH settled the bill with the woman's guardian.

Measures to cut expenses became increasingly severe in 1932 and 1933. In April, 1932, pensions were reduced by five to twenty dollars a month, and Frost oversaw specific plans to economize, such as moving clients to cheaper quarters, reducing fees to doctors, using free clinics for dental and eye exams, and reducing staff salaries by 10 percent. In March 1933, pensions were again reduced by five to twenty dollars a month, and staff salaries were reduced by 25 percent. The following month all clothing orders were temporarily cancelled.

During 1933, at the height of the Great Depression in Detroit, the LHMH took measures to bolster its resources, as well as reduce expenses. The Board approached the Trustees of the local Rackham Foundation for the purpose of "obtaining some relief" in the form of a grant (later determined to be $60,000) to cover the expenses of providing old-age assistance to clients. This effort, pursued over the next few months, ultimately failed. In September of that year, Frost met with the newly appointed State Director of the Old Age Pension Law regarding the possible transfer of some LHMH clients to the state's Old Age Pension list. However, this did not provide a workable solution to the organization's financial problems, because the state's old-age pension program accepted only people who were seventy and older, and the bureaucracy moved at a glacial pace. As a result, the state already had a long list of applicants waiting to be considered. Additionally, the state pensions, at less than ten dollars per month, were considered supplemental income only and were not enough to support LHMH clients, who (by the terms of their admission to the fund) had no other source of income.

Finally, in 1934, the LHMH sought and was granted court permission to invade the principle of the Hannan Trust to support existing clients, with the stipulation that no new clients be added until the deficit was returned. The Board also instructed Frost to make a "careful survey" of clients to see if any could now be cared for by relatives and removed from the rolls. After 1934, the Board accepted no more cases until 1946, by which time the principle of the trust had been replenished. In the remaining years of the Depression, the Trustees spent most of their time discussing investment strategies, although they did approve small cost-of-living increases in pensions, along with gradual increases in the salaries of Leon Frost and Anna Wentink.

The financial problems of the LHMH during the first half of the Great Depression clearly reflect the inadequacy of private charities in meeting the needs of old people. What we see in the minutes of the LHMH Board of Trustees is a microcosm of what was happening around the country within the charity network. Similar organizations, such as the Benjamin Rose Institute in Cleveland, established in 1908 "to provide relief and assistance . . . for respectable and deserving needy, aged people" (Beal 2008, 9) also incurred major financial losses during the Depression and was forced to cut expenses dramatically in order to meet its charitable obligations. Such organizations struggled with many of the same issues as the LHMH, questioning whether it was better to give a smaller number of people a better standard of living or to help a larger number with smaller pensions. Indeed, this very issue is raised by some LHMH clients in their negotiations for higher benefits. Both the Benjamin Rose Institute and the LHMH decided to keep their clientele relatively small. Their rationale is perhaps best described in the 1911 annual report from the Benjamin Rose Institute, which reflects the ideology of private charities devoted to working with elders of the refined class. They believed their work would be "better and more thoroughly done if the monthly allowance [was] made sufficiently large to relieve beneficiaries . . . from the constant pinch of poverty and to place them upon a comfortable and self-respecting basis of living" (Beal 2008, 18). But the Depression put that belief to the test, and both organizations began to provide some emergency and temporary relief in response to the tremendous cry for help from old people and their families. Still, by the end of 1931, both organizations were accepting only emergency cases, and the Benjamin Rose Institute would take on such a case only after another beneficiary had died.

The financial stresses on these private charities reflect the lack of adequate assistance for older people at the levels of the city and state. Although Michigan and Ohio finally began to offer assistance to old people in 1934, it was minimal, and the state agencies were overwhelmed, inexperienced, and underprepared to meet the need. As a result, one of the first advocacy roles taken on by the Benjamin Rose Institute was to protest the incompetence and abuse in the early administration of Ohio's Aid for the Aged Program (Beal 2008). What was needed was not only more financial and social assistance for old people, but also much better organization and integration of the public and private sources of this assistance. This would require an understanding at all levels of society that people, organizations, and governments had to depend on each other for social wellbeing. Franklin D. Roosevelt, in accepting the Democratic nomination for president in 1933, articulated the importance of this concept in his speech to the national convention in Chicago: "We are going to make the voters understand this year that this nation is not merely a nation of independence, but it is, if we are to survive, bound to be a nation of interdependence" (Brands 2008, 253).

Notes

1. The increase in philanthropic funds and foundations was prompted by the 1913 passage of the sixteenth amendment to the U.S. Constitution, which gave the federal government power to collect income taxes, along with the 1917 Congressional decision to allow tax deductions for charitable contributions (Mason 2008, 158).

2. These figures have not been verified, but they do coincide fairly closely with data from the Department of Public Welfare and Eloise cited by Jankowski in chapter 2.

3. These were modest wages but better than most. In 1929, the average yearly salary in urban areas, according to one source, was "well below $1500" (Billikopf 1931). Sources from the 1920s estimated that the proportion of men to women in the field of social work was one to ten, with women serving primarily as visitors and stenographers and men holding the executive positions (see Tice 1998, 48).

4. The LHMH directed clients to specific doctors and dentists with whom it had arranged for reduced rates. The organization also urged them to use free clinics whenever possible and to seek care at the Detroit Receiving Hospital, which took charity cases. However, the LHMH sometimes paid for services from specialists and the family doctors of clients who had been receiving long-term care for chronic conditions.

5. I thank Mary Durocher and Gillian Gray, members of the Hannan Archival Research Group, for the statistics and some of the examples in this section and the next.

6. This type of cooperation was not apparent in all cities during the Great Depression. Jones (1990) documents the conflicts in Chicago between private charities and the Bureau of Public Welfare. At issue was the political dominance of Catholic Charities over other charitable organizations. In 1932, Catholic Charities was made an agent of the Illinois Emergency Relief Commission through the Cook County Emergency Welfare Fund, from which it received $1,000,000 of the $7,500,000 funds available that year. There was much controversy, locally and nationally, over the fact that public funds were being administered by a private organization.

7. In fact, the LHMH considered itself and its clientele to be distinct from the DAC. The corporate minutes of the LHMH Board of Trustees indicate that on September 8, 1930, the Board declined an invitation to become a member of the Detroit Community Union, the organization that had replaced the DAC, even though the offices of the LHMH were located in the Community Union Building at 51 W. Warren, along with the offices of the Children's Aid Society, the Visiting Nurses' Association, and the Legal Aid Society—long-time DAC members. Frost was instructed to "so advise Mr. [Percival] Dodge, expressing to him our willingness to cooperate in every practical way with the Union." Shortly after that, the LHMH moved next door and established its offices at 71 W. Warren.

8. The Detroit Security and Trust Co. also held the Hannan trust, the difference between the two funds being leadership: Hannan had a board of trustees, one member of which was a high-level employee of the Detroit Bank and Trust. The Scudder trust apparently had no governing body until it was assumed by the LHMH.

9. In fact, late in 1929, Miss James was transferred to the Scudder fund.

10. In her 1917 book *Social Diagnosis*, Mary Richmond, then Director of the Charity Organization Department of the Russell Sage Foundation, prescribed standards for investigating and documenting cases, providing protocols for interviews and templates for face sheets.

11. Sometimes a case was closed and re-opened one or more times, as a result of new information or increased availability of funds; occasionally a previously closed case was later funded.

12. In 2006, when the LHMH case files were transferred from the offices of Luella Hannan Memorial Foundation to the Walter Reuther Library of Labor and Urban Affairs at Wayne State University, all photographs were removed from the case files and catalogued separately by the audio-visual department. Researchers wishing to see these photos must request the photo file separately from the archive of case files.

13. At this time, Visitors received their primary social-work training on the job, although the Russell Sage Foundation and some Charity Organization Societies offered workshops and training materials.

14. According to Tice (1998), gender greatly influenced the perception of social work as a field in the 1920s and 1930s. Male academics and professionals in other fields often judged visitors to be "unduly sentimental, meddlesome, sexually abnormal, or to be women who made gender trouble of one sort or another" (48). How the visitors perceived themselves is not well documented, other than through the work of spokespeople like Richmond who were working to establish social work as a profession during this time.

15. In addition to Harvey (previous case discussed), an example of an applicant's negative attitude toward charity is Case #167, a woman who withdrew her application after an acquaintance "accused her of accepting charity" and who did not want to talk about finances with the Visitor. Another woman, Case #489, approached the LHMH about a "loan," rather than a pension, and would not tell the Visitor the names of family members, stating, according to the Visitor's

notes, "that they would rather have her die than to apply for assistance from a charitable organization." Hannan applicants were the "new poor" among the old.

16. In March, 1933, the Board of Trustees gave employees of the Madison-Lennox Hotel the option to take a 50 percent pay cut, with a guaranteed minimum wage of thirty dollars per month, in order to keep the hotel open, or lose their jobs altogether. The employees voted in support of the pay reduction.

17. See Briller and Durocher, this volume, for a description of the Ambrose sisters, who benefitted from this new policy.

References

Agnew, Elizabeth N. 2004. *From Charity to Social Work: Mary E. Richmond and the Creation of an American Profession*. Urbana: University of Illinois Press.

Beal, Eileen. 2008. *The First 100 Years*. Cleveland: Benjamin Rose Institute.

Benjamin, Paul J. 1932. "The Family Society and the Depression." *Annals of the American Academy of Political and Social Science* 160: 135-143.

Billikopf, Jacob. 1931. "The Social Duty to the Unemployed." *Annals of the American Academy of Political and Social Science* 154: 65-72.

Board of Trustees. 1930. *The Luella Hannan Memorial Home: A Living Remembrance of William W. and Luella Hannan*. First annual report. Detroit, Michigan.

Bowman, LeRoy E. 1932. "Community Organization." *The American Journal of Sociology*, 37, 924-929.

Brands, H. W. 2008. *Traitor to His Class: The Privileged Life and Radical Presidency of Franklin Delano Roosevelt*. New York: Doubleday.

Corporate Minutes, Luella Hannan Memorial Home, 1925-1939. Offices of the Luella Hannan Memorial Foundation, Detroit, Michigan.

Editorial. 1935. "This Business of Relief." *The Nation* 141: 581. http://newdeal.feri.org/nation/na33667.htm.

Fine, Sidney. 1975. *Frank Murphy: The Detroit Years*. Ann Arbor: University of Michigan Press.

Haber, Carol and Brian Gratton. 1994. *Old Age and the Search for Security: An American Social History*. Bloomington, IN: Indiana University Press.

Henry Ford Museum. http://www.thehenryford.org/rouge/historyofrouge.aspx.

How the Depression Changed Detroit. 1999. *Detroit News*, March 4. http://apps.detnews.com/apps/history/Index.php?id=49

Jones, Gene D. L. 1990. "The Chicago Catholic Charities, the Great Depression, and the Public." *Illinois Historical Journal* 83:13-30.

Kayrod, Ellen. 2006, August 25. Personal Interview. Luella Hannan Memorial Foundation. Detroit, Michigan.

Luella Hannan Memorial Foundation Collection (LHMFC). Walter Reuther Library of Labor and Urban Affairs, Wayne State University.

Mason, Philip P. 2008. *Tracy W. McGregor: Humanitarian, Philanthropist, and Detroit Civic Leader*. Detroit: Wayne State University.

Mueller, John H. 1936. "Some Social Characteristics of the Urban Relief Population." *Social Forces* 15: 64-70.

Rashid, Frank D. 2009. Rouge. http://www.marygrove.edu/component/content/article/163-literary-map/763-rouge.html

Richmond, Mary E. 1906. *Friendly Visiting among the Poor: A Handbook for Charity Workers*. New York: McMillan.

Richmond, Mary E. 1917. *Social Diagnosis*. New York: Russell Sage Foundation.

Romer, Samuel. 1933. "The Detroit Strike." *The Nation* 136: 167. http://new deal.feri.org/nation/na33667.htm.

Roosevelt, Franklin D. 1933. An Extemporaneous Address Before the 1933 Conference on Mobilization for Human Needs. http://newdeal.feri.org/speeches/1933h.htm

Tice, Karen. 1998. *Tales of Wayward Girls and Immoral Woman: Case Records and the Professionalization of Social Work.* Urbana: University of Illinois Press.

Zunz, Olivier. 1983. *The Changing Face of Inequality: Urbanization, Industrial Development, and Immigrants in Detroit, 1880-1920.* Chicago: University of Chicago Press.

Part 2

Part Two

This Old Man and That Old Woman

In this section, contributors provide brief biographical sketches of the pensioners whose cases they analyze in Part 3. Authors of these sketches have drawn heavily on the Visitors' case notes, although clients' views are also represented whenever their correspondence is available in the files. Our purpose is to provide a snapshot of each individual, showing that older adults were as diverse in 1929 as they are now in terms of their backgrounds, education, interests, experiences, family and social life. We agree with philosopher Simone de Beauvoir in *Coming of Age* that, in order to secure a good old age for all, we must first "recognize ourselves in this old man or in that old woman" (1970/1996, 5).

Part 2

Client Sketches

Ambrose Sisters: Cora, Rose, and Sally

The Ambrose sisters were born in Aylmer, Ontario. Their father, Ezra Ambrose, was a wealthy farmer who educated his daughters in the Woodstock Ladies' College. The sisters grew up among what the Visitor referred to as "pleasant surroundings." They came from a "good family" and were used to "associating with good people." They had a brother, Leonard, who married and had two daughters. All three sisters were recipients of pensions from the LHMH—Cora and Rose for a period of ten years and Sally for the final year of her life when she lived with Cora and Rose.

Sally, the eldest of the three sisters, was born on September 3, 1854. She married Paul McGovern, a Scotch physician, at twenty-two years of age. At the age of forty, Dr. McGovern died, leaving Sally enough money to raise their son. In 1888, Sally and her son came to Detroit. Her devoted son, Willis, died of diabetes at the age of thirty-four, leaving his mother $12,000 in life insurance. Soon after, a friend of her son borrowed $5,000 and later skipped town. With the remainder of her money, Sally bought a home, fixed it up and sold it at a profit. She bought and sold five other houses in this fashion, sometimes renting a room or two out to a "congenial person." She was able to remain independent in this way until her money ran out and ill health struck in 1930.

Rose was born on September 9, 1856. Because of poor health, she remained at home with the family until she moved with her sister Cora to Detroit.

Cora was born February 1, 1866. At eighteen years of age, after finishing Woodstock Ladies' College, she and her sister Rose moved to Detroit, where Cora took a position as a bookkeeper. Cora's last job of sixteen years was for an athletic outfitter. Cora earned the living while Rose remained at home and kept house, but they shared everything equally and were "very devoted to each other."

On April 3, 1930, Cora (age sixty-four) came to the LHMH office seeking assistance for herself and Rose (age seventy-four), as she felt she was "now too old to make a living for them." The in-take notes describe Cora as "inclined to be tall and somewhat slender. Her hair is turning gray. Her pale blue eyes and her florid complexion are her outstanding characteristics." Rose is described as being "somewhat shorter than her sister and inclined to be stout. She has the same graying hair, pale blue eyes and florid complexion." The sisters seemed to the Visitor "very nervous and excitable," with thin, high-pitched voices that "in moments of intense feeling break off rather abruptly." Both sisters are described as "fine gentlewomen" who are "rather crushed by the burden of worry" which they have been carrying for a number of years.

At this time, Cora's health was good, although she needed new glasses and was very deaf in her left ear. Rose had had poor health for many years, being afflicted with high blood pressure and the results of a stroke.

From letters of recommendation the LHMH ascertained that the Misses Ambrose had "done all they could—all in their power to stem the tide and carry on" but now had no money. They were living on the first floor of a two-family home, which they owned jointly. Further investigation revealed that Cora and Rose owned several parcels of property that were partially paid for but which they "could not sell to advantage at that time, or realize sufficient income to maintain themselves." The house they were living in was the only asset the LHMH was interested in, and the sisters were advised to "otherwise dispose of their properties by gift or in any other way possible." The Board of Trustees approved a grant of fifty dollars per month for each sister. Due to their reduced circumstances, the sisters could not afford to pay rent to the Detroit Trust Company that now owned their former home, so they moved to an apartment. Cora and Rose did not stay in that apartment long, as the accommodations didn't suit them, and they were return to their former neighborhood, where they had many friends. The sisters continued to keep up domestic duties of cleaning, canning, baking, and gardening, even during bouts of severe illness.

Cora took care of Rose and the home during Rose's many illnesses, especially after she had another stroke. However, in early May of 1940, the Visitor learned that Cora had been ill for several weeks. Their long-time family physician finally advised that she be moved to a nursing home, where she died later that month. Cause of death was given as "cerebral hemorrhage, arteriosclerosis and senile dementia."

After Cora's death, Rose also moved to a nursing care facility, where her health continued to fail. She died the following year, and her body was taken by relatives to Aylmer, Ontario, where she was buried alongside Cora in the family plot. Cause of death was given as "immediate cerebral thrombosis and contributory causes as senility, arterio-sclerosis and myocarditis."

David Burke

The Reverend David Burke was seventy-one years of age in 1929 when he was referred to the Luella Hannan Memorial Home (LHMH) and taken on in June as one of the only two Black clients of the Scudder Trust. He was born in South Carolina, and the family moved to Georgia when David was age seven. His parents were both slaves, and he himself had been a slave for several years. He attended public school in Augusta through the eighth grade and later went to Beach Institute in Savannah. He attended Fisk University and graduated from New Orleans University and Gammon Theological Seminary in Atlanta, Georgia. He had taught at various places in Georgia, Arkansas, and at the Tuskegee Institute in Alabama. In her notes on the initial interview, the Visitor writes, "One can tell at once that Reverend Burke is cultured and educated. He is also an intelligent man."

The Visitor describes Rev. Burke as having "a pleasing personality." She does not describe his appearance but focuses instead on his estranged wife, upon whom the Visitor had to call in order to find an address for the Reverend. But from a picture taken by the Visitor in July 9, 1930, Rev. Burke presented a neat and dignified appearance. He wore a suit and tie, and had a handkerchief in his pocket. His white hair was receding in front and on top, and he sported a neat mustache. His hands look weathered. He told the Visitor that he enjoyed reading, walks, and was fond of lectures. He also enjoyed movies, but was not able to afford the cost of seeing them very often.

Rev. Burke was, according to the Visitor, "a teacher and preacher." He had taught school until 1923, and then relied upon preaching at Baptist churches for income. Because of continued poor health, particularly diabetes and poor vision, he was unable to have his own church and could preach only occasionally. He was married but had been separated from his wife for ten years. Of his six living children (one had died), two daughters helped support his wife (who also made paper flowers and funeral wreaths for a living); two sons were show men and had no certain addresses; and the other two sons were married and had their own families to support. Of his siblings, one brother died at age thirteen of tuberculosis; a half-sister had also died. No other siblings were mentioned.

Throughout his time as a Scudder client, Rev. Burke was very careful not to run afoul of the organization, constantly inquiring as to whether it would be permissible to engage in one activity or another. More than once he expressed concern about making a mistake that would jeopardize his pension, and he sometimes became anxious if he did not see the Visitor for a while, believing it was bad news.

In November 1931, Rev. Burke told the Visitor a story from his past that shed additional light on his family relationships. He explained that while he was teaching in Savannah, GA, he met and married a young lady, and a daughter was born of this union. He wanted to go to college and further his education, but his wife objected. He left, nevertheless, leaving his daughter in the custody of his parents and his wife to fend for herself. A few months after he enrolled at Fiske University, he learned that his ailing wife had taken the daughter and gone to her parents; she died within a year. Over the ensuing years, he had tried to find his daughter but was unable to do so. Recently, however, through correspondence with residents of the town in which he had been teaching, he had learned the whereabouts of his wife's family and, through them, had located his now fifty-one year-old–daughter, who was living with her husband in Cincinnati. After telling the Visitor this story, Rev. Burke spent the Christmas holidays with his daughter. He told the Visitor that he "was delighted to find that he had a number of grandchildren and great grandchildren whom he had never seen or known about heretofore."

Rev. Burke's joy at reconnecting with his daughter and her family speaks to the importance of family for him and the pride he took in family members despite his marital situations. When the Visitor attended Rev. Burke's seventy-third birthday party at his request, she found that he was surrounded by many of his children and grandchildren. She noted that he "took the affair quite seriously and stated several times that he probably would never live to see so many of his children and grandchildren together again." Then, as well as on subsequent birthdays and Christmas holidays, Rev. Burke proudly showed the Visitor gifts he had received from them. He also offered to have his son, a chorister in Chicago, give a concert to benefit the LHMH when he visited Detroit.

In the end, Rev. Burke violated LHMH rules about running up bills, and he was dropped from the rolls. The last entry in his case file states that a worker from the Department of Public Welfare had come in to the LHMH office to read Rev. Burke's file, as he had applied for aid from this agency.

Ada Dreyfuss

Ada Dreyfuss was sixty-four years of age when she was referred to the Luella Hannan Memorial Home (LHMH). She was born in Ontario, Canada. Ada had been a sickly child who was so incapacitated by her ailments that she was unable to attend school until the age of twelve. While confined to her home, she studied under a private tutor and eventually went on to attend the Young Ladies Academy in Shirbrook, Ontario. Ada later graduated from a business college in Ypsilanti, Michigan. She worked during her younger years as a secretary and then was employed as a social service worker for most of her adult life. She was married for a short time, but her husband died during their fourth year of marriage. Ada bore one child who died in infancy. After her arrival in Detroit (about 1912), she adopted a child from the Children's Aid Society.

In August of 1930, Ada was referred to the LHMH by Mrs. Samuel Mumford, whose husband was the president of the Detroit Edison Company. Ada was funded by the LHMH as a result of her failing health and dwindling finances. During the in-take process, the Visitor described Ada as having a "pleasing personality" and a "dignified manner." She appeared to be "a woman who has associated with a better class of people. . . . Her associates seem to be among the best in the city."

In exchange for a pension from the LHMH, Ada signed over a two-family flat that she owned, but she refused to relinquish a lot in Traverse City, a resort area on Lake Michigan, or her $300 in savings. Ada consulted with the former president of the American State Bank—a good friend of hers and Mrs. Mumford's—and he advised her against turning all of her assets over to the LHMH. The LHMH let Ada keep the property, as well as her savings but ruled that she use her own money to cover clothing, dental, and medical expenses and required that she produce an itemized list of expenditures. Ada requested a formal letter from the LHMH at this time, however, to the "effect that she would receive sixty dollars per month for the rest of her life." The LHMH denied this request.

In January of 1931, Ada rented a cottage in Florida with Mrs. Mumford for five months and had her pension checks sent there. When she returned to the Detroit area, she then spent the summer in Traverse City, with her adopted daughter and her family. This marked the beginning of Ada's yearly excursions. Ada convinced the LHMH to make extra allowances for her travel during the summer months, citing her health as "necessitating that she live out-of-doors in a cool climate during the summer." The LHMH board agreed to augment her pension during the summer months "contingent absolutely upon this matter being strictly confidential." The Visitor wrote that Ada "would use most any argument to win her point. She enjoys using her state of health as a whip to get her own way."

Over the course of Ada's fifteen year involvement with the LHMH, she made a number of residential moves, never being as satisfied with the rooms she rented as she was with the summer quarters she inhabited. She made various and frequent complaints about every residence. Despite being a woman in "reduced circumstances," she continued to keep her club memberships and leisure activities up-to-date. Even when doctors advised her to slow down and take care of herself, she continued her busy social agenda.

In the early 1940s, Ada's health began to deteriorate, and she was placed in various nursing homes around the city of Detroit. Some of these homes requested that the LHMH never admit her to their facilities again because of the "fuss" she caused. When Ada became gravely ill and in need of more serious care, her reputation as "extremely disagreeable" and "incorrigible" made it difficult for the LHMH to secure a facility for her. Ultimately, Ada's physical health declined to such a point that her family stepped in to help manage her affairs. The LHMH began to send Ada's pension checks to her niece, who was seeking guardianship. When Ada learned of this plan, she threatened that she would seek legal counsel. The family frankly stated that all parties needed to "close ranks" and do what was best for her, even if it was against her will. For the next few months, Ada's physical health continued to wane. The Visitor noted that she "finally resigned herself to life at the Arnold Home, and her health grew continually worse." Ada died on July 17, 1945, of chronic myocarditis, at the age of seventy-nine.

Jane and Jacob Lewis

Jane Lewis was born in Champagne, Illinois, in 1862, one of two children. Her father, who owned a large farm, died when she was four years of age. Her mother brought her and her brother to Detroit to be near relatives. Her mother worked as a janitress in one of the schools in the city. Jane and her brother attended common school until 13 years of age, when Jane started to make a living for herself. She became an apprentice to a dressmaker at age fifteen. Her brother died at the age of twenty.

In 1895, Jane married Jacob Lewis, a truck driver, and no children were born of this union. Mrs. Lewis was a home-loving woman. She worked hard at sewing, and through her efforts the couple owned their own home. Jane was proud and anxious to earn her own living and keep up the home as long as possible. According to the Visitor's case notes, Mr. Lewis had a rather negative personality. He appeared to be sullen and not very congenial. The Visitor notes that it seemed "impossible for him to smile or see the bright side of life." He depended a great deal on his wife, and she accepted this responsibility.

At the time of their application for a pension in June, 1929, Mrs. Lewis was "short and very fleshy" with "a large round face." Mrs. Lewis had no recreation, stating that her time was taken up with her household duties and working on her garden and lawn. In the winter she put in her time sewing, and if she had a few spare moments, she spent them resting. Mr. and Mrs. Lewis rented one side of their house, and they occupied the other side. The visitor describes their home as very large, airy and well kept, and the furniture was "well chosen." Mrs. Lewis had made the drapes for her home. Mr. Lewis had been employed as a truck driver until he was injured on the way to work one morning and from then on worked as a watchman in the yard of the trucking company. He had been with the same company for nearly forty years until he was no longer able to work but had no pension from this company.

Mr. and Mrs. Lewis had spent their lives planning carefully for the future and had sacrificed enough to purchase and almost entirely pay for their home. They had hoped to have an income from it sufficient to meet their needs in old age. However, their plans were shattered by the Depression, and Mrs. Lewis lamented that everything she attempted from then on was "doomed to failure and disappointment."

The Lewis' case was opened and closed twice due to the resistance of Mrs. Lewis to signing over their home to the LHMH. She felt that they could manage their own affairs by taking in boarders. On April 30, 1930, however, Mr. and Mrs. Lewis accepted the terms of the organization because of their declining health and financial situation and reluctantly signed over their property and life insurance policies. Despite frequent attempts by Visitors to persuade them to move into smaller living quarters, both Mr. and Mrs. Lewis begged to be allowed to remain in their own home.

Mr. Lewis died on October 25, 1931, of a heart attack. At this time, Mrs. Lewis suffered from neuritis and a light form of palsy. The LHMH Board of Trustees recommended that she be allowed sixty dollars per month and permitted to remain in her home. In addition, her medical bills were to be paid by the organization. At monthly intervals she was also reimbursed for massage treatments.

Because Mrs. Lewis's expenses were so high, the Visitor tried to talk her into going to a convalescent home for a few months until she could regain her strength. However, Mrs. Lewis was violently opposed to this plan, and the LHMH allowed her to continue living at home. In April 1932, however, her condition became worse, and she was moved to a convalescent home. Mrs. Lewis cried a great deal while there and continually made plans to return home. Eventually, she persuaded her masseur, Mrs. York, and Mrs. York's family to move into her house and care for her in exchange for their rent. Doctors approved, and she was permitted to return home.

On August 15, 1932, Mrs. Lewis suffered a paralytic stroke from which she did not regain consciousness. She died at home three days later.

Rachel Little

"Excellent, but blind." This was the way Rachel Little's health was first described on the intake sheet in her case file. Mrs. Little, who lived in an old frame house in a very poor and rundown neighborhood with her adopted daughter, Cora, was a sixty-five year-old Black woman who was referred to the LHMH by someone from the Detroit League for the Handicapped. During the initial visit to the home on June 11, 1929, the caseworker described Mrs. Little as having black hair streaked with gray. "She wears bone rimmed glasses, the left lens being frosted as her left eye has been removed. She was neatly dressed in a gingham housedress, light hose and orchid bedroom slippers." The house was "sparsely furnished, not dirty, but was in a bit of disarray as the bed wasn't made." Mrs. Little also was described as having, "a rather negative personality. At first she seemed very pleasant, but when [the Visitor] asked her so many questions regarding her life she became rather indignant and thought it was hardly necessary." The Visitor noted, however, that over the course of the interview, Mrs. Little warmed to her and said it would be all right for her to stop by any time she was in the neighborhood.

Mrs. Little was born in 1863 in Leesburg, Virginia, one of six children, only one of whom, a sister, was still living. Many years later, when the sister—who remembered many events from the Civil War—was visiting Detroit, Mrs. Little told the Visitor that their father had been a slave, but their mother "had been freed by an 'enlightened master,' so her children were all considered free even before the Emancipation Proclamation."

Mrs. Little went to common school through the eighth grade, after which she left to get a job doing housework. She married James Richards in 1883; they had no children but adopted Cora at age five. James owned a barber shop in which Mrs. Little helped by giving scalp treatments. James died of pneumonia in 1902, at which point Mrs. Little earned her living by doing housekeeping. Five years later, she married Jud Little, who worked as a salesman in North Branch, Michigan. In 1916, after nine years of marriage, they separated, and Mrs. Little moved to Detroit to live with Cora. Mrs. Little said of her second husband that, "she had heard nothing from him for twelve years, does not know whether he is dead or living, and states that he was not worth 'three rows of pins.'"

Neither she, nor Cora, who had been separated from her husband for five years at the time of the interview, received any money from their spouses. Mrs. Little had been a nursemaid for several families in Detroit and had also done day work—dishes and housecleaning—until glaucoma caused her to lose her sight. At the time of application, her only source of income was from hemming wash clothes for the Detroit League for the Handicapped, for which she earned between two to three dollars twice a month.

Mrs. Little said that she attended the Metropolitan Church for Colored People, and "that she would like to attend every Sunday if she could find somebody to take her," as she enjoyed singing hymns during the service. Her other favorite past time was reading the Bible using the Braille system. She explained to the Visitor how she came to learn Braille:

The teacher said she was too old to learn, as she was 61 years at the time she asked to be taught. [Mrs. Little] told the teacher that "only one thing beats a trial, and that is a failure." So the teacher said that as long as she was so anxious she would give her a trial, which she did, and [she] very readily learned the Braille System.

Mrs. Little described her adopted daughter Cora, with whom she was residing, as caring and giving. She was grateful to Cora for being "so good to her." When asked by the Visitor what kind of assistance Cora needed to support her mother, Cora asked for thirty dollars a month to help with room and board expenses. "She stated that she was very economical and would not run a grocery bill. What she could not afford to buy, she went without."

Mrs. Little was awarded a thirty dollar pension from the Scudder trust in late July, 1929, and the Visitor described her as "elated" when she received the news: "She stated that we would never know how much she appreciates that check each month." Mrs. Little continued to hem washcloths for the League for the Handicapped to supplement this grant and because "it [kept] her mind occupied." She read by Braille constantly, and listened to the radio, following politics as well as the Detroit Tigers' baseball team, of whom she was a great fan.

During the thirteen years in which Mrs. Little was a Scudder client, she lived either with Cora or a stepdaughter, Mrs. Mather, with the exception of a short time when she lived with a friend. Cora had become ill with goiter, and she could no longer provide care for Mrs. Little or perform housekeeping duties. When Mrs. Little moved to the stepdaughter's home, the Visitor noted that she now lived "in a home nicer than many of our white clients occupy." Cora died in September 1939, and Mrs. Little stayed with her stepdaughter the rest of her life, except during times when Mrs. Mather was ill. She interacted frequently with her sister, and they visited back and forth between Detroit and her sister's residence in Ohio. In 1940, a stepson moved in with Mrs. Mather and Mrs. Little for a short while, and she enjoyed his company greatly.

Over the years, Mrs. Little battled various health conditions, although she also had periods of feeling quite well. She was in and out of the hospital and was visited by the doctor frequently. In addition to some heart issues and high blood pressure, she had particular difficulty with her right foot and ankle, which would become ulcerated and would not heal. She often had difficulty walking up and down the stairs at her stepdaughter's home, but she did it so as not to put more burden on Mrs. Mather.

In 1942, upon her return from visiting relatives, Mrs. Little came down with a cold, which became pneumonia. She slipped into a coma, during which she suffered a stroke, and died several days later. She was buried alongside James Richards, her first husband.

Jennie McGinnis

Jennie McGinnis, referred to as "Miss M" in her case file, was single and age sixty-four when approved for a pension in March of 1929. She was the first client of the Luella Hannan Memorial Home. Miss M had always been a strong, self-supporting woman who enjoyed hard work and was "very thrifty," according to the Visitor's notes. These qualities, along with a keen intelligence, a positive attitude, and supportive friends, kept her going during the Great Depression.

Miss M was the first-born child of Scottish immigrants. She was raised and received a public school education in Ontario, Canada. At the age of twenty-one, she moved to Detroit and remained there for the rest of her life, working as a seamstress in the homes of many wealthy families and later teaching Sunday School at the Presbyterian church. She shared expenses with her three sisters and saved as much money as possible, while also helping support three nephews in Canada for several years after their father (her brother) died. According to one of her references, she had "always assumed responsibility of others."

When the Visitor first met Miss M on March 15, 1929, she was living in a seven-room apartment in a "second class residential district" of the city. The Visitor found the home to be clean but simple. The furniture was "very plain and not much of it," and the house gave the general impression of "austerity." The Visitor described Miss M as "sturdy, Scotch, proud, clean, unrelenting and honest." Physically, she was a "tall massive figure" with a "florid complexion, auburn toupee, soft voice, [and] deliberate movements." She wore a steel brace on her left ankle, covered by a specially constructed high shoe, which caused her to walk with a pronounced limp. Miss M's clothing was "of the past generation—skirts to the floor and very full." Her health was "good," although she trembled as a result of "nervous shock." A doctor's examination later revealed that she was nearly blind in one eye and had "exceptionally high blood pressure."

The Visitor found Miss M living with two roomers, a nurse and an elderly woman. She had had a falling out with her sisters, who had left and taken most of the furniture. The sisters were no longer speaking to each other, and Miss M did not want her siblings to know that she was applying for aid. She had been drawing on her savings but could not continue this much longer. She had no other relatives who could help her and told the Visitor that she would not ask them for assistance if she had. By 1929, she was "unable to get the kind of work she used to do, and would be unable to do it if she could."

Miss M liked her apartment and wanted to stay there, renting out two rooms and taking in sewing to pay the bills. She received a fifty dollars monthly pension from the LHMH to supplement this plan. Over time, however, she had trouble finding and keeping roomers, and they sometimes didn't pay. By August 1929, one of her rooms was vacant, and the woman in the other room had not paid for six weeks. Although the Visitor advised Miss M strongly to "either get the money or get rid of the woman," she rented out the room to someone else but allowed the first woman to sleep for free on a cot in the dining room. On Christmas day, 1931, one of her renters died in his room, and the Visitor later found Miss M in a "nervous upset" about it. Up until that time, the roomer "had insisted that [Miss M] do everything for her." Although this loss also meant a loss of income, the Visitor noted approvingly that Miss M was a "good manager and [would] do her best to get along." She continued to sew, taking in as much work as possible during the spring and summer months to get her through the slow winter months.

As the Depression worsened, the LHMH itself began to experience financial problems, and Miss M's grant, along with many others, was reduced in April 1932 by five dollars a month. Fortunately, her rent was also being reduced at intervals, from $70 to $50 in 1931, from $50 to $40 in 1932, and from $40 to $32.50 in January of 1933. By 1933, however, at the height of the Depression, Miss M was contemplating a move from her seven-room apartment, as she had lost another boarder and was having trouble finding needlework.

In mid February 1933, President Franklin D. Roosevelt declared a bank holiday, and Miss M could not access the forty dollars she had left in the bank to carry her through the rest of the month. Perhaps the prolonged stress of trying to make ends meet was too much for her. Miss M suffered a stroke the following Sunday evening while attending church services and died early the next day.

Miss M had already paid for a crypt in a mausoleum and had laid aside money toward her burial expenses. Her brother in Canada, Rev.

John McGinnis, paid for the rest of the funeral, including passage of the body to Ontario for burial.

Despite a life of hard work, scrimping and saving, Miss M died nearly penniless. Her brother found among her possessions three bank books containing records of small deposits, the largest of which was twenty dollars.

Madeline Landen Nuit

Madeline Landen Nuit was born in 1866 near Sarnia, Ontario; she died in 1963 in Detroit, Michigan, at age ninety-seven, of a "cerebral hemorrhage." Madeline's mother tended to the family, and her father was a fur dealer who "provided well for his family." Madeline was educated both in public school and a convent and studied music, as women of her standing were expected to do.

At the age of twenty-seven she married. Her husband, Gevrey Nuit, was of French nobility and held the title of Marquis, giving Madeline a significant boost in economic, social, and political privilege. No children were born of this union. In 1900, Mrs. Nuit and her husband sailed to France and lived with her (very prominent) mother-in-law. After the mother-in-law's death, Mr. and Mrs. Nuit returned to Windsor, Ontario, for a few years and then moved to Detroit. Mr. Nuit worked as a French teacher at a Detroit high school and gave private French lessons from home. In 1918, the couple bought a twenty-three acre farm in Lapeer County, Michigan, and spent the summers there. In 1928, Mr. Nuit died of heart problems, leaving very little money to support his widow, and Mrs. Nuit was forced to sell pieces of antique furniture they had brought from France. This gave her an income for a few months; however, she was soon "homeless and almost penniless."

"Unhappy and dissatisfied with her present quarters" in early June 1929, Mrs. Nuit formally applied to the LHMH, seeking financial assistance. Illustrative of her place in Detroit's social networks, Percival Dodge (of the automobile family by the same name) referred her case to the organization. On June 14, 1929, she was interviewed by an LHMH Visitor, who described her as "tall, thin, [with] a stately walk and air about her. She was neatly dressed in black, and the material in her coat and dress was of excellent quality." Mrs. Nuit was also described as having a "striking personality. She is very refined and cultured, also is very alert and intellectual." She had never done remunerative work but had traveled extensively with her husband.

In late June 1929, the LHMH Board of Trustees agreed that Mrs. Nuit was "deserving of an old age pension" and recommended that she be placed in a boarding home and given an allotment of fifty dollars per month. The LHMH attempted to ascertain her financial holdings. In late July 1929, Mrs. Nuit wrote a letter stating that she didn't want to "give up her home to anyone" and "accept just what total strangers" wished to give her. Resisting LHMH requirements to sign over her assets in exchange for care, she would attempt to hold on to her property for several years while receiving a pension.

In the ensuing years, Mrs. Nuit made numerous residential changes. Most of these moves were usually predicated on some complaint she had of the boarding house or room. There are instances of landlords complaining to the LHMH about her contrariness. According to the case notes, Mrs. Nuit's stubbornness was not reserved for strangers or those she thought of as beneath her station; she also treated the members of her family high-handedly. While somewhat close to her niece, she did not care for her niece's husband because of his ethnicity and the type of business for which he was the proprietor. Mrs. Nuit's disdain for this man would ultimately hurt her financially as the years wore on and she became frail. Towards the end of her life, however, Mrs. Nuit did repair this relationship, at least slightly. Nonetheless, she was always suspicious of her niece's husband. At one point later in life, she tried to get the LHMH to sell a pearl pin for her so that the niece and her husband would not inherit it.

Until the end of her life, Mrs. Nuit also kept her husband's family at arm's length, never revealing her reduced circumstances. She continually lied to them in an effort to disguise her situation and appear better off than she actually was.

Over the course of Madeline Nuit's thirty-four year involvement with the LHMH and despite the poverty she experienced during the Great Depression, she maintained an air of nobility. In many of her dealings with the LHMH staff and in her other relationships, she struggled to retain the upper hand.

Kate Shields

Kate Shields was born in Conanduaga, New York, in 1870. Her father owned a flour store. She had four sisters, all of whom died young. She graduated from Granger Place School, New York, and passed the entrance examination for the University of New York, but married instead and did not enroll. After she married, she moved to Albany, New York, where they lived a few years before coming to Detroit. The couple had no children.

Mrs. Shields had taught school for five years before marrying. Later she worked in the office of her husband's store and also at an art gallery. According to the notes of the Visitor, Mrs. Shield was a woman of good education, refined, and accustomed to moving in "good society." Mr. Shields had owned a company for fifteen years. His health became so poor, however, that he was forced to sell the store. They had owned two homes in Detroit until Mr. Shield's health failed, at which time they sold one of the properties and moved into an apartment. Later, Mr. Shields died, leaving Mrs. Shields with some insurance after all the expenses were paid. She then sold their second property and moved to a hotel. When her money was gone, she was forced to move to the St. Luke's Home operated by the Episcopalian church.

Mrs. Shields was living at the church-supported St. Luke's Home when she applied for an LHMH pension. She had also been receiving money for incidentals from that organization since 1926. However, she felt herself decidedly superior to the other women in the Home. Mrs. Shields stated that she had no companionship there. According to the notes of the LHMH Visitor, she was "very sensitive and proud." Mrs. Shields admitted this fact and stated that she was not used to associating with people of the type living at St. Luke's.

On April 20, 1929, when Mrs. Shields was fifty-nine, her case was referred by Detroit Associated Charities, which asked the LHMH to relieve St. Luke's of the responsibility for her care. The Board of Trustees declined but granted her six dollars per month for incidentals while she remained in the Home. Mrs. Shields supplemented her small grant from the LHMH by selling occasional pieces of silver, linens and pictures. She also wrote short articles for the *Detroit Free Press*. The *Free Press* began experiencing financial difficulties and published fewer and fewer of her articles. In late 1931, they stopped buying them altogether.

Certain difficulties arose from time to time regarding the type of food that Mrs. Shields was receiving at St. Luke's, and she spent more of her incidental money on special diabetic food. When the LHMH began to experience financial difficulties of its own, the Board of Trustees decided to withdraw entirely from her case, since Mrs. Shields was assured by St. Luke's Home of care for the remainder of her life. Mrs. Shields' case was closed on November 1, 1932. She presumably lived out her days in the St. Luke's Home.

Arlene Smith

Mrs. Arlene Smith applied for a pension in September 1929, at the age of sixty-one. The Visitor's notes describe her as "a refined looking person of medium height; [her] hair is gray bobbed and neatly combed back. She was dressed plainly but well in a black dress with a small white collar." Her demeanor and dress confirmed the Visitor's assessment that she was a "business type of woman, intelligent, ambitious" and that she appeared to be "a woman of culture with numerous interests," including reading, studying, attending "good theater and symphony orchestras" and associating with "the most cultured and educated people." She belonged to the Episcopal Church and had been actively associated with several churches as parish visitor or secretary. The Visitor notes that Mrs. Smith was "extremely nervous and mentally tired from worry. Her only physical ailment seems to be arthritis, which is quite bad. When walking, she limps and holds onto her back. On the street she uses a cane."

Mrs. Smith was born in a small Michigan town in 1869. The family moved to Detroit when she was a baby. She had two brothers, William and Henry. She was raised by her mother after their father died when she was fourteen. Later she went to New York to work and in 1901 married Chauncey Smith but left him a few months later, she stated, "for a good reason." She later procured a divorce but never remarried.

Independent since leaving her brief marriage, Mrs. Smith had supported herself for over twenty-five years as a secretary or a financial manager with "reputable institutions," but now she had no income. According to the Visitor's notes on interviews with her two married brothers, Mrs. Smith had moved back to Detroit about a year earlier and had lived alternately with them. Both brothers were bankers who were then having financial problems themselves. One brother, who made an investment in the stock market and had taken great losses, had to choose between supporting his sister and a foster son.

Mrs. Smith "did not get along well" with either of her brothers, and she "wished to be independent." She was granted a pension of fifty-five dollars a month for a three-month trial period, with the proviso that her brothers would also contribute financially to her care at thirty dollars a month. The brothers agreed to do so and requested that the LHMH continue to supervise their sister in private facilities. In May 1931, the brothers, who were then in very poor financial circumstances, were relieved of their responsibility, and the LHMH provided for all of Mrs. Smith's care from then on.

During the first few years of her pension, Mrs. Smith moved about from one small town to the other. She liked to be in the country where it was "quiet and away from the traffic." She was always very exacting in her demands, having been used to "the highest standards of living" and "all the conveniences and beauty of a modern home." During the eight years in which she received a pension, she moved thirty-nine times. She was always very neat and tidy about herself and her room and surrounded herself with pictures and little mementos of her former days. She did not care to mingle with other people and did not get along with them.

Religion was a troublesome factor in Mrs. Smith's life. She seemed to be constantly searching for some type of comfort, which she was never able to find. In this search she went from practicing Christian Science back to the Episcopalian faith and then to Catholicism. She was also a steady user of patent medicine and drugs and at times took doses of things that were not good for her. In January 1940, Mrs. Smith moved from a Christian Science boarding home because she had friction with her landlady over medicine. Shortly after that, she began to show a definite physical and mental change. The Visitor noted, "she became quite childish in her attitude and from time to time would ask her if she thought she ever acted peculiarly." Later, she became a convert to the Catholic Church and moved to the Carmelite Sisters Home. For a while she was very happy but ultimately became dissatisfied by the rigorous practices of the Catholic Church.

While with the Carmelite Sisters, Mrs. Smith continued to fail mentally, and the home advised that she be taken to the city hospital's psychopathic ward. Although this had been her greatest fear, her brothers were in no position to make any other arrangements. On October 22, 1941, Mrs. Smith was committed to Eloise, the Wayne County poor house, or to Ypsilanti Hospital (it is unclear from the records which), and her case was closed.

Stein Siblings: Eleanor, Flora, and Mike

Mrs. Eleanor (Stein) Drake, sixty-seven, had been a music teacher of stringed instruments, employed at the Grinnel Music Store prior to her application to the LHMH on January 12, 1931. The store could no longer refer students to Mrs. Drake, due to her "outdated methods," age, and students' lack of interest. At the time of their application to LHMH, Mrs. Drake, her sister, Flora Stein, age sixty-six, and their brother, Mike Stein, age fifty-five, had lived together in a two-bedroom apartment for the past twelve years. The siblings were born and raised in Detroit, and the sisters had studied music with their father, who had been a well-known music professor in the city.

Mrs. Drake was married in 1903 to the owner of a leather goods store in Detroit. They had no children, and her husband died of tuberculosis six years after they were married. Three years after her husband's death, Mrs. Drake resumed teaching music and was noted to be an accomplished teacher of stringed-instrument students. Mrs. Drake had not seen a doctor or dentist in years before her application in 1931. Consequently, she had only one of her upper teeth and a few lower teeth remaining and believed she had liver trouble and high blood pressure. In her initial description of Mrs. Drake, the Visitor described her as a woman who "talks almost incessantly and is somewhat evasive when direct questions are asked."

Flora Stein, who never married, had lived in her parents' home all her life. Financial assistance from her late father's estate provided enough money to maintain the home and cover the costs of a housekeeper. However, in 1909, when Miss Stein was forty-three, her mother died, and her deceased brother's wife sued the sisters for what they perceived as a "just share" of the estate. The sisters eventually lost their portion of the estate to court costs and legal fees.

For the next twenty-four years, Miss Stein worked as a saleslady in three different department stores. When she was sixty-three, her second sales position was terminated due to her age. She obtained a job at another local department store by falsifying her age. She held this position for four years. At the time of the Visitor's first contact with the sisters, Miss Stein was still working, and, although her boss had said that her services were no longer needed, she "begged to be allowed to remain and her wish was granted."

Two years later, Miss Stein had a heart attack and was no longer able to work. The Visitor observed that she appeared to be dying, which she attributed to years of overwork and malnutrition. Although the LHMH had stopped accepting clients, the Visitor appealed to the Board of Trustees to support this emergency case. Miss Stein was accepted as a Hannan client, even though LHMH finances were "taxed to capacity."

The case notes describe many conflicts between Mrs. Drake and the LHMH. There are many letters written by Mrs. Drake, complaining about her financial situation and imploring Hannan staff to increase her stipend. Mrs. Drake also complained frequently about her treatment by the staff. In a 1931 letter, written directly to a member of the LHMH Board of Trustees, Mrs. Drake complained that Executive Secretary Mr. Frost treated her "worse than a dog." Mrs. Drake's case was transferred to another Visitor in 1932, after Mr. Frost intervened because Mrs. Drake complained that the first Visitor had not treated her well. However, Mr. Frost warned her that if her relationships with the LHMH did not improve, the organization would terminate her pension.

Mike Stein, identified throughout the files by his first name only, and as their "mentally defective brother," had been able to hold a job as a wood turner's assistant but had been laid off prior to Mrs. Drake's application to the LHMH. Although the LHMH showed interest and concern for Mike's welfare, he was not formally an LHMH client. Consequently, he did not have his own case file, but information on his situation is available from the files of both of the sisters. Mr. Frost and the LHMH initially concurred that it was "in the interest of good social work that [Mike] should be placed in an institution where he would be provided regularly with his three meals per day." However, when the Visitor attempted to convince Mrs. Drake and Miss Stein to institutionalize their brother, they refused, stating that they had promised their mother on her death bed that they would care for Mike. In 1936, the two sisters were supporting themselves and Mike on a combined income of seventy-five dollars per month from the LHMH, while Mike received a small amount of money and clothing from the Department of Public Welfare.

Mike died in 1938 at the age of sixty-two. His death was extremely upsetting to both sisters. They remained together despite their very different personalities. Through the years the Visitor documented several concerns regarding Mrs. Drake's "domineering qualities," "aggressive mood," and the fact that she dominated her sister's "entire life, thoughts and actions." The Visitor also noted problems with Mrs. Drake's temper, writing that "everything must go her way or she flies into a rage and swears" and that "Miss Stein is afraid Mrs. Drake might do her physical harm if she crossed her in any way." As she grew older, Mrs. Drake grew more volatile, and at one point the Visitor recorded that Mrs. Drake was physically abusive to her sister. When Mrs. Drake was eighty-one years old, the Visitor noted that she was "of the opinion that [Mrs. Drake] is failing rapidly and that it might be dangerous for her sister to continue rooming with her if she has many more such outbursts of temper."

Mrs. Drake died of heart disease at the age of eighty-two. Four months after the death of Mrs. Drake, the Visitor noted that Miss Stein "clung to [the Visitor] and insisted upon telling all the details of her sister, Mrs. Drake's, death at Receiving Hospital and then poured out the humiliation she had suffered for years at the hands of her sister." Mrs. Stein then became seriously ill herself but refused medical care. She said she wanted "to be left alone to die in peace rather than have anything done which would bother or pain her." Miss Stein died two years after Mrs. Drake, like her sister at the age of eighty-two, after falling and breaking a hip.

Minnie Thomas

Minnie Thomas was born on February 26, 1838, in Germany, and came to the United States at the age of six. The family lived near Utica, New York. At the age of eleven, she went to work with a dressmaker, learned the trade and worked at it until nineteen years of age. She never received formal schooling, but she made few mistakes in English and read a great deal. According to the notes of the Visitor, she had an "innate culture" which overshadowed her lack of academic training.

Minnie married at the age of nineteen, but her husband drowned five months later. She gave birth to a son and went back to dressmaking to support him. When the boy was five, she married Earl Thomas, a tailor, and they moved to New York City. When her son was fourteen, the family came to Detroit. Her second husband eventually became ill. After ten years of fighting this illness, he died.

Mrs. Thomas and her son lived together for many years until he married, and then she moved to an old-age home at the age of eighty-six. She stayed for eighteen months but left out of boredom. She told the

Visitor "she could not endure having nothing to do." Mrs. Thomas took a light-housekeeping room in a large old-fashioned house, and her son paid the rent until early 1929. At the time of her pension application, her son had been unemployed for a year and had no prospects for work. He had used up his savings and was unable to support his mother financially. Mrs. Thomas was ninety years old. Her health was good, although she walked with a slight limp and arose from a chair with difficulty. She asked only that she be cared for until her son obtained employment.

In 1930, the Visitor discovered that Mrs. Thomas sometimes went without food so that she could give her pension money to her son and grandson. The Visitor made arrangements to pay her bills directly to discourage her from doing this.

Over the next few years, Mrs. Thomas' mental health declined, and her personal habits deteriorated to the point where she could no longer keep herself clean and fed. In 1932, the Visitor placed her in a boarding home, where she caused some trouble with the management because she visited some of the men's rooms in the middle of the night.

In her last days, Mrs. Thomas refused to eat or get up from bed. In late 1934, she was transferred to Detroit Receiving Hospital, where she died three days later, according to the death report, as a result of "senile dementia."

Part 3

Part Three

Old Age in Hard Times

By 1929, many old people had been able to buy homes and amass wealth to the extent that they expected to continue living independently in later life. However, financial reversals through widowhood, illness, and job loss, as well as the onset of the Depression, made this impossible for many, and elders had to turn to families for assistance. Not only were family members sometimes non-existent or unable to help, but old people and their adult children were also concerned about the possibility that elders would be become dependent on family care. In this section, contributors examine the differences between independence and dependence and show how different clients from the working class, middle class and upper class challenged and resisted this binary.

Each chapter presents one or more specific cases to illustrate how pensioners tried to maintain their sense of self and retain some measure of autonomy (personal choice) and independence (ability to act on their own behalf), despite their dependence on a charitable organization. Clients managed to assert their strength within dependence by focusing on aspects of their lives in which they were still independent. As Padgett and Cheng explain, there are many kinds of dependence, and clients who were financially dependent were not always physically or emotionally dependent. Some clients, however, were more skilled than others in negotiating their dependency needs with the Luella Hannan Memorial Home (LHMH), because they knew how to persuade the Visitors and Mr. Frost and because they had more social capital to leverage on their behalf.

Padgett and Cheng illustrate how three middle-class clients, each in her own way, refused to assume the culturally constructed role of dependent old lady. Similarly, Bailey-Fakhoury and Dillaway explain how two

119

formerly wealthy women worked to maintain their dignity and status, including a sense of social superiority while receiving assistance from a charity. Briller and Durocher describe two sisters who tried to maintain their independent identities through material items, including a home they had owned together for many years. Although the LHMH took ownership of this home, the sisters continued to care for it as if it were their own, reasoning that their caretaking made them "partners with rather than dependents of the LHMH."

Other contributors focus on how clients used their pensions to sustain their independent identities as caregivers. Hopp and Thornton, for example, describe the consistently assertive efforts of Mrs. Drake (one of the Stein siblings profiled in part 2) to increase her grant in order to maintain her role as primary supporter for an ailing sister and their mentally disabled brother. They demonstrate how Visitor Anna Wentink served as client advocate in this case, assisting Mrs. Drake in her negotiations with the LHMH. Hopp and Thornton conclude that, even with entitlement programs such as Social Security and Medicare, what social worker Mary Richmond wrote in 1930 is still true in 2010: "The family continues to be the pivotal institution around which our human destinies revolve."

Clients' abilities to maintain identity, choice and independence varied in terms of their class, gender, and race. This became even more apparent as the Depression wore on and the LHMH began scrutinizing every request, reducing benefits, and cutting off pensions entirely. Calasanti and Harrison describe how the two Black clients had to be especially careful not to break the rules of the organization and how each took pains to show gratitude and appreciation for any assistance given. Even then, the male client, Rev. Burke, was dropped from the rolls after he bought items on credit. Calasanti and Harrison point out that charitable organizations like the LHMH saw dependence as more or less "burdensome" based on an elder's social location and his/her engagement in "needs talk" that appropriately reflected this location from the perspective of the organization. Clients who asked for more than they "deserved" were seen as burdens.

Finally, Langlois and Durocher explain that the emotional tone of the Depression era was one of great fear and anxiety, especially for older people who had no way of supporting themselves. Indeed, in 1929, anyone who applied for assistance from a charitable organization, at a time when accepting charity was stigmatized as a failure of the individual and the family, was surely acting out of this fear. In the notes on their intake interviews, LHMH Visitors often described clients as "nervous," suffering from "nervous disorders," or "worn down by worry." Langlois and Durocher claim that the common dread of the poorhouse was an expression of a larger cultural anxiety over becoming dependent on others. It therefore reflected not just physical concerns but existential ones as well. They describe the case of one LHMH client who was "haunted" by loss and her fear of the future. Drawing on Carole Haber and Brian Gratton's historical accounts of the almshouse (Cite, chapter 9), they suggest that similar hauntings occur today as elder Americans contemplate their futures in nursing homes.

In his book *What are Old People For?*, geriatric physician and nursing home abolitionist William Thomas confirms that fear and the dread of becoming a burden still haunt most older people in the twenty-first century. He concludes that we can avoid being "imprisoned" by these beliefs if we "allow ourselves to acknowledge the simultaneous truths of our dependence and independence. The word that is usually used to signify such unification is *interdependence*" (2004, 242).

Chapter 4

The Multiple Roles of Social Workers in the Great Depression

Faith P. Hopp and Nancy Thornton

Although men are now to be found more and more often in better-paid jobs, the typical social worker is a devoted, hard working, college-trained woman who has dedicated her life to the service of those afflicted in mind, body, or estate. Busy almost constantly day and night, the social worker is valiantly trying to ease the suffering and the despair of a few of the many caught in the utter breakdown of an industrial system. . . . The truth is, the depression has swamped social work.
—June Purcell Guild

Introduction

The Depression was a cataclysmic event that impacted both social work Visitors, (also known as "caseworkers") and those whom they served, in a profound way. The Luella Hannan Memorial Home (LHMH) Visitors in Detroit, Michigan, were among the first geriatric social workers in the United States, and they played multiple roles as they coped with the challenging, perplexing, and often overwhelming situations of old people in the Great Depression. Visitors worked long hours with low wages; social workers during the Great Depression typically made 30 percent less than high school teachers of the era (Huff n.d.).They encountered people in a variety of circumstances and attempted to employ meager funds to provide basic services and support. The older men and women helped by the LHMH had little or no family support and were experiencing economic hardships that were often difficult, distressing, and embarrassing. Money was scarce, both for those providing assistance and for those in need, and the relationship between Visitors and those they served were forged within this environment of limited resources. Although much has been written about prominent social workers such as Frances Perkins, Harry Hopkins, and Jane Addams, in terms of their influences on social welfare policy during this era (e.g., Adams 1977; Downey 2009; Elshtain 2002; Hopkins 2009; Linn 1935), much less is known about the day-to-day work of Visitors.

As Lipsky (1980) notes, case workers and other "street level" workers are primarily employed by bureaucracies, such as police and welfare departments, schools and community agencies. They play a key role in implementing social welfare policies because they "interact with and have a wide discretion over the dispensation of benefits or the allocation of public sanctions" (p. 11). He stresses that street-level workers have a profound impact, because they set client expectations for services and because they provide and supervise the services and treatments received through social programs. A defining feature of street-level workers is that they deal directly with immediate, personal reactions of individuals to organizational decisions. Although Lipsky's research is based on workers in public agencies in modern times, his depiction of street-level workers can help us to better understand the role played by workers in a private agency during the Depression era.

A review of the LHMH archives provides a unique glimpse into the lives of the Visitors during these difficult years. By reviewing social casework records from these archives, we are able to observe Visitors encountering people in a variety of circumstances as they developed street-level policies and procedures. Within the broad constraints of organizational, local, and national policies for people in dire financial circumstances, LHMH Visitors were able to exercise considerable discretion, and, in this way, influenced the lives of countless elders and their families during this period.

In this chapter, we begin with a narrative of one family (a sibling group of two sisters and a brother) who received support from the LHMH. We will draw on this narrative to describe the Visitors' role, in terms of three related functions: managing interpersonal relationships, coordinating family support, and mediating between the organization and its clients. Through discussion of these roles, we describe how the Visitors sought to assure elderly men and women that they would be able to live their later years with dignity, but within the constraints imposed by the LHMH and the larger social, economic, and policy environment. We conclude with a discussion of the implications of this narrative for contemporary social work.

Encounters with Mrs. Drake and Her Family

Although the LHMH initially provided services only to Mrs. Drake (Case #486), the organization eventually took an interest in the entire family, which included Mrs. Drake, her younger sister, Miss Stein (Case #510), and a younger brother, always referred to in the case notes by his first name, Mike, but who we will refer to as Mr. Stein. Mr. Stein appears to have had a developmental disability; the records indicate that he had had a "mental condition" since infancy and received help from his sisters during adulthood that allowed him to live in the community. We divide our narrative of this family into two phases. Phase I encompasses the initial encounters between Mrs. Drake and the Visitor, Mrs. Slack, and the challenges they faced in forging a mutually trusting relationship. Phase II begins as a new Visitor, Mrs. Wentink, takes over the case, obtains financial assistance for Miss Stein, takes an active interest in advocating for Mr. Stein, and provides on-going mediation between Mrs. Drake and the LHMH.

Phase I: Initial Encounters with Mrs. Slack

Mrs. Slack was the Visitor first assigned to the case of Mrs. Drake, age sixty-seven, who had been a music teacher of stringed instruments and employed by the Grinnell Music Store for forty years. In 1931, Mrs. Drake directly contacted the LHMH for financial assistance, listing Mr. Guest of Grinnell's as a reference. During an interview with the Visitor, Mr. Guest indicated that he had known Mrs. Drake for twenty-five years, during which she had taught music and been self-supporting. He described her as "a sincere, ambitious woman who, until the present, has always been anxious and capable of making her own way. In her day she was a first class mandolin teacher. . . ." He further stated that "recently her methods have become more or less out of date and her age is also against her," and that, consequently, they could no longer refer students to her.

Mrs. Drake's unmarried sister, Miss Stein, lived with her and worked at Kline's Department Store at the time of referral. The household also included their brother, Mr. Stein, age fifty-five at the time of the referral, and described in the records as "mentally defective." Their father, a German immigrant, had been a well-known professor of music in Detroit. Mrs. Drake had been married for six years and was widowed following the death of her husband from tuberculosis. The Visitor conducted the initial interview with Mrs. Drake, and described her as coming from "a family of unusual culture and refinement" and identifying her "definite problem" as "to supply an income whereby [Mrs. Drake] may pay part of her expenses."

The LHMH approved Mrs. Drake for fifty dollars per month in support. However, Mrs. Drake did not initially reveal that she was also receiving income from another source, the Masonic Welfare Organization, a violation of the LHMH eligibility rules, which required full disclosure of all income. When the Visitor (Mrs. Slack) learned of this omission and confronted Mrs. Drake on the issue, a series of tense discussions between the two women ensued. Mrs. Drake expressed the belief that it was appropriate for her to withhold information about financial support she was receiving from the Masons. However, Mrs. Slack relayed the Mason's view that she had been deceptive. Pursuant to these discussions, the Masonic organization withdrew its support from Mrs. Drake. Mrs. Slack, through a series of discussions and negotiations with the Masons, arranged for their financial support to resume. However, Mrs. Drake's combined income from both sources was reduced from eighty dollars to fifty dollars per month.

In response to these developments, Mrs. Drake wrote a letter of complaint to Rev. Vance, a trustee of the LHMH, on July 31, 1931. In this letter, she relates to him that she was "a very successful and prominent music teacher," noting that "I am extremely well known throughout the city in the best circles of society" and reminding him that she had previously ("seventeen or eighteen years ago") instructed his daughter in music. She further relates that, once LHMH staff learned that she was receiving assistance from the Masons:

> This instantly started a fire for me to burn up in the next day, by being called over the phone to face Mrs. Slack for a case of dishonesty, which Mr. Frost [Mrs. Slack's superior] called it, and was extremely angry and rough with me in every respect . . . I was too well known here for such talk as that. It was disgraceful the way he treated me—worse than a dog (LHMFC, Case #486).

A letter of response from Rev. Vance, dated September 15, 1931, and included in the file, is summarized by Mrs. Slack in her case notes. According to the summary, Rev. Vance informed Mrs. Drake that

> . . . all dealings were received through the office of Mr. Frost and the Visitors . . . the Board members were busy men and could not handle the details of the case. He advised [Mrs. Drake] that both Mr. Frost and the Visitor were her friends, and that it is a desire of the Board that all contacts be as pleasant as possible (LHMFC, Case #486).

Executive Director Leon Frost, on September 16, 1931, subsequently wrote a letter of thank you to Rev. Vance for his "splendid letter" to Mrs. Drake, noting that:

> I realize . . . that from her standpoint she feels justified, or, at least, has worked up a defense reaction to fortify herself in her own mind. Do not feel, however, that I will take advantage of this, but will assume in my relations to her, a kindly and considerate attitude (LHMFC, Case #486).

In the meantime, the Masons, like all other charitable organizations at the time, were experiencing their own financial difficulties, and they soon cut off financial support to Mrs. Drake. When Mrs. Slack subsequently visited Mrs. Drake in her home on October 2, 1931, she recorded her observations as follows:

> [Visitor] was quite shocked at the change in [Mrs. Drake]'s physical appearance. She has apparently lost a great deal of weight and did not look at all well. [Mrs. Drake] came into the room crying and was almost hysterical. She stated that she could not stand the treatment she had been receiving and added that she had been hungry most of the month. [Mrs. Drake] did not for an instance admit that she had not been absolutely fair in her dealings with the Home. She talked at length in order to attempt to justify herself and the action which she took (LHMFC, Case #486).

At this time, Mrs. Slack considered Mrs. Drake on the "verge of physical and mental collapse."

Informed of the financial constraints on the LHMH and urged by Mr. Frost to cut expenses wherever possible, Mrs. Slack looked for ways to lower Mrs. Drake's budget. On December 30, 1931, she inquired at the apartment office and learned that Mrs. Drake could move to another apartment for three dollars less per week. This would have saved Mrs.

Drake the sum of twelve dollars per month; however, Mrs. Drake could not be convinced, as she believed the apartment was less desirable than the one she occupied. Mrs. Slack indicates in her case notes that she "feels that if [Mrs. Drake] and her sister are in straitened financial circumstances as they claim, they would welcome a chance to save three dollars a week on their rent." At this point, the notes suggest that the relationship between Mrs. Slack and Mrs. Drake was deteriorating. After this visit, Mrs. Slack documented the growing antagonism between them:

> Throughout [Visitor's] entire call, [Mrs. Drake] seemed antagonistic and quarrelsome. [Mrs. Drake] stated that [Visitor]'s first two calls on her had been quite pleasant and enjoyable, but that recently everything had changed. She stated that from the questions [Mrs. Slack] asked it seemed that her veracity was being questioned. She stated further that if [Mrs. Slack] could not see her like she had in the beginning she saw no reason for [Mrs. Slack]'s calling on her at all. [Mrs. Drake] insists she is not getting a square deal and severely criticized the organization for not giving preference to those people who were born in Detroit. [Mrs. Drake] made several references to the salaries of staff workers and stated that none of those workers would be able to get along if their incomes were cut in half as hers had been (LHMFC, Case #486).

In a meeting shortly afterwards between Mrs. Slack and Mr. Frost on January 8, 1932, Mrs. Slack's notes relay that Mrs. Drake:

> . . . did not think [Mrs. Slack] had treated her very well, and she stated she was satisfied with everyone else with whom she had come in contact. Mr. Frost asked if a change in Visitors would bring an entirely different attitude on her part. [Mrs. Drake] stated that it certainly would. Mr. Frost, therefore, told [Mrs. Drake] that he would transfer her to another worker in order to give her a chance to prove that her assertions were correct. He warned her, however, that if any antagonism was shown in the future, or if her attitude toward the Home did not entirely change, the relations between the Home and herself would be terminated and the money which she was receiving would be used for someone who was happy to receive it and appreciative (LHMFC, Case #486).

The case was transferred to Anna Wentink on the same day that this discussion took place.

Phase II: Mrs. Wentink Takes the Case

Mrs. Wentink conducted a new assessment upon taking over the case. In her notes dated January 28, 1932, she remarks that Mrs. Drake:

> . . . has the feeling that she has been grossly misunderstood by the people she previously had contacted through this office. She went to great length to justify her conduct to [Mrs. Wentink] and expressed the hope that she and [Mrs. Wentink] would get along well together (LHMFC, Case #486).

Unlike Mrs. Slack, whose notes focus primarily on Mrs. Drake, Mrs. Wentink from the beginning took an active interest in the entire family, including Mrs. Drake, her sister Miss Stein, and their brother Mr. Stein. She assesses the home situation, noting that "these three people have lived together since the death of their mother in the sense that they all come back to the same place to sleep at night." Mrs. Wentink also worked with the LHMH to obtain money for Miss Stein. After visiting the home on October 21, 1932, she describes Miss Stein as "a woman of medium height, exceedingly thin, whose face has a death-like pallor" and further notes that "her health is completely broken" due to acute heart trouble, anemia, and varicose veins. She further expresses the view that Miss Stein appeared to be dying from overwork and malnutrition. The case files document that Miss Stein had been confined to bed for six weeks due to a heart attack, and that "doubtlessly, she will never be able to work again, for in addition to her heart trouble she is suffering from anemia and a dreadful case of varicose veins."

Mrs. Wentink documents that Miss Stein had begun working twenty-four years earlier, after her mother's death and "the breaking up of the family home." She further notes that Miss Stein had worked for the Siegel Company for ten years until being let go four years ago "because of her age." Miss Stein then got a job at the Kline Company "by giving her age falsely," but was now unable to work because of declining health. Because of the severity of the situation and the fact that her sister was already a client, Miss Stein was accepted as a client, even though the organization's finances "were already taxed to capacity." The LHMH agreed to provide Miss Stein with fifteen dollars per month to cover the cost of food.

Mrs. Wentink also attended to the needs of Mr. Stein, even though he was not an LHMH client. She noted that Mr. Frost considered the subject of Mrs. Drake's brother to be "a problem for this office" and initially thought he should be removed from the home, stating that "in the interest of good social work [Mr. Stein] should be placed in an institution where he would be provided regularly with his three meals a day," and advising Mrs. Wentink "to talk with [Mrs. Drake] and [Miss Stein] and attempt to show them that it was for the best interest of all three that [Mr. Stein] be cared for outside of their home" (LHMFC, Case #486).

During her initial meetings with Mrs. Drake, Mrs. Wentink followed this suggestion and attempted to persuade the sisters to institutionalize their brother. However, Mrs. Drake responded that they could not abide by this suggestion, as they had made a death-bed promise to their mother to care for their brother. Mrs. Wentink summarizes the gist of this conversation, concluding that "[Mrs. Drake] would rather starve than be separated from the brother." Mrs. Wentink consulted with Mr. Frost and a week later, after another visit to the family on November 4, 1932, writes that she "explained to [Mrs. Drake] that the objection had been withdrawn to having [Mr. Stein] remain in their home," which very much pleased Mrs. Drake. This exchange indicates a willingness on the part of the LHMH to support the siblings' desire to remain together as a family unit.

Throughout her case notes, Mrs. Wentink often interprets Mrs. Drake's motives sympathetically, considering her self-appointed role as head of the family and the pressures associated with this role. For example, following a conversation on May 2, 1933, involving Mrs. Drake and a Masonic administrator, Mrs. Wentink notes that "[Mrs. Drake] showed the worst sides of her personality and . . . demanded assistance rather than asked for it." However, Mrs. Wentink acknowledges the financial stress Mrs. Drake was under and reflects that "if judgment were passed on our fellowmen when deciding whether or not to extend to them the bare necessities of life [then] perhaps it would be possible to find a reason for not helping any unfortunate person" (LHMFC, Case #486).

Despite the assurance made in 1932 and the expressed wishes of the sisters, the LHMH, as a result of its own financial distress during the Depression, later returned to the idea of having Mr. Stein move to an institutional location, such as the county poor house. Mr. Frost writes in a letter to Mrs. Drake on June 19, 1936, that "I cannot see how you can possibly get along with the money which is available from this organization to the two of you, and at the same time divert part of it for the care of your brother . . . . we are faced with a realistic situation which in my judgment does not permit a continuation of your plan." However, a subsequent meeting with Mrs. Drake appears to have convinced him that

Mr. Stein should remain with his sisters. Mrs. Wentink summarizes this meeting:

> After going over both the family home conditions and economic situation, Mr. Frost decided that it would not be wise to break up the relationship between [Mrs. Drake], her sister and their brother, [Mr. Stein]. He advised that he would have the case presented to the Board in an effort to obtain a $10 per month increase for [Mrs. Drake's] sister, [Miss Stein], another one of our clients. This would give the two women an income of $75 per month, which would maintain the family situation inasmuch as the brother, [Mr. Stein], receives money for food and is supplied clothing by the [Department of Public Welfare] (LHMFC, Case #486).

Despite these concessions, Mrs. Drake continued to protest the amounts of their stipends, which she viewed as inadequate, and met again with Mr. Frost, at his request, on May 10, 1937. Mrs. Wentink later summarized her understanding of the events that transpired. According to the case notes, Mrs. Drake attempted to convince Mr. Frost of the need to increase the grant, but "Mr. Frost explained to [Mrs. Drake] that she and [Mrs. Stein] are together getting seventy-five dollars per month which is as much or more than some of our couples, man and wife." She also relates that Mr. Frost said that "he could readily see how the brother's presence in the family group increased their living costs" but emphasized that the LHMH could not be financially responsible for Mr. Stein (who did not fall within the requirements of the Hannan fund). Mrs. Drake then wrote to Mr. Vance requesting his intervention in increasing her monthly grant, and this letter was forwarded to Mr. Frost. On June 1, 1937, Mr. Frost responded by letter to Mr. Vance, writing that Mrs. Drake had

> . . . stepped entirely out of line in writing to you as I had a long talk with her about her finances. . . . The difficulty is that she insists on keeping a feeble minded brother with her who is not a pensioner of ours and for whom we cannot assume financial responsibility. . . . She is, indeed, a very persistent woman and absolutely will not take no for an answer (LHMFC, Case #486).

Mrs. Wentink's strategy for balancing the expressed wishes of the family with the views of Mr. Frost are shown in her subsequent accounts of a conversation with a Mrs. Kane, from the Department of Public Welfare's Old Age Bureau, concerning Mr. Stein's financial assistance. Mrs.

Kane questioned whether the LHMH was providing assistance to Mr. Stein, to which Mrs. Wentink responded that "we had closed our eyes to the fact that some of our money was being used in [Mr. Stein]'s care because we felt it a shame to break up a family situation such as theirs." She also advised Mrs. Kane that "some of the sisters' money was used only through dint of self-sacrifice to help maintain [Mr. Stein]." In the following months, despite the strong views on the part of Mr. Frost concerning the need to place Mr. Stein in an institution, Mrs. Wentink continued to support the sisters in caring for their brother until his death, which occurred at home.

The Multiple Roles of the Visitor

Managing Interpersonal Relationships

The Visitors had the challenging task of establishing and maintaining good working relationships with pensioners supported by the LHMH, while at the same time conducting a thorough investigation of other sources of financial support so that unnecessary burdens were not placed on the LHMH. The Visitor's job was to investigate circumstances and enforce the rules, but within the context of a warm personal relationship and a "friendly" manner. In this respect, the LHMH Visitors, like today's social workers, could be described as "soft cops" (Goroff 1977), charged with the task of enforcing conformity to prevailing societal values as a means of social control (Day 2009). The obligation to maintain friendly relationships was a part of the culture of the LHMH and extended to senior leadership, as shown in Mr. Frost's letter to Mr. Vance, in which he assured the Trustee that he would maintain a "kindly and considerate attitude" with regards to Mrs. Drake.

To the extent that Visitors could develop friendly relationships with their elder clients, they were in a good position to conduct a thorough and accurate assessment of their financial needs. However, Mrs. Slack's investigatory activities in regards to Mrs. Drake appeared to get in the way of developing a warm relationship. Instead, their relationship appears to have been distrustful and adversarial on both sides. Mrs. Drake refused to admit Mrs. Slack into her apartment for their scheduled visits and instead arranged to meet her in the lobby. Mrs. Slack, while waiting in the building lobby on one such occasion, quietly inquired of the manager about the availability of less expensive rooms for Mrs. Drake. She informed Mrs. Drake that she would like for her to move to a new room, to which Mrs. Drake expressed adamant opposition. Their relationship ultimately deteriorated to such an extent that Mr. Frost transferred the case to another Visitor. He did so with the admonition that Mrs. Drake be more forthcoming in her relationship with the second Visitor and with the stipulation that Mrs. Wentink (the newly assigned Visitor) be allowed access to her home.

The transfer of the case is an important action because it demonstrates the authority of Mr. Frost over the activities of the Visitors, and it also emphasizes the importance he places on strong interpersonal relationships between Visitors and clients. Thus, although the case notes do not clearly indicate Mr. Frost's motives for transferring the case, it seems likely that his decision was due to a desire to maintain positive relations with Mrs. Drake, as well as his opinion that establishing a new relationship with another Visitor would provide a "fresh start" in Mrs. Drake's relationship with the LHMH. The transfer also provides Mr. Frost with the opportunity to impose his authority over Mrs. Drake, stipulating that the new Visitor be allowed access to the Drake home. In summary, Mrs. Slack's focus on a thorough investigation, while potentially reducing the financial burden of the LHMH with respect to Mrs. Drake, contributed to a decline in her relationship with that particular client. Mrs. Slack experienced challenges in balancing the friendly and investigative functions of her role, and the resulting adversarial relationship was not in keeping with the professional expectations for a Visitor.

Coordinating Family Support

In contrast with Mrs. Slack, who focused primarily on investigating and providing services to Mrs. Drake, Mrs. Wentink took a broader perspective and considered the entire family situation in her assessment and interventions. In this regard, she was acting consistently with the social casework approach advocated by Mary Richmond (1917), which stressed that the family, rather than the individual, was the appropriate unit of attention for caseworkers. Upon taking over the case, Mrs. Wentink turned her attention to Miss Stein, Mrs. Drake's sister, who by this time was in poor health and unable to support herself. By persuading the LHMH Board of Trustees that Miss Stein was in dire circumstances, Mrs. Wentink was able to obtain financial support for her, even though the resources of the LHMH were, by this time, strained to capacity.

Mrs. Wentink, however, was much more constrained in her ability to help Mr. Stein, who had previously been employed but was now unable

to work. Mr. Stein, only fifty-five at the time of referral, was too young
to qualify for LHMH assistance, and also, because of his disability, may
not have been considered a "Hannan type." Moreover, although the 1935
Social Security Act provided a retirement pension for workers, it was not
until 1956, long after Mr. Stein's death, that federal funds were provided
through the Social Security Disability Insurance (SSDI) for disabled persons, such as Mr. Stein, who had a previous work history.[1] The only
available source of assistance appears to have been from a local organization, the Department of Public Welfare, which provided an extremely
small stipend of sixteen dollars per month to him in 1936. Social policies
of the time provided a minimal, subsistence level of support or "outdoor
relief" for persons with disabilities living at home, with the expectation
that those who needed more extensive services and support would utilize
"indoor relief" available through placement at institutions such as insane
asylums or the county poor house, in this case, the Eloise facility for Detroit residents. This rationale is reflected in the letter, written by Mr.
Frost, suggesting that a placement of Mr. Stein at Eloise would be "in the
interests of good social work," a statement that is somewhat odds with
his earlier comment that it "would not be wise to break up the family."
Interestingly, a 1930 newspaper article quotes Mr. Frost promoting the
benefits of encouraging community care for older adults:

> It has been said recently that those in dire need should, when old, be
> made comfortable among friends and relatives that they may spend
> their declining years as members of the community in which they have
> been active members. This fact seems difficult for public opinion at
> large to grasp. While increasing age only too frequently brings infirmi-
> ties of a physical nature, this is not by any means universally the case.
> If infirmities do exist in any particular instance, the institution may be
> the logical solution, but surely economic lack alone should not be the
> deciding factor. (*Detroit Free Press,* March 7, 1930)

Most likely, Mr. Frost's opinions on Mr. Stein's care, were based on the
financial distress of the LHMH and Mr. Stein's lack of eligibility for
LHMH funds because of his age. It is also possible that Mr. Frost, while
progressive on the issue of community care for older adults, nonetheless
subscribed to the widely held belief of that period that persons with disabilities should be cared for in institutions.

    As a direct provider of services for a large caseload of vulnerable
elders, (dealing in what Mary Richmond (1930) referred to as "retail"
social work), Anna Wentink must have had little time to advocate for
changes in larger social welfare policies that would better serve the needs

of disabled persons and their family members. In particular, she was constrained by the fact that, since Mr. Stein was not eligible for LHMH services, he was not a formal client of the organization. She was therefore unable to fully support Mrs. Drake and Miss Stein, who, like other single women, had family needs that were not supported by existing policy frameworks (Abramovitz, 1996). However, despite these constraints, Mrs. Wentink had considerable discretion as a "street level" policy maker, as she attempted to forge solutions to the issues and problems posed by Mr. Stein's situation. As a woman and a lower-level employee of the LHMH, in her professional discourse, Mrs. Wentink did not directly oppose Mr. Frost's initial recommendation that Mr. Stein be placed at Eloise. The records reflect that she initially followed Frost's directive to encourage placement for Mr. Stein. In her actions, however, she supported the family's desire for him to remain at home and conducted casework services to help make this a reality.

Consistent with LHMH policy, Mr. Stein, since he was not a formal client of LHMH, did not have his own case file. Consequently, Mrs. Wentink's activities regarding Mr. Stein can only be surmised by examining the case notes for his two sisters. However, through her interactions with the DPW, Mrs. Wentink stressed the LHMH's ongoing care and concern for Mr. Stein, while suggesting that the DPW was the appropriate entity for assuming the financial burden of his care. Within this context, she admitted to the DPW that the LHMH had essentially "looked the other way" with respect to the financial support provided to Mr. Stein by his sisters, which was essentially indirect support from the LHMH.

In summary, Mrs. Wentink appears to have been aware of the full picture of the siblings' situation and was supportive of their aspirations to remain together in one home as a family. However, the policy context of the time (including those of both the LHMH and the local DPW) forced her to deal with each family member in a piecemeal fashion. Her "street level" approach entailed maintaining separate files (and, eventually, separate but equal stipends)—for the sisters, while advocating for Mr. Stein's assistance by other sources. Operating within these limits, Mrs. Wentink admitted to being aware of the likelihood that some of the LHMH funds were being used for his support. Although the strategies used by Mrs. Wentink were not entirely satisfactory to anyone involved, including the LHMH and the family, her actions were ultimately successful in helping the sisters to keep their "deathbed promise" to their mother. Mrs. Wentink helped Mr. Stein to continue living with his sisters for the rest of his life and also provided solace for his sisters after his death.

Mediating Between Organization and Client

Abraham Flexner, in a famous speech to the National Conference of Charities and Corrections in 1915 (Kirk and Reid 2001), asserted that social work was not a profession and further claimed that the social workers were simply acting as mediators between "professionals" (physicians, attorneys, etc.) and people in need (Trattner 1999). Our reading of the Hannan case files suggests that this depiction vastly underestimates the high level of knowledge, interpersonal skills and diplomacy required by the Visitors in their mediating role. They were not, as Flexner suggested, simply carrying out the orders of more qualified professionals but were instead actively shaping the implementation of policies through a series of negotiations that reflected knowledge of complex interpersonal dynamics. They were assigned the often incongruous tasks of determining persons as "worthy" or "unworthy" of assistance during times of wide-spread need, protecting the dwindling financial assets of the charitable organizations for which they worked, and maintaining harmonious relationships with often desperate clients. This mediating role also assigned power: the Visitors had the authority to go into client homes and make recommendations regarding their welfare. For their work, in return, they received a salary. However, as Flexner's speech suggests, they did not have the status of the medical (male-dominated) professions, and their skills were frequently underestimated and devalued by other professionals, the social workers' clients, and the larger public.

Although this mediator role is only partially discernable in the day-to-day activities recounted in the case files, it often became explicit when the expectations for successful mediation were violated. For example, Mrs. Drake circumvented the Visitor by writing directly to Rev. Vance, a Presbyterian minister and a member of the LHMH Board of Trustees. Quite possibly, she recognized that the Visitor had limited authority and therefore felt justified in taking her plea for an increase in pension to the highest authority of the LHMH. Moreover, her actions in writing the letter, and her other interactions with Mrs. Slack, indicate that Mrs. Drake was hesitant to accept the authority of the social worker as a mediator between herself and the LHMH. The multiple letters written by Mr. Frost to Mr. Vance in reference to Mrs. Drake's situation appear as a type of "damage control," an attempt to clarify and reinforce the "friendly" motives and disposition of the LHMH, which were threatened by Mrs. Drake's sidestepping of established lines of authority.

In short, the mediator role required a high level of skill and allowed for considerable discretion on the part of the Visitor. Moreover, this role appears to have been an essential part of a broader strategy that allowed the LHMH, and similar organizations, to preserve their financial assets as much as possible, while at the same time maintaining a positive, warm, and friendly image with their clients, board members, donors, and the larger public. When the Visitor's mediator role was sidestepped, challenged, or disturbed, Mr. Frost, as the top administrator in the organization, took quick and decisive actions to reinforce the public face of the LHMH and thereby re-establish his authority and that of his organization.

Visitors and their Perception of Older Adults

Consideration of the historical era in which the case notes were written provides insight into the attitudes that the Visitors had towards older adults at that time. By the early twentieth century, a "cult of youth" was prominent in the United States. A growing number of elders faced mandatory retirement, and older people were increasingly marginalized (Fischer 1978). At the same time, increasing migration and industrialization during this era meant that, by the time of the Great Depression, there was growing recognition that some families were not able to financially sustain and protect their members (Haber and Gratton 1994).

The profession of social work was established within this context and was strongly influenced by two leading social work pioneers: Mary Ellen Richmond and Jane Addams. The Charity Organization Society (COS), led by Richmond, trained "Friendly Visitors" in casework principles. These early social workers, such as Marie Slack and Anna Wentink, visited the poor in their homes, using scientific-method investigation procedures that stressed the determination of who was "worthy" as opposed to "unworthy" of assistance (Barusch 2009). Charity under COS was carefully dispensed, with Richmond criticizing "haphazard benevolence" with the admonishment that "every form of human weakness is intensified by the charity that asks no questions" (Richmond 1899, 157). Mary Richmond's book, *Friendly Visiting Among the Poor: A Handbook for Charity Workers* (1899) depicted older adults neglected by their children as the "worthy poor," along with "illegitimate offspring, children crippled by drunken fathers, juvenile offenders who began as child-beggars" (157). By the time of the Great Depression, this book had been widely distributed and likely influenced the LHMH Visitors' attitudes towards "deserving" older adults during the Depression era.

The other major social work approach that may have influenced the Visitors at this time was the Settlement House Movement, established in the United States by Jane Addams. While poverty was generally seen as being caused by the individual, the settlement workers looked to social causes (Walkowitz 1999). By the end of the nineteenth century, there were fifty settlement houses in the United States, with settlement workers living in the neighborhoods among the poor and demanding better living conditions for those living in poverty (Boyer, Clark, Kett, Salisbury, and Sitkoff 2008). During the early twentieth century, there were three settlement houses in close proximity to the office of the Luella Hannan Memorial Home in Detroit (Bliss 1909). Settlement House workers generally opposed the "degrading experience" of procedures used by other charities (NASW), while many of the COS workers found the settlement house workers to be "too radical and too unscientific and coddled the poor" (Walkowitz 1999, 39). In her handbook for friendly visitors, Richmond states that "the charity worker and the settlement work have need of each other" (8) but also remarked:

> . . . those who are engaged in social service often exaggerate the causes of poverty that are external to the individual . . . Settlement workers are likely to say that the sufferings of the poor are due to conditions over which they have no control (7-8).

The Settlement House work is an early example of what is now known as strengths-based social work. Addams also reached out to older adults in her settlement work, looking for their attributes and reinforcing independence. In her reflection on her twenty years at Hull House, the first Settlement House in the United States, Addams described three "impressive old women" who expressed themselves in the arts and sciences. She stated that they were:

> . . . but three out of many whom I might instance to prove that those who are handicapped in the race for life's goods, sometimes play a magnificent trick upon the jade, life herself, by ceasing to know whether or not they possess any of her tawdry goods and chattels (Addams 1910, 174-176).

The influence of both Richmond and Addams is reflected in the work of the Hannan Visitors. Mrs. Slack, followed COS procedures and was diligent in her assessment, determining that Mrs. Drake did not have any other family members who could financially contribute to her care. She also monitored how Mrs. Drake spent her stipend as the Visitor incorporated an ongoing investigation into her casework. Mrs. Slack's efforts exemplify the work that most challenged the Visitors: to fully investigate the worthiness of the clients, while building and managing supportive relationships. The limits of this approach, in terms of client relations, are seen as Mrs. Drake became angry and resentful of her treatment at the hands of Mrs. Slack. Although there is no direct evidence in the case notes that Mrs. Wentink was influenced by the Settlement House movement, her holistic view of the family needs and their ability to help one another nonetheless reflects the Settlement House emphasis on amplifying and celebrating individual strengths.

Going beyond investigating the family members to ascertain their ability to contribute to Mrs. Drake's sustenance, Mrs. Wentink also assessed their needs as individuals and as a family unit and responded with advocacy and direct service. It is important to emphasize, too, that, in the case of LHMH Visitors, their attitude and treatment of older adults was also influenced by Luella Hannan's understanding of the "worthy" poor as people of refinement who had seen better times.

The Social Worker as "Street-Level" Worker

The narrative of Mrs. Drake and her family, as derived from the case notes, illustrates the unique and difficult role of Visitors as street-level workers during the Great Depression. The importance placed on personal relationships suggests a frequently overlooked component of social welfare policy, namely that the *way* in which policies are enforced (in this case, through a friendly demeanor and a kindly and considerate attitude) are a key factor in the success of the policy itself. As noted by Lipsky (1980), "street level bureaucrats are also the focus of citizen reactions because their discretion opens up the possibility that they will respond favorably on behalf of people" (p.9). He further notes that "it is not only the *decisions* that become satisfactory rather than optimal, but also the mental and organizational *processes* that must become satisfactory" (82). Mrs. Slack is clearly within LHMH policy in questioning Mrs. Drake about her assistance from the Masons. However, perhaps because Mrs. Drake's expectation of a favorable interaction with Mrs. Slack are disappointed by this exchange, a feeling of mutual distrust develops that makes it difficult for the two women to maintain an effective relationship. Mrs. Slack's struggles with Mrs. Drake suggest that she had a hard

time maintaining a "soft cop" demeanor toward her, keeping cordial relations while enforcing agency policies.[2]

Mrs. Wentink appears to have been more successful in forging a
trusting relationship with Mrs. Drake, and, once this trust was established, she was able to focus on the goal of coordinating family support.
Mrs. Wentink clearly saw the family as the unit of attention, but her intervention was constrained by organizational policies that prevented Mr.
Stein from formally receiving LHMH assistance and that encouraged his
institutionalization. Her own day-to-day actions with regards to the family were forged within these limitations. She could not provide Mr. Stein
with LHMH financial assistance; but she took an active interest in his
well-being, advocating for his financial assistance from the Department
of Public Welfare, and supporting the sisters in their determination to
keep him living with his family. Mrs. Wentink's more flexible approach
in meeting the needs of the family allowed her to use practices that were
more innovative and progressive than the prevailing social policies for
people with disabilities would encourage or allow. She was able to maintain Mr. Stein in the community support system, an achievement that is
particularly notable, given that her actions occurred several decades before community placement and deinstitutionalization became part of the
public policy discussion.

The Visitors, through their role as mediators, functioned in a critical
juncture between the LHMH and the older men and women who were
served by the organization. As "street-level" workers, they were asked to
develop close and empathetic relationships with persons in financial and
personal distress, while acting as organizational agents charged with protecting and maintaining the financial viability of organizations such as
the LHMH. From a feminist perspective, it is also important to note that,
since most of the LHMH pensioners were female, the Visitors' role as
street-level workers was likely influenced by expectations of close relationships that often develop among women. Within the limits connected
to their positions as women, and by organizational and economic conditions, the Visitors were able to advocate for assistance, provide emotional support, and address family dynamics as a means of helping both men
and women struggle through the difficult personal and economic challenges of the Depression.[3]

Connections to Contemporary Social Work

As we read the narratives of Mrs. Drake and her family, we are reminded of our own earlier experiences as employees of social-service organizations. Social workers, the majority of whom are women, continue to act as "street-level" workers through their multiple roles in managing interpersonal relationships, coordinating family support, and mediating relationships between organizations and families, and their efforts continue to be largely invisible and marginalized, within the larger social-welfare system. Further, despite the strong pull of the mental hygiene movement and psychoanalytic movements to focus on individual issues in treatment in the earlier part of the twentieth century (Hartman and Laird, 1983), most contemporary social workers would agree with Mary Richmond that "the family continues to be the pivotal institution around which our human destinies revolve" (Richmond, 1930, 262).

Relevance of the Family Preservation Practice Model

The Family Preservation Model stresses the importance of maintaining and strengthening families and avoiding institutional placement. Originally depicted as a practice model for social welfare agencies helping families who were at risk of losing custody of their children (e.g. Littell and Schuerman 2002), this model has also been depicted as a way for social workers to help families in meeting the caregiving needs of elders (Chandler, Marlow, and Rosa 1997) and as a strategy to prevent elder abuse (e.g. Bergeron 2001; Nerenberg 2007). The Family Preservation Model emphasizes that it is in a person's best interest to remain with his/her family and that families can serve as an important resource. The family is self-defined, and the family's uniqueness and diversity is valued. This is a non-hierarchical approach, in which family members are seen as partners in the planning and implementation of care (Bergeron 2001; Chandler et al. 1997).

This Family Preservation Model is a contemporary model that has relevance for the situation described in the case archives. The narrative of the Drake/Stein family suggests that these individuals formed a non-traditional family because they were elder siblings who identified as a family and were determined to stay together. They had valuable historical perspective on each other's needs and abilities, as well as each other's medical conditions, including Mr. Stein's developmental disability, and this information was relevant for planning interventions that might help the family to stay together. Mrs. Wentink's actions, which involved working with the entire family, were consistent with the emerging emphasis on families, as promoted by the Charity Organization Society movement.

The modern family preservation model would take Mrs. Wentink's approach one step further by coordinating caregiver respite services and increasing in-home medical support. Such an approach requires that caseloads be reduced to compensate for intensive treatment, with the need for social workers who are trained in implementing a range of services, including caregiver education, family crisis intervention, and case management (Bergeron, 2001). These services, especially when more intensive monitoring is needed to ameliorate the risk of elder abuse, can be costly. However, if the family unit is not preserved, the alternative is often placement of the elder in a long-term care facility. Family preservation is much less expensive than care in a nursing facility, as indicated by the recent AARP study of long-term care that found, on average, three older persons can be supported in their home or other community setting with the money that Medicaid spends to fund nursing home placement for one individual. These are critical issues to consider, with the dramatic growth in the aging population and the dependency in the United States on informal caregiving provided by family members as the means for caring for this population (Houser, Fox-Grage, and Gibson 2009).

Policy Implications

Although the national economic crisis of 2008-2010 has not reached the enormity of the Great Depression, economists tell us that there are many parallels (Robbins 2009), and some fear that another major depression is close. We regularly witness important and vital social service agencies facing financial difficulties that result in the elimination of staff positions. We are aware of social work colleagues who struggle with higher caseloads and other increased responsibilities as a consequence of increased need and reduced staffing, and they sometimes feel the burdens of "survival guilt" when the jobs of colleagues are eliminated.

Given the challenges facing the social work profession today, we have a tremendous respect and admiration for the Hannan Visitors of yesterday. The commitment to their work was evident in their careful documentation of persistent efforts to improve the lives of the elders they served. They also faced salary reductions during that period. Mrs. Slack began her employment at LHMH on April 1, 1930, at $100 per month; her salary peaked at $135 a month in 1932 and declined thereafter, with regular reductions in pay because of economic conditions. When she resigned on March 4, 1933, with the LHMH proposing yet another pay reduction, she was receiving a salary of $91.13 per month. Mrs. Wentink experienced similar reductions and was also making $91.13 per month as of March 1, 1933, when the staff of Visitors was reduced and she became the only Hannan Visitor with sole responsibility for all LHMH clients. Similarly, many social workers today are accepting pay reductions and taking on new and challenging responsibilities that are nearly overwhelming.

Although social work as a profession has made many academic and professional strides since the 1930s, social workers continue to do the same kind of work that the early Visitors documented in their case notes: coordinating services, providing family support, and mediating between the bureaucracies and the people they serve. Faced then and now with an under-funded and fragmented social welfare system, social workers are required to make the best of a difficult situation by finding the most workable solution to support clients, while maintaining a warm and friendly demeanor. At the street level, contemporary social workers implement social welfare policies with considerable discretion and skill, striving to meet the needs of older adults with limited resources in a rapidly changing society.

Notes

1. Even today, unless Mr. Stein had a sufficient number of work credits for the Social Security Disability program, he would qualify only for the much less financially generous SSI program, and would be restricted in the types of assets that he would be allowed to keep in order to qualify for the program

2. These difficulties were surely personal, as well as professional and institutional: Mrs. Slack was a young woman in her early thirties working for a male-dominated institution that had charged her with negotiating the daily needs of hard-pressed clients twice her age during a time of social upheaval.

3. See, for example, Abrams and Curran (2004), "Between Women: Gender and Social Work in Historical Perspective" on the intersections of professionalism and maternalism in client-worker relations.

References

Abramovitz, Mimi. 1996. *Regulating the Lives of Women: Social Welfare Policy from ColonialTimes to the Present.* Cambridge: South End Press.

Abrams, Laura. S. and Laura Curran. 2004. "Between Women: Gender and Social Work in Historical Perspective." *Social Service Review, 78,* no. 3: 429-446.

Adams, Henry Hitch. 1977. *Harry Hopkins: A Biography.* New York: Putnam.

Addams, Jane. 1910. *Twenty Years at Hull-House with Autobiographical Notes.* New York: The Macmillan Company

Association of University Centers on Disabilities. *AUCD Special Report on FY 2010 Funding.* http://www.aucd.org/docs/Special%20Report%20on%20FY %202010%20Appropriations%20Final%20(2).pdf. Accessed on Dec. 23, 2009.

Barusch, Amanda. 2009. *Foundations of Social Policy: Social Justice in Human Perspective,* 3rd ed., Belmont, CA: Brooks/Cole

Bergeron, L. Rene. 2001. "Family Preservation: An Unidentified Approach in Elder Abuse Protection." *Families in Society: The Journal of Contemporary Human Services, 83,* no. 5/6: 547-556.

Bliss, William, Ed. 1909. *The New Encyclopedia of Social Reform (vol. 2).* London and New York: Funk and Wagnalls.

Boyer, Paul, Clifford Clark, Joseph Kett, Neal Salisbury, and Harvard Sitkoff. 2008. *The Enduring Vision: A History of the American People (6th ed.).* Boston: Houghton Mifflin.

Chandler, Barbara, Christine Marlow, and Myrna Rosa. 1997. "Family Preservation and Elders." *Journal of Gerontological Social Work, 29,* no. 1: 57-76.

Colello, Kirsten. 2008. *Family Caregiving to the Older Population: Legislation Enacted in the 109th Congress and Proposals in the 110th Congress.* Congressional Research Services (CRS) Report for Congress. http://aging.senate.gov/crs/aging11.pdf.

Day, Phyllis. 2009. *A New History of Social Welfare.* Boston: Pearson Education.

(n.a). 1930. 378 in Life's Twilight Aided in Year by Fund. *The Detroit Free Press*, March 7, 1930.

Downey, Kirsten. 2009. *The Woman Behind the New Deal: The Life of Frances Perkins, FDR'S Secretary of Labor and His Moral Conscience.* New York: Nan A. Talese/Doubleday.

Elshtain, Jean Bethke. 2002. *Jane Addams and the Dream of American Democracy: A Life.* New York: Basic Books.

Fischer, David. 1978. *Growing Old in America* (3rd ed.). New York: Oxford.

Goroff, Norman. 1977. *Humanism and Social Work: Paradoxes, Problems, and Promises* [mimeograph]. West Hartford, CT: University of Connecticut School of Social Work. Cited in: Phyllis Day. 2009. *A New History of Social Welfare.* Boston: Pearson Education.

Guild, June. 1933. "The Social Worker and the Depression." *The Nation, 136,* no. 3545: 667. http://newdeal.feri.org/nation/na33667.htm.

Haber, Carole and Brian Gratton. 1994. *Old and Age and Search for Security: An American Social History.* Bloomington: Indiana University Press.

Hopkins, June. 2009. *Harry Hopkins: Sudden Hero, Brash Reformer.* New York: Palgrave Macmillan.

Houser, Ari, Wendy Fox-Grage, and Mary Jo Gibson. 2009. *Across the States 2009: Profiles Of Long-Term Care And Independent Living, 8th ed.*; AARP, Public Policy Institute, Washington, DC (Feb 2009) 368 pp. Publication No. D19105.

Huff, Dan. (n.d.). Progress and Reform: A Cyberhistory of Social Work's Formative Years. Boise, ID: Boise State University. http://www.boisestate.edu /SOCWORK/DHUFF/history/chapts/5-1.htm.

Kirk, Stuart and Willilam Reid. 2001. *Science and Social Work: A Critical Appraisal.* New York: Columbia University Press.

Linn, James. 1935. *Jane Addams: A Biography.* New York: Appleton-Century.

Lipsky, Michael. 1980. *Street-Level Bureaucracy: Dilemmas of the Individual in Public Services.* New York: Russell Sage Foundation.

Littell, Julia and John Schuerman. 2002. "What Works Best for Whom? A Closer Look at Intensive Family Preservation Services." *Children and Youth Services Review 24* no. 9-10: 673-699.

Luella Hannan Memorial Foundation Collection (LHMFC). Walter Reuther Library of Labor and Urban Affairs, Wayne State University, Detroit, Michigan.

NASW Foundation National Programs (n.d). *NASW Social Work, Pioneers, Jane Addams (1860-1935).* http://www.naswfoundation.org/pioneers/a /addams.htm.

Nerenberg, Lisa. 2007. *Elder Abuse Prevention: Emerging Trends and Promising Strategies.* New York: Springer Publishing Company.

Richmond, Mary Ellen. 1899. *Friendly Visiting among the Poor: A Handbook for Charity Workers.* http://www.scribd.com/doc/2334857/Friendly-Visiting-among-the-PoorA-Handbook-for-Charity-Workers-by-Richmond-Mary-Ellen-18611928

———. 1917. *Social Diagnosis.* New York: Russell Sage Foundation.

———. 1930. *The Long View.* New York: Russell Sage Foundation.

Robbins, Lionel. 2009. *The Great Depression.* Edison, NJ: Transaction Publishers

Trattner, Walter. 1999. *From Poor Law to Welfare State: A History of Social Welfare in America.* New York: The Free Press.

Walkowitz, Daniel. 1999. *Working with Class: Social Workers and the Politics of Middle-Class Identity.* Chapel Hill, NC: The University of North Carolina Press.

Chapter 5

Resisting Dependence and Burden: On Refusing to Become a "Little Old Lady"

Donyale R. Griffin Padgett and Shu-hui Sophy Cheng

A Case Narrative Approach

As Fine and Glendinning note, research and theorizing on dependency have been explored across a number of disciplinary perspectives, perhaps without realizing that we are "explaining different aspects of the same phenomena" (2005, 602). That is why this multidisciplinary archival research is so unique. The uniting factor represented in this combined work is in fact the realization that a multi-lens approach has not only led to a greater understanding of the lived experiences of old people during the Great Depression, but also contributes to our understandings of how women, especially, moved from privileged positions in society to positions on the margins of dependency, as economic hardships drove many to seek institutional help from human service organizations (HSOs) like the Luella Hannan Memorial Home (LHMH).

In this chapter, we use the LHMH archives to explore how the performance of social identity among some female clients is influenced by their unwillingness to accept the position of dependence brought on by their declining economic status and health. The terms *dependency* and *burden* are interconnected and collectively represent the experience of many old women during the Great Depression and today, as well. We focus on three cases: Jane Lewis, Kate Shields, and Minnie Thomas, paying close attention to their enactment of "burden" as a discursive practice.

147

From the three case files, we compiled narrative summaries from in-take data, case notes of the Visitor (social worker), letters from friends and associates in support of their petition for aid and various personal correspondences. An examination of the case files reveals that these women lived among the middle class earlier in life when they were able to work and live independent of external support, but they found them-selves living near poverty in their later years. These cases reflect the American economic downturn during the Great Depression and the chal-lenges old women faced during that period in American history.

Human Service Organizations as Sites of Identity

Human service organizations are particularly beneficial to women during times of great economic crises, and as Trethewey (1997) argues, they are sites of identity formation and often even sites of resistance. While wom-en are the majority of welfare recipients today (and were the majority of LHMH clients in 1929, as well), their displacement from mainstream society marginalizes them, placing them in a cycle of desperately need-ing services from "typically underfunded" agencies (Trethewey 1997, 282). Ferguson (1984) further contends that HSOs reinforce the socially accepted view of clients as submissive and dependent on social support. This view is of particular importance for elderly women recipients of social service benefits because, as Fine and Glendinning point out, they have a greater vulnerability to institutionalized care when they demon-strate a "lack of physical or mental capacity" (2005, 614).

In their role as "client," women are typically considered "recipients of predefined services rather than agents involved in interpreting their needs and shaping their life conditions" (Fraser 1989, 174). Through the LHMH clients' ongoing dialogue with the Visitor, we can begin to see how they used conversation to negotiate the exchange value of their identities, and how they progressively lost status as the patterns of their interactions succumbed to ageism (Dowd 1981). This dialogue also re-flects the power dynamic between clients and the LHMH, as older wom-en attempted to subvert and co-opt "the notion of 'frailty' on an individ-ual and collective level" (Grenier and Hanley 2007, 211).

Identity, in our understanding, is created through "the dialectical process between [recipients of care] and the social environment" that pre-defines their social identity as aged and dependent, particularly when they can no longer rely on their own resources (Baltes and Wahl 1996, 218). In this case, that social environment is not only the LHMH and its staff, but also the broader environment that does not center the experiences of elderly individuals. As old age becomes synonymous with declined health and dependency, "it defies the cultural ideals of youth, activity and independence, which are seen as characteristic of the 'normal' human condition" (Hennessy 1989, 40). Here, social identity theory (SIT) becomes a lens through which we can understand how individuals come to enact or perform certain identities. Scott argues that "various identities are made known to us, [along with] the social costs and rewards of maintaining those various identities" through our communication with others (2007, 124). SIT helps us to see human service organizations such as the LHMH as complex organizational systems providing an "institutional" concept of care sustained by "organizational discourses [that] create and recreate power structures" (Trethewey 1997, 282). Clients use their own discourse strategies to negotiate these power structures in an on-going attempt to meet their needs and desires. But as they deteriorate mentally and physically, this negotiation becomes increasingly difficult.

As Scott's (2007) research points out, there are two dimensions of SIT that run parallel: one centered on cognitive processes that relate to being placed in a particular social category and another centered on communicative processes used to construct these categorizations or identifications with certain categories. The *cognitive level* deals with how old women made sense of becoming recipients of social service benefits and the degree to which they saw such benefits as representing a loss of independence and the acceptance of dependency. Nichols and Leonard (1994) suggest that elderly women are assigned devalued status in our society because of ageist stereotypes; the social devaluation of old persons prevails in society's expectations and negative depictions of older adults. In fact, as Hurd points out, "stereotypical images of older adults have served to constrain and define" the behaviors we consider to be appropriate for elderly people (1999, 420). This was true in 1929, and it is still true today. SIT helps us to understand the stigma often associated with being an old woman and the shame associated with reliance on social support.

The other dimension of SIT, the *communicative level*, deals with the enactment of certain identities through discourse, in other words, how the women expressed or performed these identities "primarily through language [and their] interactions with others" (Scott 2007, 126). For instance, in her argument for frailty as a social construction, Kaufman contends that frailty is "socially produced through the interaction of older individuals, their caregivers, and their health providers" (1994, 49). This

leads us to wonder, what is in fact created through clients' ongoing conversations with the Visitor? Does talk with the Visitor reify notions of
dependence and burden? Whether they come willingly or reluctantly to
receive social services, most clients "do not come with the expectation
that behaviors, habits, and patterns of a lifetime will be scrutinized along
with the symptoms they choose to identify and present as troublesome"
(Kaufman 1994, 54). Communication, therefore, functions as the process
by which clients define their status; it reflects the interpretation of their
self and social identities and the tensions among them. Finally, communication is the tool by which clients negotiate resources within complex
organizational systems such as the LHMH.

Discourses of Dependency and Burden: Constructing the "Little Old Lady"

Characterizing Achenbaum's (1985) work, Arber and Ginn note that
there is a dichotomy in perceptions about old age that has been in existence since Ancient times. In early Christian and Graeco-Roman writings, there were "exhortations to respect and protect the elderly" as well
as "cruel, pitying, or satirical portrayals of the frailties of age" (1991,
33). They go on to argue that while many societies expressed traditional
respect for elderly people even into the twentieth century, modernization
in Western societies brought with it a more pronounced focus on the value that individuals bring to the social collective—values that "reflect the
interests of the most powerful social groups" (Arber and Ginn 1991, 34-
35). The social identity that emerges among elderly recipients of social
services often represents the power dynamic in relationships between
institutional actors (in the case of the LHMH, Visitors, Executive Director Leon Frost, and the Board of Trustees) and the old women; the
LHMH case files therefore provide a narrative glimpse into the experience of being old in harsh economic times.

In making choices about how to enact their social identity, older
women with limited resources are often caught "between the expectations of compliance (e.g. grateful receipt of limited services) and the implications of such classification and compliance" (Grenier and Hanley
2007). This struggle causes many older recipients of care to display acts
of resistance by insisting on their entitlement to services in order to preserve their dignity. This research is consistent with our findings that the
social identity among the women we describe in this chapter seemed to

be influenced most by an inability to part with their old lifestyle and the status of being middle-classed.

Fraser and Gordon (1994) characterize dependency as an ideological and social construct that includes economic aspects as well as socio-legal, political and psychological aspects. Over time, old people are seen as a burden essentially because over the course of life, they become dependent on socio-institutional support. For many women who find themselves in need of social services, the persona of being dependent and therefore a burden is not only inflicted upon them because of the social category they belong to, but also because they are expected to enact this role in their quest to secure services. Shakespeare (2000) tells us that the concept of dependency too often connotes negative burden and deficiencies on the part of the person needing help. While dependency is not only associated with old age, it is often a consequence of the aging process, and as Baltes notes, "is influenced strongly by social environmental conditions" (1996, 9). In the case of the LHMH clients, dependency and burden are interconnected and further heightened by the environmental conditions of the Great Depression. Often, clients negotiated their circumstances in ways that revealed a resistance not only to the dependence brought on by the cycle of life, but magnified by the fear of becoming an economic, physical and emotional burden (see Langlois and Durocher, this volume). To better understand various types of dependence, Gibson (1998) proposes a typology that includes economic, political, legal, psychological and emotional dependencies, each of which could be distinguished from dependency that arises from age-related ill health or frailty. Each of these types of dependency has special significance for older women. Specifically, we look at dependency in terms of the *financial* burden, *physical* burden, and *emotional* burden of three women in order to understand their experiences of disability, frailty, and decline in the latter part of their lives.

Brief Histories:
Jane Lewis, Kate Shields, and Minnie Thomas

Jane Lewis was born in Champagne, Illinois, in 1862, and attended common school in Detroit until thirteen years of age, when she began to make a living for herself. She became an apprentice to a dressmaker at the age of fifteen. In 1895, she married Justin Lewis, and no children were born of this union. She had been a hard worker all her life, and it was largely through her efforts that they owned their home. She was proud and anxious to earn her own living and keep up the home as long as possible.

At the time of her first application for a pension in 1929, Mrs. Lewis was sixty-seven years old. Although she no longer worked for pay, she kept busy with household duties and garden work. The couple rented out one side of their house and occupied the other side. Mr. Lewis had been employed as a truck driver and a night watchman until he was no longer able to work. Although he had been with the same company for forty years, he had no pension.

The Lewis' case was opened and closed twice due to Mrs. Lewis' resistance to signing over their home. In April, 1930, however, the couple accepted the terms of the LHMH because of their declining health and financial situation. Although the LHMH owned their home, the couple remained there and lived on a $100 per month grant, the highest amount awarded to couples.[1] When Mr. Lewis died of a heart attack in October, 1931, the LHMH reduced Mrs. Lewis' stipend to $60 per month, still one of the highest pensions for individuals at the time. She continued to live in her home until August, 1932, when declining health made it necessary for her to move to a convalescent home. Shortly after, she suffered a paralytic stroke from which she did not regain consciousness. She died three days later at the age of seventy.

Kate Shields was born in Conanduaga, New York, in 1870. After she married, she moved to Albany, New York, where the couple lived a few years before coming to Detroit. They had no children. According to one of her references, Mrs. Shields was "a woman of good education, refined, and accustomed to moving in good society" (LHMFC Case #71). Mr. Shields had owned his own company in Detroit. His health became so poor, however, that he was forced to sell the business. He died in 1918, leaving Mrs. Shields a small amount of insurance money.

After this money was gone, Mrs. Shields derived income from the sale of her furniture, rugs, pictures and linens. When this money had been used up, in 1926 she was forced to move to the St. Luke's Home, operated by the Episcopalian church. At the time of her application to the LHMH in April, 1929, Mrs. Shields was 59 years old. Her case was referred by Associated Charities, which asked the LHMH to relieve them of the responsibility for her care. The Board of Trustees declined to take over the case but granted her six dollars per month for incidentals while she remained at St. Luke's. In late 1932, when the LHMH was experiencing its own financial difficulties, the Board voted to discontinue her grant, inasmuch as Mrs. Shields was assured by St. Luke's Home of necessary care for the remainder of her life.

Minnie Thomas was born on February 26, 1838, in Germany, and, at the age of six, came to the United States with her parents to settle near Utica, New York. At the age of eleven, she went to work with a dressmaker, learned the trade and worked at it until nineteen years of age. She never received formal schooling, yet she made few mistakes in English and read a great deal. According to the notes of the Visitor, she had an "innate culture" which overshadowed her lack of academic training (LHMFC Case #48).

Minnie married at the age of nineteen, but her husband drowned five months later. She gave birth to a son and went back to dressmaking to support him. When the boy was five, she married Earl Thomas, a tailor, and the family moved to New York City. About ten years later, they came to Detroit, where her second husband died after a long illness.

At the time of her application for a pension, Mrs. Thomas was ninety years old. Her son had not been employed for a year, had used up his savings, and could no longer assist his mother financially. In applying to the LHMH, Mrs. Thomas asked only that she be cared for until her son obtained employment. She was initially funded as a Hannan client but was shifted to the Scudder fund in 1932.

Resisting Financial Burdenhood

Although the women were different in many ways and their ages ranged widely from fifty-nine to ninety, each feared becoming a financial burden to their families. They recognized that they had become financially dependent, despite their efforts to remain independent. Initially, Mrs. Lewis did not want assistance from the LHMH; she felt that she could manage her own affairs by taking in boarders. However, she began having trouble finding and keeping boarders during the Depression, and the sporadic income they provided was not sufficient to support her and her husband. One of the people who recommended the couple for a pension wrote, "she [Mrs. Lewis] has been a hard worker, very frugal and is quite independent, but at this time her health is breaking, and she should have some financial assistance in order that she might be relieved from the great financial strain from their home" (LHMFC Case #115). Another letter by Rev. Clyde Vance of First Presbyterian Church in Illinois, confirmed that, "the house was their sole resource except for a small life insurance policy worth $15-20,000" (LHMFC Case #115). Mr. and Mrs.

Lewis accepted assistance from the LHMH only because they did not have an adequate income to supply their needs, and the prospects for future income were slim: they could not sell their home during the Depression and were reluctant to leave it anyway. After much consideration, they agreed to the terms of the LHMH. Mrs. Lewis' monthly grant was supplemented from time to time to cover the additional expenses necessitated by her prolonged illness. The expenses included the family doctor, Swedish massage treatments and various housekeepers who were employed to care for her. Although she had more privileges than many other LHMH clients, such as massage, medical treatments and housekeeping service, she regretted very much that she had had to turn over property. But by 1930, Mrs. Lewis had looked at the situation from every possible angle and could see no other way out. The Visitor reports that she felt:

> Her life has been a continual series of disappointments, and she has known very little happiness. She has worked and saved all her life in order that she might have something upon to which to rely in her old age and now she feels that all her efforts have been failures (LHMFC Case #115).

Despite these challenging circumstances, Mrs. Lewis seemed intent on maintaining her composure and demonstrated refinement in her correspondence to LHMH. For example, when the LHMH voted to cancel the Lewis' pension on January 17, 1930, due to their refusal to turn over assets, she wrote a letter of response to Leon Frost, dated January 20, 1930: "Thank you for your past kindness and consideration. I want to assure you that I will make every effort to repay the loan made me at my earliest convenience. We deeply appreciate all favor granted us" (LHMFC Case #115). She did, however, make it clear that she wanted to retain their pension, concluding, "I beg to remain" (LHMFC Case #115). The Board determined that the couple did not have to repay the amount they had received, and Mr. and Mrs. Lewis soon decided to sign over their assets. They subsequently received notice that their monthly pension had been renewed.

As for Mrs. Shields, the Visitor found that she had been socially prominent and in wealthy circumstances until her husband died in 1918, at which time she discovered that Mr. Shields had left practically no estate. Her various friends tried, unsuccessfully, to secure work for her. She turned down several offers as unsuitable to her social position, continuing to live in a style incompatible with her reduced circumstances. She confided in the Visitor that she had been "extravagant" after her husband's death and had not conserved her resources when she had them. Her friends gave her money and clothes. Finally, in 1926, when her money was gone, she was forced to move to the St. Luke's Home, where she was living free of charge when she was referred to the LHMH in 1929. Although the Board of Trustees agreed to supply her with a small amount for incidentals (six dollars per month), she argued that this amount was insufficient, and on June 19, 1929, was successful in getting her grant increased to twelve dollars per month.

Mrs. Shields was fond of writing and had been trying to sell some of her writings but had been unable to do so. The Visitor's notes indicate that "the *Free Press* has several of her manuscripts which they do nothing about, and she has been unable to make any other contact for selling her work" (LHMFC Case #71). She was extremely bitter because she felt that she never had enough spending money. Additionally, certain difficulties arose from time to time regarding her diet at St. Luke's Home, and she spent more of her incidental money for special diabetic food. The Visitor notes that "she stated that if she could only have twenty-five dollars a month she would with careful management be able to get along and to maintain her self-respect" (LHMFC Case #71). However, she said that she did not want money that was not rightfully hers and was anxious to obtain it by disposing of her belongings or by earning it. She told the Visitor that at one time she had been offered six thousand dollars for the portrait of her mother, which hung in her room, but she had refused the offer. Mrs. Shields asked if the LHMH would consider buying this picture and paying for it in monthly installments. The Visitor advised her that the Home would have no use for a picture of that sort and that she thought it hardly worthwhile to even raise the matter with the Board of Trustees.

In August, 1930, Mrs. Shields asked if it would be possible for her to have a little more money so that she would have fifteen dollars per month. The Visitor told her that it would not be possible as the organization's funds were being "taxed to their capacity," and they had a long waiting list. Mrs. Shields stated that it was all right and asked the Visitor not to mention the fact that she had asked for more money. The Visitor notes that "she is extremely sensitive and is extremely hurt to think that she must receive money from an outside source" (LHMFC Case #71). The Visitor interpreted her behavior in terms of pride and a desire for autonomy, explaining "she was blue and discouraged and a great deal of her trouble seemed to be due to the fact that she was financially unable to be as independent as she would like to be" (LHMFC Case #71). Yet Mrs. Shields was far better off than many others during the Great Depression, and in November of 1932, the LHMH withdrew her grant. In her a letter of response, dated November 13, 1932, Mrs. Shields wrote that Mr. Frost's letter had been "a great disappointment to me (at this season)." She said that she "had been expecting a reduction, not withdrawal." However, she expressed gratitude for the assistance to date: "I want to thank you most sincerely for all the happiness your interest in me has made possible the past years." She signed the letter "with deep regret, but sincere appreciation and heartfelt thanks, K. Shields" (LHMFC Case #71).

When the Visitor first met Minnie Thomas' son, Mr. Katz, in April 13, 1929, he told her a good deal about his struggles to provide for his wife, his mother, and himself. He seemed to be in desperate circumstances, as he had been unable to obtain employment and had no prospects of any. In her investigation of the case, the Visitor called on Mrs. Thomas' relative, Dr. Carroll, who told her that his family had at various times assisted her. However, he felt Mrs. Thomas was not their responsibility and that Mr. Katz should take her into his home. According to the Visitor's notes, Dr. Carroll believed, "she had been a problem for a number of years because of her dislike of any home or place considered suitable for her to stay" (LHMFC Case #48). Dr. Carroll further mentioned that Mr. Katz was a well-meaning man who had been unfortunate. Mrs. Thomas told the Visitor that she had a cousin who was able to help her if he wanted to, but he had apparently forgotten she existed. The Visitor advised her not to worry because the LHMH would take care of her and would see to it that she always had a nice place to live and plenty of food.

Mrs. Thomas was granted a pension of fifty-five dollars, but soon her management of these funds came into question. According to the Visitor's notes, she complained that she hadn't gotten a five dollars Christmas check from LHMH. When the Visitor investigated, she learned that the original check had indeed been honored at the bank. During another of the Visitor's calls, Mrs. Thomas' landlady, Mrs. Cummings, whispered to the Visitor to drive around to the alley because she wanted to talk without Mrs. Thomas hearing. Mrs. Cummings stated that Mrs. Thomas was being imposed upon by her son and added that she knew Mrs. Thomas to be giving money to him. She also told the Visitor that Mrs. Thomas scarcely bought enough food to keep her alive and that she and the neighbors both contributed several meals a week. Mrs. Thomas spent only a few dollars a month on groceries and gave the remainder to her son and grandson. Mrs. Cummings also stated that Mrs. Thomas had given forty dollars to her son for a birthday present. The Visitor then questioned Mrs. Thomas closely about her expenditures, and she stated that she had found it necessary to give about five dollars to the church for the relief of some poor families. The Visitor told her that she should "under no circumstances give any money away to anybody" (LHMFC Case #48). The Visitor then made a plan with Mrs. Thomas that she was to charge all of her food at the local store and instructed her to keep the charge slips and turn them over to the LHMH. Mrs. Thomas was resistant, stating that she preferred to manage her own money, but the Visitor was persistent in pursuing an arrangement where the LHMH would pay her bills directly. Mrs. Thomas finally admitted that she had given money away to families who had needed it worse than she, but would not admit that she had ever given any to her son.

What we see here are different types and levels of financial dependence and various efforts, even within dependency, to keep from becoming a "burden." Mrs. Lewis did not need a home, but she needed medical assistance and an income on which to live. She and her husband held out as long as possible before becoming dependent on the LHMH for financial and medical support, and they signed over assets in exchange for this care. Mrs. Shields needed neither a home nor medical care, but she did need dental care, which the LHMH provided. She asked the LHMH only for a small amount of spending money. She attempted to provide some of this money herself by selling personal items and earning it through story writing. Mrs. Thomas needed both a home and an income on which to live but did not need medical care until the very end of her long life. She wanted to remain independent for as long as possible and asked to live in a place where she could do her own housekeeping. She also wanted to control her own finances and be able to give money away when she encountered people who needed assistance.

Resisting Physical Burdenhood

As they experience physical problems, older women also experience a loss of control over themselves and their lives, yet most struggle for whatever independence they can still manage. In early February of 1932, for example, Mrs. Lewis became ill after suffering a light stroke and also severe burns on both feet caused by the application of hot water bottles not properly wrapped. This health condition was a threat to what was left of her independence. She was afraid to notify the Visitor of the incident out of concern that she would be placed in a convalescent home, and she continued to care for herself at home.

Mrs. Lewis, an exacting woman, at first paid housekeepers to assist with her care. One of the housekeepers, Mrs. Miller, told the Visitor that she did not feel she could care for Mrs. Lewis much longer as her own health would not permit it; she had lost ten pounds and had had no opportunity to sleep since coming to Mrs. Lewis' home. On her part, Mrs. Lewis indicated that Mrs. Miller scolded her constantly (because she was "so much care") and threatened to leave. In April 1932, Mrs. Lewis' condition became worse, and her mental attitude deteriorated. She turned against most of her friends and was extremely bitter and critical. There seemed no alternative for the Visitor other than to place her in a convalescent home against her will. Mrs. Lewis was moved to the Willows Convalescent Home at the age of seventy, and in order to make her more contented, her own bed and chair were also moved to that location. However, Mrs. Lewis was dissatisfied, and at times it was almost impossible for the staff to manage her. The Visitor reported that "she refused to eat, would not take her medicine, demanded the attention of the nurses during the night at eight to ten minute intervals and frequently threatened suicide if not permitted to return to her home" (LHMFC Case #115). Mrs. Lewis also quarreled with the nurses and would not permit one of them to enter her room. In her case, the personal defeat that she experienced and expressed became more of a burden to the caregivers than her actual physical care. Whenever Mrs. Lewis had company she burst into tears and told them how unhappy she was away from home. Finally, resistance to the social identity attached to dependency propelled her into action. In May, 1932, Mrs. Lewis persuaded her masseur and her family to move into the Lewis house and take care of her in exchange for rent. The LHMH approved of this plan and allowed her to return home.

Mrs. Shields also had high expectations for her physical care and was often unhappy with the care provided by the LHMH doctors. She told the LHMH Visitor that her dentures were extremely painful and that her gums bled almost constantly and were extremely sore and irritated. She complained that she bit her inner lip when she tried to wear the teeth, and it was an absolute impossibility for her to chew food with them. However, she did not want the Visitor to think that she was complaining and said she realized that the trouble was due to her own "peculiar type of mouth." The dentist told the Visitor that he had done all that he could do for her. He had made over her dentures three times and felt that she could wear them if she really tried to do so. The doctor frankly told the Visitor that he could not improve her dentures and offered to refund the money that the LHMH had paid for them. Mrs. Shields told the Visitor she would wait until it became possible for her to sell something or to raise some money in some other way, at which time she would go to another dentist who would make over the teeth in such a way that she might be able to wear them comfortably.[2] The problems with her teeth influenced her social life. She was not able to wear the dentures more than a few minutes at a time, and she would not accept invitations to the homes of friends because "her teeth had to be removed at the most inopportune time" (LHMFC Case #71).

Mrs. Shields also had her own ideas about what constituted appropriate care, and they were not always compatible with the ideas of her caregivers. When she had trouble digesting the food at St. Luke's Home, she consulted the St. Luke's doctor, who informed her that she could eat any kind of food and did not have to be on a diet for diabetes. This made her angry, and she went to her own physician, who took a blood test and informed her that she should continue her diabetic diet. Mrs. Shields took the matter up with the superintendent of St. Luke's Home, who responded that "a little learning was a dangerous thing" (LHMFC Case #71). She stated that St. Luke's could not give Mrs. Shields a special diet, and they were doing the best they could for her. Angry at the dismissal of her health concerns, Mrs. Shields went downtown, purchased some diabetic food, warmed it on the radiator, and ate it in her room. The Visitor notes that the superintendent at St. Luke's considered Mrs. Shields to be "most unreasonable, but she sympathizes with her to a certain extent and tries not to antagonize her" (LHMFC Case #71). From Mrs. Shields's perspective, she was trying to meet her own needs in an institution that was not prepared to provide *individualized* care.

As for Mrs. Thomas, her chief complaint was that she did not have enough to do and that she had too much time to think about her troubles and to feel sorry for herself. Mrs. Thomas was handicapped by cataracts and was no longer able to sew or read. Her son was willing to assist her in any way he could aside from giving material aid. He begged her to allow him to do her shopping, but Mrs. Thomas usually refused. Despite her insistence on doing things for herself, there was evidence that Mrs. Thomas was failing. Mrs. Cummings, her landlady, told the Visitor that Mrs. Thomas was not keeping her room in order and on two different occasions had been careless and had almost set the house on fire. Mrs. Cummings said she had to watch Mrs. Thomas carefully and had zinc strips placed about the stove to eliminate the possible danger from fire. Mrs. Katz, the daughter-in-law, also told the Visitor that her mother-in-law was "very difficult to care for; that she objects to having a bath, etc. . ." (LHMFC Case #48).

Over the years in which she received a pension, Mrs. Thomas moved several times to various light-housekeeping rooms and then a boarding room. In April, 1931, when she was ninety-three, she was placed in a sanatorium, where she could be relieved of the responsibility of cooking and caring for herself. However, Mrs. Thomas was dissatisfied and was anxious to get back into a housekeeping room. According to the Visitor's notes, "she refused to be convinced [that she could not take care of herself] and was more unhappy than she had ever been before in her life, and [said] that she would rather commit suicide than to remain there" (LHMFC Case #48). She told the Visitor that she did not get outdoors or get sufficient fresh air. However, since she had always complained of this same thing, the Visitor felt that she was getting good care and all the attention she needed in the convalescent home. After conducting a medical exam in 1932, the LHMH doctor reported that Mrs. Thomas was "an old lady, not actually ill, but able to be up and about" (LHMFC Case #48). In his report nearly a year later, the doctor wrote that, while "physically, she is in excellent condition," she could be "classified as a mild mental case" (LHMFC Case #48).

These cases again reveal considerable diversity in the type and level of dependence. Mrs. Lewis was ill and needed direct care from paid caregivers, having no children or other family members on which to rely. Mrs. Shields had diabetes and struggled with deteriorating sight. The Visitor reports that "she is so nearly blind that she is afraid to try the street cars, finding buses more convenient and more easily traveled" (LHMFC Case #71). Yet Mrs. Shields asked only for special consideration in regards to her diet, which the institution where she lived would not provide. She therefore took matters into her own hands and prepared diabetic foods for herself. Mrs. Thomas was the strongest of the three women physically, although she was the oldest. Over time, she became senile and needed others to cook and clean for her, but she never did become as physically dependent as Mrs. Lewis.

Resisting Emotional Burdenhood

As they suffer from physical problems and experience less control over their material lives, older people lose not only self-esteem but also self-identity. To various degrees, depending on the person, such losses result in a diminished self. Mrs. Lewis, Mrs. Shields, and Mrs. Thomas were all aware that they could not do the things they had once enjoyed and maintain identities based upon prior activities, interests and pursuits (Charmaz

1983). This loss of social identity was especially burdensome to Mrs. Shields, the youngest of the three women. The Visitor found that, although Mrs. Shields always seemed to be in a fairly "comfortable frame of mind," she told the Visitor about her discontent at being "of no use in the world," at the treatment of her friends, and at her inability to entertain friends in her home (LHMFC Case #71). The Visitor encouraged her to talk about these concerns and agreed to try to find some way for her to feel of use in the world. For Mrs. Shields, being "of use" meant being able to maintain former social connections, as well as meeting at least some of her financial and physical needs through her own efforts.

When older people become more dependent upon others to provide for their needs, their loss of independence is also accompanied by a loss of power in relationships. Communication scholars indicate that this power loss is not only reflected but also created through communication within these relationships (Nussbaum et al. 2000). As an example, Mrs. Thomas was most dissatisfied with her living quarters in the boarding and convalescent homes and desired to get back into a light housekeeping room where she felt she was competent to do her own housework. However, her son and daughter-in-law were afraid that she would not take proper care of herself. While family members and the Visitor believed that an assisted-living facility would be more appropriate, Mrs. Thomas resented the suggestion because it challenged her sense of independence. At one point, Mrs. Thomas criticized her son severely for not having found her a housekeeping room, but when the Visitor asked if she would like for her to talk with him, Mrs. Thomas stated that it would "only make matters worse, and he would be more irritable and cross with her than ever" (LHMFC Case #48). Obviously, Mrs. Thomas was not able to argue convincingly with her son or the Visitor that she could still live on her own.

The unpredictable course of their aging fosters worry, uncertainty and fear in most old people. This anxiety affects their forms communication, as well as their self-concepts and relationships (Taylor 1994). According to the Visitor's notes, Mrs. Shields had several spells of hysteria during which she left the dining room and "created quite a disturbance by screaming at the top of her voice" (LHMFC Case #71). The Visitor notes that she seemed to be worried because the *Free Press* was not publishing her articles and because her teeth would not fit. She had also attempted to sell certain of her personal belongings but had been unable to do so. She was dissatisfied with her clothing and felt that her friends were neglecting her because she had no money. All of these things indicated to her that she had lost control over her life. Similarly, Mrs. Lewis suffered social losses as a result of her reduced circumstances. She told the Visitor that several of her friends and cousins had invited her out, but due to lack of proper clothing she had been unable to go. As their financial difficulties increased, both of these women became more socially isolated.

Charmaz (1983) points out that social isolation is a major consequence of a restricted life and fosters loss of self. Many studies have linked social isolation with greater psychological distress in late life (Krause 1991). Mrs. Thomas was perhaps the most assertive of the three women in seeking out the company of others. She knew that she became depressed when she spent too much time alone. The superintendent of the boarding home where she moved after she could no longer keep up her own room told the Visitor that, although she was over 90, Mrs. Thomas was "man crazy and played up to every man who would give her the slightest attention" (LHMFC Case #48). The superintendent reported that, on one occasion, she heard Mrs. Thomas get up in the night and go into one of the male resident's rooms. Later, she reported that Mrs. Thomas had made advances to two other men and had been seen coming out of their rooms and they out of hers "at all hours of the night." On another occasion, Mrs. Thomas insisted that she was very ill and needed a physician, although the superintendent did not believe this was true. Mrs. Thomas was emphatic that she had no faith in the woman doctor retained by the LHMH and desired a man doctor. After this incident, the Visitor talked with her for quite a while, and Mrs. Thomas admitted that most of her trouble was due to loneliness, as she was now the only woman boarder in the house. The other woman with whom she used to talk a great deal had been sent to Eloise.

Charmaz reminds us that even "minimal social contacts, such as the visits from an attentive neighbor or a call from a relative, assume tremendous significance" in the lives of older adults, particularly when they are dependent on others for care (1983, 180). Reflecting upon her isolation, Mrs. Thomas at one point scolded the Visitor roundly for not coming to see her more often, suggesting that the Visitor was neglecting her. The Visitor (Anna Wentink) explained that since she was the only social worker then employed by the LHMH, it was impossible for her to visit every month. Mrs. Thomas replied that the LHMH "should employ enough people so that their old folks could properly be taken care of" (LHMFC Case #48). The Visitor notes, however, that Mrs. Thomas "could give no particulars as to how she was neglected, and evidently was in need of nothing she did not have" (LHMFC Case #48). Mrs. Thomas' requests for attention reflect how selves are situated in networks of social relationships. She valued the company of others and expected to be equally valued as an emotional being who needed intimacy, as well.

When these three women attempted to return to aspects of their previous lives and failed, they felt profound disappointment and grief for their lost selves. As devaluing events occurred more frequently, Mrs. Lewis, Mrs. Shields, and Mrs. Thomas began to see themselves as burdens to others. Yet they continued to try and meet their emotional needs through friendships and associations, including their relationships with the Visitor.

The Discourse of Independence

Traditionally, Americans emphasize the values of independence and self-assurance. Dependency, therefore, involves a negative image and a diminished sense of self. Moreover, becoming a social or financial burden demeans identity because it means one has little power over situations and the quality of life (Charmaz 1983). As noted earlier, Mrs. Lewis, Mrs. Shields, and Mrs. Thomas projected an identity of dependence, emphasizing their economic hardship, loneliness, and illness when they needed assistance, but they also resisted an identity of dependence, exercising choice and trying to maintain their independence in whatever ways possible. Understandably, they resisted the negative images of a dependent old age, constructing an alternative identity by distancing themselves from those they considered to be frail and incompetent.

Autonomy (Freedom of Choice)

Older people also feel devalued when the arrangements for their care reflect an undesirable identity. For example, after her husband died, Mrs. Lewis opposed the idea of going into a convalescent home, even for a temporary period of time. She wanted to believe that she was still competent and able to care for herself. She said to the Visitor that it would cost the LHMH more if she moved out of her house. More importantly, she claimed that her health depended upon her being able to move about freely and to keep on working about her house. Her main argument to the Visitor was that she and her husband had spent practically an entire lifetime in saving and sacrificing to establish this home. The Visitor notes that "the matter of remaining in her own home was of paramount importance to her, and that if allowed to do that she would be willing to make whatever sacrifices were necessitated by the reduction in her monthly grant" (LHMFC Case #115). Mrs. Lewis felt a sense of responsibility toward her home and firmly believed that she was the best person to take care of it. She also felt most like "herself" when she was at home. Taylor (1994) confirms that a home is both a material and a symbolic construction, embodying the resident's values concerning independence, space, comfort and security.[3]

Mrs. Shields also insisted on making her own choices whenever possible. She was an intelligent and sensitive woman who "kept up appearances" unusually well and insisted on having her own way whenever possible. After her husband died, she had had an offer of marriage from an acquaintance in Savannah, Georgia, who was still interested in her. Mrs. Shields told the Visitor that she had given the man no encouragement, but each letter that came from him referred to the subject of marriage. A friend of Mrs. Shields who was a manager in one of the downtown banks looked up the man's account in Savannah and found that he was worth between $150,000 and $175,000. He was the largest stockholder in a firm that manufactured overalls and men's working clothes. The friend also stated that he was well thought of in the community and a very good businessman. Mrs. Shields told the Visitor that if she had the proper clothing and could afford to buy the things she needed, she would marry him. However, she had lost her hair during an illness and had been wearing toupees since that time. She was using mange cure and olive oil on her hair and told the Visitor that she would not think of getting married with her hair in that condition. Although Mrs. Shields wished to keep her financial circumstances private, the Visitor advised her to tell the man that she had no money. Mrs. Shields asked the Visitor to keep his interest in her a secret, as she did not care to have anyone at St. Luke's Home or any of her outside friends know of the affair. Later, the Visitor's notes indicate that Mrs. Shields did not accept the man's proposal because "she felt she [would] be much happier as she is now situated, and can be her own boss" (LHMFC Case #71).

The extent of Mrs. Shields' desire to keep her financial and social losses private is reflected in her discussions with the Visitor about funeral arrangements. She stated that she "did not want her funeral to cost more than one hundred dollars" (LHMFC Case #71). She wanted to be taken from St. Luke's Home to the funeral home and did not want a soul to see her. She did not even want a minister to say a prayer. She wanted to be cremated and her ashes "thrown to the wind." The Visitor assured her that the LHMH would carry out her wishes as far as possible.

Mrs. Thomas asserted her autonomy primarily by attempting to influence where and how she lived. The choice of room in her case symbolized independence and freedom of action. She insisted on taking rooms in which she could prepare her own meals. She did not like either the boarding homes or the sanatorium in which she was finally placed. Although the Visitor tried to make her see the advantages of living with the assistance of others, such arrangements underscored Mrs. Thomas' fears of incompetence and dependence. Consequently, she would not be convinced and insisted that she was perfectly well and able to "do her own work."

Over the years, the Visitor went to considerable lengths to accommodate her needs and concerns, once investigating six different rooming homes before she found a suitable one. The room was near a downstairs bathroom, and there was a large airy porch where Mrs. Thomas might sit when she cared to; a large grocery store was located less than half a block away, all of which greatly appealed to Mrs. Thomas. When finally situated in a room that suited her, she told the Visitor that she was "ashamed of herself for having caused so much trouble," and had figured that she had cost the Home quite a sum in moving expenses over the course of a year (LHMFC Case #48). She suggested that the Visitor keep part of the five dollars Christmas gift annually given to LHMH pensioners to partially reimburse the Home for moving expenses. The Visitor told her "not to worry about the moving bills and assured her that as long as she remained happy and contented where she now is," the organization would gladly forget all of the troubles which she had caused in the past (LHMFC Case #48).

Toward the end, when Mrs. Thomas was placed in a sanatorium because she could not care for herself, she resented the fact that she had to associate so closely with people who were dying. Hurd explains that "human beings deny [deaths] inevitability and strive to distance themselves from anything and anyone that reminds them of the fragility of life and the indignities of dying" (1999, 421). In this vein, Mrs. Thomas told the Visitor that she was not in a physical condition that justified her being in a sanatorium and would much prefer to live on her own.

Dignity and Pride

To the people around them, these women's assertions of independence and self-reliance sometimes made them seem overly proud and disdainful of the help they received from others. In the beginning, Mrs. Shields expressed indignation when asked for references to support her application for a grant, stating that her own word should be enough. But she finally consented to give the names of two people who could write on her behalf. According to the Visitor's notes, Mrs. Shields did not want people to know that she was requesting help. She also did not want any additional help from the LHMH if she could get along without it. She prided herself on the fact that she did not mingle with other people at St. Luke's and tried very hard to "keep out of the affairs in St. Luke's Home inasmuch as she felt that most of the people in the home were below her social standing" (LHMFC Case #71).

Mrs. Lewis, too, was proud and reluctant to depend on others for assistance. On one occasion, when she told her cousins that the LHMH was hard pressed for funds, one of them stated that if the Board insisted upon her going to St. Luke's convalescent home merely to cut down expenses, she would be glad to assume the responsibility for paying for her massage and medical treatments for at least a month. Mrs. Lewis resented this offer because she had never been very friendly with the cousin. She instead applied to the LHMH for help because she did not want to discuss her private affairs with family members. She stated that she would rather do without the treatments than ask this cousin for help.

Mrs. Lewis also resented having to apply for assistance to the LHMH. The Visitor urged her to think of her relations with the organization as a business transaction, but Mrs. Lewis was unable to lose sight of the fact that her assistance was coming from a charitable organization. The Visitor notes that "her only hope and remaining ambition seems to be that her friends and acquaintances shall not know of her dependency, or of what she considers to be the loss of her home and life savings" (LHMFC Case #115). If the LHMH were to force her to move from this home, Mrs. Lewis believed that "her spirit would be entirely broken and that her only active interest in life would be taken away" (LHMFC Case #115). In staying in this home while receiving her pension, Mrs. Lewis was able to sustain some of her social status and enjoy the privilege of presumed independence, despite her financial constraints and health problems.

Mrs. Thomas, a working-class woman with less "refinement" than Mrs. Lewis and Mrs. Shields, was more concerned about keeping busy than keeping others from knowing about her financial situation. Prior to applying for assistance from the LHMH, Mrs. Thomas had left an old-age home because she could not endure having nothing to do. According to the Visitor's notes on the first interview, "there was about her the simple dignity of conscious accomplishment with no resentment of life's compensation" (LHMFC Case #48). On one occasion, Mrs. Thomas asked the Visitor to take her to see a woman who was an invalid, because she wanted to "visit someone worse off than herself" (LHMFC Case #48).

In short, these three women continued to use language and relationships to assert their power of choice and to express their dignity and pride, even though they were dependent on a charitable organization for assistance. They did not accept the dependent social status of "little old lady" but worked to maintain their own sense of identity.

Conclusion

These cases suggest ways in which older women can actually gain a sense of power in struggling against dependence and burdenhood. Although Jane Lewis, Kate Shields, and Minnie Thomas experienced a decline in personal control and social status, they still worked constantly to assert their needs and negotiate their social status. They were, however, variously successful in their negotiations with the LHMH. Jane Lewis and Kate Shields, who still had some assets, were able to exercise more choice and negotiate more independence than Minnie Thomas, who was older and had no social or financial assets with which to bargain.

Jane Lewis' increasingly desperate attempts to remain in her home demonstrated her need to hold on to the social status that it provided. She used the only leverage she had—property and possessions. While she was the wealthiest of the three women financially, when her health began to decline, she had to relinquish her assets, which included furniture, linens, rugs, silverware and jewelry, as well as property and life insurance, in exchange for sixty dollars per month. However, she was able to stay in her home for most of her time with the LHMH, with the help of live-in caregivers and medical treatments paid for by the LHMH.

Kate Shields attempted to increase her stipend but didn't want anyone to know that she had made such requests. When she got articles published in the *Detroit Free Press*, this demonstrated her ability to support herself, at least in part. When the paper finally sent a letter saying that it would no longer be able to publish her work because of its own financial troubles, she refused to take "no" for an answer, pushing her friends to write in and request to read more of her work. For Kate, being productive in this way was the key to independence.

Perhaps least successful was Minnie Thomas, who interacted with the Visitor mostly by complaining. The Visitor's reports indicate that "as usual, [Mrs. Thomas] is very dissatisfied with everything in general," that she was "irritable and cross," "extremely dissatisfied," and "more unhappy than she had ever been in her life" (LHMFC Case #48). Over time, her constant complaints came across to the Visitor and the LHMH doctors as mild mental illness, which ultimately landed her in the Noble Sanatorium. Mrs. Thomas most wanted to live independently and control her money. However, when the Visitor discovered that she had used her pension to help her son and grandson, the LHMH took control over Mrs. Thomas' bills and paid them directly. After this, her mental state began to deteriorate.

What is perhaps most telling in these cases is that each of the women understood that there is a diminished space in American society for individuals who cannot remain in control of their physical, financial and emotional wellbeing. Older women who lose control of these things become "little old ladies." As Grenier and Hanley point out, accepting this diminished identity "would mean relinquishing their sense of 'self'" (2007, 218). The image of the little old lady is derogatory in U.S. society because it emphasizes the marginal status women have in relation to both men and younger women. This term signifies the decline of the female body—the source of life, reproduction, and caregiving. However, by drawing on the experiences of older women, as we have done in this chapter, "we can begin to understand the complex interplay of gender, age, and the body as resistance to powerful social constructs and organizational processes" (Grenier and Hanley 2007, 216, emphasis added). Even in their decline, all of these women resisted others' control over their finances, health, and living arrangements.

In the cases of Mrs. Lewis, Mrs. Shields and Mrs. Thomas, how did resistance lead to personal empowerment? These cases highlight the diverse ways that agency can be enacted across different circumstances. Wray encourages us to think of agency not as simply an effect of a relation to power and domination or actions to gain freedom but as "creative and generative . . . allowing for the recognition of different strategies used by women to deal with constraint and potentially disempowering experiences" (2004, 26). Each of these women defined "successful aging" for herself by coping with and adapting to the changes that shaped her final years. This gives us further insight into the unique ways in which women establish their social identities and resist the negative image of "little old lady."

Notes

1. This comparatively generous amount, especially in 1930, was probably awarded in exchange for the assets the couple signed over to the LHMH, including the deed to their home and a life insurance policy.

2. The LHMH referred all its clients to its own physician, dentist and eye doctor, who gave them special rates as charity cases. Clients who wished to see other doctors were expected to pay for those visits themselves. Mrs. Shields probably did not regard the LHMH doctor with the same respect as she regarded her own dentist.

3. See Briller and Durocher, this volume, for more on the connection between identity, material culture and home in later life.

References

Achenbaum, W. Andrew. 1985. "Societal Perceptions of Aging and the Aged." Pp. 129-47 in *Handbook of Aging and the Social Science,* edited by Robert Binstock and Ethel Shanas. New York: Van Nostrand Reinhold Co.

Arber, Sara and Jay Ginn. 1991. *Gender and Later Life: A Sociological Analysis of Resources and Constraints.* Newbury Park, CA: Sage.

Baltes, Margaret M. 1996. *The Many Faces of Dependency in Old Age.* New York, NY: Cambridge University Press.

Baltes, Margaret. M. and Hans-Werner Wahl. 1996. "Patterns of Communication in Old Age: The Dependence-Support and Independence-Ignore Script." *Health Communication* 8, no. 3: 217-231.

Charmaz, Kathy. 1983. "Loss of Self: A Fundamental Form of Suffering in the Chronically Ill." *Sociology of Health and Illness* 5: 168-195.

Dowd, James J. 1981. "Conversation and Social Exchange: Managing Identities in Old Age." *Human Relations* 34: 541-553.

Ferguson, Kathy E. 1984. *The Feminist Case against Bureaucracy.* Philadelphia, PA: Temple University Press.

Fine, Michael and Caroline Glendinning. 2005. "Dependence, Independence or Inter-Dependence? Revisiting the Concepts of 'Care' and 'Dependency.'" *Aging & Society* 25: 601-621.

Fraser, Nancy. 1989. *Unruly Practices: Power, Discourse and Gender in Contemporary Social Theory.* Minneapolis, MN: University of Minnesota Press.

Fraser, Nancy and Linda Gordon. 1994. "A Genealogy of Dependency: Tracing a Keyword of the US Welfare State." *Signs* 19, no. 2: 309-334.

Gibson, Diane. 1998. *Aged Care: Old Policies, New Problems.* New York: Cambridge University Press.

Grenier, Amanda and Jill Hanley. 2007. "Older Women and 'Frailty': Aged, Gendered And Embodied Resistance." *Current Sociology* 55, no. 2: 211-228.

Hennessy, Catherine Hagan. 1989. "Culture in the Use, Care, and Control of the Aging Body." *Journal of Aging Studies* 3, no. 1: 39-54.

Hurd, Laura C. 1999. "We're Not Old!: Older Women's Negotiation of Aging and Oldness." *Journal of Aging Studies* 13, no. 4: 419-439.

Kaufman, Sharon R. 1994. "The Social Construction of Frailty: An Anthropological Perspective." *Journal of Aging Studies* 8: 45-58.

Krause, Neal. 1991. "Stress and Isolation from Close Ties in Later Life." *Journal of Gerontology: Social Sciences* 46, no. 4: S183-S194.

Luella Hannan Memorial Foundation Collection (LHMFC). Walter Reuther Library of Labor and Urban Affairs. Wayne State University, Detroit, Michigan.

Nichols, Barbara and Peter Leonard. 1994. *Gender, Aging and the State.* New York: Black Rose Books.

Nussbaum, Jon F., Loretta L. Pecchioni, James D. Robinson, and Teresa L. Thompson 2000. *Communication and Aging*. Mahwah, NJ: Lawrence Erlbaum Associates, Inc.

Scott, Craig R. 2007. "Communication and Social Identity Theory: Existing and Potential Connections in Organizational Identification Research." *Communication Studies* 58, no. 2: 123-138.

Shakespeare, Tom. 2000. "The Social Relations of Care." Pp. 52-65 in *Rethinking Social Policy*, edited by Gail Lewis, Sharon Gerwirtz, and John Clarke. London: Sage.

Taylor, Bryan C. 1994. "Frailty, Language, and Elderly Identity: Interpretive and Critical Perspectives on the Aging Subject." Pp. 185-208 in *Interpersonal Communication and Older Adulthood: Interdisciplinary Research*, edited by Mary Lee Hummert, John M. Wiemann, and John F. Nussbaum. Newbury Park, CA: Sage.

Trethewey, Angela. 1997. "Resistance, Identity and Empowerment: A Postmodern Feminist Analysis of Clients in a Human Service Organization." *Communication Monographs* 64: 281-301.

Wray, Sharon. 2004. "What Constitutes Agency and Empowerment for Women in Later Life?" *The Sociological Review* 52, no. 1: 22-38.

Chapter 6

Privileged But Pensioned? How Two Formerly Well-Off Women Experienced Receiving Aid

Chasity Bailey-Fakhoury and Heather E. Dillaway

What is Privilege?

On an everyday basis, we might think of a privilege as something "extra," a "benefit" of sorts, which perhaps we are just lucky to get. For instance, it is a "privilege" to meet someone for the first time, or it is a "privilege" to be able to take the afternoon off from paid work and spend it with our children. However, we can also think about privilege in more academic, sociological terms. As sociologist Allan Johnson notes, privilege "exists when one group has something of value that is denied to others simply because of the groups they belong to, rather than because of anything they've done or failed to do" (2006, 21). Privilege is also often based on one's access to economic, political and social resources and opportunities, and one's ability to use these resources and opportunities to one's advantage (Weber 2001). Privilege of this kind can often be ascribed by one's membership in certain racial-ethnic, gender, class, or age categories (Calasanti et al. 2006; Calasanti and Slevin 2001; Reskin 2003; Weber 2001). Thus, privilege exists because systems of inequality exist.

Economic and Social Dimensions of Privilege

In this chapter, we explore the economic and social dimensions of privilege. The economic dimension of privilege includes one's access to and control over resources such as income (through paid employment), savings, credit, and ownership of property and other assets (e.g., cars and other material valuables). While most individuals have access to some sort of income (however small), fewer people (and primarily certain types of people by race, class, gender, and age) have access to other economic resources (Calasanti and Slevin 2001; Weber 2001). Thus, an individual may be considered to be privileged economically if he or she has ownership of private property, access to savings, and good credit, along with income. The economic dimension of privilege may be experienced rather poignantly in both hard economic times and in times of aging, because some individuals' wealth or assets may exist long past their income. Elderly individuals who hold onto economic assets in their later lives are often better off than those who do not, because income decreases in old age (Calasanti and Slevin 2001; Gray 2009; Wilson 2008). For instance, in lieu of income, privileged older adults could sell economic assets in order to continue to secure a certain quality of life or a certain kind of medical care. Individuals without property ownership, savings, credit, and other assets can fall quickly into poverty in old age.

Along with (and often because of) one's economic position, some individuals experience and come to take for granted the social dimension of privilege, and this social dimension often bolsters one's economic standing (and vice versa) (Ostrander 1984). As with the economic dimension, the social dimension of privilege is multifaceted and includes access to social capital and ability to make choices, as well as social status.

French sociologist Pierre Bourdieu defines social capital as "an asset of the individual or group that participates in social networks, which can be used to obtain information and assistance of various kinds" (as cited in Gray 2009, 7; see also Portes 1998). Social capital is an individual resource because the networks within which individuals participate influence "the practical and emotional support available to those same individuals" (Gray 2009, 5). These networks could be based on both memberships in formal organizations (such as women's clubs and churches) and informal social ties (with extended family, friends, neighbors, and well-placed community members) (Gray 2009). Social networks are critical for individuals because they provide individuals with access to informational resources (e.g., tips on running a successful business, information on legal or economic resources in difficult times, and access to other social opportunities such as vacationing and leisure activities) possessed by their associates (Portes 1998). Gray (2009) suggests that as intimate partners and other, similarly-aged family members die, aging adults are more likely to rely on non-kin individuals and groups for practical and emotional support; this is especially true for elderly women who live longer than their male counterparts. Thus, social capital can affect how individuals experience aging.

The social dimension of privilege also can encompass one's ability to "make and implement choices" (Wilson 2008, 1). Audre Lorde (2003, 26) suggests further that the ability to make choices includes the ability to both a) envision a desirable future, and b) effect the changes necessary to bring that future into being for oneself. Ultimately this dimension of privilege is representative of one's own "personal power" or control within society (Lorde 2003), and one's "independence" (Wilson 2008) as well. In old age, one's ability to make choices on one's own is "associated with the ability to drive a car, to use public transport, to shop when and where one chooses, to decorate the house, or to visit friends whenever one wants" and "a major ingredient in the maintenance of self-identity and self-respect" (Wilson 2008, 3).

Finally, the social dimension of privilege includes a seemingly guaranteed type of social status or prestige (Turner 1988; Weber 1978). According to social theorist Max Weber "status" is "an effective claim to social esteem . . . typically founded on a) style of life, b) formal education, and c) hereditary or occupational prestige" (1978, 305-306). Weber continues in saying that status groups are "stratified according to the principles of their consumption of goods as represented by special styles of life" (1978, 937). Theorist and cultural critic Bryan Turner explains further that "status relates simply to one's position in society" and "may be conceptualized therefore as lifestyle; that is, as the totality of cultural practices such as dress, speech, outlook, and bodily dispositions" (1988, 66). As formerly well-off individuals age (particularly women), asserting and sustaining social status may represent an important part of their daily activities because it is what can remain constant from a former identity and lifestyle (especially as health and finances decline as part of normal aging processes).

Situating Our Analysis of Privilege

A key to understanding privilege more generally is in comprehending how one's access to its economic and social dimensions must be constantly sustained, renewed, and recreated on a micro (individual) level. Critical theorist R. W. Connell (1995) reminds us, for example, while certain federal policies or organizational guidelines might garner all men more economic privilege than women, individual men must constantly showcase their strength to remain dominant in comparison to women and other men. Political theorist Nancy Fraser (1989, 26) and French historian and philosopher Michel Foucault (as cited in Fraser 1989, 26) also show us how power/privilege is gained only through constant interactions with others in the "mundane social practices and relations" of everyday life, thus showing that all individuals potentially could attempt to grasp privilege. Acquiring and sustaining privilege is a never-ending, interactive process (Reskin 2003).

This conceptualization of privilege is especially relevant to the social work case files discussed in this collection, because thinking about privilege as (1) both economic and social and (2) constantly reproduced allows us to see more clearly the thoughts and experiences of those who have grasped privilege but then feel it slipping through their fingers. Indeed, in certain phases of the life course (e.g. old age) and in particular economic times (e.g., the Great Depression era, or our contemporary economic climate), individuals find themselves faced with the fact that they might not be able to sustain the economic and social dimensions of privilege that they have taken for granted. When individuals are faced with economic burden for the first time, they confront a glaring discrepancy between their previous and current abilities to make ends meet (Abbott 2006; National Economic Council Interagency Working Group on Social Security 2007; Newman 1994; Rubin 1994; Wood 2008). Not only must individuals adjust to the loss of economic resources within these moments, but also they experience disconnections between how they think of themselves and how others might see them and their recent economic constraints. In these unique moments, they may call upon their remaining economic assets to attempt to secure a certain quality of life. Even more importantly for our purposes in this chapter, they may attempt to assert and sustain their social capital, choices, and social status, as they resist the loss of the economic dimensions of privilege that they took for granted and the new ways in which others look upon them.

It is in the situations of *recently* downtrodden individuals, then, that we may see more clearly the micro-level "mechanisms" (Reskin 2003) that sustain dimensions of privilege—particularly the social dimension. To illustrate these interactive, micro-level processes by which privilege might be sustained, we review the cases of "Madeline Landen Nuit"[1] (Case #131) and "Ada Dreyfuss" (Case #443), recipients of Luella Hannan Memorial Home (LHMH) pensions during the era of the Great Depression. We argue that both of these LHMH clients—once wealthy but then impoverished— are examples of individuals who attempt to sustain privilege, despite a lack of economic resources. We also suggest that these two women might feel the loss of the social dimension of their privilege much more poignantly than their male counterparts, because of their lack of control over economic resources and the fact that women of privilege are often assigned the job of maintaining social status over time (Ostrander 1984).

Intersections of Race, Class, Gender, and Age

The intersections of race, class, gender, and age provide an important lens through which to analyze how these two women struggled to sustain privilege while receiving an old-age pension. Feminist theorist Patricia Hill Collins suggests that an intersectional analysis:

> explores and unpacks relations of domination and subordination, privilege and agency, in the structural arrangements through which various services, resources, and other social rewards are delivered; in the interpersonal experiences of individuals and groups; in the practices that characterize and sustain bureaucratic hierarchies; and in the ideas, images, symbols and ideologies that shape social consciousness (as cited by Dill and Zambrana, 2009, 5).

Therefore, situating our research within an intersectional analysis allows us to use personal narratives to "[flesh] out our understandings of how people experience and construct identities within intersecting systems of power" (Dill and Zambrana, 2009, ix).

The main argument proposed by an intersections perspective is that individuals do not share equal opportunities or equal conditions of living (Dill and Zambrana 2009; Weber 2001). Individuals' and/or groups' access to resources, opportunities and, ultimately, experiences of privilege, is structured by a combination of their "social locations" defined by race/ethnicity, class, gender, age, sexuality, national origin, and other social background characteristics. Thinking about Madeline's and Ada's case stories, we must think about what it must have been like to be simultaneously older, White, formerly yet no longer upper class, and female in the midst of the Great Depression and directly afterwards.

For the purposes of this book, a particularly salient social location is age, in that we are analyzing the cases of those who received an old age pension specifically because they fell upon hard times in later life (see Ray, chapter 3, this volume). However, age intersects with class, gender, and race in the story of any LHMH pensioner, as these two women were receiving pensions specifically because they were above the age of sixty, but also only recently impoverished and formerly well-to-do, and usually White (see Calasanti and Harrison, chapter 8, this volume). Madeline and Ada were also specifically receiving a pension because Luella Hannan established her foundation primarily to take care of *women* who were "used to the comforts of life," just like her (see Ray, chapter 3, this volume). Thus, these social locations are all important simultaneously for their effects on these two women's abilities to survive and assert any dimension of privilege during the Depression in Detroit. The specific intersections of class, gender, race, and age in these two women's lives—and the fact that these women experienced economic and social dimensions of privilege before their impoverishment and old age—also provided them with unique opportunities to act on their own behalf and react in certain ways while receiving a pension from a private foundation. In the pages that follow, we embark on an analysis of how Madeline Landen Nuit and Ada Dreyfuss *experienced* receiving an old-age pension, and how they interacted with others to assert and sustain dimensions of their privilege over time.

How Two Formerly Privileged Women Receive an Old-Age Pension

Formerly Privileged and Therefore Pensioned

LHMH was established to "provide for the aged and infirm persons of the City of Detroit who have been accustomed to enjoying the comforts of life, but who, through change of fortune, have come to reduced circumstances" and for clients who had "lived comfortably in the middle and upper classes during their lives" (see Ray, chapter 3, this volume; see also Bowers 1930). Therefore, it seems that the Hannan funds (as distinct from the Scudder funds, as described by Ray, chapter 3) were designated for aging women and men (although mostly women) who were accustomed to defining their own identities, making their own decisions, experiencing a "comfortable" lifestyle, and controlling their own finances. Because of this designation, the LHMH staff investigated each potential pensioner's economic assets, family history and background, social status, and social networks around the city of Detroit before providing funds to any individual.

"Madeline Landen Nuit" and "Ada Dreyfuss" were typical clients of the LHMH in many ways. Both women were deemed "worthy" of aid by the LHMH because of their previous economic standing, their current social connections, and their refined, cultured manner and/or lifestyle. In the case files it is written that Madeline "never [did] remunerative work" and "traveled with her husband"; she enjoyed the "comforts of life," and came to her "reduced circumstances" only through a change of fortune. Madeline's noble background (through marriage) is noted numerous times by the LHMH staff (and in correspondence between Madeline, landlords, doctors, family members, and the LHMH staff as well). Madeline was referred to the LHMH by a member of the Dodge (automobile) family and, based on how many times the Dodge family is discussed in the first few months of her case notes, we presume that her noble status and this social connection is of importance to the LHMH staff. Her case file also notes pastimes and hobbies such as music, painting, and reading, all important activities (and good choices) for a woman of her social and economic standing (Ostrander 1984). Thus, both the economic and social dimensions of Madeline's former privilege are documented in the LHMH intake process.

Ada's story, as written in the LHMH case notes, is different from Madeline's, yet similar in key ways. While she did come from a well-off family, as evidenced by her private tutoring for several years, she had engaged in paid work for the majority of her adult life and managed to acquire residential property as a widow. Therefore, based on our reading of her case, we believe that Ada had to invest more individual effort than Madeline into maintaining the economic and social dimensions of privilege over her lifetime. In addition, while Madeline acquired a stable economic and social position through a long marriage, Ada had to maintain her social location through paid work (because of young widowhood and also perhaps because her family of origin did not have access to as much wealth as Madeline's husband's family did). Nonetheless, Ada was referred to the LHMH by Mrs. Mumford, the wife of the president of the Detroit Edison Company, and this well-documented social connection provided endless options to Ada in her efforts to sustain her own independent choices and lifestyle. For instance, the LHMH case notes tell a story about how Ada sought out and gained legal advice from a friend of Mrs. Mumford's in order to keep her Traverse City, Michigan, property in her own name and initiated her "summering" away from Detroit with a trip to Florida with Mrs. Mumford as well. Ada's numerous memberships to social clubs around the city are noted in the case files, as are her volunteering and charity efforts. These social connections and activities provided Ada with a "knapsack" full of tools and guide maps for how to navigate her life and sustain privilege (McIntosh 2000). While Ada may have had less economic privilege than Madeline over her lifetime, she made up for it in being able to secure the social dimensions of her privilege.

Case notes document that the LHMH visitors relied upon descriptions of social capital and social status to determine Madeline's and Ada's eligibility for old-age pensions. These women qualified as deserving of pensions from the LHMH precisely because they had never represented an economic burden in their younger years—expressly the type of women for whom Luella Hannan had established her fund. Therefore, both economic and social dimensions of privilege are acknowledged as the LHMH makes decisions about pensions. Because of the women's impoverishment (as evidenced by the need for a pension), however, case notes emphasize the social dimensions of Madeline's and Ada's privilege more than the economic dimensions after they began receiving a pension.

The Potential for Losing Privilege
While Receiving a Pension

Being approved for the LHMH pension was positive for impoverished women like Madeline and Ada in many respects, yet also potentially damaging to the remainder of their privilege in other ways. In this section, then, we detail the types of situations within which these formerly well-off women might have felt constricted while receiving a pension, and the ways in which they reacted to these situations. In each case we attempt to highlight interactions within which Madeline and Ada might have attempted to assert or sustain economic and social dimensions of privilege while receiving the LHMH pension.

Losing the Economic Dimension of Privilege

After being granted a pension, Madeline and Ada both encountered pension rules that challenged their abilities to exercise control over the economic and social dimensions of their former privilege. The LHMH's rules stipulated that anyone receiving a pension would sign over insurance policies, savings, belongings, and property to the LHMH, to be administered and/or disposed of on behalf of the client (see Ray, chapter 3, this volume). Pensioners who may have been living in their own homes were oftentimes moved from that dwelling to an apartment or boarding house/room; their homes were then sold by the LHMH. In this property transfer, LHMH pensioners were stripped not only of their physical place, but also what was left of their wealth. Once economic assets were turned over to the LHMH, the organization also instituted guidelines regarding how the monthly pension could be spent. The LHMH visitors often monitored the spending and the remaining assets of their clients as well, to insure that clients were following LHMH rules about spending (such as paying bills on time, incurring no debts, and making only necessary purchases) and did not have extra expenses or extra funds that might warrant a shift in the amounts of monthly pensions. For instance, Ada was asked to provide itemized lists of her expenditures in her early pension years and Madeline's financial relationship with her niece and nephew-in-law was monitored closely. The LHMH most likely created these stipulations and guidelines to protect and promote the welfare of its clients and its own organization during the Great Depression, as well as to standardize the types of pensions that their aid recipients received. Nonetheless, many formerly well-off women like Madeline and Ada, experienced the implementation of such rules and guidelines as the end of financial freedom and influence. In giving up these remaining economic assets, all that they had left was the social dimension of privilege.

Trying to Maintain Control over Everyday Life

Another tangible challenge Madeline and Ada faced when awarded a pension was the loss of control over their everyday lives once the LHMH rules were implemented—ultimately, the loss of choice and/or decline of their abilities to make decisions over their own lives and others' lives. Thus, Madeline and Ada potentially lost a portion of the social dimension of their privilege, once they no longer held economic assets and relied on the LHMH pension for support. Similar to the ways in which

younger women in poverty have had their actions and expenses monitored in contemporary economic times (Abromovitz 1996; Dodson and
Schmalzbauer 2005; Edin and Lein 1996), the LHMH's clients oftentimes had to make requests to the LHMH staff for toiletries, undergar-
ments, clothing, shoes and other sundries, material items that previously
had been easy to acquire and taken for granted. Requests for vision care,
dental care, or various medical specialists also had to be fielded through
the LHMH. Even one's physician was no longer one's own; a pensioner
had to utilize those who were approved LHMH service providers. Furthermore, the LHMH staff would frequently contact the family and
friends of pensioners about the women's circumstances and welfare.
There was also constant contact between staff members and pensioners
via home visits and phone calls, as well as monitoring of their relationships and activities. Madeline and Ada never became accustomed to such
close scrutiny over their private lives. Perhaps the most challenging aspect of the aid process for both was the fact that they lost control over the
boundaries of their private lives and their everyday decision-making.
Indeed, Madeline's and Ada's case files frequently include notes and
correspondence that suggest that Madeline and Ada both felt a lack of
choice and/or independence at times. We suspect that this lack of choice
and independence was as jarring to them as the actual loss of economic
resources, because it affected their daily lives considerably. In response,
then, both Madeline and Ada attempted to assert and sustain their privilege by refusing to give up their remaining economic assets, taking
charge over residential changes, defining their own standards for health
care, talking continually about past and present social connections, and
defining themselves as different from other impoverished people.

Refusing to Give up Assets

Madeline resisted turning over a summer home in Lapeer, Michigan,
for four years, because she thought that she could get more money from
its sale than the LHMH would; she did not relinquish until it was in significant disrepair and she could no longer maintain it. Ada agreed to deed
a two-family flat in Detroit over to the LHMH but fought successfully to
keep her savings and another property in Traverse City, Michigan. With
the help of legal advice, Ada also got the LHMH to agree to allow her
adopted daughter to take possession of the Traverse City property and all
of her personal belongings, in the event of Ada's death, thus finalizing
the fact that the LHMH would never see the proceeds from a sale of
Ada's property or personal belongings. Quite often, the LHMH visitors
would make notes in their case files about how pensioners initially

fussed about relinquishing property and assets to the LHMH, but most eventually agreed to sign property and assets over in exchange for a pension. The LHMH Board of Trustees and the executive secretary, Leon Frost, made exceptions for Madeline and Ada, however. These exceptions were made in response to the efforts that both Madeline and Ada exerted on their own behalf. Ada, in particular, successfully utilized social capital as well as her business and legal knowledge to protect herself against LHMH rules. Madeline and Ada both temporarily sustained a small part of the economic dimension of their privilege by pulling on both social capital and their own decision-making abilities in negotiations with the LHMH staff and board. The fact that Madeline and Ada still held onto the social dimension of privilege (in particular, social capital and the ability to make choices) meant that they could save their remaining economic resources more ably than less privileged pensioners could.

Managing Residential Changes

Madeline and Ada both made numerous residential changes over their pension years. Some residential changes were cumbersome—as they were initiated by LHMH—but many represented their struggles against the confines of LHMH rules. For Madeline, some residential changes came as a result of health problems and subsequent hospitalizations (for vision difficulties, kidney problems, a tonsillectomy, appendicitis, a nervous breakdown, sinus problems, "bronchitis that developed into pleurisy," "angina pectoris," "heart problems," "hemorrhoids and pelyope," etc.). In later life, Ada's changes in residence were also due to her diabetic and cardiac conditions, which necessitated living in a boarding home where she could eat meals fulfilling her special dietary concerns or in a convalescent home where she could receive more comprehensive health care. Initial moves, however, were the result of Madeline's and Ada's attempts to live where each desired in order to preserve their social status and lifestyle choices—assertions of the social dimension of their privilege.

For instance, in early October 1929, the Visitor's notes indicate that Madeline was "very discouraged with [her second boarding] home. . . . [S]he was very much upset to think that [the Visitor] found her a place near a church that had wooden pews and where it tired her to walk to church." Later in the same month, the Visitor notes that Madeline complained about the same residence because of the fact that the owners would not let her cook vegetables on the stove because cooking used too much gas. Interestingly, the landlady and her daughter also complained about Madeline. Here, we cite a letter from October 19, 1929, that the Visitor received from the landlady's daughter at this residence, complaining about Madeline's "contrariness and unreasonableness":

> [Madeline Nuit's] horizon is so small all she has to amuse herself is eating three meals a day. Ma has been kind enough to sit by hour and listen to her high falutin talk about homes in France, her trip to Spain, Germany, [and] Switzerland, her servants, her homes here, her clothes, food, wines, etc., ad infinitum. If she still thinks she is a marquise [sic] it's time someone brought her down to terra firma (LHMFC, Case #131).

In mid-May 1930, when Madeline moved in with her niece, her landlady "stated that [she] is much relieved at [Madeline's] departure as she demanded a great deal of attention and was at times unreasonable and hard to please." According to the Visitor's case notes and correspondence in the file, most people were unwilling to challenge Madeline's contrariness directly. Therefore, not only did Madeline assert her own identity, but she also made sure that her interactions with others helped sustain her ability to make decisions, remain independent, and reaffirm her social status.

In the beginning, most of Ada's residential moves reflected summer excursions and her efforts to maintain physical freedom and a life of leisure. Even with declining physical health, however, Ada attempted to remain involved in decisions about her living conditions and, in doing so, asserted the social dimension of her privilege. When given a particular room in a hotel or nursing home, Ada usually found something wrong with it and relocated at least once or twice within that dwelling. She was also able to get the hotel managers, boarding room providers, and nursing home proprietors to make the changes in rooms which she required. While in one home, the Visitor noted that "she has been in three different rooms in the house since she arrived and was constantly wanting a different mattress, bed, chair, or stand." This is illustrative of Ada's attempt to assert the social status and lifestyle to which she was accustomed, as well as some control over her daily life. According to the case notes, one nursing home proprietor became so fed up with Ada's antics and idiosyncrasies that she made a special request that the LHMH not ask her to take Ada back again because she had created such a disturbance upon her last visit. It is significant that Ada never voiced concerns about any room she occupied during her summer excursions, because she alone selected those residences.

Negotiating Health Care

Because these women were older and inevitably faced certain health conditions, a considerable portion of the case notes and correspondence in their case files concern health care. Yet, because health care is a commonly discussed topic in these cases, it also reflects Madeline's and Ada's negotiations with the Visitors and doctors about pension rules. As in their negotiations over residence, Madeline and Ada often attempted to sustain social status through negotiations around health conditions and health care. For instance, in May of 1930, according to the case notes, Madeline told the Visitor that "she had always been accustomed to the best medical care available, and she objected to receiving treatment from student nurses. . . . [Madeline further] stated she could not understand why the [LHMH] should place their clients in charity beds [in the hospital] when they had money which had been left for the purpose of paying such expenses."

Once when Madeline became ill, the Visitor offered to take her to the clinic at one of the local hospitals, but Madeline is quoted as stating unequivocally that she "absolutely will not go to the free clinic as long as she has anything she can sell in order to pay." A doctor also made a note in February 1930, that her health "trouble" was "largely mental and a result of the brooding about her reduced circumstances." In these notes, we find others acknowledging Madeline's continual reaffirmation of both the economic and social dimensions of her privilege. Madeline threatens to utilize some of her remaining assets (e.g., paintings, jewelry, other household items, etc.) to secure a certain type of care that she deems appropriate for her social status.

From what we can piece together from Ada's case files, Ada also was willing to pay out of pocket for medical expenses if it meant that she could see *her* doctor. She indicated at one point that she did not mind visiting a local hospital clinic because *her* doctor was on staff there and she had "the utmost confidence in him." Even as her savings dwindled—the savings that she fought to keep from the LHMH—Ada was reluctant to make use of the LHMH doctors (even when this seemed to be the best economic decision). In May of 1934, for instance, Ada had a heart attack and was placed in a local hospital to convalesce. While there, Ada let everyone know of her dissatisfaction with the room. One of the matrons told the Visitor that Ada was a difficult patient because "she [had] helped furnish a room at [the hospital] years ago and she feels entitled to go as she pleases and pay what she thinks her care is worth." A few years later Ada was placed in a nursing home after another heart attack. She quickly moved herself from this establishment, however, complaining that "she [did] not receive sufficient baths and that the bed linen [had] 'tattle-tale gray.'" Upon hearing this, her LHMH doctor lamented that she had "been used to too much service," distinguishing her from perhaps the less privileged clients he usually saw. In late 1935, Ada developed pneumonia and was placed in a private hospital room endowed by a wealthy member of her Episcopal congregation for "worthy people without funds." This special accommodation was looked upon quite favorably by Ada. In this moment, Ada was successful in sustaining social status and the social dimension of her privilege.

Ada often cited her health as a justification for fighting against pension rules. In 1933, for instance, the visitor notes that Ada, in the process of getting the LHMH Board to approve her annual summer excursions, "would use any argument to win her point. She enjoys using her health as a whip to get her own way." Case notes illustrate that the Visitor and Board of Trustees, as well as Ada's own family, often felt exasperated and burdened by the constant negotiations Ada initiated around her health. Yet she usually succeeded in getting her way.

Constructing the Social Dimension of Privilege

As is already clear from the above recounting of Madeline and Ada's interactions with the LHMH, health care providers and landlords, these two women remained committed to renewing and sustaining their social capital, ability to choose, and social status. This meant, however, that they also had to actively and continually assert the social dimension of their privilege in their interactions with others in the face of their impoverished status and LHMH pension rules.

Everyone from the Visitors to doctors, landlords, and family members all regularly reported that Madeline talked incessantly about her past life, clear evidence that she still connected herself with the social dimensions of her former economic privilege. While talking about one's past does not automatically designate privilege, the ways in which these conversations are described in the case files illustrates Madeline's particular construction of her social status within the city of Detroit. On April 16, 1935, for instance, according to the Visitor's case notes, Madeline "talked at length" with her:

[A]bout some of the more prominent families in Detroit and how they had bought the valuable things she had brought over with her from her mother-in-law's chateau in France. They apparently gave her very little for her linens, silver, copper, etc. She was quite bitter about their neglect of her and said that many of them, though they consider themselves the prominent women of Detroit, would not have been received in her mother-in-law's home. [Madeline] told V[isitor] of an offer she had received for two hundred thousand dollars if she would divorce her husband and let a socially prominent woman have him (LHMFC, Case #131).

In the years that follow, case records indicate that the Visitor considered Madeline's condition to be "pathetic" because she lived "entirely in the past" and dwelt "on the greatness of her husband's family."

Another way in which Madeline attempted to maintain social status was through hiding her poverty from family members (both her own family in Windsor and Detroit, and her late husband's family in France). Dodson and Schmalzbauer (2005) found the practice of hiding information to be common among contemporary welfare recipients as well. In May 1930, for instance, the Visitor found that Madeline had not yet told her niece in St. Clair County, Michigan, that she was poor and receiving an LHMH pension. The Visitor encouraged Madeline to tell her niece about the aid, and she eventually did, though under duress. Madeline's interactions with her late husband's family in France were especially focused on reaffirming her privileged status. Case notes from May 1937 read:

[Madeline] feels that a great injustice was done her husband, the Marquise des [Nuit], since his mother divided the remains of the family estate in three portions, one for himself, one for his sister, and one for the sister's daughter. The Marquise's sister. . . and her daughter . . . have also lost financially. . . [Madeline] writes them glowing accounts of how wealthy she is due to some imaginary oil wells in order to make them feel badly (LHMFC, Case #131).

The re-creation of the economic and social dimensions of her privilege (especially her economic assets, social capital, and social status) seemed essential for Madeline when she could no longer hold onto privilege in any tangible way. Her efforts to hide her impoverishment are evidence that she publicly constructed herself as a privileged woman, long after the economic dimension of this privilege had disappeared. Madeline's discourse about her past and present situations weaves together both the economic and social dimensions of privilege, suggesting that they bolstered each other. The fact that she needed to hide her impoverishment means that the social dimension of privilege *is* harder to sustain when it is not accompanied by income and wealth.

Although Ada was not the wife of a Marquise and did not garner as much economic advantage over her lifetime as Madeline did, she also felt it necessary to reify her social status in conversations with others. The Visitor notes on one occasion that she was "reminiscent and brought out a picture of . . . her mother's home in Summersetshire, [England; her] father . . . occupied a castle near Dublin, Ireland, and one branch of the family still owns it." By clinging to and verbalizing this detail of her family history, Ada was attempting to maintain social status, just like Madeline.

The lengths to which Ada was able to assert and utilize her social capital, personal choice, and social status are worth noting as well. Unlike Madeline, Ada kept her women's club memberships current for the majority of her pension years and attended functions at her clubs on a weekly basis—even when she was supposed to be home recuperating from heart attacks or other illnesses. One day Ada took the Visitor to lunch at one of her clubs. The corresponding case notes turned to the cost of maintaining these memberships. The Visitor notes that "to some it might appear an extravagance for a person in her [economic] position to keep up the club membership. . . . It entitles her to so many privileges and to so many free lectures and entertainment that [Ada] feels justified in spending her money for recreation in this manner."

Although Ada had come to reduced circumstances, she still believed it important to stay engaged in the activities associated with women of upper-class position (Ostrander 1984) and exercised choice in order to do so. To Ada, the privileges that club activities afforded her were more important than the benefits she would gain by using dues money to purchase more mundane items. Ada seemed to find activities that highlighted her membership in particular social networks to be even more important than her health, supporting the idea that sustaining social capital was vital for women like Ada and Madeline. Ada's persistence in this regard is noted by the Visitor in May of 1941: "[Ada] was preparing to go to the [club election] that day in spite of the fact that she had had a very serious heart attack two nights before." Ada even took on the duty of chairing more club committees at this time.

Ada also asserted privilege by encouraging others to do things for her, thereby maintaining control over her own and others' decisions and actions, as evidenced by the Visitor's comments about her ability to "use any argument to win her point." At times, the Visitor seemed impressed by Ada's "sensible and businesslike" dealings with the LHMH, realizing the extent of her negotiation skills. We can see this dynamic at work in Ada's first encounter with the LHMH, in which she was able to get the Board of Trustees to agree to handle her assets as she saw fit, requiring them to make a special exception for her on this and many subsequent occasions. Later on, after much prodding, the Board agreed to augment Ada's pension so that she would be able to continue her summer excursions, as long as this arrangement was kept confidential by all parties. While Madeline complained more loudly and reminisced more regularly than Ada overall, Ada seemed to have a greater ability to pull on her social capital and her own experiences as a social worker in younger years. Thus, Ada seemed more adept than Madeline in sustaining three aspects of the social dimensions of privilege—social status, ability to exercise choice, and social capital—even in her final years.

A major similarity between Madeline and Ada is that they both used racial-ethnic slurs as discursive tools to solidify their social standing above others, and they constructed their privilege in comparison to others' lack of privilege. Madeline talked negatively about her niece, for instance, because she had married an Italian man who worked in the "pool trade." For more than a decade, case notes detail her refusal of his monetary help because of his presumably "unsavory" and "dirty" ethnic background. In all of the conversations within which Madeline talked about her niece's husband, however, his Italian background and consequent choice of paid work was the only "unsavory" or "dirty" detail provided about his character. Thus, readers of this case file are forced to conclude that his ethnic background was the main reason for Madeline's disdain. Likewise, Ada discussed a visit to the dentist, during which she realized that the dentist saw "Negro" patients because she witnessed a Black patient sitting in the chair before her. Not only did the dentist not "wipe down the chair" before Ada sat down, but also the case notes from June 1938 specifically report that:

> The dentist protected himself by wearing a pair of rubber gloves. [Ada] followed a colored man into the dentist chair. At first the dentist used a wooden probe but later touched portions of her mouth and teeth with

his rubber covered fingers. He had done the same for the colored man and had not washed or disinfected his gloves in any way. [Ada] resented this fact and did not care about having her dental work done there [again] (LHMFC, Case #443).

In her continual pursuit of better-quality health care, Ada mentioned this race-based story to the Visitor as evidence that her current dental care was insufficient, indicating that to be in contact with other races was to experience a lowered quality of life. The racial-ethnic discourse used by both Madeline and Ada seemed purposeful, as they both tried to separate themselves from those they deemed less fortunate in order to reify their "higher" (White, wealthy, connected) position within Detroit society (Lipsitz 1998).

The racial-ethnic discourse in which Madeline and Ada engage serves as a tool or wedge to help them separate themselves from others (even other, "lesser" Whites, such as Italians, in Madeline's case), and allows them to benefit from the "unearned skin privilege" which their whiteness affords them (McIntosh 2000). George Lipsitz also suggests that whiteness is not a passive social fact but is engaged actively: "[W]hiteness has a cash value . . . [it is] an identity created and continued with all-too-real consequences for the distribution of wealth, prestige, and opportunity" (1998, vii). Conversations about race and ethnicity helped Madeline and Ada cement the fact that neither of them were "charity cases" and that they had social status that other poor and elderly people did not have.

Conclusions

An intersectional approach includes a thorough analysis of the similarities as well as the differences among individuals (Dill and Zambrana 2009; Weber 2001). Thus, we organize this conclusion to highlight the similarities and differences between the two women we analyze in this chapter as well as between these two women and other LHMH pensioners. Madeline and Ada were different from each other in many ways. Madeline lived a noble married life and came into poverty only because of a lawsuit vaguely described in case notes and her husband's death in 1927. Madeline had never worked to support herself. Ada, on the other hand, was widowed many years before receiving a pension and thereafter worked to support herself. Nonetheless, Madeline and Ada experienced many similar things, both before and during their receipt of an old-age pension. Both were widows who reached old age in poverty. Neither woman had children who could support them. Both experienced the economic dimensions of privilege before old age and, thus, were accustomed to social capital, personal choice, and social status. Based on case notes, both spent considerable time and energy negotiating with the LHMH staff, doctors, landlords, and others around them in order to exert influence over decisions made about their residences, health care, lifestyles, and spending, while complying with LHMH rules enough to continue receiving a pension.

The greatest similarity between Madeline and Ada, however, may be in how their gendered and age-based position in society facilitated their poverty. Most elderly women, then and now, do not have as much direct access to economic resources as men because of the lack of full-time paid work, thus making it difficult for them to control their economic situations, especially after retirement or the death of wealthy spouses (Calasanti and Slevin 2001). Yet, their loss of economic position, while extremely difficult and life-shaping, may not affect these women's identities as much as the loss of social capital, personal choice, and social status. Ostrander makes it clear that it is the upper-class woman's responsibility to "uphold the power and privilege of her own class in the social order of things" (1984, 3), and that this is a very gendered responsibility, if not a gendered burden. Formerly well-off aging women still feel the responsibility to keep up the social dimension of privilege, even after the economic dimensions of privilege are long-gone.

While we do not analyze the case files of older male pensioners served by the LHMH in this chapter, we hypothesize that formerly wealthy men might not have struggled in their interactions with landlords, doctors, and the LHMH staff as much as Madeline and Ada did, specifically because they might not have felt the need to sustain the social dimension of privilege. On the other hand, older, formerly privileged men were probably much harder hit by the loss of economic position because of how central the breadwinner role has been to men's individual identities over time (Abbott 2006; Rubin 1994; Wood 2008). Robert McElvaine suggests that men who lost their jobs during the Great Depression "became dependent in ways that women had been thought to be," and had to create other ways of being masculine during this "crisis" of masculinity (as cited in Abbott 2006, 463; see also Wood 2008, 21). Either men had to become passive within the context of their lack of economic resources, or they had to redefine who they were (Abbott 2006; Wood

2008). Future research on male clients of the LHMH (or male poverty during the Depression era more broadly) should explore the balance of case notes about purely economic dimensions of men's lives versus their social position and daily life, and consider whether male pensioners were more attuned to finding additional income rather than engaging in the interactional work that occupied Madeline and Ada's later years.

Even though these women may be among the most privileged of LHMH clients, we believe that Madeline and Ada were similar to other women designated by the LHMH as "Hannan types." For instance, Ray (2008) tells the story of "Jennie McGinnis," the very first LHMH pensioner (see also Ray, chapter 3, this volume). In 1927, Jennie independently contacted the LHMH to inquire about aid, when she could no longer work as a seamstress because of her failing health. She was unwilling to ask her other two sisters for help and, according to the case notes, had "no relatives who [could] help her, and surely none she would ask for assistance." After she was granted a pension in 1929, the LHMH requested that she turn over her savings and other asserts. Ray (2008, 168) quotes from her case file:

> Miss M became very much upset and stated that she is sure that Mrs. Hannan never meant to pauperize her people; that she had had a personal message from Mrs. Hannan telling her that she need never worry, a home would be provided for her, it would not be charity and it would not cost her one cent. She feels that if she turns over her savings she will have no resources at times of emergency. She will be forced to ask for every little thing she wants and will thereby feel so dependent that she will not be happy (LHMFC, Case #1).

The Visitor's note of this conversation illustrates Jennie's resistance to the burdensome pension rules and her attempts to maintain control over economic assets, residential locations, health care, and social status despite poverty. Stating her concern that LHMH rules might "pauperize" her, Jennie also implies how different she is from other poor people in Detroit during the Depression. Even if the LHMH case files do not document it, many other pensioners probably resisted the lack of control over their daily lives, as the LHMH took charge of (or at least monitored) their daily spending and material needs. Especially the "Hannan types"— older women accustomed to the "comforts of life" and economic independence—most likely experienced the subsequent lack of control over decision-making and the constriction in their spending and social activities as highly intrusive.

On the other hand, the LHMH pensioners were very different in other ways. Many women and men coming to the LHMH were already failing in health and had been poor for longer than Madeline and Ada. Most likely, the majority of pensioners could not sustain their resistance to pension rules as Madeline and Ada did, specifically because of health or poverty concerns or both. Despite facing physical health conditions from time to time, Madeline and Ada were fairly healthy when compared to others their age, and their good health, along with their remaining economic and social privileges (however partial), helped them assert and sustain their privilege. These two women come close to representing the exclusive category of "successful" agers that contemporary gerontologists so often praise (Dillaway and Byrnes 2009), in that they were able to fight off physical and cognitive decline, sustain portions of their independence, and remain socially engaged despite poverty. We cannot deny the important differences between these two women and some of the other LHMH pensioners.

Nevertheless, there are some general parallels between contemporary poor women's experience of receiving welfare and formerly well-off, elderly women's experiences of receiving an old-age pension in the 1930s (e.g., Dodson and Schmalzbaue, 2005; Edin and Lein 1996). Many comparisons also can be made about how aging individuals (especially women) think about and experience economic decline in both the Depression era and contemporary times, particularly in light of aging women's high poverty rates across history (Calasanti and Slevin 2001). Comparisons of the recently downtrodden in both the Depression era and today might also be instructive as we find ourselves in another era of great economic decline in America. Parallels between historical and contemporary cases should be explored further because, as scholars like Abromovitz (1996) and Estes (2001) argue, one of the threads through U.S. history is the monitoring of poor women's and older people's lives through policies and organizational rules. Resistance to pension rules meant that Madeline and Ada could attempt to assert and sustain their social position as "nobody's burden" despite poverty, reifying Luella Hannan's original desire to help women who had never *been* a burden to *stay* that way. Yet, the simple fact that these individuals even had the opportunity to receive an old-age pension from the Luella Hannan Memorial Home before any type of governmental social security existed also designates them as privileged within their time.

This analysis of the economic and social dimensions of privilege and the micro-level processes by which specific older women asserted and reproduced their privilege can be expanded considerably if we apply it to similar and different scenarios in the present day. In this way, we can understand better the ways in which entire systems of inequality, including privilege and oppression, might be maintained on a larger scale.

Notes

1. For purposes of confidentiality we use pseudonyms.

References

Abbott, Philip. 2006. "Titans/Planners, Bohemians/Revolutionaries: Male Empowerment in the 1930s." *Journal of American Studies* 40, no. 3: 463-485.

Abromovitz, Mimi. 1996. *Regulating the Lives of Women: Social Welfare Policy from Colonial to Present Times.* Boston, MA: South End Press.

Bowers, H. C. 1930. "239 Live in Comfort Under Hannan Will: Clients are Those Who Have Been Accustomed to Higher Standards." *The Detroit Free Press*, January 25, Sunday Section.

Calasanti, Toni, and Kathleen Slevin. 2001. *Gender, Social Inequalities, and Aging.* Walnut Creek, CA: Altamira Press.

Calasanti, Toni, Kathleen Slevin, and Neal King. 2006. "Ageism and Feminism: From "Et Cetera" to Center." *NWSA Journal* 18, no. 1: 13-30.

Connell, R. W. 1995. *Masculinities.* Berkeley, CA: University of California Press.

Dill, Bonnie Thornton, and Ruth Enid Zambrana. 2009. *Emerging Intersections: Race, Class, Gender in Theory, Policy, and Practice.* New Brunswick, NJ: Rutgers University Press.

Dillaway, Heather, and Chasity Bailey-Fakhoury. 2008. "What Price Accommodation? An Exploration of One Woman's Struggle to Sustain Privilege While Receiving an Old Age Pension." *Journal of Aging, Humanities, and the Arts* 2: 207-216.

Dillaway, Heather, and Mary Byrnes. 2009. "Reconsidering Successful Aging: A Call for Renewed and Expanded Academic Critiques and Conceptualizations." *Journal of Applied Gerontology* 28, no. 6: 702-722.

Dodson, Lisa, and Leah Schmalzbauer. 2005. "Poor Mothers and Habits of Hiding: Participatory Methods in Poverty Research." *Journal of Marriage and Family* 67, no. 4: 949-959.

Edin, Kathryn, and Laura Lein. 1996. *Making Ends Meet: How Single Mothers Survive Welfare and Low-Wage Work.* New York, NY: Russell Sage.

Estes, Carroll L., ed. 2001. *Social Policy and Aging: A Critical Perspective.* Thousand Oaks, CA: Sage.

Fraser, Nancy. 1989. *Unruly Practices: Power, Discourse and Gender in Contemporary Social Theory.* Minneapolis, MN: University of Minnesota Press.

Gray, Anne. 2009. "The Social Capital of Older People." *Ageing and Society* 29: 5-31.

Johnson, Allan. 2006. *Privilege, Power, and Difference* (2nd ed.). New York, NY: McGraw-Hill Publishers.

Lipsitz, George. 1998. *The Possessive Investment in Whiteness: How White People Profit from Identity Politics.* Philadelphia, PA: Temple University Press.

Lorde, Audre. 2003. "A Master's Tools Will Never Dismantle the Master's House." Pp. 25-8 in *Feminist Postcolonial Theory: A Reader*, edited by Reina Lewis and Sara Mills. New York, NY: Routledge.

Luella Hannan Memorial Foundation Collection (LHMFC). Walter Reuther Library of Labor and Urban Affairs, Wayne State University, Detroit, MI.

McIntosh, Peggy. 2000. "White Privilege and Male Privilege: A Personal Account of Coming to See Correspondences through Work in Women's Studies." Pp. 30-8 in *Gender Basics: Feminist Perspectives of Women and Men,* edited by Anne Minas, 2nd ed. Belmont, CA: Wadsworth.

National Economic Council Interagency Working Group on Social Security. "Women and Retirement Security." http://www.socialsecurity.gov/history/ reports/women.html

Newman, Katherine. S. 1994. "Troubled Times: The Cultural Dimensions of Economic Decline." Pp. 330-57 in *Understanding American Economic Decline,* edited by Michael Alan Bernstein and David E. Adler. New York, NY: Cambridge University Press.

Ostrander, Susan. 1984. *Women of the Upper Class*. Philadelphia, PA: Temple University Press.

Portes, Alejandro. 1998. "Social Capital: Its Origins and Applications in Modern Sociology." *Annual Review of Sociology* 24: 1-24.

Ray, Ruth. 2008. "Relations of Power: Issues of Gender and Class in the Struggle for 'Security' in Old Age." *Journal of Aging, Humanities, and the Arts* 2: 158-174.

Reskin, Barbara. 2003. "Including Mechanisms in Our Models of Ascriptive Inequality: 2002 Presidential Address." *American Sociological Review* 68, no. 1: 1-21.

Rubin, Lillian. 1994. *Families on the Fault Line: America's Working Class Speaks About the Family, the Economy, Race, and Ethnicity*. New York, NY: HarperCollins Publishers.

Turner, Bryan. S. 1988. *Status*. Milton Keynes, England: Open University Press.

Weber, Lynn. 2001. *Understanding Race, Class, Gender, and Sexuality: A Conceptual Framework*. New York, NY: McGraw-Hill Publishers.

Weber, Max. 1978. *Economy and Society: An Outline of Interpretive Sociology.* (G. Roth and C. Wittich, Trans.). Berkeley, CA: University of California Press. (Original work published 1914).

Wilson, Gail. 2008. "Money and Independence in Old Age." In *Ageing, Independence and the Life Course,* edited by Sara Arber and Maria Evandrou. LSE Research Online database. http://eprints.lse.ac.uk/21491/

Wood, Gregory. 2008. "Forty Plus Clubs and White-Collar Manhood." Pp 21-33 in *The Great Depression. Essays in Economic and Business History: The Journal of the Economic and Business Historical Society* 26.

Chapter 7

What is Held Dear: Personhood and Material Culture in Old Age

Sherylyn H. Briller and Mary E. Durocher

[Cora] sat in the car and talked with [the Visitor]. She stated that the reason she had asked [the Visitor] to call was to report that she had visited friends in the neighborhood of her old home recently and had been grieved to see the run down condition of the yard surrounding their house. She stated that the shrubs were untrimmed, that the grass had not been mowed for a long time and that things looked rather dilapidated. She stated that she did not want to complain, and that it was really none of her affair, but that she had believed that it would be easier to rent the place if a little more attention could be paid to the outside.

[Cora] is very desirous of knowing that both flats of her home are rented because she feels that in this way she is reimbursing the organization for money advanced her, and is, therefore, not living on charity.

[Cora] continues to look after the interests of the property as she did in the days when she was its owner.

These excerpts from the file of Cora Ambrose (LHMFC Case #400) about revisiting the house that she and her sister Rose (LHMFC Case #402) formerly owned is a fitting start for this chapter. We consider how *personhood* in old age, including sense of self and the ways individuals are socially recognized, is often negotiated through *material culture*, including homes and the objects within them. Material culture can tell us much about old people and the social worlds in which they live. We investigate how two sisters understood themselves in old age through their interactions with each other and the material world they shared during

197

the Great Depression.

Within the archives of the Luella Hannan Memorial Home, (LHMH), the Ambrose sisters' case files contain rich descriptions of their relationships with material culture and its meanings to them. This particular set of files documents how the sisters, two maiden ladies unable to work any longer and without family support, strove not to become a burden on the LHMH, making every effort to remain responsible for themselves and their property. By examining their files, we can learn more about how the sisters were viewed by and interacted with the LHMH, an organization established to assist Detroit residents like them—those who had "seen better days" but who had come to "reduced circumstances" in old age. Our analysis provides insight into how formerly middle-class women adjusted to financial and physical decline as they continued to interact with their changing social and material worlds.

Personhood

Anthropologists have argued that being a biological individual is not the same as being a "person" (Fortes 1987; Geertz 1984; Hallowell 1955; Mauss 1938/1985). The forces that determine who is or is not a person include ideas about the value and meaning of certain kinds of human relationships, who is worthy, concepts of productivity or contribution to society, forms of legal systems, notions of gender roles, competence, frailty and so forth (e.g., Douglas and Ney 1998; Fortes 1987; Frank 2000; Geertz 1984; Leibing and Cohen 2006; Luborsky 1994; McLean 2007; Murphy 1990; Shweder and Bourne 1984; Strathern 1992). The particular constellation of forces that makes an individual a person in one cultural setting may or may not be the same as the constellation at work in another.

In addition to studying the cultural category of personhood generally, social scientists have explored the meaning of "full personhood" and the requirements for achieving and maintaining it in various contexts. In defining "full adult personhood" in the United States, Luborsky (1994) makes the case that it is "earned during the adult phase . . . of the life course by being a responsible and (re)productive worker, spouse, family and community member" (240). This definition is important to (re)consider when considering older people's struggles to maintain personhood.

While Luborsky specifically examines the effect of physical disabilities, other challenges can erode adults' abilities to maintain full personhood, including poverty. Douglas and Ney (1998) emphasize several key points salient to our discussion here. First, personhood is relational, and ideas about what constitute "acceptable" wants and needs are culturally formed. As these authors note, "Not nature but culture defines what a full belly is, how full it should be, and what is needed to fill it up" (49). Second, "society and tastes are co-produced" (54); that is, individuals form their value judgments and ideas about appropriate ways of living through interactions with others.

Age and gender are also important aspects of the socially mediated process of personhood (Lamb 1997, 2000). Specifically, we will see that the Ambrose sisters, consistent with the expectations of "proper" womanhood for those of their social class, sought to uphold their personhood by managing how they looked and kept house, as well as by giving gifts to signal that they were still "refined" ladies, even as they lost property and became increasingly frail.

Material Culture

For anthropologists, material culture is any *object* or *thing* that is part of the everyday world. The two terms, "objects" and "things" represent categories that overlap but are not totally interchangeable. An object refers to pieces of the world that have physical substance and can be handled (e.g., books, furniture, paintings). Things can include objects but are also tangible pieces of nature or culture that are not movable, such as rivers, trees, plants, or property. These objects or things have a physical presence that we experience primarily through our bodily and sensual perceptions in our daily interactions with them (Langer 1953/1977; Miller 1994; Pearce 1992).

As they negotiate the material world, humans interact in meaningful ways with objects and things. Even when they must divest themselves of personal belongings, humans continue to derive a sense of personhood from the myriad objects and things they encounter daily, including the familiar surroundings of their environment. Historically, social scientists have focused on the symbolic or representational value of objects and things, but more recently they have begun to consider how people establish *relationships* with objects and things. Using this relational approach, objects and things acquire their significance in the ways people relate to them, and persons continually negotiate their sense of self through their interactions with the objects that surround them. In other words, "through making, using, exchanging, consuming, interacting and living with things, people make themselves in the process" (Tilley 2007, 61). Thus, the things we surround ourselves with tell a story of who we are and where we have been (Gell 1998; Miller 1994). This notion is a powerful one for investigating how specific LHMH clients, including the Ambrose sisters,[1] used familiar objects and activities to reinforce identity and try to maintain their social position. Csikszentmihalyi and Rochberg-Halton (1981) define household objects or activities as "those selected by the person to attend to regularly or to have close at hand, that create permanence in the intimate life of a person, and therefore that are most involved in making up his or her identity" (17). Of specific interest to us are the meanings the Ambrose sisters made of various household objects, such as furniture and knick knacks, and things they produced through domestic activities like gardening, baking, canning, and sewing.

Bearing these concepts in mind, we will demonstrate how people's interaction with objects and things in their everyday lives, as well their interactions with "persons-through-things," shape their experiences, the objects they use (Belk 1988; Chapman 2006; Gell 1998; Kopytoff 1986; Tilley 2007) and the stories they tell about them (Hoskins 1998, 2006; Ochs and Capps 1996). Objects and things in this sense become part of the "biography" of a person. They become associated with life-transforming events and therefore become filled with special meaning (Kopytoff 1986). It is not the physical characteristics of an object that make it biographical but the meaning given to it as a significant personal possession. This is why some objects are never given away and are often considered heirlooms that are passed on from generation to generation. Weiner (1985, 1992, 1994) considers such things to be "symbolically 'dense,' filled with cultural meanings and values, and this density accrues through association with owners, ancestral histories, sacred connotations, etc." (Weiner 1994, 394). A painting, piece of furniture, or pair of earrings may become irreplaceable because of associations with a particular life event. The Ambrose sisters mention several objects of this kind, an especially noteworthy example being their grandmother's wedding shawl.

In addition to such individually meaningful possessions, objects or things given as gifts also play an important role in forming and maintaining social relations and thereby supporting personhood. In giving, receiving and exchanging gifts, people form a moral bond (Mauss 1925/1990). In giving a gift, part of the person doing the giving remains attached to the gift—what Strathern (1990) calls a *partible* person; that part serves to bind and maintain the relationship between giver and receiver. The act of giving creates a social bond with an obligation to reciprocate in some way on the part of the recipient. By giving, one shows oneself as generous, and thus as deserving of respect. Failure to reciprocate may break the bond between giver and receiver.

Gerontologists have long been interested in the role of gift giving for older adults and its impact on social relations. Dowd (1975) proposed a classic framework known as exchange theory, which focused on the economic and social bargaining power and related esteem that older adults receive from gift giving. This model purports that older adults in contemporary industrial societies have fewer resources for exchange than those in more "traditional" societies. With much less ability to bargain, older adults in these settings must do what they can to maximize the benefits they receive from various forms of social exchange. Dowd subscribed to a popular premise that the social position of older adults had lessened with increasing modernization; however that premise has since been widely critiqued in the gerontological literature cross-culturally. Yet, Dowd's concerns remain relevant today, more than 30 years later: What social bargaining power do older adults have at particular times and in particular situations? What role does gift giving and social exchange play in their lives? To what extent are they supported and burdened in old age by these forms of social exchange?

Contemporary scholars from many fields have examined the distinctions between "house" and "home" (Rowles 2006), along with the meaning-making processes involved when older adults disband their homes (Chaudhury 2008; Ekerdt and Sergeant 2006; Ekerdt et al. 2004). A home is far more than a physical structure providing shelter, and "home" takes on special significance when older adults must make a transition to new living quarters (Boschetti 1995; Chaudhury 2008; Ekerdt and Sergeant 2006; Ekerdt, Sergeant, Dingel and Bowen 2004; Marsden et al. 2001; McCracken 1987; Wiles et al. 2009). For many people, the home is the central setting of life experiences and the primary locus for the production and reproduction of social relations (Chaudhury 2008). People act on their physical surroundings, selecting and adapting the home environment to shape experience and identity: "To enter a house is to enter a body, a mind, a sensibility, a specific mode of dwelling and being in the world" (Tilley 2007, 263). Thus, a home and its contents is another form of biography—"the untold story of a life being lived" (Berger 1984, 64; see also Csikszentmihalyi and Rochberg-Halton 1981). It therefore makes sense that Ekerdt et al. (2004, 265) characterize household disbandment for older individuals as "an acute episode of a more general lifelong process of possession management."

In sum, the ways we interact with the material world, including our homes, are key to understanding personhood and sense of self. Ideas, values and social relations are "actively created" through our personal relations with things in the world—both the things we make and the things we use. In effect, personhood is produced through the act of living with and through material culture (Chapman 2006; Dant 1999; Gell 1998; Tilley 2007).

Personhood and Material Culture for the Ambrose Sisters

Many aspects of the Ambrose sisters' material culture, including property, home furnishings, domestic objects and activities, were highly salient to their process of telling others (and themselves) who they were and what their place was in the world. The sisters had a particularly strong commitment to objects that represented home ownership, domesticity and the life of social engagement and "refinement." As their circumstances changed over time, especially at the onset of the Great Depression, their material culture (especially land and property) began to burden them financially, although it continued to support them socially.

Our discussion in this section focuses primarily on material taken from the files of Cora Ambrose (LHMFC Case #400), age sixty-four at the time of application, and Rose Ambrose (LHMFC Case #402), age seventy-four at the time of application. The two sisters referred themselves to the LHMH for assistance in April, 1930, when the organization was beginning to limit applications to the most qualified Hannan clients only. Later, their widowed sister Sally (nee Ambrose) McGovern (LHMFC Case #501), age seventy-six at the time of application, also received support from the LHMH between 1931-1932. We refer to the sisters by their first names, as did the Visitor in her interactions with them.

Property and Home

The Ambrose sisters had been raised on a farm, through which their father had acquired both wealth and social status. It is not surprising, then, that they valued property ownership. Notes from the LHMH intake interviews conducted with Cora and Rose in April, 1930, reveal that the sisters jointly owned a home and several parcels of land that were partially paid for. However, due to the Depression, they could not afford to pay the taxes on these properties, nor could they sell or generate sufficient income from them to cover their living expenses. Several people who wrote letters in support of their applications agreed that the sisters had handled their money and properties well but that the economic circumstances of the Depression now necessitated their seeking financial aid. The Visitor summarizes a letter from Mr. A. S. Hampton of the Detroit Historical Society, who said that he had "known the Misses [Ambrose] for twelve years and his wife had known them for twenty-five years and they have found them always delightful friends; that they [had] been thrifty and careful in money matters, and he wishes to take this opportunity to endorse them in every possible way, unreservedly" (LHMFC Case #400). Several similar letters confirmed that "they [were] refined ladies with simple tastes, worthy of assistance" and "in jeopardy of losing their properties if they did not receive the needed assistance" (LHMFC Case #400).

When they applied for assistance, Cora and Rose were living in the downstairs flat of a two-family house they owned together in an "upper-middle class neighborhood" on the west side of Detroit. Cora had earned a living for both of them as a bookkeeper, while Rose kept house. After investigating their assets, the treasurer of the Board of Trustees informed the Board that the house they were living in was the only asset the LHMH would be interested in and that the sisters should "divest of their other lots by any means possible." The Board concluded that it would then give each sister an adequate income to support her needs. It was not easy for Cora and Rose to follow this business plan, which required that they sell at a considerable loss or give away their properties.

However, the sisters agreed to go along with the plan and turned over their home to the Detroit Trust Company, which managed property for the LHMH, while disposing of the other properties themselves. Arrangements were then quickly made for them to move to a less expensive place. On May 20, 1930, the Visitor documented that Cora and Rose were by then "comfortably situated in a five room apartment" in Highland Park, Michigan, a prosperous suburb of Detroit. Yet it soon became apparent that the sisters were not fully satisfied either with the business methods of the LHMH or their new home. When the Visitor called again on June 13, 1930, she noted that "[Rose] and her sister Cora were very much upset to think that they had not received an agreement or even a piece of paper showing that they had turned their property over to the Luella Hannan Memorial Home" (LHMFC Case #402). The Visitor promised to look into this matter. On July 11, 1930, Rose reiterated to the Visitor their worries that they had not received any paperwork about the property that they had transferred to the LHMH. Again, the Visitor promised to make inquires and get these papers for them. This instance is evidence that the sisters were careful to protect their interests and also wished to maintain some connection to the home they had once owned.

From the beginning, the sisters were unhappy with the living conditions in their new apartment, which the Visitor described as large and comfortable. Rose told the Visitor that they lacked janitor service and were concerned that they would not be able to keep up with shoveling snow in the winter. Three months later, Rose complained of problems with the laundry and said that she and Cora had found several other things about the apartment that did "not just suit them." She reported that they were "thinking of making a change" (LHMFC Case #400). On October 14, 1930, the Visitor called to find Rose suffering from a bad cold that she blamed on their living conditions, stating that "the apartment had very little fire during the cold days and that the rooms were exceedingly damp" (LHMFC Case #402). Cora echoed Rose's dislike of the apartment and indicated that they would not be able to stay there much longer. Rose later went on to say that she and her sister were "anxious to be located in the Grand River section near their friends and neighbors, among whom they formerly lived" (LHMFC Case #402). This statement suggests that, along with the importance of property ownership and their home environment, the sisters were also concerned about the neighborhood in which they lived, as this reflected (and reinforced) their social status. Proximity to former social networks helped them sustain their personhood.

The sisters later successfully negotiated with the LHMH to move to a house they had located on the same street in Highland Park. The fact that they were not able to move back to their former neighborhood, though, is significant; Cora and Rose had to begin the process of adapting to reduced circumstances. When the Visitor came to the new apartment on November 12, 1930, she recorded that the sisters "seemed to be well pleased" and believed that they would be much more contented in their new location, even though it was not in the more desirable Grand River area. Proud of their new home, the sisters took the Visitor on a tour through the apartment, after which the Visitor reported, "Everything was clean and neat, not a speck of dust to be seen" (LHMFC Case #400). As for their state of mind and health, the Visitor added that both sisters "seem to be unusually well."

However, the sisters expressed concern about how their former home was being handled by the LHMH, as demonstrated in the excerpts that begin this chapter. In late 1931, Cora spoke to the Visitor about the dilapidated condition into which their home had fallen and suggested that it would be in the LHMH's best interests to attend to needed repairs. The Visitor notes that "[Cora] is very desirous of knowing that both flats of her home are rented because she feels that in this way she is reimbursing the organization for money advanced to her, and is therefore, *not living on charity*" (LHMFC Case #400, emphasis added). By taking action to make the LHMH aware of this problem, Cora was not only trying to retain her own status as the former property owner but also establishing her relationship to the LHMH. Rather than merely receiving support as an old age pensioner, Cora saw herself as *assisting* the LHMH by pointing out these needed repairs. Similar sentiments can be read into letters that Cora and Rose later wrote to the LHMH about how grateful they were when they were eventually able to move back into their former house and how they would "endeavor to take such good care of 5059 Ivanhoe that we [LHMH] will have no cause to regret having placed them there" (LHMHC Case #402). In December of 1933, the Visitor reports that the sisters wrote to the LHMH again "thanking the Home for their Christmas greetings and for the fact that they are living back in their old home among their former neighbors" (LHMFC Case #402). From these examples, we can see that the sisters viewed their good stewardship of the property as central to their concept of themselves as invested and committed owners and as partners *with*, rather than dependents *of*, the LHMH.

The sisters' subsequent return to the family home reflects a business decision on the part of the LHMH. In April, 1933, Detroit was beginning its worst year of the Depression. Foreclosures were widespread, many homeowners were seeking renters to help make their mortgage payments, and rental rates were dramatically declining as a result of the number of available properties on the market. The LHMH, like everyone else, was struggling to find renters for its properties, including the house on Ivanhoe Street. In January of 1933, the Board decided that pensioners should be placed in LHMH-owned properties "wherever feasible" (LHMFC Case #400), as the LHMH could receive a tax credit for housing "charity" cases. The LHMH determined that the Ambrose sisters could therefore move back into their old home. The sisters were eager to do so and agreed to cooperate in any way possible.

On August 31, 1933, despite Rose's poor health, the sisters moved back to the house they had once owned. They found the house "in good repair with a few exceptions" (LHMFC Case #400). The sisters made a detailed listing of things that needed to be fixed or were missing, including five Tiffany glass lamp shades from the living room that had been replaced with "cheap" ones. We might assume that this was an attempt on their part to return the house to its former state. Despite these small problems, Cora and Rose were happy to be back home, and they continued to feel responsible for maintaining the house, even as renters, "spending some of their money to keep it in better repair than the Trust Company had done" (LHMFC Case #400).

The Ambrose sisters continued to assume responsibility for the property, as documented in the Visitor's notes. In October, 1933, when the tenants occupying the other half of this two-family home moved, Cora told the Visitor she was concerned that the Trust Company was not making sufficient effort to rent out the upper flat. She stated that she was "desirous of having a good tenant this winter, not only for the sake of the Hannan Foundation but for her own comfort" (LHMFC Case #400). What ensued next shows how Cora and Rose took the notion of serving as good stewards so seriously that it caused them trouble with both the Detroit Trust Company and the LHMH. Mr. Thompson, a representative of the Real Estate Division of the Detroit Trust Company, insinuated to the Visitor that the sisters' behavior when they showed the upper flat to prospective tenants was the reason it had not rented. The Visitor had to defend the sisters by pointing out that times had changed, it was now much more difficult to rent out upper flats in general, and the sisters should not be held responsible for the failure to find a tenant.

While Cora and Rose may have relished the first-hand opportunity to look after their former home, surely it was a bittersweet experience for them. One can imagine that this role shift was quite burdensome to them psychologically. This altered burden of care may account for their interactions with potential tenants and explain why Mr. Thompson declared that people looking at the property found the sisters to have "a fussy and proprietary" attitude (LHMFC Case #400). The case notes demonstrate that the property continued to hold deep meaning for the sisters, even though they no longer owned it. The selection of tenants was more than just a business deal for Cora and Rose. The sisters wished to surround themselves with like-minded people who would be good neighbors and value the property as they did.

Domestic Objects, Things and Gifts

Presiding over a well-kept home was especially important to Rose, who had always seen herself as the homemaker, while Cora worked outside the home and provided the family income. It is not surprising then that Rose, struggling with her physical decline and lessening abilities to continue running the household, would use domesticity as a way to try to maintain "full adult personhood" as long as possible.

Rose discussed at length with the Visitor her various domestic activities and how she was keeping busy with them. A typical conversation occurred on September 24, 1930, when the Visitor came to interview their eldest sister, Sally McGovern, as a potential LHMH client at the Ambrose sisters' apartment. Rose greeted her at the door and proceeded to tell her that she was "boiling cabbage, canning peaches, making peach pickles and some muffins" and then excused herself to return to the kitchen (LHMFC Case #402). Such detailed listings of domestic tasks appear frequently in Rose's file.

Eventually, however, Rose's diminishing strength and endurance began to impact her ability to keep house, and Cora took over many of the domestic duties. Cora expressed surprise to the Visitor that she was able to handle the housework (LHMFC Case #400). As Rose's health deteriorated, the Visitor noted that Rose seemed "to worry a great deal because it is necessary for her sister to do most of the work in addition to caring for her. However, her sister does it gladly and is extremely kind to [Rose] and never complains" (LHMFC Case #402). Both Rose and Cora seemed to adjust to their changing domestic roles fairly well.

Eventually, Cora's health began to worsen too. On September 24, 1937, when Cora was seventy-one and Rose was eighty-one, Rose confided in the Visitor that she realized "that her sister on whom she has leaned all of these years, is not well either and it adds to her burden of worries" (LHMFC Case #402). Despite this realization, Rose did not fully change her old ways. The Visitor writes on March 4, 1938, that she found Rose "up and about again and in violation of the doctor's orders in helping with the house cleaning." The Visitor then reports that she "urged her not to do this as it may bring on another illness." The sisters managed to regain some equilibrium, and on August 22, 1938, the Visitor called and found them "cutting up fresh yellow beans to make a particular kind of pickle for winter use" (LHMFC Case #400).

The sisters' health continued to decline, however. On January 8, 1940, the Visitor called and reported that "even though [Rose] was scarcely able to get about due to her infirmities she insisted on going to the kitchen and getting a piece of the five different kinds of fruit cake and cookies that they had had for [Christmas] some of which had been sent in to them by friends. With it [the Visitor] was served a glass of homemade grape juice." The Visitor goes on to comment, "Even though [Rose] and her sister are both infirm they insist on keeping up their housework under the greatest difficulties—and persist in cooking and baking as they have always done" (LHMFC Case #402). Through this offering of food to their guest, the sisters continued to demonstrate many elements that were integral to their sense of self and maintaining personhood, including good hospitality, successful domesticity, and appropriate social exchange. It is not incidental that there were *five* kinds of dessert, including those the sisters had received as gifts, or that the grape juice was homemade. Even though it was difficult for the sisters to entertain as readily as they had in prior times, it was still important to try and do so in the manner they considered proper.

Despite their ill health and increasingly limited resources (LHMH pensions were reduced twice during the Depression), the sisters were resolved to keep up the image of their home and themselves. On March 16, 1939, the Visitor noted that Cora had walked several blocks to find suitable kitchen curtains. The Detroit Trust Company had just redecorated the kitchen, and a niece had given them a set of canisters with red tops. The Visitor reported that the sisters had bought red dotted curtains and a red sink pad and that Cora considered it "the gayest kitchen they had ever had" (LHMFC Case #400).

There are several other examples of the sisters' continued efforts to keep up their home. Cora, especially, took an interest in flowers and gardening. They had numerous paintings of flowers hanging in their home, and they had nurtured over the years and many moves a particularly rare plant that we will discuss at the end of this chapter. Cora also did china painting and displayed several pieces in their home. The Visitor documented that on one occasion Cora did not have much time to talk because she "was painting a vase . . . and had her hands covered with paint." On seeing the completed vase the following week, the Visitor commented on the "beautiful piece of work" (LHMFC Case #400). The sisters set such high value on these paintings and pieces of china that many of them appear on the list of possessions they planned to bequeath to their relatives.

Just as the sisters wanted their home to be seen in flawless condition, they were also sensitive about being seen when their physical appearance was less than perfect. When the Visitor called one time in midsummer, she reported that Cora had been resting and "seemed truly distressed because of the fact that she was wearing an old house dress, and that her hair was not in order. She stated that she rarely looks so untidy in the afternoon, but that she had suffered so from the heat that she had become careless" (LHMFC Case #400). For these gentlewomen, maintaining who they were was linked to physical signs of self-management, and showing frailty, lack of competence or lack of control was very damaging.

When Rose experienced severe health crises and was not able to keep up her regular lifestyle, it particularly disturbed her sense of self. One telling example is when she suffered a paralytic stroke in July, 1931. When the Visitor called the following month, Cora would not permit her to see Rose, stating that "her [Rose's] mouth is drawn to one side and her entire face is misshapen" (LHMFC Case #402). Later on, Rose was still upset by the fact that her voice remained husky, and she had trouble pronouncing many words. The Visitor documented that Rose was "sensitive about this fact and apologizes frequently for not being able to express herself in a better manner." These examples demonstrate how the sisters used dress, grooming and physical appearance to try to manage their personhood as "refined" women.

Following Rose's stroke, the sisters were faced for the first time with medical bills that they could not cover themselves. Embarrassed, they asked the Visitor to consult with Mr. Frost to see if the LHMH would assist them with these payments. Mr. Frost agreed to do so "because of the fact that [Rose] and her sister have always been co-operative and reasonable in their demands from the Home" (LHMFC Case #402). This pattern of asking and receiving occurred repeatedly during their final years and is another example of their attempt to maintain personhood through social exchange.

When their various requests were granted, Cora and Rose expressed gratitude by giving homemade gifts to the Visitor, which represent tangible evidence of their domestic selves. Many of these "thanks for listening" gifts are reported in the Visitor's notes, such as plants from the garden, homemade cookies and muffins, jams and marmalade, or pickled fruits and vegetables. One example of the sisters' pattern of laying out a series of worries to the Visitor and then presenting her with homemade goods occurs during the visit on July 28, 1932. Rose was very stressed by the critical condition of her sister Sally, who was dying of cancer; the strain upon Cora, who now had to run the household by herself; and her own physical condition, including blood pressure that was prone to spiking to dangerously high levels. The sisters needed to ask the LHMH to pay a new round of doctor's bills. After expressing all of these concerns, Rose insisted upon giving the Visitor "a pint of pickled beans which she herself had canned the week before" (LHMFC Case #402).

However, on July 30, 1932, Rose telephoned the Visitor to tell her that "she was afraid the pickles that she had given her were not good and to ask the Visitor to stop at her house at her earliest convenience to get another jar" (LHMFC Case #402). What makes this incident particularly significant is that, although Rose desperately wanted to continue the pattern of reciprocity with the Visitor, the circumstances of their lives made this increasingly difficult. It is unclear from the notes how Rose determined that the pickles were "not good," but Rose took action to rectify the matter as soon as possible. Rather than conclude that making pickles might be too much for her at the time, Rose was determined to present a new jar of pickles to the Visitor that would make the situation right. An especially poignant aspect is how Rose asked the Visitor to "stop by at her earliest convenience to get another jar." Related to our earlier discussion of social exchange, we can see why Rose needed to reinforce her status as an accomplished and capable homemaker. While giving the pickles was important, the fact that Rose had made this gift with her own hands was essential to the negotiation of her personhood. Rose would have been quite burdened by the tangible evidence of the bad pickles. In effect, the act of making pickles was an act of making her *self*, and the act of giving them was not only a sharing of that self but a reinforcement of social relations.

As the sisters' health deteriorated, their abilities to maintain domestic activities declined as well. First, Cora had to take over the long-ailing

Rose's domestic duties. Eventually Cora became too frail, and Rose had to resume these activities, albeit at a lower level. Sadly, after Cora's death, Rose's health failed rapidly, and she was forced to move to a boarding house where others could care for her.

Prized Possessions & Household Disbandment

In 1939, the Visitor had several conversations with the sisters about the disposition of their furniture and personal effects upon their deaths. From the Visitor's notes on these conversations, we gain many insights into the objects and things that were important to Cora and Rose. In June of that year, the Visitor asked the sisters to conduct an inventory of their possessions and sign a special agreement listing the items and their recipients. The sisters somewhat reluctantly agreed to participate in this process. The Visitor was informed that Rose "would want her sister Cora to have her effects if she survived and Cora wants Rose to have her effects in a like situation" (LHMFC Case #402). Initially, neither of the sisters wanted to designate any belongings to their brother and sister-in-law or nieces and nephews. The sisters told the Visitor that "they will think the matter over for a time and when they are ready to definitely sign the agreements will notify the Visitor" (LHMFC Case #400).

At the next visit on June 22, 1939, the sisters informed the Visitor that they had changed their minds about not wanting to leave anything to their relatives and had made a detailed list of which people should receive what objects. No explanation is given in the files for this change of heart. It is possible that, at first, Cora and Rose found it difficult to think beyond their life together. It is also possible that they felt that others would not value their possessions as they did. Drawing on Weiner's ideas about "inalienable possessions"—objects that are saved over time and given as heirlooms to succeeding generations—we wonder whether the Ambrose sisters came to view the passing on of their prized possessions as further expression of their personhood.

In any case, the handwritten list of objects is not long; the sisters may have sold or given away items over the course of their moves during the Great Depression. Yet it helps to tell the story of their lives in words not written by the Visitor. The list (LHMFC Case #400) includes the following items, left to seven different people:

- grandmother's white wedding shawl
- cut glass pitcher
- hand-painted china kettle
- hand-painted china dresser set
- silver fan vase
- Wedgewood vase
- table linens
- club bag
- victrola
- piano and piano chair
- anglo-persian rug
- small mahogany table
- small walnut table
- oak dining table
- leather coach
- davenport
- oak library table
- assorted paintings (mostly flowers)
- small radio
- washing machine
- stone porch crocks
- porch chairs
- brass fernery
- all hand-painted china except for items specifically mentioned

Cora had probably made the hand-painted items on the list. The washing machine, a modern convenience, reflects the importance of domesticity and cleanliness to the sisters. This list includes other items that played a special role in the lives of Cora and Rose, as evident from the Visitor's notes in May, 1931. At that time, Rose told the Visitor how happy she was that "a friend of theirs had fixed their victrola for them and they were very happy now to think they could have some kind of music in their home" (LHMFC Case #402).

Not long after making this list, Rose was confronted with the actual task of dividing up their belongings. By May, 1940, Cora was so critically ill that Rose reluctantly agreed to have her moved to the Walter Nursing Home and decided to come along if a double room could be provided for them. Cora arrived in a coma and lived only two days following the transfer; she died on May 29, 1940. At that point, Rose decided to take a single room in a boarding house that she preferred due to its location. The Visitor advised Rose, as per the earlier agreement, that she would receive all of Cora's personal effects. However, Rose was not able to keep all of these objects, due to the small size of her room. She had to decide quickly which things to keep for her own use. Ultimately, Rose took "her own mahogany dresser into which she packed many items of bric-a-brac as well as her clothing, the davenport, the large mahogany library table, beaded chair, mahogany desk chair, several pictures and a throw rug" (LHMFC Case #402). On June 3, 1940, the Visitor transported Rose to the boarding house in advance of the truck coming to move her personal effects, because Rose "did not want to see the van drive up to the front of the house and begin to carry out furniture," as this would be too upsetting (LHMFC Case #402).

Rose lived in a small rented room crammed with these personal items until her death on November 22, 1941. Arrangements were made for her body, like Cora's, "to be transported to Aylmer, Ontario, Canada for interment in the family lot." After the sisters' deaths, their possessions were distributed according to the list they had compiled together.

We find that the Ambrose sisters' experiences of dealing with inheritance and household disbandment mirror key issues raised in the gerontological literature on this topic. As is true for many older adults, Cora and Rose were hesitant to think about such concerns and only reluctantly engaged in the planning process after it was initiated by the Visitor. For her part, the Visitor introduced this topic to the Ambrose sisters because she needed to fill out paperwork required by the LHMH. There is no concrete evidence, but we wonder whether dealing with this sensitive topic could have been more highly charged because it was being managed through the bureaucratic institution of the LHMH, rather than handled as a more intimate family matter. While Cora and Rose appeared to have a warm personal relationship with the Visitor over the years, we conjecture that there may still likely have been an important qualitative difference in addressing such a touchy subject with a charity worker, as opposed to their own family members. Indeed, we are left to wonder: what else might it say about Cora and Rose's relationship with their relatives that this topic was not taken care of with their own family members beforehand? Yet, this unwillingness to contemplate the end of their lives is not so surprising in a highly death averse culture such as ours.

In reflecting on what Cora and Rose ultimately left to their relatives, it seems very much in line with what Marx, Solomon and Miller (2004) present in their aptly entitled article, *Gift Wrapping Ourselves: The Final Gift Exchange*. In describing how older adults' bequests of meaningful objects follow the social norms of gift exchange, these authors state, "When a person gives an object, which is an extension of the self, to friends, family members or charity, s/he expects in return that the object be appreciated in ways consistent with her/his own definitions of the object's nature and value" (Marx, Solomon and Miller 2004, S274). This sentiment seems relevant in considering how Cora and Rose thought about themselves, their cherished possessions, and what should happen in the final gift-giving process.

Things Held Dear

One last story beautifully represents who the Ambrose sisters were, their domestic life together, and their relationship to special objects. Cora had always taken a keen interest in gardening. She often took the Visitor to the back yard and showed her the different flowers she had cultivated. The Visitor reported that she found these flowers quite attractive. On occasion, Cora gave the Visitor cuttings of the plants that she had admired.

On August 26, 1932, Cora telephoned the Visitor to tell her that the night-blooming cereus plant the sisters had cultivated for over twenty years would be blossoming that evening. This was a rare plant that did not bloom until its seventh year, after which it bloomed only once a year. It was expected that the flowers would begin to open about 8:30 p.m. and would be completely opened by midnight, after which they would fully close and not bloom again until the following year. Cora and Rose invited the Visitor to come and see the blossoming plant that night, and she agreed to do so. This celebration took place in the second of their rented apartments, indicating that the sisters had carried the plant with them from their former homes.

When the Visitor arrived, she found that many people had gathered on the front porch to watch the opening of two enormous white blossoms. Rose had not been feeling well recently. In fact, she had been so ill that she had not been able to attend her sister Sally's funeral three weeks earlier. But on the night of the plant blooming celebration, Rose was able to get up for the party. It was a remarkable occasion; even the local newspaper came out to report on the night-blooming cereus plant.

The story of this plant celebration provides a fitting end for our discussion of aging, personhood and material culture. The joyous event affirmed the sisters' lives together and their successful domesticity. The night-blooming cereus, a very special object, had been nurtured over many years, culminating in a short-lived but glorious blossoming. Cora and Rose invited all of their friends, including the Visitor, to share in this event, which for us symbolizes their use of material culture to help define and enact their personhood.

Conclusions

We began this chapter by asserting that material culture can tell us much about old people and the social worlds in which they live. We demonstrated this process by describing the relationships between the Ambrose sisters and various objects in their lives—how they used objects in their relationships with other people and how the objects themselves helped shape or maintain their image of themselves as "refined ladies" and productive members of society. Clearly, the sisters had to make many adjustments in later life due to changes in their personal and economic situations and the loss of many possessions, not the least of which was their home. Evidence from the files provides insight into the relationship between the Ambrose sisters and their remaining objects and things, right up to the end of their lives. We have seen how Cora and Rose sought time and time again to use various aspects of material culture to support their sense of self and to negotiate their personhood, even as economic insecurities and frailty became a focus in their lives.

Cora and Rose were both different from and similar to the other LHMH pensioners. They were maiden sisters who had supported each other throughout their lives, unlike other pensioners who were married couples or widowed men and women. In some respects, these sisters' relationship paralleled many marriages of the time in that Cora worked outside of the home and provided an income while Rose ran their household. There is no information in the case-files regarding the earning power of Cora over the years, but we are left to wonder to what extent the gendered structure of their household and Cora's overall earning capabilities may have further jeopardized them, even though many Americans at that time were losing hold of middle-class status economically. While their domestic arrangement appeared to have worked financially for the sisters over many years (others vouched that they had managed their money well), they became quite vulnerable during the Depression. Like the other LHMH pensioners, they were left without crucial economic and social support.

What we learn from a close examination of the Ambrose sisters' case files, and indeed those of many other LHMH pensioners, is how they reacted to their reduced circumstances and the loss of "the comforts of life" in old age. As can be seen throughout the chapters of this book, the files provide clues about how different people adjusted to hardship in old age during the Great Depression. A few pensioners had been members of the privileged class. Others, particularly the Scudder clients, had worked hard all of their lives, had fewer material items to lose, and were also more accustomed to struggling.

In the wake of these losses, we wonder about how age, gender and socio-economic class, taken together, influenced how clients used material culture to try to negotiate their personhood. There is evidence in the case files that many other clients, both male and female, considered how material culture impacted perceptions of their personal wellbeing. For example, we find numerous instances of clients negotiating with the LHMH over clothing budgets and the purchase of specific items of clothing. One woman (LHMFC Case # 526) recalls days past when she never appeared at the dining table without being dressed in an evening gown. These lost images are important, and this instance particularly highlights the struggle to renegotiate that sense of self—who am I now that I don't wear evening gowns (and am not *expected* to do so)? Even those who have not fallen as far in social class must still renegotiate their personhood. A man (LHMFC Case #244) laments that a suit that he bought a year and a half ago is badly worn and in need of repair, recognizing that it is no longer an option to buy something new. His concern is a social one: he wants to attend church services without feeling ashamed of his shabby appearance. These examples fit with Douglas and Ney's (1998) ideas about poverty and personhood. Because personhood is relational, individuals form value judgments about appropriate ways of living through their interactions with others. In these cases, we see how class-structured notions of self-presentation not only play into older people's sense of self, but also influence their choice about whether to engage in activities that were once important to them.

As we saw with the Ambrose sisters, appearances as well as activities are important. Some LHMH pensioners made efforts to maintain past friendships and memberships to exclusive clubs, such as Ada Dreyfus, described by Bailey Fakhoury and Dillaway.[2] Others maintained their sense of self through familiar activities, as Cora and Rose did with their plants and gardening. The following excerpt, dated February 11, 1931, from the Visitor's notes on Mrs. Clarissa Bradley (LHMFC Case #39) emphasizes the joy that some clients found in keeping up their home or gardens even (or especially) during distressing times:

> [She] is happy in the flowers and birds she has around her. A florist friend of [Mrs. Bradley's] built in a large flower box across the entire end of her solarium in which she has cultivated some beautiful ferns and flowering plants. . . . She takes great pride in her home, particularly in view of the fact that she is unable to get away from it except once or twice a year when someone takes her out in a car (LHMFC Case #39).

While the examples we used to illustrate the linkages between aging, personhood and material culture came from the Great Depression era, it is equally important to consider how these issues play out for many old people today. As gerontologists continue to examine the meanings of people's relationships with cherished and everyday objects and activities, and the multiple meanings of "home," we will learn even more about the social construction of personhood at different moments in the life course, but especially in old age. More work can certainly be done to explore how specific historical periods and economic times influence older individuals' relationships with material culture. What we do know, however, and what we see in the case of the Ambrose sisters, is that throughout the life course, humans continually interact with and relate to the social and material worlds. If we want to better understand aging in all its variety, we need to respect and learn from these important relationships.

Notes

1. Not all pensioners were as successful in getting what they asked for, especially between 1930 and 1934, when the LHMH was experiencing financial hardships of its own. Requests for additional funds from Scudder clients were almost always turned down due to "insufficient funds." Requests from Hannan clients were variously successful, depending on how well the clients could justify their needs. In comparing the files of the Ambrose sisters with those of other clients, such as Mrs. Train (see Ray, chapter 3) and Mr. Brown (see Ray, chapter 12), we see that socio-economic class figured into the Visitor's assessment of needs and the willingness of the LHMH to negotiate those needs. Race was also

clearly a factor (see Calasanti and Harrison, chapter 8).

2. See Bailey-Fakhoury and Dillaway (chapter 6) for descriptions of how other older women used property to maintain both personhood and privilege.

References

Belk, Russell. 1988. "Possessions and the Extended Self." *The Journal of Consumer Research* 15, no. 2: 139-68.

Berger, John. 1984. *And Our Faces, My Heart, Brief as Photos.* New York: Pantheon.

Boschetti, Margaret. 1995. "Attachment to Personal Possessions: An Interpretive Study of the Older Person's Experience." *Journal of Interior Design* 21, no. 1: 1-12.

Chaudhury, Habib. 2008. *Remembering Home: Rediscovering the Self in Dementia.* Baltimore, MD: John Hopkins University Press.

Chapman, Sherry Ann. (2006). "A New 'Materialist' Lens on Aging Well: Special Things in Later Life." *Journal of Aging Studies* 20: 206-16.

Csikszentmihalyi, Mihalyi and Eugene Rochberg-Halton. 1981. *The Meaning of Things: Domestic Symbols and the Self.* Cambridge: Cambridge University Press.

Dant, Tim. 1999. *Material Culture in the Social World: Values, Activities, Lifestyles.* Buckingham: Open University Press.

Douglas, Mary and Steven Ney. 1998. *Missing Persons: A Critique of Personhood in the Social Sciences.* Berkeley, CA: University of California Press.

Dowd, James J. 1975. "Aging as Exchange: A Preface to Theory." *Journal of Gerontology* 30, no. 5: 584-94.

Ekerdt, David J., Julie F. Sergeant, Molly Dingel, and Mary Elizabeth Bowen. 2004. "Household Disbandment in Later Life." *The Journals of Gerontology: Series B.* 59, no. 5: S265-S73.

Ekerdt, David J. and Julie F. Sergeant. 2006. "Family Things: Attending the Household Disbandment of Older Adults." *Journal of Aging Studies.* 20, no. 3: 193-205.

Fortes, Meyer. 1987. "The Concept of the Person." Pp. 247-86 in *Religion, Morality and the Person,* edited by J. Goody. Cambridge: Cambridge University Press.

Frank, Gelya. 2000. *Venus on Wheels: Two Decades of Dialogue on Disability, Biography And Being Female In America.* Berkeley, CA: University of California Press.

Geertz, Clifford. 1984. "From the Native's Point of View: On the Nature of Anthropological Understanding." Pp 221-37 in *Culture Theory: Essays On Mind, Self And Emotion,* edited by Richard A. Shweder and Robert A. LeVine. New York: Cambridge University Press.

Gell, Alfred. 1998. *Art and Agency: An Anthropological Theory.* New York: Oxford University Press.

Hallowell, Irving A. 1955. "Ojibwa Metaphysics of Being and the Perceptions of Persons." In *Culture and Experience,* edited by Irving A. Hallowell. Philadelphia: University of Pennsylvania Press.

Hoskins, Janet. 1998. *Biographical Objects: How Things Tell the Stories of*

People's Lives. New York: Routledge.

———. 2006. "Agency, Biography and Objects." Chapter 5 in *Handbook of Material Culture,* edited by Christopher Tilley, Webb Keane, Susanne Kuchler, Mike Rowlands and Patricia Spyer. New York: Sage.

Kopytoff, Igor. 1986. "The Cultural Biography of Things: Commoditization as Process." Pp. 64-91 in *The Social Life of Things: Commodities in Cultural Perspective,* edited by Arjun Appadurai. Cambridge: Cambridge University Press.

Lamb, Sarah. 1997. "The Making and Unmaking of Persons: Notes on Aging and Gender in North India." *Ethos* 25: 279-302.

———. 2000. *White Saris and Sweet Mangoes: Aging, Gender and Body in North India.* Berkeley, CA: University of California Press.

Langer, Susanne. K. 1977 [1953]. *Feeling and Form: A Theory of Art Developed from Philosophy in a New Key.* Upper Saddle River, NJ: Prentice Hall.

Leibing, Annette. 2006. "Divided Gazes: Alzheimer's Diseases, the Person within Life and Death." Pp. 240-68 in *Thinking about Dementia: Culture, Loss and the Anthropology of Senility,* edited by Annette Leibing and Lawrence Cohen. New Brunswick, NJ: Rutgers University Press.

Luborsky, Mark R. 1994. "The Cultural Adversity of Physical Disability: Erosion of Full Adult Personhood." *Journal of Aging Studies* 8, no. 3: 239-53.

Luella Hannan Memorial Foundation Collection (LHMFC). Walter Reuther Library of Labor and Urban Affairs, Wayne State University, Detroit, MI.

Mc Lean, Athena. 2007. *The Person in Dementia: A Study of Nursing Home Care in the U.S.* Peterborough, Ontario: Broadview Press.

Marsden, John, Sherylyn Briller, Margaret Calkins, and Mark Proffitt. 2001. "Enhancing Identity and Sense of Home Vol 4." In *Creating Successful Dementia Care Settings* (series), M.P. Calkins. Baltimore, MD: Health Professions Press.

Marx, Jonathan. I., Jennifer C. Solomon, and Lee Q. Miller. 2004. "Gift Wrapping Ourselves: The Final Gift Exchange." *Journal of Gerontology: Social Sciences* 59B, 5: S274-S80.

Mauss, Marcel. 1985. "A Category of the Human Mind: The Notion of Person; the Notion of Self." Pp. 1-25 in *The Category of the Person: Anthropology, Philosophy, History,* edited by M. Carrithers, S. Collins and S. Lukes, 1-25. Cambridge: Cambridge University Press. Originally published as Une Catégorie de L'esprit Humain: La Notion de Personne, Cellede "Moi." In *Sociologie et Anthropologie, 331-62.* (Paris: Presses Universitaires de France, 1935).

———. 1990. *The Gift: Forms and Functions of Exchange in Archaic Societies.* W.D. Hall, trans,. London: Routledge. Originally published as Essai Sur Le Don: Forme et Raison de L'échange dans Les Sociétés Archaïques. in *Sociologie et Anthropologie, 143-279.* (Paris: Presses Universitaires de France, 1925).

McCracken, Grant. 1987. "Culture and Consumption among the Elderly: Three

Research Objectives in an Emerging Field." *Aging and Society* 7, no. 2: 203-24.

Miller, Daniel. 1994. "Artifacts and the Meanings of Things." In *Companion Encyclopedia of Anthropology,* edited by T. Ingold. London: Routledge.

Murphy, Robert F. 1990. *The Body Silent: The Different World of the Disabled.* New York: W.W. Norton.

Ochs, Elinor and Lisa Capps. 1996. "Narrating the Self." *Annual Review of Anthropology* 25, no. 1: 19-43.

Pearce, Susan. M. 1992. *Museums, Objects, and Collections: A Cultural Study.* Washington, D.C.: Smithsonian Institute Press.

Rowles, Graham. D. 2006. "A House Is Not a Home; But Can It Become One?" Pp. 25-32 in *The Many Faces of Health, Competence and Well Being in Old Age: Integrating Epidemiological, Psychological and Social Perspectives,* edited by H-W Wahl, H. Brenner, H. Mollenkopf, D. Rothenbacher and C. Rott. Netherlands: Springer.

Shweder, Richard and Edmund Bourne. 1984. "Does the Concept of the Person Vary Cross-Culturally?" Pp. 113-55 in *Culture Theory: Essays on Mind, Self and Emotion,* edited by R. Shweder and R. LeVine. New York, NY: Cambridge University Press.

Strathern, Marilyn. 1992. *Reproducing the Future: Essays on Anthropology, Kinship and the New Reproductive Technologies.* New York: Routledge.

Tilley, Christopher. 2007. "Ethnography and Material Culture." Pp. 258-72 in *Handbook of Ethnography,* edited by P. A. Atkinson, S. Delamont, A. J. Coffey, and J. Lofland. London: Sage.

Weiner, Annette. B. 1985. "Inalienable Wealth." *American Ethnologist* 12, no. 2: 210-27.

———. 1992. *Inalienable Possessions.* Berkely, CA: University of California Press.

———. 1994. "Cultural Difference and the Density of Objects." *American Ethnologist,* 21 no. 2: 391-403.

Wiles, Janine, Ruth Allen, Anthea Palmer, Karen Hayman, Sally Keeling, and Ngaire Kerse. 2009. "Older People and Their Social Spaces: A Study of Well-Being and Attachment to Place in Aotearoa New Zealand." *Social Science and Medicine* 68, no. 4: 664-71.

Chapter 8

Race, Class, Gender, and the Social Construction of "Burden" in Old Age

Toni Calasanti and Jill Harrison

Introduction

In this chapter, we look at the intersections of race, class, and gender through a focus on African-American clients, comparing them with white clients to show how social location influences the construction of "burden" and "deservingness" in old age. We begin with economic dependence and ask, how it is that some clients are seen to deserve help while others are not? To the extent that interpretations of such client data as income levels depend upon other ascribed characteristics, we can see these to be related to social location. Thus, while we recognize that a range of economic factors, policies, and the like, place people in positions in which they are more or less likely to become economically dependent, we focus on how such dependence is assessed as more or less burdensome or deserved. Further, we show that these evaluations alter over the courses of clients' careers with the institution, and thus that the maintenance of worth is an on-going project.

When Visitors determined whether an applicant was in "need" (recognized as dependent) they negotiated deservingness and appropriate burden for the organization to assume, with potential clients who presented themselves in ways designed to ensure that the Visitors recommended them for aid. In this chapter, we refer to this process as "needs talk," a term used by Fraser (1989) to describe the process by which experts, such as caseworkers, decide whom should be allocated charitable funds, how much, and why. Our analysis is an extension of the needs talk concept as a process related to the moral economy (Kail, Quadagno, and

Keene 2009) of decision-making about the (un)deservingness of LHMH clients. Not only do we find that the organization's experts (Visitors, and ultimately Leon Frost and the board of trustees) made decisions about the needs and allocation of funds to clients, but clients also influenced this process by engaging in their own "needs talk" with the experts.

Because the publicized mission of the LHMH indicated that the pension funds were to help older adults who had "seen better days," applicants demonstrated their deservingness through various types of interactions with Visitors, such as interviews, home visits, shopping trips, and correspondence. Using case files of African-American clients, we compare "worthy Black" clients to "worthy white" clients. We argue that securing and maintaining funding as a client of the LHMH was based on engaging in needs talk deemed appropriate based on social location. In general, "deserving whites" received more latitude in the negotiation of their needs with the LHMH organization than did "deserving Blacks," a finding that coincides with race relations in Detroit during this time period.

Deservingness and Burden as Social Constructions

When one is viewed as a burden, the issue is not so much whether or not one must rely on others but whether or not one is deemed to be worthy of receiving such support. Those who need support are thus constructed as more or less deserving versus more or less burdensome. Because such designations are socially derived, they can also change in application over time.

Previous research on old age has shown that ageism plays an important part in constructing old people as (potential) burdens rather than worthy recipients of support. Children, for example, are dependent; nevertheless, they generally are not viewed as burdens (Calasanti 2003). Indeed, the construction of old people as burdensome is often used to frame debates about intergenerational equity, wherein old people are depicted as taking valuable resources away from children (Binstock 2005; Pampel 1998). At the same time, old people's dependence is not labeled similarly across the board; we argue that age intersects with race, class, and gender in designating the extent to which *particular* old people are seen to be burdens.

Political economists who study aging explore "the social, political, and economic processes involved in the distribution of scarce resources and the ways that the state and market economy" influence resource re-allocation (Kail, Quadagno, and Keene 2009, 555). Those who have the greatest power within a political economic system and garner the most resources also have the greatest ability to promote their beliefs about who deserves social largesse. Thus, the prevalent "moral economy" tends to contain values that reflect and reinforce the prevalent distribution of resources (Kail, et al. 2009, 560). Evaluations of deservingness are based on the extent to which recipients are seen to reflect such values, and policies that address their needs are designed accordingly. In looking at Hannan clients, we argue that the designations of deservingness varied by class, gender, and—our main focus in this chapter—race.

Within the capitalist economy of the U.S. in the 1920s, paid work was (and still is) highly valued. Such values can be seen in the different kinds of public assistance given. For example, social assistance programs for poor people, which are derived from the old British poor laws, are meant to provide benefits that are less desirable than what the lowest wage earners would receive, in order to ensure that recipients would not become dependent upon such assistance (Kail et al. 2009). Implicit in this model is the idea that such beneficiaries are not worthy of assistance; they need to be taught to value work, even if poorly paid. The LHMH reflects similar values. According to Zunz (1982, 261), "middle-class Protestant charity workers" who worked with the poor in Detroit at that time exemplified the broader national ideology that "attributed destitution to personal failings such as idleness, intemperance, or simply ignorance." They thus sought to serve the "'deserving poor,' destitute through no fault of their own"—who could be recognized as somehow different from those who were poor because of their individual traits. As we will show, then, potential Hannan clients needed to show they had middle-class work values, by demonstrating possession of previous wealth or a steady work history in a reputable job (or jobs), in order to be "entitled" to help—i.e., deserving. Middle-class and wealthy women of this era could demonstrate deservingness through their husband's work (i.e., he earned enough to support his wife); such wives were to take care of public and private reproductive labor. Of course, single women and working-class women whose husbands were not well to do were expected to have engaged in paid labor to be seen as deserving.

Race intersects with class and gender in determining potential clients' deservingness, and we focus on this in particular. Certainly, race influences class such that Black men and women of this era were likely to be working-class. In this pre-Civil Rights era, racial discrimination in the workplace was such that Blacks were both occupationally segregated and paid less than whites for similar work.

Race also has its own impact. Though Detroit had no Jim Crow laws, Blacks and whites were segregated, by residence and in every other way. Potential clients of the Hannan Foundation worked and raised families during the late nineteenth and early twentieth centuries. According to Zunz's (1982) history of race relations in Detroit at that time, Blacks did not experience the frequency of racial violence that occurred in such places as Chicago. It occurred but was generally confined to small areas and rarely erupted into riots. Zunz (1982, 374) notes that "Racist impulses were expressed . . . in many other ways than killing Blacks on the street." Blacks faced "continuous form[s] of local discrimination," including being relegated to living in only one part of the city, a result of private agreements in other areas not to sell real estate to Blacks.

Racism thus influenced all Blacks, regardless of class, and influenced the work of many civic institutions. In her discussion of Detroit race relations at the time, Martin (2007) notes that agencies that served the Black community "proudly boasted of their work among African-Americans, all the while emphasizing the separateness of the two races and the superiority of the white race to the African-American race." Likewise, health care facilities segregated services to Blacks and whites, which caused some difficulties for Visitors wanting to arrange medical or convalescent care for Black clients.

In this chapter, we argue that race shaped the deservingness of clients, such that Blacks and whites differed in terms of presentation of selves and outcomes of their cases. That is, while all applicants for LHMH funds were economically dependent and thus shared some situations, we find differences based on race in the process of receiving and maintaining funding. We compare the only five Black applicants during this period—only two of whom were funded—with white cases. While the small number of Black cases—itself a reflection of race relations—may give pause, we have many examples of white clients who present themselves differently, and yet still received funding; and still others whose behavior is similar but who drew different responses. We argue that initial decisions and duration of funding were shaped by race, class and gender.

"Needs Talk" and Evidence Used

Determining applicant worthiness for aid is tied to assessment by an authority of what a group of people really needs (Fraser 1989). This type of "needs talk" reflects the categories used by experts (social workers, politicians, and the like) to determine and develop policies related to the appropriate allocation of charitable and government funds (Brush 1997; Fraser 1989). Brush (1997), for example, found that case workers evaluated single mothers who applied for charitable or governmental support based on their conformity to race and class-based ideals of proper womanhood in a particular socio-historical context (i.e., "worthy widows and welfare cheats"). Similarly, Mohr (1994) found that relief organizations in New York City in the early 1900s assessed clients' "worthiness" based on moral categories related to the political and economic climate at the time. Soldiers and widows were more likely to be entitled to benefits because their status was linked to highly valued morals, for example. These designations of worthiness refer to a type of "moral economy" that is meant to justify differential distributions of resources. Analyzing needs talk as a discourse between those who confer aid and those who receive or are denied such help illuminates the power relations that shaped the moral economy of the time. Zunz (1982, 261) notes that Visitors of that era both used their middle class status to judge clients, and also "saw in their roles a chance to offer the poor a model of middle-class life."

In our analysis, we rely on two sources of data for needs talk. The first reflects assessments by the organizations experts (Visitors, Mr. Frost, and board of trustees) about what the clients needed; these data are found in the Visitor's case notes, described earlier by Ray (see also Ray 2008; Durocher and Gray 2008). While these data do not come directly from clients, Visitors took great pains to detail as much as possible concerning each clients visit, request, and the like. In addition, these notes are an excellent source of data concerning how clients' self-presentations were perceived.

Our second source of data comes from the correspondence included in all case files, and reflects clients' notions of what they needed. While Visitors' notes reference these, and summarize the contents of letters, the letters themselves provide important clues about self-presentations, in particular. That is, letters are the only source of data that we have about clients that is not mediated by Visitors' perceptions. Letters were a more common means of communication at that time (telephones were also used, though some clients appeared to have less access to these than others), and these missives give us some idea of the relationship between the

LHMH and clients. Typically, letters from clients revolved around requests (for such things as clothing, doctor or dental appointments, permission to travel, etc.), updating their addresses so that checks would be sent to the proper location (moving could be quite frequent as clients sought cheaper or more suitable housing), or thanks (for birthday and Christmas cards, clothing, and the like). In addition, clients sometimes wrote to object to a policy or some other aspect of the LHMH.

Constructions of Deservingness and Race, Class and Gender

We begin with examples of deservingness in relation to social location.

Class was critical to being considered a deserving client in two ways. First, as discussed in previous chapters (e.g., Ray), clients were funded from either the original Hannan fund—which was granted to those who had been "accustomed to enjoying the comforts of life," a class-based yardstick that encompassed both material access and a particular lifestyle and access to social resources; or the Scudder fund, which could be distributed "without regard to race, creed, sex or color" (Ray 2008, 161).

Thus, Jane Dowdy (case #329), for example, a white woman who received Hannan funds for fourteen years was described by her Visitor after her intake interview as "refined, respectable, and proud. She is a woman who had many advantages in her girlhood and childhood, being of a family who were well to do." Second, all clients—of either fund—needed to display traits that reflected the morality of white, middle class men and women, regardless of a his or her previous financial situation. The role of class and class-based morality is apparent in the following examples.

Betsy Matthews (#415) was interviewed on May 16, 1930, in the Visitor's office. Having been widowed from her first husband of ten years, Mrs. Matthews was divorced from a husband who deserted her when she became very ill. She worked thereafter as a housekeeper and practical nurse. The Visitor described her as having a pleasing manner and used other similarly positive terms. The file then states that "This case is to be kept on file and considered later for Scudder Fund." Evidently, Mrs. Matthews displayed the appropriate middle-class values for a positive evaluation, but her work as a housekeeper and practical nurse designated her as working class. However, when the Visitor went to visit Mrs. Matthews to see if she had applied to the Department of Public Welfare, she found Mrs. Matthews was out. The woman with whom Mrs. Matthews was living temporarily talked with the Visitor, and the latter reported "that W[oman] is a refined and likeable sort of person with an admirable disposition and many friends. V learned that W has traveled some during her life having been to Boston and other eastern cities and west as far as Oklahoma" (LHMFC, Case #415). This information caused the Visitor to reconsider, and she noted that "Further investigation proved W to be of a higher type than had first been supposed." She then asked the Board to approve Mrs. Matthews for a Hannan grant, which was approved. Having displayed both the appropriate moral economy and class, Mrs. Matthews became a Hannan client.

By contrast, we have the case of Amy Bateman (Case #356), a seventy-five year-old, white woman who was quite deaf. According to the Visitor's notes, at her initial visit she found Mrs. Bateman with "six or seven Mexicans" who said they had been caring for her but could no longer. Further investigation found Mrs. Bateman and her deceased husband to have been "two of the most disreputable characters" who were reported to have been "involved in underworld activities, drunken orgies and common-law marriages." He presumably had a venereal disease, and since he died, Mrs. Bateman was found to be living in a "room in a filthy condition." Mrs. Bateman's evident lack of deservingness was apparent in the Visitor's assertion that "it was decided at the time that this case could not be considered even as a Scudder case, not to mention a Luella Hannan case" (LHMFC, Case #356).

This class distinction is shaped by race and gender relations, however. The Visitor's notes in relation to the Black applicants make clear that they all demonstrated the appropriate middle-class values, although they did not all share the same class background. For instance, the Visitor's notes on Hannah Steele (Case #104) refer to such class-based cultural capital as education, reading interests, and travel. An eighty-five year old Black woman, Mrs. Steele was referred to LHMH by a member of the Detroit Urban League who wrote that he "was happy, indeed to learn that something is being done for old people of the refined class." The Visitor's description of Mrs. Steele placed her as a part of "a very intelligent negro family, who have undoubtedly seen better days." Her deservingness was further supported by the fact that Hannah went to college in Washington, D.C., and her home had an aged mahogany piano, "bookcases well filled with good books, among which might be seen *Fifteen Plays* by Shakespeare, Emerson's Works, Mrs. Browning's Poems, twenty-three volumes of the *New International Encyclopedia*, Tennyson's *Idylls of the King*, and many others" (LHMFC, Case #104). Had Mrs.

Steele not withdrawn her case from consideration, it seems likely she would have been recommended for funding.

By contrast, we have the cases of both Cora Price (Case #196) and Amelia Gardner (Case #188), old Black women who were illiterate as they had received no education. Given their race and gender, they were even more constrained than white women in employment options, and thus worked in domestic labor, as cooks in private homes. Interestingly, the Visitor describes them in similar ways. Cora is "fairly well mannered, and aside from that has no outstanding characteristic." Amelia is "fickle, sympathetic and kind, but has no outstanding characteristics." Neither was funded as Scudder funds are exhausted by that time. In Cora's case, the Visitor recommends she be reconsidered for Scudder funds should that trust be increased; Amelia is simply referred to DPW.

Despite these apparent class differences, however, no Blacks clients were considered for Hannan funds. While the Hannan mandate does not explicitly exclude Blacks, race relations were such that they were implicitly excluded—i.e., if a policy, etc., did not explicitly state Blacks *were* eligible, they were not. Thus we see that Reverend Burke (Case #122), a Black man, was first referred to the LHMH in March, 1929. However, his case was not investigated at that time as, according to Mr. Frost's letter, the foundation was "unable to undertake the care of colored people." It was only in June, when Scudder funds, which explicitly stated that no discrimination was to occur on the basis of race became available, that Rev. Burke's case was investigated and, ultimately, approved.

Beyond the policy differences that shaped possibilities for Black and white clients, race mattered in other important ways: through (potential) clients' presentation of self, and in terms of outcomes. In our discussion of these areas below, we also point to ways that gender intersected with race to shape Rev. Burke's and Rachel Little's experiences with LHMH.

Clients' Presentation of Self

Race, class and gender shaped the ways that applicants and clients of the LHMH presented themselves, as evidenced by clients' correspondence.

Regardless of social location, correspondence tended to be polite, and often appreciative; in terms of the latter, religion or God was often invoked. Since much of the correspondence was related to requests of various types, it could sometimes be quite businesslike. Interestingly, while all clients might reference their lives, women were more likely to include personal comments about the Visitor's lives. Letters also often reflected clients' knowledge that they were dependent, and to the extent that this is the case, we found letters from both Blacks and whites that expressed some level of deference. Still, the letters from the Black clients differed from those of whites in two important ways. First, they never were assertive or tried to negotiate their status (in contrast to the behaviors seen in other chapters, such as Bailey-Fakhoury and Dillaway's). Second, they were far more deferential than any of the white clients. While white Scudder clients were functionally in the same position as the two Black clients, none of the whites expressed the kind of deference that the Blacks did. And, as we will show, this deference reflected gender as well.

In her history of race relations in Detroit in the 1920s, Martin (2007) notes that Blacks—regardless of class—needed to demonstrate deference to whites in order to receive help. She says that "As much as [Black leaders of the Urban League] and other Blacks despised the condescension of their benefactors, they generally found it necessary to submit in silence. . . . Whenever there was a conflict between whites and Black elites, Blacks usually retreated. . . . Though Black elites were often humiliated by the subservient position they had to assume, they did what they believed would best serve the interest of their community." We see this deference in the letters of Black clients; a kind and level of deference that differs dramatically from that displayed by white clients.

For instance, and beginning with white clients, when he finds he has been approved to receive funds, James Wilkinson (Case #454, letter 14) writes[1]:

> My dear Mr. Frost
> Your kind letter of Dec. 8 rec'd and content noted. You can rest assured that I will comply strictly with your instructions.
> I cannot expressed [sic] to you what a God send it was to me in my febbel condition! as my Christmas and New Year this year was becoming a nightmare to me. And I'm sure you will never regret your kindness to me.
> Respectfully Yours,
> James J. Wilkinson

Subsequent letters are polite, sometimes grateful (e.g., thanking LHMH for Christmas money received), and sometimes included requests for dental and medical care. At one point, he runs afoul of the organization as they learn that he has been getting some money from the DPW as well. He is able to negotiate this, however, by giving up his additional funds and thus retaining his Hannan grant (he was transferred to the

Scudder fund later). He writes to them (letter #29) on September 27, thanking them for the continued grant, closing his letter with "thank you again for all past favors. Your Respectfully."

Letters from other white men receiving Hannan funds are quite similar. What we want to emphasize here are two points. First, Mr. Wilkinson is always polite and often grateful, and expresses this; second, he violates rules, yet is able to continue to receive funds. Similarly, we have the case of Paul Baker (Case #171), who was funded by the Scudder trust for 15 years, 1929-1944. While he began as part of a couple, his wife died in 1930 and he continued as a client thereafter. His letters also express gratitude, and acknowledge his dependence. After his wife died, he wrote (letter #19):

> Kindly accept my Sincerest thanks for the Kindly Interest the Board has taken In regards to our Marital Welfare and I Wish to thank the Board once More for the fine Burial Service extended to the Departed My beloved [Carrie Baker] and I further Wish to thank the Board for their fine Increase in my Monthly Allowance.
> Thanking you all again for Both of us
> I Remain your
> Respectfully
> Paul Baker

Similarly, in response to a birthday greeting, he writes (letter 22)

> Your kindly Greeting Received and I Wish to thank you very kindly as I enjoyed It More than all the Money you Could have Send In Its Place so please except my hearty thanks and appreciation
> Your Respectfully
> Paul Baker
> My Regards and Best Wishes to you all

Other letters (e.g., #28 and 29) began by saying "To my Kind Benefactor," and often ended with such closures as "Your Kind and Real Friend"—and elsewhere, in letter texts, referred to the LHMH staff as friends.

Yet, he too violated rules. For instance, in Sept. 1932, he borrowed money from a friend in order to pay for room and board for a month. He paid back the friend, but he did not get permission to do all of this in advance. And on another occasion (letter #53) he wrote that he had spent more money than was allotted for a suit because he needed one that was heavier; LHMH paid this bill without objection.

Contrast Wilkinson and Baker with Rev. David Burke (Case #122), a Black male client. Throughout Rev. Burke's correspondence we hear gratitude and appreciation. When he finds out he is to receive Scudder funds he writes to Leon Frost,

> I am unable to find words that will exactly express my gratitude to you [and the Visitor] for deciding and causing the Board of Trustees to decide in favor [of] my receiving a pension. . . . I shall strive to use every dollar of it judiciously and with due consideration for the spirit of benevolence it expresses. I am thankfully
> Yours, D.W. Burke. (Letter #10)

But his writings often express far more deference and appreciation than what we hear from white clients, male or female. For instance, in letter #15 he wrote:

> Since you and your duties have touched my otherwise barren existence, I have experienced a period of peace and cessation of worry. My regret is in writing you this note, I realize that words often proved very poor vehicles sometimes futile in conveying those thanks wherein there is 100% of genuine heartfelt, gratitude.

And in letter #43 he wrote to thank the Visitor for arranging medical care, saying that "You see you have very greatly increased my debt of gratitude. I thank, thank, thank [double underline] you, and hope for you the reward which the Master above bestows upon the good."

In addition, we find in his letters (as well as the Visitors' case notes) frequent concern expressed that he not overstep, or do anything that would offend his benefactors or cause him to lose funding. For instance, when reminding the Visitor that she had promised to get him needed medical help, he wrote (letter #26)

> I am reminding you of your kind promise to get the doctor for me. As I am very much in need of medical attention. I truly hope that I am not too great a burden to you.
> "Life has a burden for every one's shoulder;
> None can escape from its trouble snare
> Miss it in youth it will come when you're older
> And fit you as close as the garment you wear."
> Just trying to modify anything unpleasant in asking after you had promised.

And again, when he needed dental work:

I am anxious to prove myself grateful to those who are managing the
Hannan Fund, of which I am a grateful beneficiary. . . . Do you think I
am making too great a draft upon your fund of sympathy of responsibility to ask if you would feel free to ask if I can have my teeth attended
to? . . . [T]he condition of my mouth . . . is giving me considerable
pain. I know this is not discretionary with you, but I want you to say
whether you think it advisable for me to make this additional request
for favor from a source which has wonderfully helped me? . . . Please
dismiss and forget it if you think this will in any way strain the relation
existing between my benefactors and me. (letter #44)

Finally, as happened with many clients as the trust ran low on funds,
Rev. Burke found his pension cut. While some clients expressed great
dismay or disappointment at this turn of events, Rev. Burke writes in a
way which clearly references race relations, deference, acceptance of this
decrease and his related anxiety about his future:

From the beginning of the beneficience, I have felt myself extremely
fortunate in the reception of this gratuity. No day has past that I have
not expressed my gratitude to God and prayed for those who administer
the fund. I now thank you Mr. Frost and all concerned for what has
come to me through you. I have been fearful that I might do something
to make you change your attitude toward me, as a pensioner and I assure you I am thankful it is no worse Yes Sir I regard your treatment of
me as a consideration of my group far beyond anything that could have
been expected. I hope I have come within the requirements of a benefactor of the fund. If there is anything I can do to prove myself grateful,
let me know. . . . I write [lest] my not writing would be misunderstood.
Again thanking you I am yours very gratefully (letter 44, Case #122).

In later correspondence, Rev. Burke offers to show his gratitude to
the foundation by having his son, a chorister from Chicago, give a "free
recital at which a voluntary offering would be taken to be used in any
way Mr. Frost saw fit" (Case #122). He makes clear that only a "few"
Blacks would be in attendance and thus whites would not be made to feel
uncomfortable. Mr. Frost promptly directs the Visitor to write that such a
plan "is neither necessary or desirable." Implicit recognition of race relations and a constant concern that lack of contact with the Visitor pres-
aged a loss of funding, Rev. Burke then went to the office "to learn why
V and not been to see him recently. He stated that he was afraid he had
said something in his last letter which he should not have said" (Case
#122).

Letters from the lone female Black client, Rachel Little (Case #132), also express great deference, but in a manner that differs from Burke's and points to the gendered nature of race relations. Despite the fact that Black women would be expected to work throughout their lives, the white, middle-class notion of women as dependent beings influences Black women as well. Thus, we find that in her letters, Mrs. Little often evokes not only gendered relational imagery—of friendship, and of family—but also that of a dependent child, an image that reflects race relations as well. We see this in the following excerpts, mostly written in response to various holiday and birthday greetings she has received:

> Letter #17: "Your loving thoughts of me are like rays of sunshine in my life, and I am deeply grateful to you, and thank my Heavenly Father for giving me friends like you."
>
> Letter #19: "I thank God for giving me friends like you, for you have made life for me much more worth living, and I am happy in knowing there is always a cheery message coming from you, even though time is growing shorter each year, and by most people I am forgotten. For when we get old, we are sometimes in the way. . . . [M]y heart is made glad when I hear [your message] read."
>
> Letter #20: "May this New Year bring to you all the treasures worth possessing—love, health, wealth, and happiness. Not a day without a blessing is the sincere wish of your grateful child, R.D. Little."
>
> Letter #24: "I take this opportunity to thank you for your wonderful kindness and and [sic] generosity extended me during all the time I have been in your family. . . . [F]rom the very innermost recesses of my being I thank you."
>
> Letter #25 "Words fail me to express my thanks and gratitude to you for the comforts you have given me since I became a member of your great family. And you can never realize the joy and comfort you are bringing to your aged children."
>
> Letter #26 "May this year be filled with blessings and may 'the children' give you less work is the desire of a very grateful child." (LHMFC, Case #132)

No other letter from any client that we (or other members of the research team) read expressed this sort of "child" imagery. Family might be alluded to; but not being a child.

Client Outcomes

Finally, race and gender shaped client outcomes, through Visitors' perceptions of clients' actions. A brief overview of the two Black clients and comparison with others helps make this clear.

In the case of Rachel Little, her continued conformity to appropriate behavior based on her race and gender allowed her to continue to be seen as deserving and maintain funding until her death. In conforming to middle-class notions of productivity for aging Black women, she needed to demonstrate industriousness for as long as possible; she also needed to evince an attitude of deference and gratitude that also displays an appropriate view of race relations. The overview of her case, which helps to illuminate these points, follows.

Mrs. Little, who lived in an old frame house in a very poor and run-down neighborhood with her adopted daughter, was a 65 year-old, blind Black woman who was referred to LHMH by the Detroit League for the Handicapped. She was born in 1863 in Leesburg, Virginia, one of six children of which only one other, a sister, remained alive. Many years later, when her sister—who remembered many events from the Civil War—was visiting her in Detroit, the Visitor learned that their father was a slave but their mother "had been freed by an 'enlightened master' so her children were all considered free even before the Emancipation Proclamation."

Mrs. Little went to school through the eighth grade, after which she left to earn her living doing housework. She married James Richards in 1883; they had no children but adopted a five year-old daughter. James owned a barber shop in which Mrs. Little helped by giving scalp treatments. Unfortunately, James died of pneumonia in 1902, at which point Mrs. Little returned to housekeeping. Five years later, she married Jud Little, who worked as a salesman in North Branch, Michigan. In 1916, after 9 years of marriage, they separated and Mrs. Little moved to Detroit to live with her daughter. Of her husband, Mrs. Little said that, "she had heard nothing from him for twelve years, does not know whether he is dead or living, and states that he was not worth 'three rows of pins' (file#132)." Mrs. Little worked as a nursemaid for several families in Detroit and also did day work—dishes and housework—until glaucoma caused her to lose her sight. Her only source of income was from hemming wash clothes for the Detroit League for the Handicapped for which she earned, at that time, between two to three dollars twice a month.

Mrs. Little attended the Metropolitan Church for Colored People, and said that she enjoyed singing hymns during the service. Her other favorite past time included reading the Bible using the Braille system. How she came to learn Braille is important for showing her work ethic and resolve, and is described in the Visitor's notes as follows:

> The teacher said she was too old to learn as she was 61 years at the time she asked to be taught. [Mrs. Little] told the teacher that "Only one thing beats a trial, and that is a failure." So the teacher said that as long as she was so anxious she would give her a trial . . . and [she] very readily learned the Braille System (LHMFC, Case #132).

Mrs. Little was awarded a thirty dollar pension from the Scudder trust in late July 1929. She continued to hem washcloths for the League for the Handicapped to supplement this grant and because "it keeps her mind occupied." She read by Braille constantly, and listened to the radio, following politics as well as the exploits of the Detroit Tigers' baseball team, of whom she was a great fan.

Over the thirteen years that Mrs. Little received a pension, she was repeatedly described by the Visitor (of which she had four) as "uncomplaining" and "cheerful." For example, in March, 1930, the Visitor writes, "Mrs. Little never complains about anything and enjoys all advantages given her." In April, 1930, the Visitor writes that "she is intelligent, cheerful, and uncomplaining," and again in January, 1931, she note that when she visited, Mrs. Little "was reading her Bible. She seemed to be in good health and was cheerful and uncomplaining as usual (file#132)." Similar descriptions appear throughout the years in the file.

In addition, the notations in Mrs. Little's file characterize her as displaying traits in accordance with middle-class values. Her blindness did not deter her from learning Braille, saving her money to purchase the Bible in Braille, writing letters, sewing towels for the Handicapped League, attending parties at the League and interacting with friends. She also displays attitudes concerning race relations of which the Visitor apparently approved. As we saw in her letters above, Mrs. Little constantly expressed gratitude to the organization for her pension; indeed in December, 1931, the Visitor wrote that Mrs. Little "asked that she be reported as the happiest client on the list." But the Visitor's notes also tell us that:

> W showed an amazing grasp of local and foreign political affairs and of the problems of her own race. W feels that the colored people are better off in the South where their social status is definitely set. She feels these conditions are better both for the colored and the white race. In the South because the two have their own separate schools, churches, stores, etc., the colored people are more stable. More of them engage in

small businesses and the professions. [Here] . . . since they can associate on a wider basis with the white people yet are not accepted as
equals, it creates inharmonious and contradictory situations which
make the colored people unhappy and envious (LHMFC, Case #132).

Overall, then, Mrs. Little displays white, middle-class views of race,
class, gender. As a Black woman, she is expected to have a paid work
history and to continue to earn money as long as possible; in addition to
industriousness, she should hold the appropriate racial attitudes not only
in terms of what she says, but also by expressing the kind of deference
and gratitude that shows that she understand that she is being helped by
those who are "superior." A part of this is the unspoken mandate that she
should act in ways that never challenge or presents difficulties for the
foundation—a reality that Rev. Burke's constant worry about offending
LHMH staff echoes.

By contrast, for whites, maintaining "deservingness" and funding
was possible even if one did present problems or violate rules. Earlier,
we gave examples of two white men who violated rules. There are many
similar examples in the files, including men and women, both Scudder
and Hannan clients, and much more serious rule violations. What stands
out in all these cases is the latitude that white clients are given relative to
Blacks. Many white clients repeatedly violated rules or caused problems
and were never taken off funding; others did so for quite some time before losing their pensions. For instance, Fred Carter (Case #) was funded
for seven years before his pension was ended. Based on the Visitor's investigation, it was found that Mr. Carter, who had worked as a newspaper
reporter and as a law clerk, had not been an exceptionally kind father and
had not been able to get along with his wife and his relatives. There were
also reports that he drank to excess. However, because of his class background and despite these negatives, he was accepted as a Hannan client.
Because of continued reports about his drinking from landlords and others, about which he was continually warned, after four years, he was
moved to the Scudder fund. At this point, according to the case notes, the
V "told him point-blank" that if he did not stop drinking, the Board
might drop him altogether. They did, eventually, but not for another three
years.

The contrast between Mr. Carter, and many similar cases involving
white clients and that of Rev. Burke (Case #122), the Black male recipient is striking. The Rev. Burke was seventy-one years of age in 1929
when he was referred to LHMH. He had been born in South Carolina to
parents who were both slaves; he was also a slave for several years. He

moved to Georgia at age seven, and attended public school through the eighth grade. Later he attended Fisk University, graduated from New Orleans University, and Gammon Theological Seminary in Atlanta, Georgia. He had taught at various places in Georgia, Arkansas, and at the Tuskegee Institute in Alabama, and this background led to the Visitor's positive depiction that "One can tell at once that Reverend Burke is cultured and educated. He is also an intelligent man."

Rev. Burke had suffered poor health for some years, particularly diabetes and poor vision, and as a result was unable to earn his living by preaching at his own church. He was married, but had been separated from his wife for ten years. Of his six living children, two daughters helped support his wife; two sons were show men and had no certain addresses; the other two sons were married and had their own families to support.

As we noted earlier, both his letters and the V's notes demonstrate a level of anxiety about being cut off funding that we found in no other case. Throughout his time as a Scudder client, Rev. Burke was very careful to not run afoul of the organization, constantly inquiring as to whether or not it would be permissible to engage in a variety of activities, and making clear that he neither wanted to violate rules nor cause the staff any inconvenience. He sometimes became anxious if he did not see the Visitor for a while, believing it was bad news. The fact that he is not a white client seemed to be one reason for his concern; on one occasion he told the V that he was uncomfortable at his present residence because the landlord's wife was white, and he was uncomfortable around white people. He then asked her how many Blacks were clients of the LHMH.

He lived for a short while with one daughter, a situation which changed when she needed to care for her ailing husband. This same daughter also undertook to help with his care when he became hospitalized in January, 1933, due to a serious "heart block." During his convalescence, he appears to have become confused, and doesn't realize that he has already endorsed his pension check, and thus sends a letter of inquiry. While Mr. Frost takes this to mean that Rev. Burke is "no doubt psychopathic" and will likely need to go to Eloise soon, the Visitor (then Marie Slack) explains that he is simply suffering from poor memory. However, shortly thereafter, Rev. Burke requests four dollars to pay a bill. Despite being cautioned not to run up bills on credit, he did so, buying two chairs and a rug with his daughter. When the Visitor (now Anna Wentink) suggested that he simply let the furniture company repossess the goods, he became upset at the prospect. The case notes, which are followed by Leon Frost's initials, then say that "In view of the fact that this man seems unable to co-operate properly and also that there is grave doubt as to his mental competency . . . it was unanimously recommended that we withdraw our support as of March 15." Found to have violated LHMH rules, he was thus dropped from the rolls. He protested, as did Reverend Bradby on his behalf, but LHMH does not re-consider, saying that "he has repeatedly refused to cooperate with us." The last entry states that a worker from the Department of Public Welfare has come in to read Rev. Burke's file as he has applied for aid from this agency.

Like Mr. Carter and other white clients, Rev. Burke was a well-educated and well-written man. But similar behavior—belief on the part of the Visitor that rules have been violated—leads to different vastly different outcomes and, in Rev. Burke's case, after only one incident.

Conclusion

Deservingness—in Detroit of the 1920s and 30s, as well as today—is shaped not only by age but by race, class, and gender. It is not simply that race influences class but, as we see in the cases of Black clients of the LHMH, race has an additional impact. Black clients were less likely to apply for and to be considered by LHMH for pensions in general. Among the Black clients who were funded, we see that they had to demonstrate greater deference and also had much less latitude to live and age in the ways they might prefer.

For example, despite rules forbidding clients to run up bills or assume debts, patterns of excess spending found among white middle class women (who wished to keep up appearances or simply maintain their lifestyles) were often overlooked. However, in the case of Rev. Burke, a Black male client, a furniture debt of a few dollars was viewed as outside the boundaries of "need" and was ascribed to dementia (which ascription owes to the influence of ageism) and, ultimately, psychopathology, and resulted in the withdrawal of support. Although the mission of the Hannan Foundation was to benefit older adults who had "seen better days," constructions of deservingness, and the degree and kind of applications of the mission varied with the race, class, and gender of the clients. Historical accounts of race relations in Detroit during this period suggest a dependency of Blacks on whites for economic security that hinged on blacks "knowing their place" and acting accordingly (Martin 2007). Black applicants who were funded by the LHMH negotiated their identities as deserving vs. burdensome within the boundaries of such relations.

Thus, impression management by "worthy Black" clients included acknowledgement of race relations, gratitude, deference, and compliance in ways that "worthy white" clients were less likely to encounter. When they did, whites enjoyed greater tolerance by the organization.

At the same time, gender influenced both presentation of self and outcomes. While we have only one Black male and one Black female client to use for evidence, the contrasts by race and gender are suggestive. As we have shown, both of the Black clients exhibited far more deference than did white ones. But Rev. Burke also expressed much greater anxiety about being dropped from the rolls—a fear that turned out to be well-founded. Rachel Little did nothing to challenge the organization, so we cannot be sure that she would not have received equally swift punishment for rule violations. By the same token, her adoption of childlike dependence was quite unlike Rev. Burke's deference or, indeed, the pose adopted by any other client. This posture is all the more striking in light of Mrs. Little's industriousness and never-say-die attitude in relation to her blindness. In this sense, then, it appears that her behaviors—and positive outcomes—reflect her position as a Black woman in an era in which such women were to be both hard-working while also acknowledging their inferior gender and racial statuses.

The comparisons of Rachel Little and Rev. Burke's cases, and of the Black and white cases, make clear the importance of moral economy and related needs talk in the distribution of social support. Among other lessons, these cases make clear the importance of individuals' self-presentations and Visitors' interpretations in determining eligibility and continued funding. To the extent that such aid is based on perceptions of deservingness, the ability to meet even basic needs in later life is partially determined by the extent to which one can be seen to fit white, male, middle-class standards.

The present Social Security program embeds some of these assumptions about deservingness within it; to be eligible, one needs to have worked in covered employment for ten years, or be a dependent of such a worker, for example. Based as it is on notions of pooled risk, however, Social Security still broadens entitlements to support in later life and does not require the demonstrations of deservingness typical of social assistance programs or private charities such as the Hannan Foundation. The more we move away from such notions of social insurance, the greater the likelihood that a good old age will become the purview and experience of fewer people. Rev. Burke's case, in particular, makes clear how easily moral economy dictates can ease the lives of marginalized people while leaving them in constant anxiety, wondering if they will soon be seen as undeserving and abandoned. As generous and important as the Hannan funds were for old persons in Detroit, they make clear the importance of the ways that social location can shape possibilities for aging well, and thus, of universal benefit programs that are not based on socially constructed notions of deservingness.

Notes

1. We reproduce the clients' letters verbatim, including choice of words, spelling, and punctuation.

References

Binstock, Robert H. 2005. "Old-Age Policies, Politics, and Ageism." *Generations* 29, no. 3: 73-78.

Brush, Lisa D. 1997. "Worthy widows, welfare cheats: Proper womanhood in expert needs talk about single mothers in the United States, 1900 to 1988." *Gender and Society* 11, no. 6: 720-46.

Calasanti, Toni. 2008. "Gender and Class Relations in the Struggle for Old-Age Security." *Journal of Aging, Humanities, and the Arts* 2: 238-250.

Calasanti, Toni. 2003. "Theorizing Age Relations." Pp. 199-218 in *The Need for Theory: Critical Approaches to Social Gerontology for the 21st Century*, edited by Simon Biggs, Ariela Lowenstein, and Jon Hendricks. MA: Baywood Press.

Durocher, Mary and Gillian Gray. 2008. "Establishing a Clientele: Cases of Acceptance and Denial for Pensions in Old Age." *Journal of Aging, Humanities, and the Arts* 2: 175-185.

Fraser, Nancy. 1989. *Unruly practices: Power, Discourse, and Gender in Contemporary Social Theory*. Minneapolis: University of Minnesota Press, 1989.

Hendricks, Jon. 2005. "Ageism: Looking Across the Margin in the New Millenium." *Generations* 29, no. 3: 5-7.

Kail, Ben Lennox, Jill Quadagno, and Jennifer Reid Keene. 2009. "The Political Economy Perspective of Aging." Pp. 555-571 in *Handbook of Theories of Aging*, edited by Vern L. Bengtson, Merril Silverstein, Norella M. Putney, and Daphne Gans. NY: Springer.

Luella Hannan Memorial Foundation Collection in the Walter Reuther Library of Labor and Urban Affairs at Wayne State University, Detroit Michigan.

Martin, Emily Anne. 2007. "Detroit and the Great Migration: The Migration and Relations Between the Races in Detroit. " Bentley Historical Library, University of Michigan. Retrieved on March 17, 2009 from http://bentley.umich.edu/research/publications/migration/ch7.php

Mohr, J.W. 1994. "Soldiers, Mothers, Tramps, and Others: Discourse Roles in the 1907 New York City Charity Directory." *Poetics* 22: 327-57.

Pampel, Fred C. 1998. *Aging, Social Inequality, and Public Policy*. Thousand Oaks, CA: Sage.

Ray, Ruth E. 2008. "Relations of Power: Issues of Gender and Class in the Struggle for 'Security' in Old Age, 1927-1933," *Journal of Aging, Humanities, and the Arts* 2: 158-174.

Zunz, Olivier. 1982. *The Changing Face of Inequality: Urbanization, Industrial Development, and Immigrants in Detroit, 1880-1920*. Chicago: The University of Chicago Press.

Chapter 9

The Haunting Fear: Narrative Burdens in the Great Depression

Janet L. Langlois and Mary E. Durocher

This is preeminently the time to speak the truth, the whole truth, frankly and boldly. Nor need we shrink from honestly facing conditions in our country today. This great Nation will endure as it has endured, will revive and will prosper. So, first of all, let me assert my firm belief that the only thing we have to fear is fear itself—nameless, unreasoning, unjustified terror which paralyzes needed efforts to convert retreat into advance.

—Franklin Delano Roosevelt

Introduction: Fear Itself

Franklin D. Roosevelt's famous lines in his March 4, 1933, inaugural speech framed a strategy for political action in the face of devastating financial and social reverses. Yet, as David M. Kennedy has noted in his *Freedom From Fear: The American People in Depression and War, 1929-1945*, it took Roosevelt's ebullient political personality and family wealth to carry off such statements, which promised change that seemed impossible to attain for most in the heart of the Great Depression, and which would wear thin only two years later (1999, 104-30, 218-48). Kennedy has made the case that fear was the predominant emotion in the Depression decade; fear was "the ordeal of the American people" that fueled the social legislation for which the New Deal is ultimately remembered (160-89). When Roosevelt told the press on June 7, 1935, that his administration's objective was "to try to increase the security and

245

happiness of a larger number of people in all occupations of life and in all parts of the country . . . *to give them assurance that they are not going to starve in their old age,"* his statements were predicated on that fear (as quoted by Kennedy 1999, 249; emphasis added). Supreme Court Justice Benjamin Cardozo, speaking for the majority in 1937, upheld the constitutionality of the Social Security Act of 1935 in writing that "the hope behind this statute is to save men and women from the rigors of the poorhouse *as well as from the haunting fear that such a lot awaits them when journey's end is near"* (as quoted in Haber 1993, 5; Haber and Gratton 1994, 139; emphasis added). Cardozo's statement articulated what Roosevelt's remarks had implied: fear haunted the Depression era, it was particularly acute for old people, and its alleviation was the *hope* of federal social reform.

In this chapter, we two authors, the first a folklorist, the second a cultural anthropologist, explore "the haunting fear" that burdened many elderly people in the metropolitan Detroit area, both prior to and after the passage of the Social Security Act. We draw evidence from our preliminary survey of case files from the Luella Hannan Memorial Home (LHMH) and from our analysis of one case in particular to explore older people's experiences of loss, loneliness, fear and anxiety during the Great Depression. We see the case files in general as partial "life stories or narratives," (Luborsky 1987) constructed from, and mediated through, the Visitors' field notes and interviews, Board reports, and correspondence, including applicants' and clients' own letters to Board members and Visitors. While we realize that ethnographic gaps and cultural misreadings are possible in a narrative approach, we believe that such an approach can also lead to insights and cultural connections that would not have been made otherwise. Therefore, following Luborsky's (1993; Luborsky and Rubenstein 1995) methods of content analysis of life narratives, we reviewed the 508 applications submitted to the LHMH between 1929 and 1934, using relevant keywords already devised for data searches by earlier cataloguers.

We found that fully 209 case files revealed applicants being *nervous* or *worried* [1] about their financial, health or social circumstances, understandably so as these conditions were the very basis for their applications for aid. Thirty-two files noted applicants' generalized *fears* and twelve their *dread*, terms that we read as evidence of escalated anxieties. Individuals of every socio-economic class feared losing their homes, being put out by relatives, or not being able to pay their rent if they were apartment or boarding house dwellers. They feared not being able to pay their doctors' and medical bills, having strokes, getting cancer, going blind or becoming too crippled to feed themselves. They dreaded growing old without adequate money or family support, being alone, and the uncertainty of the future. They did, indeed, need assurance that they were not going to starve in old age, as Roosevelt had stated.

We found that clients' fears coalesced around end-of-life issues in particular, again understandably so, as these individuals were, by the LHMH's very terms of eligibility, usually at least sixty years old, and some were much older. Yet we recognize that, above and beyond the practical matters of asking for and receiving continued aid from the LHMH, clients' haunting fears concerning their journey's end were also grounded in specific cultural beliefs about aging, about identity, and about what loss of a good and satisfying life might entail (Haber 1993; Haber and Gratton 1994). They dreaded going to hospitals, for example, unless absolutely necessary, as they saw them as end points, institutions from which they would not return, where "their bodies might be turned over to medical students" at their death, as one grantee clearly stated (LHMFC Case #236).

Their greatest fear, however, was of going to the poor house, Eloise Hospital in the greater metropolitan Detroit area, confirming locally Justice Cardozo's recognition of a national anxiety. While six case files mention fear of going to the *poor house*, sixty-five case files specifically mention fear or dread of "going to *Eloise*." One applicant's daughter put this fear in perspective, stating that "the family would not listen to her going to Eloise or to scrubbing kitchens" (LHMFC Case #368) highlighting a particular fear of loss of social status. Four files specifically mention that the applicants would rather commit suicide than be sent to Eloise (LHMFC Case #160, Case #217, Case #294, Case #391). Eloise was such a predominant fear for many that in some cases it was even used as a threat by the Visitors to keep grantees in line. The case notes in one instance state that "if she [the grantee] were not satisfied now [with her living arrangements] that she might be sent to Eloise" (LHMFC Case #465). In another case the Visitor suggested that the best thing was "for the daughter to tell her mother that she should settle down and make up her mind to be happy or else she would eventually end up in Eloise (LHMFC Case #315). As gerontologist Carol Haber (1993) has noted, "the horror of the poorhouse *cast a long shadow*" in early twentieth-century America, despite the fact that only two percent of the elderly population was institutionalized during this period (1900-1930) (2; emphasis added), although the numbers had risen considerably, at least at Eloise, by the 1940s (Luxenberg 2009, 234-37).

In our narrative analysis, we examine one woman's case file carefully because "the horror of the poorhouse" appeared to cast a particularly long shadow over Arlene Smith's extensive record (LHMFC Case #217). On the one hand, her file is fairly typical for the type of cultured woman who became a Hannan client because of financial loss and lack of familial support during this period as evidenced in the Visitor's intake interview.

> [Mrs. Smith] appears to be a woman of culture with numerous interests who is pleasant and would seem to be kind and generous and appreciative. [She] belongs to the Episcopal Church. She has been actively associated with several churches (Episcopal) as parish visitor or secretary . . . [Mrs. Smith] is a student and finds her greatest enjoyment in books. However, she likes to sew and enjoys a good theater and symphony orchestras. . . . She left [her last position] because of ill health and the fact that she could no longer live on a half time position salary.

She applied for assistance to the LHMH in September, 1929 when she was 60 years old, one month before the stock market crash that marked the beginning of the Depression era. She died twelve years later, in November, 1941, one month before the bombing of Pearl Harbor that marked its end as the United States entered the Second World War. Entries in her file, running to 700 pages of documents, including her own letters, exemplify the widespread fears among old people in Detroit, culminating in the dread of Eloise, which she shared with many other LHMH applicants and clients.

On the other hand, Mrs. Smith's case history has unique qualities that we find arresting. Her apparent recognition of her own fears and the tactics she employed to be reassured bring another level of participant self-awareness to our discussion. The way in which her fears came to be manifested—she was literally haunted by them—makes Justice Cardozo's "haunting fear" open to a more specific analysis through compelling stories of *evil spirits* and *ghosts*,[2] as well. We see her case file, then, as one that both reveals and complicates the broader Depression-era anxieties of elders, both locally and nationally, and one that speaks to our concerns about elder care today.

The Case of Arlene Smith: Escalating Anxiety and Spectral Snakes on the Walls

The Visitor wrote in her intake notes of September 13, 1929, that Mrs. Smith was a "business type of woman, intelligent, sociable, reserved and ambitious." The Visitor's summary of the applicant's long work history—"The last thirty years of her life she has devoted herself to social work, either directly or indirectly as secretary or financial manager"—confirmed her business acumen, work ethic and service orientation. She had been financially and socially independent until job reduction and ill health forced her to apply for a pension. One might assume that Mrs. Smith, once a member of the professional class, with some financial support from her two brothers employed in Detroit's banking industry, would have fewer fears than other applicants with less support, but such was not the case. She appeared to be very anxious from the beginning of her association with the LHMH.

Under the categories Personality and Health in the notes of the intake interview, the Visitor wrote that Mrs. Smith was "extremely *nervous* and mentally tired from worry" and that she was "nervous acting and sensitive at present." In her summary diagnosis, the Visitor noted that Mrs. Smith had a "worried condition and [was] hard to please." On September 20, 1929, the Visitor reported that Mrs. Smith had apologized for "the bother she had made us [LHMH] because of the anxiety, strain and nervousness she was under" (LHMFC Case #217). Like other applicants who had been middle-class, white-collar workers, Mrs. Smith, a divorced woman, seemed not to have had the coping skills for such economic downturns when family support was lacking or insufficient (Haber and Gratton 1994, 133-34). This situation was not uncommon for the "new poor" during the Great Depression (Abelson 2003, 104-12).

Mrs. Smith's initial nervousness and worry appeared to grow over the years that she was a client. One of her brothers had made stock investments just before the 1929 crash and had lost much of his income; the other brother lost his job at the bank where he worked when it failed during the Depression. Mrs. Smith's case file indicates that she could not continue to drain their resources but would not live with their families. Her wish for economic and social independence appeared to come at a price, as its loss was her continual fear. While Mrs. Smith did not specifically mention her dread of "going to Eloise" until 1940, her letters and the Visitors' entries over the years show her deepening anxieties and foreshadow that fear.

When she first applied to the LHMH, Mrs. Smith worried about getting approved for a pension. Later, she worried that people would find out that she *was* a pensioner. The files detail her on-going concern that her pension would be insufficient for basic living—adequate lodging, clothing and food—and that needed prescriptions and surgical expenses would not be covered. The entries also indicate her health concerns: she feared that she had cancer, but an examination proved otherwise, although her debilitating arthritis and severe digestive problems were confirmed. Entries also note that LHMH administrators, Visitors, and doctors saw her worries as unfounded to some extent and believed that her finances and medical support were adequate, even when her support was reduced, along with that of other pensioners, during the early years of the Depression.

We see how these fears and worries eventually took a toll on both Mrs. Smith and her Visitor in the notes of Anna Wentink, who took over her case in 1930 and would retain it until her client's death in 1941. Mrs. Wentink summarized one of their conversations in a March 6, 1940, entry when Mrs. Smith was living at the home of Mrs. Baxter in "a very good neighborhood" in Detroit:

> [Mrs. Smith] told [the Visitor] how she feared becoming unable to wait on herself and being a burden. She advised that she had been able to help others through her prayers for them but seemed unable to help herself. She asked [the Visitor] to pray for her that her fears may be cast away. [The Visitor] attempted to assure her that most of her difficulty was the result of this fear (LHMFC Case #217).

We see this entry representing both the fear that had saturated Mrs. Smith's life and the Visitor's sense of her own possible inadequacy in responding to a client whose problems eerily echoed Roosevelt's 1933 dictum about fear itself. We find that this entry takes narrative shape as reported dialogue in a "call-and-response"[3] pattern, repeated throughout Mrs. Smith's case file, in which she articulated her fear, asked for reassurance, and received it to some degree through conversations with her Visitor, who seemed to interpret this fear, as did Mrs. Smith, as the very burden she must overcome.

A similar antiphonal pattern occurs six months later, in notes of September 6, 1940, in the first entry that reports Mrs. Smith's fear of Eloise, yet one that also indicates that her dread of the institution was probably longstanding. Mrs. Wentink reported that Mrs. Smith, then living at a boarding house in Hazel Park, Michigan, had told her that she "had felt much better since talking with her and Dr. Barton, [the LHMH physician]." The doctor "had assured her that if she became incapacitated that [the Visitor] would find a place for her in a nursing home and that she would not need to go to Receiving Hospital[4] or Eloise." The entry ends with the Visitor's coda: *"This had evidently been her dread"* (LHMFC Case #217; emphasis added).

Dr. Barton's reported assurances were apparently not completely effective for Mrs. Smith because her particular fear of "going to Eloise" took on disturbing, palpable, haunting forms by the following spring when she was seventy-one years old and in failing health, both physically and mentally, according to the doctor's and the Visitor's assessments. At this time, she was living in a single room at the Carmelite Sisters' Home, a Roman Catholic facility in Detroit, which would be her last place of residence. We examine the Visitor's entry for May 27, 1941 in some detail here, for it shows both the ethnographic quality of Mrs. Wentink's reporting and the spectral turn that Mrs. Smith's end-of-life experiences took. This entry becomes the basis for our analysis in the following sections.

In the first part of the May, 1941 entry, Mrs. Wentink summarizes Mrs. Smith's description of a haunting experience in the same call-and-response pattern we noted earlier: Mrs. Smith asks for and receives some assurance that she will not be sent to Eloise, here from the Mother Superior, Sister Bernadette, director of the Home:

> [Mrs. Smith] telephoned advising she wants to see [the Visitor] today or tomorrow morning. [Mrs. Smith] says it is urgent. [The Visitor later called at the Carmelite Sisters Home.] [Mrs. Smith] expressed great satisfaction in seeing [the Visitor] and explained that several days previously she had had a brainstorm. [Mrs. Smith] advised that she had seen snakes on the walls and had somehow held the idea that the Home was going to have the Probate Court come and take her to Eloise. [Mrs. Smith] told step by step how she dressed at 8:45 one night and went out in front of the building walking up and down in order to avoid being taken.
>
> Later she came in to the Home, told Sister Bernadette about it and had been reassured that this was not the case. [Mrs. Smith] advised, however, that she did get confused on occasion and was worried about this condition. However, she asserted she was all right today (LHMFC Case #217).

The Visitor then reported a series of three additional requests for reassurance that Mrs. Smith asked of her that day and which she gave to her client. Each of Mrs. Smith's requests was nested within the one before it, spiraling out from her initial report of seeing "snakes on the walls." The Visitor described the first instance:

> Shortly after, a peculiar expression came over [Mrs. Smith's] face. She wanted [the Visitor] to hold her hands and asked because of [the Visitor and Mrs. Smith's] long friendship to tell her the truth about some things. She then pointed to shadows on the wall, asked [the Visitor] if she saw them and how she could account for them. They were simply shadows from the chairs, the bed, etc. [Mrs. Smith] then took [the Visitor's] hand[s] and guided them along the shadows and then went along them with her own hand (LHMFC Case #217).

In the second instance, the Visitor reported that Mrs. Smith "also took [the Visitor] to the sunroom and asked for an explanation of a piece of old palm which was stuck up in a picture. It did look like a snake but [the Visitor] explained just what it was to her. This seemed to satisfy her." And in the third instance, the Visitor reported:

> [The Visitor] then went back to [Mrs. Smith's] room with her and [Mrs. Smith] asked [the Visitor] to step in the coat closet while she hung up her coat and hat as she was afraid to go in alone. [Mrs. Smith] advised it was the nights which were so bad as she could not sleep and heard evil spirits in her room. [The Visitor] reassured her and suggested that she let a lamp burn all night (LHMFC Case #217).

The Visitor concluded her entry for that day by summarizing her own discussion about Mrs. Smith with the Home staff and their debate about her care:

> Later [the Visitor] talked with the Mother Superior and Sister Martin. Sister Martin was of the opinion that [Mrs. Smith] should be committed but the Mother Superior advised they would keep [Mrs. Smith] as long as possible. It was finally agreed, however, that after Labor Day, [the Visitor] should ask our psychiatrist, Dr. Stanton, to call on [Mrs. Smith] (LHMFC Case #217).

Three months later, the Visitor called at the Home to check on Mrs. Smith. In her August 29, 1941, entry, she reported first on her conversation with her client: "[Mrs. Smith's] condition was about the same except that she begged [the Visitor] to stay all night with her and [the Visitor] had to promise to speak to a Sister and see if someone could not drop in on [Mrs. Smith] a time or two during the night." Then the Visitor reported on her discussion with the Mother Superior: "Later talked with Sister Bernadette. Advised her of the above. Sister Bernadette agreed to let [Mrs. Smith] have her door open and keep a light on during the night and have a nurse who is on duty nights drop in to see [Mrs. Smith]."

Yet, only four days later, on September 2, 1941, the Mother Superior telephoned the Visitor, telling her that they had had to take Mrs. Smith to Receiving Hospital the day before, coincidentally Labor Day, because "[Mrs. Smith] became increasingly worse and was a source of great annoyance and fright to the other patients." The Visitor went to see Mrs. Smith one last time, either later that day or soon after, as the entry is not dated. After an initial sign of recognition, Mrs. Smith refused to speak with her. The Visitor reported:

[The Visitor] called at Receiving Hospital Psychopathic Ward. [Mrs. Smith] immediately recognized [the Visitor] and said, "Oh, Mrs. Wentink, go right back home. I don't want you to have to call on me in a place like this." Following that she refused to carry on any conversation and pulled away from [the Visitor] when [the Visitor] attempted to touch her hand. [Mrs. Smith] was strapped in a wheel chair but had changed radically in appearance since [the Visitor] had seen her last (LHMFC Case #217).

LHMH Board minutes, summarized in the case file of September 17, 1941, corroborated the Visitor's entry of September 1, 1941: "[Mrs. Smith's] mental condition took a decided turn for the worse and she was taken by one of the Sisters to Receiving Hospital." The minutes also provided a conclusion to Mrs. Smith's life story, but not one of her own making: "Dr. Craig, Receiving Hospital Psychiatrist, has examined her there and holds out very little hope for any recovery. It is expected that she will be committed to either Eloise or Ypsilanti in the near future." As noted in her biographic sketch in this volume, Mrs. Smith was committed to one of the two hospitals on October 22, 1941, and the case was closed. Upon her death in the first week of November, 1941, Anna Wentink arranged for her burial.

Discussion I: Haunting as Metaphor for Loss and Loneliness

Medical anthropologist Mark Luborsky has suggested that researchers who analyze elders' life narratives should consider the underlying metaphors that structure their stories (1987, 1990). In his own analysis of older Americans' retirement stories, he found that the metaphor of nature as organic growth shaped many retirees' perceptions of their life course (1987). Our interpretations of Mrs. Smith's case file rest not on natural metaphors, but on supernatural ones. Although archival records are all we have to conjure up her presence, and we cannot speak to her directly about haunting experiences, we take seriously Mrs. Smith's reports of spectral snakes, shadows and evil spirits, as well as her requests for reassurance. We recognize that she was a haunted woman.

We have not yet defined the term "haunting," relying on common cultural knowledge of its meaning up to this point. The term comes from the Old French verb *hanter*, to frequent a place or location, but took on a supernatural connotation in the Middle Ages. The contemporary definition, "frequented or much visited by spirits, imaginary beings, apparitions, specters, etc.," can be interpreted literally or metaphorically (Oxford English Dictionary). Our readings include both these possibilities, but we focus on figurative meanings in this section. We take as a starting point literary critic Jeffrey Andrew Weinstock's observations in *Spectral America: Phantoms and the National Imagination* that America has always been a haunted place and that "[g]hosts...reflect the ethos and anxieties of the eras of their production" (2004, 3-17). Mrs. Smith's particular "haunting fear" of "going to Eloise," represented in her striking juxtaposition of "seeing snakes on the walls" and "holding the idea that the Home was going to have the Probate Court come and take her to Eloise," is a specific example of anxious America. What was it that so frightened Mrs. Smith and countless others about the poorhouses and hospitals that loomed as specters in the Depression era and beyond?

Steven Luxenberg (2009), researching the hidden history of his aunt, a patient at Eloise Hospital for over thirty years (1940-1972), gives us a clue in his *Annie's Ghosts: A Journey into a Family Secret*:

> By 1945, the overcrowding would have impinged on whatever privacy or sense of home [Annie] possessed after five years at Eloise. One female ward, designed for 18, had 45 patients; several others, built for 100, had 140. When no more space could be found for female patients, the staff began a nightly ritual of clearing the heavy dining room tables to make way for temporary cots. The next morning, patients had to be roused from bed early so that the dining tables could be returned in time for breakfast. It was unsafe, and more to the point, it violated the spirit of the state's declared philosophy of providing humane care for society's least fortunate (237).

Luxenberg's concerns about whatever privacy or sense of home his Aunt Annie might have retained in Eloise Hospital resonate for us when we consider the particular ways Mrs. Smith's haunting fears manifested. We argue that her spectral experiences related specifically to her concept of home as a place to reside physically, spiritually, and emotionally, ever elusive and ultimately unobtainable, as evidenced by her many moves over the years. We look at the shadows she saw on the wall at the Carmelite Sisters Home in 1941, the ones that the Visitor told her "were simply shadows from the chairs, the bed, etc." and we see them as emanations of the many furnished rooms in a descending series of boarding houses and group homes that never quite suited her.

In her notes of September 13, 1929, the Visitor wrote that Mrs. Smith was very particular about her housing arrangements, as "she has been used to the highest standards of living and must have all the conveniences and beauty of a modern home." She also reported on the beauty of Mrs. Smith's accommodations at the boarding house where she was living when she first requested aid:

> [Mrs. Smith] has an exceedingly clean and pleasant room in a modern lower-home duplex. [Mrs. Smith] has the privilege of any place in the home which is expensively and beautifully furnished. Her back room has plenty of light and ventilation and a beautiful outlook. This is in a very respectable residential district (LHMFC Case #217).

Yet the Visitor also noted that Mrs. Smith said her landlady was "a large, gruff German person who does not fit in with her expensive and artistic furnishings." She also feared that the landlady "was too inquisitive" and stated that she wished to move from her home because it was too expensive.

And move she did, thirty-eight more times before she reached the Carmelite Sisters Home in 1940, from which she planned to move also, but her commitment to the hospital and her death intervened. The Visitor, who had listened to Mrs. Smith's successive praises and then complaints about boarding house facilities, staff, and services; who had helped her find new lodgings and get settled over and over; and who had negotiated moving expenses many times with LHMH Secretary Leon Frost, was often frustrated by the woman. An entry dated June, 21, 1932, is indicative:

> As soon as [the Visitor] arrived [Mrs. Smith] began to complain about her present living conditions. [The Visitor] feels that she has an unusually nice room and is in a place where she can take care of herself

when able, and if ill, can receive nursing care. When [the Visitor] talked rather plainly with [Mrs. Smith] about her constant moving about and finding fault with every place in which she lived, [Mrs. Smith] attempted to throw hysterics, began to cry and appeal to [the Visitor's] tender sensibilities. . . . [Mrs. Smith] said that she would go insane if she had to stay there the rest of her days (LHMFC Case #217).

Others seemed frustrated by Mrs. Smith as well. In her notes of May, 1939 the Visitor reported a conversation, which has elements of the antiphonal pattern we discussed earlier, in which Mrs. Smith's brother urged her to stop moving around:

[Mrs. Smith] was in a peculiar frame of mind. On one hand she has decided to remain where she is until the end of her days. Her brother has advised her recently and cautioned her about moving around anymore saying that he was afraid the Home [LHMH] might cut her off if she persisted in this. [The Visitor] did not say that the Home would cut her off for her frequent moving but advised that this frequent moving suggested a mental attitude which might lead [Mrs. Smith] into difficulties. [The Visitor] explained that she did not want [Mrs. Smith] to get a reputation among the various boarding and nursing homes that she was a transient and difficult to please. [Mrs. Smith] asked several times for [the Visitor] to reassure [her] of [the Visitor's] friendship for [her]. [Mrs. Smith] appears to want to do the right thing and fears that she will not because she realizes a certain unrest and discontent within herself (LHMFC Case #217).

The Visitor's tender sensibilities did win out as she continued to help her client relocate until her case was closed. From hints in earlier notes, we guess that the Visitor sensed Mrs. Smith's yearning for a home, which mitigated her irritation at her client's incessant moving. In her notes of December 8, 1930, she discussed an Ann Arbor, Michigan boarding house where her client had recently moved.

Found [Mrs. Smith] comfortably situated in her new boarding home. She occupies a bedroom to the front of the house which is always kept comfortably warm. Although there is no bathroom on the second floor, [Mrs. Smith] has a little dressing room off of her bedroom which contains a wash stand. Each morning her landlady brings up warm water for a sponge bath and carries down the waste water. She said the food was excellent, the best she has ever had. *[Mrs. Smith] feels that this place is almost too good to last* (emphasis added) (LHMFC Case #217).

And in her February 2, 1932, notes, the Visitor wrote that, after looking at three boarding houses with her client, who was moving again, "There were things at each place which did not suit [Mrs. Smith], *but [the Visitor] tried to tell her that she would never find the ideal boarding home*" (emphasis added).

Although we do not want to whitewash Mrs. Smith's "certain unrest and discontent within herself," we do see her desire for an ideal home as a personally and culturally valid one. However, this ideal was hard to realize, given that affordable housing in the Detroit area generally, and for elderly clients in particular, consisted of a patchwork of rooms in hotels, boarding houses and nursing homes. In addition, the situation for the "non-family woman" with no assets was dire; Mrs. Smith's social location lay somewhere between the culturally-valued home and family domesticity underlying national reform policies and the "emergency relief" provided by local service agencies to the poor and destitute (Abelson 2003).

Although we do not see the psychoanalytic tenor of Sigmund Freud's (2003) classic essay on *The Uncanny* completely relevant to our more culturally- and socially-based reading of Mrs. Smith's fears, Freud's concept of "the uncanny," that which haunts, in relation to one's sense of that which is homelike, *Heimlich,* and that which is not, *Unheimlich,* captures Mrs. Smith's dread particularly well. The living situation for Eloise patients during the Depression and early war years was the antithesis of the beautiful "room of her own" that eluded Mrs. Smith and other women in comparable circumstances. The situation then may not be so different from the situation of old people now who live in a traditional nursing home, which gerontologist Ruth Ray describes as "a workplace structured around the staff's needs for cleanliness, order, and efficiency, rather than the residents' need for a 'home'" (2008, 64).

There are indications, too, that Mrs. Smith never found the religious or spiritual home for which we believe that she was searching. When we look at her next haunted experience, when she took the Visitor into the sunroom at the Carmelite Sisters Home to ask about the shadow of a palm frond stuck in a picture on the wall, we read this request metaphorically as well. We see the palm frond as a blessed artifact given to the faithful on Palm Sunday, the Sunday before Easter, and often displayed in homes throughout the year; this symbol evokes the Lenten calendar and the whole liturgical framework of the Christian church. We can only conjecture that Mrs. Smith's questioning whether the palm's shadow on the wall was a spectral snake might have in some way marked her religious concerns, questions, and doubts.

In September 1940, for example, the Visitor reported that she had talked with Dr. Barton about Mrs. Smith. She summarizes his response: "He advises that most of [Mrs. Smith's] troubles are imaginary. She had talked with him about becoming a Catholic. Dr. Barton knows that she fluctuates from Catholicism to Christian Science and back again to the Episcopal Church of which she is a member." The Visitor had received a letter from Mrs. Smith in 1937 that indicated similar theological shifting by "advising that while she was interested in Christian Science and the Roman Catholic Church, she is really an Episcopalian and wants an Episcopal clergymen when she is sick or dying."

We see Mrs. Smith's religious quest and her search for suitable lodgings over the years as being intertwined. One of the first homes that she found much to her liking, but later complained about, was St. Luke's Convalescent Home, an Episcopalian home located for her by the rector of her Episcopalian Church in 1932. Another boarding house where she lived in 1939, whose landlady was a Christian Scientist, mirrored her own turning toward the Church of Christ, Scientist, perhaps influenced by one of her brothers, who practiced this religion as well. Yet she turned from this home and this religion because one its major tenets as she understood it was not allowing conventional medical treatment but only healing by prayer. The Visitor's notes are instructive:

> [Mrs. Smith] advised the landlady tried to interest her in Christian Science but [Mrs. Smith] told her she was an Episcopalian and was not interested. [Mrs. Smith] advised her she would want a doctor in the event of illness. The landlady advised she could have one but knew nothing was really wrong with [Mrs. Smith] (LHMFC Case #217).

Mrs. Smith's move to the Carmelite Sisters Home in 1940 showed her shift toward Roman Catholicism, despite her protestations as an Episcopalian above. This move had been expedited by a Roman Catholic priest who became her confessor and who wanted his recent convert treated well. Through his influence, the sisters gave her a single room, even though there was a waiting list. Yet she had concerns there as well. She found that the floors of the Home were slippery and feared that she would fall while using her walker to climb the three flights to the cafeteria or the bathroom. Yet her deepest concerns and fears regarding Catholicism lay in her inability to understand, and practice, what she saw as stringent rules for fasting and other doctrinal issues.

Mrs. Smith's spiritual journey seems fraught to us, expressed in a kind of religious ricocheting among the higher-status Episcopal Church, the possibly more working-class Roman Catholic Church and the Church of Christ, Scientist whose numbers swelled during the Depression. We interpret her questioning of spectral snakes and palm fronds as a sign of negative religious experiences, whether of sorrow, disappointment or guilt. While folklorist Gillian Bennett (1999) reports that elderly women sometimes sense benevolent, as well as malevolent ghosts, evil spirits surrounded Mrs. Smith. She did not have the emotional support of either Dr. Barton or the landlady quoted above, who saw her spiritual troubles as imaginary according to the Visitor's notes. She might well have benefited from the counsel advocated recently by physician David Kuhl, who writes that "living fully and dying well involve enhancing . . . one's understanding of the transcendent, the spiritual, the supernatural" through a more joyous sense of the sacred for elderly people (as quoted in Ray 2008, 169).

There are also indications that Mrs. Smith never found the emotional home for which we believe that she was searching as well. When we look at her last reported haunted experience in 1941, when she took the Visitor into her room and told her that she particularly feared hearing evil spirits when she was alone at night, we read this haunting as a mark of loneliness, the subjective downside of independence as a personal and cultural goal. A thread running through her case file is the fear of being alone. She often articulated this fear directly to the Visitor as demonstrated in the following notes from February 10, 1930: "[Mrs. Smith] seems to be somewhat lonesome and asked [the Visitor] to tell her brother to come out to see her when he has the time" (LHMFC Case #217), and again in April 9, 1930, "[Mrs. Smith] is very lonely and appears care-worn. [The Visitor] feels that [Mrs. Smith's] health is failing, and that mentally she is not just up to par" (LHMFC Case #217).

Mrs. Smith's request for a nightlight and a door open when she was alone may be seen as a reversion to child-like behavior, as the Visitor described it in her notes at times. Yet we read it here as a symbolic gesture of existential dread that surfaced in the night. She told the Sister that on most days, she preferred her own company in her room with her books and sewing, rather than socializing with other residents. When the evening came, however, she needed the assurance of others. The Visitor noted on January 31, 1950, that another of her LHMH clients, who "sensed menacing figures in her room and would cry out," was also "awake a good bit at night, and evidently in the wee small hours in the loneliness of her room, shut off from every human contact, she becomes afraid" (LHMFC Case #56). Haunting *as a burden of loneliness* in both of these cases suggests a need for continued analysis of this issue in public and private care, which is surely as relevant today as it was during the Great Depression.[5]

Discussion II: Material Effects of Haunting

Our metaphorical reading of Mrs. Smith's reported haunting as *fear of loss*, which she shared with many elderly persons, is congruent with what Weinstock has called "spectrality studies," in which researchers examine reported hauntings in both social and literary contexts in order to explore individual and group experiences, as well as historical and cultural movements, that are not often documented (2004, 7) (See, for example, Bennett 1999; Brogan 1998; Goldstein, Grider and Thomas 2007; Gordon 1997; Richardson 2003; Tucker 2007). We draw inspiration from sociologist Avery F. Gordon's *Ghostly Matters: Haunting and the Sociological Imagination*, when she writes that haunting is "a constituent element of modern social life. It is neither pre-modern superstition nor individual psychosis; it is a generalizable social phenomenon of great import. To study social life one must confront the ghostly aspects of it (1997, 7).

We begin our discussion in this section by first examining what Gordon says haunting is *not*—"It is neither pre-modern superstition nor individual psychosis"—precisely because these perceptions of the ghostly were widely held during the Depression and beyond. The particularly graphic way that Mrs. Smith articulated her fears could, indeed, be seen as her belief in, and experience of, evil spirits, ghosts and other things that go bump in the night—a sign of "pre-modern superstition" at best, and of "individual psychosis" at worst. In the Depression era, the disciplines of anthropology and psychology were still shaped in some part by the nineteenth-century paradigm of cultural evolution, itself based on an application of Darwinian science to the concept of culture. Within this framework, in which cultures were seen to evolve from primitive societies to more complex civilizations through time, folk traditions—especially occult beliefs and superstitions—were understood as "survivals" or "leftovers" from the archaic past. Individuals or groups who shared such beliefs were "backward."

Yet even in the 1930s, folklorists were interested in ghosts. Just around the time that Mrs. Smith began to show definite physical and mental changes, 1936-1940, the Federal Writers' Project, one of Roosevelt's Works Progressive Administration programs, was designed to put unemployed artists, writers, actors and researchers back to work. It included a "Folklore Project" in which field researchers interviewed "everyday Americans" about their beliefs and superstitions and asked them if they knew, heard or told ghost stories. Many of the people interviewed were older adults, ranging from fifty to eighty years of age. They recalled the ghost stories of their youth, not as frightening experiences in the present, but, more safely, as nostalgic memories of frontier and pioneer life and the importance of storytelling there (American Life Histories).

In contrast, Mrs. Smith's haunting experiences, her present-day ghost stories, were considered by psychiatrists and the Visitor to be hallucinations, both visual and auditory. They were signs, not necessarily of psychosis, but certainly of some form of dementia or "undifferentiated schizophrenia," according to the first edition of the *DSM* (*Diagnostic and Statistical Manual*) used for evaluation at that time. These hallucinations and their accompanying diagnoses of mental impairment sometimes became the catalysts for placement into psychopathic wards. The sad irony is that, in articulating their haunting fears of hospitals like Eloise, older people may have hastened their removal to that dreaded facility.

We turn now to what Gordon says haunting *is*—"a generalizable social phenomenon of great import." Taking her admonition that to "study social life one must confront the ghostly aspects of it," we reiterate that Eloise Hospital, as a specter, loomed large for many Detroiters. As Haber notes, the almshouse could be seen as "a reality for some, and a symbol for many more" (1993, 5). Here we consider Eloise's potential as "a reality for some." Not only did Eloise Hospital haunt LHMH clients, but also LHMH administrators and staff. Although the LHMH staff were often tireless in searching for alternatives to Eloise Hospital for their clients, the possibility of being involuntarily committed to the county institution (alluded to by Mrs. Smith's reference to a Probate Court order) was very real for her and other elders of the day.

LHMH administrators, doctors and Visitors sometimes expressly stated applicants' fates when they noted on intake papers that an applicant was either "a subject for Eloise" (LHMFC Case #172) or "not a subject for Eloise" (LHMFC Case #191). The intake notes for one Scudder client in July of 1929 stated, for example, that "She does not dare ask for help from the Department of Public Welfare because they have spoken of sending her to Eloise of which she has a terrifying dread, having been there one day and one night" (LHMFC Case #169).

At other times, the decisions to send clients to Eloise were often seen as a last resort after years of care. Such decisions never appeared to be easy and were not always enacted. For example, the Visitor's notes in November, 1936 on a Scudder client reported that the client, upon learning that she would be sent to Eloise because she was a difficult boarder, "put up such a pitiful plea that it was finally decided not to carry out this plan and the action was rescinded" (LHMFC Case #294). As we saw, Mrs. Smith was committed at the end of her life in 1941 for similar reasons, after the Carmelite Sisters Home staff debated the decision and kept her in private care as long as possible, honoring her requests for reassurance that she would not be committed.

Other LHMH clients experienced hauntings similar to Mrs. Smith's, and the LHMH doctors and Visitors saw these, too, as signs of senility or insanity that warranted admission to Eloise. Anna Wentink reported on July 7, 1949, for example, that another of her Hannan clients, the woman who had sensed menacing figures in her room at St. Luke's Home, had told her that "the new superintendent, Mr. Elliott, had told her a change would have to be made if she persisted in doing this." We assume "a change" refers to involuntary commitment to Eloise, and "doing this" refers to speaking of her "visions or hallucinations, and perhaps even dreams." The client, however, celebrated her 100th birthday at St. Luke's and was admitted to Eloise only at the end of her very long life (LHMFC Case #56). In an earlier entry of June 9, 1938, the Visitor reported her discussion with Dr. Stanton, LHMH psychiatrist, concerning another of her clients, a woman who had told her that she actively communicated with departed friends and relatives through automatic writing and the use of an Ouija board, which she had learned about during the First World War when their use was common. "From the facts given by [Visitor], Dr. Stanton was of the opinion that [the client] is suffering from a form of insanity. He believes that [she] is approaching the place where she will begin to commit some act which will make her a nuisance." The client remained outside of Eloise, however, dying in 1947 in a relative's home, as LHMH staff had determined that monitoring her activities would be sufficient (LHMFC, Case #348).[6]

Luxenberg concludes his book, *Annie's Ghosts,* with a report of his visit to Eloise's secluded cemetery, where over seven thousand unmarked graves signaled the presence of those who were absent—patients whose lives remained hidden while they were living and whose deaths went unremarked—because no relatives claimed their bodies and no private foundation supported them (2009, 351-58). Gordon has called ghosts "the seething presences" of those who are absent (1997, 195). She reminds us that "to write stories concerning exclusions and invisibilities is to write ghost stories" and "[t]o write ghost stories implies that ghosts are real, that is to say, that they produce material effects" (1997, 17).[7] We have seen that the Depression-era medical interpretation of hauntings as individual psychosis or dementia, rather than as personal and cultural response to fear and loss, was itself a social phenomenon and did, indeed, have significant material effects. Sensing ghosts and summoning them could or did bring many individuals to institutions in which they were defined as mentally ill.

Conclusion: Haunting as Sign That Life is More Complicated

We conclude by considering Mrs. Smith's case in terms of Gordon's statement that "haunting [is] a paradigmatic way in which life is more complicated than those of us who study it have usually granted" (1997). As we read her case file, it is easy to see a woman who was suffering from imaginary illnesses and excessive worries, who was obsessively difficult to please, and who slipped into dementia at the end of her life. Yet she was more than this. We believe that Mrs. Smith was haunted by the possibility of becoming a ghost herself, invisible and marginalized within institutional life, and that her haunting applies not only to her case, but to the cases of many other LHMH clients, as well as all old people who are avoided and forgotten in American culture. We draw from literary critic Kathleen Brogan's insights into what she calls "cultural haunting" in our exploration of Mrs. Smith's evil spirits. Brogan suggests that one of the functions of ghostly figures is that "they signal an attempt to recover and make social use of a poorly-documented, partially erased cultural history" (1998, 2). Literary critic Judith Richardson corroborates Brogan's findings when she suggests that ghosts "operate as a particular, and peculiar, kind of social memory, an alternate form of history-making in which things usually forgotten, discarded, or repressed become foregrounded, whether as items of fear, regret, explanation or desire" (2003, 3).

We, in turn, are haunted as we retell Mrs. Smith's occulted story, a ghost story in this sense. We join those writers and researchers that Brogan calls "heirs and ethnographers" (1998, 1-29) who have inherited the historical and cultural patterns we must excavate and modify for our own time. Mrs. Smith's ghost story tells us that, contrary to both President Roosevelt's and Visitor Anna Wentink's assurances, not all fears are "unjustified." Even the best social-support measures have gaps through which individuals, particularly vulnerable people in need of care, can fall. In these situations, elders' fears may be legitimate. In our efforts to improve social policies and their implementation, we must be willing to search for "the ghosts in the machine," to take a phrase from novelist Toni Morrison, who recognizes that important issues and motivations remain invisible in any system (1992, 11). We must also be willing to admit that our policies, our research, and our practice will be ghost-ridden, in the sense that we will be engaged in "a constant negotiation between what can be seen and what is in the shadows"(Gordon 1997, 17).

For us, Mrs. Smith emerged from the case files as an emblem of "what is in the shadows." She helped us recognize that the haunting fear of illness, loss, loneliness and death, symbolized in the specter of Eloise Hospital, is a deep and widespread burden that ultimately needs to be overcome on a personal, institutional and national level. Yet that possibility is almost always complicated by factors beyond our control. As Haber and Gratton remind us, the legacy of that haunting fear of the poorhouse continues to influence current legislation and practice in nursing homes and "to trouble the national conscience in our own time" (1994, 117). Yet, if we let it, "[t]he double voice of the ghost will do its work," forcing us to look backwards at past cultural beliefs and practices concerning aging once hidden and to look forwards to emergent modifications and resulting reforms. We must keep in mind that the ghost's very opaqueness "passes itself on as our haunting burden" (Gordon 1997, 193-208).

Notes

1. Terms in bold face are keywords.
2. Also keywords in LHMH data base.
3. A stylistic feature of African American work songs and spirituals in which one person calls out a phrase and a group or chorus responds, here applied to Mrs. Smith's reported requests for help and others' responses.
4. The psychopathic ward at Detroit Receiving Hospital was the point where individuals were sent for evaluation, often before being sent to Eloise or other hospitals. Mrs. Smith had told her Visitor eight years earlier that "she would do something to put herself out of misery" rather than go to Receiving. On January 18, 1932, the Visitor had duly reported her threat of suicide to the director of St. Luke's Convalescent Home, where Mrs. Smith was living while recuperating from surgery to mend a broken arm.
5. See Ray, 2008, 138-53, for a description of modern-day hauntings experienced by an old man at the end of his life.
6. Darby Penney and Peter Stastny note in their sobering work, *The Lives They Left Behind: Suitcases from a State Hospital Attic*, that a number of pa-

tients at the Willard State Hospital in New York were brought there precisely because they spoke of "hearing voices," defined as auditory hallucinations, or of seeing apparitions, defined as "visual hallucinations," that signaled "dementia praecox" or schizophrenia. The authors' discussion of a young woman, a French intellectual named Madeline Cartier who became interested in psychics and believed that she could communicate with the dead through mental telepathy despite her psychiatrists' warnings to stay away from the supernatural, is particularly telling. Sent to Bellevue Hospital in 1932 when she was thirty-six years old for evaluation, she believed that she was going there to consult with doctors on psychic phenomena. Instead she was hospitalized for schizophrenia. The authors conclude her story by writing that "Outrage with her confinement was to become the central theme of her forty-seven-year stay within New York's state hospital system" (2008, 161-69).

7. It should come as no surprise that Eloise Hospital, whose last building closed in 1984 as the de-institutionalization of mental health care continued from the 1970s, is itself said to be haunted. Patricia Ibbotson's *Images of America: Eloise: Poorhouse, Farm, Asylum, and Hospital, 1839-1984* opens with the statement: "Local interest in the 'ghosts of Eloise' has also been strong and there have been ghostly expeditions to the grounds in search of these spirits" (2002, 7).

References

Abelson, Elaine S. 2003. "Women Who Have No Men to Work for Them: Gender and Homelessness In The Great Depression, 1930-1934." *Feminist Studies* 29, no. 1 (Spring): 104-27.

American Life Histories: Manuscripts from the Federal Writers' Project, 1936-1940. *American Memory*, Manuscript Division, Library of Congress. 19 October 1998. http://memory.loc.gov/ammem/wpaintro/wpahome.html.

Bennett, Gillian. 1999. *Alas, Poor Ghost!: Traditions of Belief in Story and Discourse*. Rev. Ed. of *Traditions of Belief: Women and the Supernatural*. Logan, UT: Utah State University Press.

Brogan, Kathleen. 1998. *Cultural Haunting: Ghosts and Ethnicity in Recent American Literature*. Charlottesville, VA: University Press of Virginia.

Freud, Sigmund. 2003. *The Uncanny*. (D. McClintock, Trans.). New York: Penguin. (Original work published 1925).

Goldstein, Diane, Sylvia Grider, and Jeannie Banks Thomas. 1997. *Haunting Experiences: Ghosts in Contemporary Folklore*. Logan, UT: Utah State University Press.

Gordon, Avery F. 1997. *Ghostly Matters: Haunting and the Sociological Imagination*. Minneapolis, MN: University of Minnesota Press.

Haber, Carol. 1993. "And the Fear of the Poorhouse: Perceptions of Old Age Impoverishment in Early Twentieth-Century America." *Generations* 17, no. 2: 46–51.

Haber, Carol and Brian Gratton. 1994. *Old Age and the Search for Security: an American Social History*. Bloomington, IN: Indiana University Press.

Ibbotson, Patricia. 2002. *Eloise: Poorhouse, Farm, Asylum, and Hospital 1839–1984*. Chicago: Arcadia.

Kennedy, David. M. 1999. *Freedom from Fear: The American People in Depression and War, 1929-1945*. New: Oxford University Press.

Luborsky, Mark R. 1987. "Analysis of Multiple Life History Narratives." *Ethos* 15, no. 4: 366-81.

———. 1993. "The Identification and Analyses of Themes and Patterns." In *Qualitative Methods in Aging Research*, ed. J. Gubrium and A. Sankar. New York: Sage.

Luborsky, Mark R. and Robert L. Rubinstein. 1995. "Sampling in Qualitative Research: Rationale, Issues and Methods." *Research on Aging* 17, no. 1: 89–113.

Luella Hannan Memorial Foundation Collection (LHMFC). Walter Reuther Library of Labor and Urban Affairs. Wayne State University, Detroit, MI.

Luxenberg, Steve. 2009. *Annie's Ghosts: A Journey into a Family Secret*. New York: Hyperion.

Morrison, Toni. 1992. *Playing in the Dark: Whiteness and the Literary Imagination*. Cambridge, MA: Harvard University Press.

Oxford English Dictionary, (Compact Edition). 1971. New York: Oxford University Press.

Penney, Darby and Peter Stastny. 2008. *The Lives They Left Behind: Suitcases from a State Hospital Attic.* New York: Bellevue Literary Press.

Ray, Ruth. E. 2008. *Endnotes: An Intimate Look at the End Of Life.* New York: Columbia University Press.

Richardson, Judith. 2003. *Possessions: The History and Uses of Haunting in the Hudson Valley.* Cambridge, MA: Harvard University Press.

Roosevelt, Franklin Delano. "First Inaugural Speech March 4, 1933." *Challenge of Democracy.* http://www.hpol.org/fdr/inaug.html.

Tucker, Elizabeth. 2007. *Haunted Halls: Ghostlore of American College Campuses.* Jackson, MS: University Press of Mississippi.

Weinstock, Jeffrey A., ed. 2004. *Spectral America: Phantoms and the National Imagination.* Madison, WI: University of Wisconsin Press/Popular Press.

Part 4

Part Four

Rethinking the "Burden" of Age

In this section, contributors take up issues raised in previous sections by examining the unequal social relations that perpetuated ageism, sexism, racism, and classism in Depression era America. When such relations exist, any form of human difference or dependency will be seen as a burden. The authors look to the present and the future to imagine an America in which old age is not a burden. They describe what is needed to create a socially just environment in which everyone has the chance to experience a good old age.

Writing in an autobiographical mode, Elizabeth Chapleski explains how ageism and sexism work together, limiting the lives of old people today, much as they did in 1929. She sees the case files as "poignant depictions" of "women desperately trying to remain independent" and recognizes that this is not just a personal desire but a reflection of "the polity, the values and the culture of their time." This desperate need to remain independent, unfortunately, still reflects the culture of our time. Chapleski writes of her own concerns as she looks ahead to the limited possibilities for long-term care on her small pension. As a wife and mother of three who stayed home to care for her family during the first half of her adult life, she "provided the free labor upon whose backs a healthy economy could function," and her meager retirement benefits are proof of it. Chapleski argues that, if Americans developed a more socially and spiritually enlightened view of aging, we would value the caring labor of women and provide for them better in old age. We would also recognize the social, as well as personal opportunities in old age and see that "ageist attitudes, ageist behaviors, and ageist policies are the burden, not the aged person."

In her chapter on old-age policies, Toni Calasanti places the construction of burden, both in 1929 and today, in a larger socioeconomic and ideological context. Beginning with a discussion of how U.S. society responds to the risks that people face in any given era, she argues that the issue is not whether the welfare state *can* respond to the needs of older people but whether it *wants* to. Old-age policies are influenced by the contradictory ideologies concerning personal responsibility and independence, on the one hand, and the dictate to care for others on the other, a tension that masks the "embeddedness of all individuals in the wider society and their reliance on it." Calasanti argues that ageism makes it easier to dismiss old people as burdens, while dependent children are rarely considered burdens. She points to the reality of interdependence across the life course and into old age. What we need are welfare state policies that reflect an ethic of interdependence.

In the final chapter, Ruth Ray describes what a just society would look like from the perspective of a feminist ethics of care. She begins by explaining that the assistance provided by the Luella Hannan Memorial Home (LHMH) and other organizations of the day was based on the paternal assumption of elder dependency. This assumption was in fact accurate because society disabled them. The LHMH also assumed that families (namely women) would care for dependent elders with little or no social assistance, which is an assumption that prevails today in American society.

Ray argues that in adopting a paternalistic attitude toward old people, the LHMH provided charity or "limited benevolence" but not care. Within a feminist ethics of care, all providers and clients, caregivers and care receivers alike, are considered social equals. Caring relations, rather than individual independence, are placed at the center of a just society, and genuine caring replaces charity. Ray draws on the work of feminist visionaries to imagine a better America in which elders, however dependent, are seen as valuable members of society and, by their own accounts, live a good life.

Chapter 10

Reflections on Ageism: Perspective of a Septuagenarian on the Avoidance of Burdenhood

Elizabeth Edson Chapleski

Do not cast me off when old age comes, nor forsake me when my strength fails

– Psalm 71:9[1]

No one wishes to become a burden. Not in tenth century B.C. or 1929 or in 2010. Traditionally women have provided care for their children, their husbands or partners, and often their parents. For those of us who have spent our lives caring, the mere thought of the role reversal is repellent. And yet I wonder if this is a sign of ageism. Does our constant wish for independence reflect the denial of aging and even death? Does it reflect societal and cultural expectations that value only youth and productivity? The stories of the Hannan clients are poignant depictions of vulnerable older women desperately trying to remain independent; their lives are affected by the economy, the polity, the values and the culture of their time.

As I read through the many Luella Hannan Memorial Foundation Collection (LHMFC) files, I tried to imagine myself in the shoes of these women, and given the economic climate in Michigan in 2010, this is not much of a stretch. I am the only member of this research group who is retired. I am a gerontologist-social worker-sociologist whose research has focused on minority aging, and specifically, American Indian Elders.

As a woman, born in the same year as Social Security (1935) and only fifteen years after women were given the right to vote, my own life bears many similarities to the lives of these women—and many differences.

In 1957, I married as I completed my undergraduate education at the University of Michigan. Before that I had shown signs of leadership, having been elected the first female mayor of my grade school (K-8) in Chicago. A few years later I worked to end the racial segregation of my high school. I was proud of my bachelor's degree in sociology and yet never worked for pay until I returned to graduate school in the 1980s. I was privileged, though never wealthy, in my middle-class upbringing and later, as the wife of a dentist. I never really questioned my choices as I became a mother of three children in five years. Living a typical suburban housewife's life ignoring my own interests (although always a voracious reader), in the mid 1960s I happened on a book that changed my outlook. Betty Friedan's (1963) *The Feminine Mystique* illuminated my unspoken, unresolved issues of "quiet desperation" and "unrest." I was the woman she wrote about, the prototypical white, middle-class housewife who felt trapped. I needed to discover myself.

I threw myself into community volunteer activities, working to start up the Everywoman's Center at the YWCA, serving on numerous boards of directors, including the local Urban League. However, after a two-year presidency for the Junior League, I was reminded by their policies that I was now expendable—the *Junior* League was intended to assist *young* women in becoming active, productive members of their communities; at the age of forty, I was to become a *sustaining* member, no longer expected to be active or productive. These policies (changed since 1975) were established in the early 1900s and reveal how age was socially constructed through the "inadvertent but pernicious ageism" described by Toni Calasanti and Kathleen Slevin (2006, 1), which functions as a "system of inequality that privileges the not-old at the expense of the old." The training I received through the AJLA (Association of Junior Leagues of America), however, did equip me with advocacy skills, as well as time management and management-by-objectives abilities, all of which facilitated my success in graduate school.

Rather than give in to the "quiet desperation" Friedan (1963) had described, I pursued an MSW and later a PhD (through the joint doctoral program in social work and social sciences at the University of

Michigan), shedding the *Mrs.* I had taken so many years earlier. I gave up the *privilege* of being a kept woman and stepped out on my own—without really thinking of the financial hardship I might later encounter. My daughter, in college at the same time, had no problem getting a credit card, yet I was turned down—because I was a middle-age woman with no credit in her own name. I was also turned down for the first mortgage I applied for after my divorce. I still don't have enough years contributing to social security (at an assistant and later associate professor's salary) to receive much more than I would have as a wife at half of the partner's rate. Political and economic reality forced me to recognize that I was, for all practical purposes within the general economy, powerless as a single, middle-aged woman. Both Social Security and the banking industry failed to recognize the contribution of unpaid work to the overall productivity required to maintain a healthy society. Women like me, along with minority groups and poor people, provided the free labor upon whose backs a healthy economic foundation could be constructed. Despite the *good intentions* of the framers of social programs, people with power maintain it. Poole's suggestion that the "visions of reformers must be scrutinized" because "altruistic dreams can mask the perpetuation of privilege" rings true (Poole 2006, cited in Calasanti 2008, 248-249). As my American Indian friends would say, walk a mile in my moccasins, and the path will become more clear.

I recall all this with no regret for my decisions. I am rich with experience that I value more highly than material advantages—my years of work with American Indian Elders, my city study of Detroit elders (Chapleski 2002), teaching and mentoring graduate students about issues of aging, and the opportunity to continue to develop my own potential and to recognize the potential in others, a developmental process described in Ruth Ray's (2006) chapter *The Personal as Political.*

I am well aware from my own experience of the importance of Social Security, however gender [and race] biased it is, and I am sad for the women whose lives depended on the LHMH safety net to keep them from the poor farm. Thus, my views of these women are informed by my own age and experience, and I think many of their stories could be my story. Their situations, shared by women in similar circumstances today and with generations of other women, is a result of structural, systemic inequities. Reading these stories in the LHMH archives, I am haunted by the knowledge that nearly a century later, many women are faced with the same economic situations.

In this chapter I will examine the shifting meanings of aging and ageism as they are reflected in theoretical approaches to social gerontology. I explore images of ageism as represented across the years in literature devoted to issues of aging, placing the LHMH women within a relational context that illuminates the Visitors' reflections and situates the lives of these women in time and place. I explore the influence of these theories on our ways of understanding the aging process today and our construction of old age as a *burden*.

My reflections are informed and influenced, not only by my biographical and cultural history, but also my fifteen years as an academic researcher at a gerontology institute, as well as over twenty years of long-term care research with Great Lakes American Indians. When I first began working with the American Indian population in 1987, I did not realize that they would change my worldview. My location at a research institute facilitated awards of funding for long-term care research (National Institute on Aging), especially given my prior collaboration with American Indians in Michigan. The prevailing positivist paradigm and the overwhelming trend toward empiricism in the gerontology field, plus the need to publish (and survive), placed a premium on writing and receiving grants. My success in this venture was due in part to being in the right place at the right time and having experience with and access to a vastly understudied population. I soon found out, however, that many of the instruments and empirical methods, normed and validated with the mainstream population, failed to represent the American Indian elders I was studying—or illuminate their cultural richness (Jackson and Chapleski 2000). As I trained Native interviewers and conducted key informant interviews in urban and rural, tribal and off-reservation locations, I became aware of many contradictions across theory, research and lived experience and the insufficiency of common theories in social gerontology to understand this unique group of elders. This is yet another reminder that the diversity of older people goes unrecognized and unappreciated in America, which is a major reason why ageism (as well as sexism and racism) prevails in the collective unconscious.

Shifting Meanings of Aging and Ageism

I do not consider myself an expert on ageism, and my conceptions are shifting as I myself grow older and am challenged to rethink many assumptions. One of the most dominant and widely quoted conceptualizations of ageism comes from sociologist Erdman Palmore (1999, 3-18). In teaching gerontology courses, I have employed quizzes on aging from this book for pre-testing student attitudes and knowledge. These quizzes were developed from the empirical findings of surveys largely focused on the physical or psychological aspects of aging. The term *ageism* is attributed to a statement made by Robert Butler in 1969 and restated by Palmore as "any prejudice or discrimination against or in favor of an age group*"* (3). In the second edition of his book *Ageism: Negative and Positive,* Palmore contended that "ageism is the ultimate prejudice, the last discrimination, the cruelest rejection" (4) and suggested that it is also ageist to ignore the many bio-psychosocial differences among older adults (14). Reflecting on Palmore's choice of wording, my understanding of ageism is that, in any form, it results in injustice toward older people and as such cannot be *positive.* Failing to recognize real differences between age cohorts seems less evidence of *positive ageism* than indifference. Prejudice can be both attitudinal and emotional, while discrimination is behavioral. Ageism is manifested in invisibility (especially of older women) and an unwillingness to see power differentials or to value difference.

Where do we see ageism? Palmore identifies obvious manifestations—overt prejudicial attitudes and beliefs, negative language, neglect, avoidance and ignorance. Feminist gerontologists identify a more pernicious, entrenched ageism by examining the confluence of institutional ageism and sexism, even as it exists within feminist scholarship and activism. In "failing to study old people on their own terms, as well as failing to study systemic inequities, feminist scholars themselves have been ageist (Calasanti and Slevin 2006, 1)." Nowhere was this scholarly ageism more evident than in the scant literature addressing long-term care among older American Indians. Disadvantage multiplies when the effects of racism combine with ageism and sexism.

Recognizing that one size does not fit all, the National Institute on Aging issued an RFA in 1991 seeking research on Long Term Care among minorities. Little if any research had focused on the conditions of aging American Indian people prior to the 1990s (Chapleski 1997). So, in my first year as an academic researcher, I was honored with one of these grants and my introduction to another culture began in earnest.[2] The studies I conducted with American Indian Elders now help me better understand the urban context of women's aging during the progressive era and the Great Depression in Detroit.

Rise of Ageism, Urbanism and Industrialization: Detroit in the 1920s and 1930s

Born in a largely agrarian society, the LHMH women were aging in a time of industrialization, a time when having husbands, siblings or children was the only insurance against poverty for women. The population over the age of sixty-five was just over 4 percent but growing rapidly and was thus increasingly viewed as a *problem*, both individually and collectively. While many of the concerns expressed in the LHMH files suggest *individual* problems and an inability to sustain lifestyles due to age and life changes, such as frail health and loss or lack of family support, the overriding issues that impacted these women were systemic and socioeconomic in origin.

In Detroit in the early 1900s, horses and carriages had been replaced by horseless carriages and all that accompanied their manufacture. Henry Ford, Billy Durant, Walter P. Chrysler, Ransom Olds and the Dodge brothers were founding what would later be called the *big three* automobile companies, the very companies that brought laborers, engineers, and their families to Detroit (Klingaman 1989). Largely because of automobiles, Detroit rose fast and fell hard. In the 1920s, Detroit experienced the largest rise in population in America (from 465,766 in 1910 to 1,568,662 in 1930) and the greatest fall in employment during the Great Depression, which left one-third of the workforce out of jobs in 1933 (Detroit History 2009).

This rise in industrialization was accompanied by a loss in status of older persons, who were viewed as unable to *keep up* and therefore expendable. Butler may have coined the term *ageism* in 1969, but prejudice toward old people existed long before Luella Hannan left her bequest; in fact, the very act of making that bequest was a response to the ageism of her time.

This was the time of mechanization. Carol Haber (2000) reviewing the conclusions of age historians, writes that "the more industrial and urbanized an area, the less likely the old were to be employed, and the more impoverished they became (31)." These same concerns about industrialization were expressed by Executive Secretary Leon W. Frost in the first Annual Report of the Luella Hannan Memorial Home (Board of Trustees 1930)[3]:

> We must view our country as one of youth, and particularly is this so in our great industrial cities, where to *do* seems to be of so much greater importance than to *be*. . . . Where is his [older worker's] place? Only too frequently he finds it has not been reserved. The machines are whirring at an even more accelerated rate of speed. . . . He has discovered that the city tends to become more impersonal. It is the unit which counts rather than the individual; it is speed which matters rather than exacting skill.

Frost was surely drawing on more than "book learning" in writing these words. He had spent the previous year responding to loss and need among Detroit's older population, granting and denying pensions on behalf of the LHMH. As a man in early middle age (Frost was forty in 1930), he may himself have begun to feel the press of ageism in the "Great city" of Detroit (See Jankowski, this volume, chapter 2), where men over 40 were increasingly turned away from employment, especially in the automobile companies, for being "too old."

Changing Perspectives on Aging: Old Age as Decline

Historians tell us that old age was generally viewed as a disease until the 1940s; there were no experts in geriatrics and gerontology, and even then, both fields referred to *medical* specializations (Katz 1996; Moody 2006). Andy Achenbaum (1978), in his landmark book, *Old Age in the New Land*, presents an excellent history of the rise in medical theories of pathological aspects of growing old, citing "Metchnikoff's assertion that old age itself was a chronic, infectious disease, both progressive and incurable" (45)! Stephen Katz (1996), in *Disciplining Old Age* also chronicles this contextualization of "aging as disease" that formed the basis for geriatrics and gerontology and framed aging in terms of loss and decline. Given the prevailing notion of aging as disease, it is little wonder that the primary "service"—other than financial aid and Visitor's calls—that the LHMH offered was medical. The Visitors' copious notes and letters devoted to discussing the aches, pains and chronic conditions experienced by the Hannan clients, as well as the many medical visits, paint a picture of aging women preoccupied with their bodies as defined for them by a rhetoric of decline. Also not surprising is the doctor's note in a client file, reporting that the seventy-three year-old woman, Hope, was "in quite bad shape, the bone fragments not in good position nor the wrist fracture in good condition . . . However, due to Hope's advanced age [I] feel it impossible to do anything further, though her arm will no doubt cause her trouble the rest of her life (LHMFC, Case #142)." Today, given modern orthopedic advancements and Medicare coverage, Hope would be treated and have a better chance of living pain-free.

In 1929, however, demographic trends, industrialization, the economic environment, and the general understanding of aging as disease came together to construct aging as a national problem (Achenbaum, 1978, 109; Katz, 1996, chapter 2; Moody, 2006, 5-7), undoubtedly aiding in the passage of the Social Security Act of 1935 and later Medicare. The huge majority of older people were *not* a problem, but the tendency to homogenize the older population resulted in opposite effects: on the one hand, it cleared the path for passage of policies and services for the entire cohort age sixty or sixty-five and older; on the other hand, it obscured the needs of the more vulnerable subpopulations (Minkler and Estes 1984), especially females, minority persons and those living in poverty. Carroll Estes and Meredith Minkler critiqued this homogenization in their political economy of aging theory, contending that the aged as a class have not been discriminated against on an equal basis and therefore have entered old age with varying degrees of status and power. We see the differences in social status in the assignment of LHMH pension applicants as "Hannan types" or Scudder clients (see Ruth Ray, this volume, chapter 3).

The differences in social status are revealed even more in who did *not* apply. Only four African-Americans applied, and two became Scudder clients. There were no American Indian applicants, as these were the "forgotten elders" of this generation, confined to reservations or rural Indian communities, with many of their children sent to government boarding schools for purposes of acculturation. They were victims of removal from their lands, termination of their tribes and later relocation to urban centers. They suffered from poor health, lower life expectancy and poverty (Chapleski 1997).[4]

Re-Framing Old Age:
Other Perspectives from the 1920s and 30s

Going against the common grain, two early gerontologists (although they did not call themselves that) presented alternative views of aging in the 1920s. Each recognized that aging was more than a biomedical problem, and each raised issues similar to today's theories of successful aging and even gerotranscendence. Both voices were responding to negative concepts of old age commonly held at the time, and both promoted positive suggestions for change in attitudes about and by older people. What these authors had in common was age and their training in psychology: both were in their late seventies and clearly had aged well, and both were asking questions and searching for meaning in and for the latter part of life, not just for others but for themselves.

The first, G. Stanley Hall (1922) in *Senescence*, expressed an ambivalence toward the biomedical views on aging, stressing an expansion of meaning in what he termed the *senescence* stage of life, "which begins in the early forties, or before in woman" (vii). (Today we would consider this attribution in itself to be ageist and perhaps sexist.) Hall extended his search for answers beyond science and biology to theology, humanities, poetry, fiction, and autobiography and in doing so identified characteristics of old persons that, to the contemporary reader, bear some resemblance to those described (approvingly) by Tornstam (2005, 41) in his theory of gerotranscendence. For example, Hall (1922) includes in personal characteristics of the aged: 1) "tendency to low ideals"; 2) "lowering and liberalizing of conduct creeds" and the loss of power to distinguish right from wrong or true from false; 3) "lessening of emotional intensity or stodginess"; 4) "failure in religious teaching"; and 5) the feeling that "church offers too little" and does not meet spiritual needs (25-27). In 2010, following Tornstam, we might reinterpret these characteristics in more positive terms: as they age, people become less competitive, less constrained by rules, less judgmental, less impulsive, and more inclined toward cosmic searching over obedience to religious doctrine.

The second scholar to challenge cultural assumptions, a clinical psychologist also in her late seventies, was Lillien J. Martin, who wrote two books with Clare de Gruchy, *Salvaging Old Age* (1930) and *Sweeping the Cobwebs* (1979/1933). The first book (Martin and de Gruchy 1930) argues the need for mental rehabilitation in most individual old people; the second, based on case studies described in the first book, presents a specific plan of exercises and practices for "that mental rehabilitation called *salvaging old age*" (53). The authors' work laid the groundwork for developing education, training and programs especially for the stage of life called senescence or old age. They lament that

> because of the physical deterioration of the old they have fallen prey to the stronger present generation which, in the name of kindness, has about choked and suffocated them. The old have been flattened out, and so have retired into boredom, obscurity and apathy as a protective measure (Martin and de Gruchy 1930, 11).

The authors suggest that the aging or old be encouraged to have a new life analogous to that of other periods. Their hope is that

> the burdens of the old will not be increased by what it [their program]contains but lightened instead, since the fruit of the labor here described gives proof that the last part of life, if well prepared for, may be the richest period of all . . . (Martin and de Gruchy 1930, 14)

Some of the women described in earlier chapters of the present volume (see especially the chapters in this volume by Langlois and Durocher, Bailey-Fakhoury and Dillaway, and Pratt-Hopp and Thornton) would be ripe for *salvaging* by Martin. The resistance and struggle seen in the cases of Kate Shields, Madeline Landin Nuit, Ada Dreyfus, and Ida Drake reflect "their strength to fight and emotions still alive to stimulation" (Martin and de Gruchy 1930, 34), a stance Martin and de Gruchy consider preferable to lethargy and passivity, even if it is based on a sense of privilege and entitlement.

Mrs. Hannan's generosity and charity clearly met a need for some in the Detroit area at the time of the Great Depression, not the least of which was preventing their placement in the dreaded poor house, where two percent of aged people were committed nationally, according to

Haber (1993). Yes, the LHMH "outdoor" assistance was preferable to Eloise, as noted by Thomas Jankowski (see chapter 2, this volume) and Faith Pratt-Hopp and Nancy Thornton (see chapter 4, this volume), but did their dependence on the LHMH mitigate the agency of these older women? Did they *believe* themselves to be burdens on this charitable organization? If given a choice, how would they have preferred to age, and where? How did their choices in 1929 differ from the choices older women make today?

The LHMH men and women, as reflected in the case files, seem basically powerless, with few avenues for choice. While the Visitors were thoughtful and responsible, the substance of what they could offer, given the structure of a charitable organization in a highly stratified society, reflected the social work culture of the times, placing the worker in a quandary when the wishes and needs of her client conflicted with the cultural assumptions about old age and the rules of the LHMH (see chapter 8, this volume, for a thoughtful consideration of the multiple role expectations of the Visitor). Fortunately for Mrs. Drake, as described in chapter 4, the visitor Mrs. Wentick was empathetic and bright and found success in her role as client advocate. More often, however, social work (then and now) fails to empower elders, and despite all the good intentions, clients are virtually powerless in their position of need.

The LHMH case files, through letters and the depictions of Visitors, reflect the times in which they were written, times of extreme economic hardship for many, especially women who had no independent means of maintaining their lifestyles. These were times when the prevailing beliefs about aging were fraught with pessimism and expectations of decline. In chapter 5 (this volume), for example, Padgett and Cheng tell us about Mrs. Thomas, a ninety-one year-old widow, through the Visitor's words. Mrs. Thomas was apparently the only female in a boarding home, the superintendent of which reported that she had seen Mrs. Thomas coming and going from the men's rooms "at all hours," which was surely a sign of senility. The superintendent apparently did not consider the possibility that Mrs. Thomas was lonely for companionship and still a sexual being.

Today's older adults do have more advocates than the LHMH clients did. Contemporary social workers, more sensitive to age issues, may not so readily dismiss the complaints of Arlene Smith (see chapter 9, this volume) as unfounded or caused by diminishing cognitive capacities. We have no way of knowing whether the "snakes" or "menacing figures" they saw were real or imaginary, because there were no comprehensive cognitive tests given then as might happen now and no check for poly-pharmaceutical causes. There were also no ombudspersons to check on the conditions of the homes—only the Visitors who came monthly for a few hours at most. Aside from the lack of technologies for diagnoses or policies for protection in 1930, what was truly missing was a social gerontology that would change attitudes, both public and private, about what it means to age well in America.

Contemporary Ageism?
Modern Theories of Social Gerontology

Though unintended, ageism still resides in many of the contemporary theories of aging—an ageism of exclusion through implicit and explicit expectations imposed on older persons as though they were a homogeneous group, rather than persons of different status, class, wealth, gender, race/ethnicity, health and age.

As one early example, Cumming and Henry's disengagement theory (Moody 2010, 10-11), presented in 1961, was a natural successor to the "age as decline" perspective, postulating the mutual withdrawal of society and the aging person and justifying laws that allowed forced retirement. Later activity and continuity theories postulated that life satisfaction was dependent on staying active and engaged but these concepts were based on understandings of "activity" and "engagement" forged in youth and midlife. None of these theories took into account the variety of ways people develop and experience old age.

In their more recent attempt to overcome the focus on decline, Rowe and Kahn (1998) funded by the MacArthur Foundation (with grants totaling over $10 million), brought together selected "research scientists" (there were none from anthropology, social work, or the humanities) to explore the positive aspects of "successful aging." At first glance, this was a welcome change, despite its biomedical bias.

On closer analysis, however, critical readers have noted that the book merely reflects a more subtle form of ageism. My own first response to Rowe and Kahn's book was visceral. As I developed a lecture in 1998 on the positive aspects of aging for the interdisciplinary gerontology course

I was teaching, I came to conclusions similar to those of Calasanti and Slevin (2001) in their feminist critique of leading theoretical perspectives on aging. The very phrase "successful aging" sounds like a destination rather than a journey, an outcome and not a process, and one that is other-defined (by the polity, the culture, the medical profession) rather than self-defined. Rowe and Kahn's model for successful aging posits three critical components: "avoiding disease or disability, maintaining mental and physical function, and continuing engagement with life" (49). In other words, successful aging is not aging at all, but an attempt to look, be and act middle-aged. Furthermore, Rowe and Kahn failed to recognize the many who fell outside this model long before old age, whose life engagements involved struggle, whose diseases and disabilities had already taken their toll, and even those whose mental faculties had diminished—a description of many of the LHMH clients. Is there no hope of aging well for them? Although Rowe and Kahn's model offered a recipe for staying young (given the right life situation and good health care), it did not offer a process for aging well in a diverse America. One of its other major omissions—the importance of spirituality and the search for meaning among people of all backgrounds—was later addressed in a critical publication by Crowther and her colleagues (2002). The latter model of "successful aging" focused on the "whole person" who lives in the social world and has spiritual, as well as physical, social and emotional needs. This model resembles the balance and wellness symbolized by the American Indian medicine wheel. This dimension of spirituality and a concept called "gerotranscendence" are presently at the cutting edge of gerontology research in terms of defining what it means to age well.

In my own search for meaning and ways to age well, despite financial limitations and health problems, I have found Tornstam's (1997) theory of gerotranscendence appealing. According to his theory, in the process of living into old age, one finds opportunity and potential which entails "a shift in meta-perspective, from a materialistic and pragmatic view of the world to a more cosmic and transcendent one, normally accompanied by an increase in life satisfaction" (143). Many aspects attributed to gerotranscendence echo the indigenous worldview I have observed in the American Indian culture.

Progress toward gerotranscendence is seen in changes that can be grouped into three categories—self, social and personal relationships, and cosmic insights. A person in this developmental period is:

- less concerned with "self" and expected roles and has the courage to be oneself;
- accepting of aging, with no need to separate mind from body;
- less likely to give advice;
- less concerned with material possessions;
- more inclined to find deeper significance in nature, relationships, and solitude;
- more likely to see time as circular and to feel an interest in ancestors and a kinship with earlier generations and earlier times;
- more accepting of life's mysteries and more likely to integrate science and faith;
- less afraid of death.

So many of these characteristics (if not all) are essential to Native indigenous cultural beliefs. Tornstam, a sociologist at Uppsala University in Sweden, developed his theory by conducting qualitative interviews with fifty people between ages fifty and ninety-seven. My own instinct about what accounts for this resonance with Native indigenous culture is more related to the nature of transcendence than the political-economic differences between the U.S. and Sweden. This is a theory of older adult development, when people shed the unnecessary, the mundane, and the need to be right; it's about becoming authentic (living one's values) and "being" rather than "doing." Indigenous cultures, more rooted in nature and the spiritual realm, may be closer to transcending materialism, scientific "truth" and busy-ness.

Choices Today: Moving Beyond Ageism

There are some themes in the study of aging that have not changed over time. One of those is the desire to age in place and to avoid institutionalization. This was a strong wish during the time of the Great Depression, as evidenced in the case of sisters Mrs. Drake and Miss Miller and their mentally disabled brother Mr. Miller (see chapter 4, this volume) and in the general dread of the poor house (see chapters 1 and 3, this volume). Dread today rests in the possibility of ending up in a nursing home. Due to financial limitations, older people in 2010, like the elders of yesterday, have few real choices at the end of life, despite the continuum of long-term care options, including home care, assisted living, continuing care retirement communities (CCRCs), foster care homes and nursing homes. I have spoken frequently at local CCRCs and am always struck by the homogeneity of the residents—mainly white, educated, and privileged. The early evidence of classism, as seen in placement decisions regarding Hannan or Scudder clients (see Ray, chapter 3), reveal the same societal values that influenced the design of our bifurcated social security system in 1935. These same values and policies maintain a bi- or tri-furcated system in 2010, seen in this array of long term care options, especially in housing choices that are costly and out of reach for people with limited resources. According to AARP (2009) the average cost for nursing home care is now over $70,000 and assisted living over $35,000 per year in 2009.

When exploring the possibilities for my own long-term care, I realized that many of the housing options are beyond my financial capabilities. CCRCs in Michigan require one to four hundred thousand dollars down just to move in, and monthly fees are in excess of $2500. There is no Eloise, thank god, although some of today's Medicaid nursing homes might prove to be no better, and some are certainly worse. The mid-range choices for assisted living or independent living offer menus of options, as well as a modicum of independence. No matter what the cost and which entitlements might defray those costs, what really matters is the care received and the possibility of spending one's latter days in a place that encourages growth and, as the body naturally declines, continued development of the soul. What options might there be for me?

My twenty-year immersion into American Indian culture continues to raise great internal debates between the culture in which I was raised and a culture I have grown to respect profoundly. The white, middle-class, protestant culture of my childhood is steeped in the values of independence, youthfulness, and busy-ness and tends to ignore those elders who have not aged "successfully" (as defined by the biomedical model). The American Indian culture, although influenced by the mainstream culture, has maintained the values of interdependence, respect for elders, and reflection (storytelling, talking circles). I contributed a chapter, "Long Term Care Among American Indians" for

Minorities, Aging and Health (Chapleski 1997), in which I discussed findings from the extant research, as well as my own longitudinal long-term care study. I reported that these indigenous elders, if they maintained tribal ties, whether urban or rural, expressed the possibility of returning to their reservations. I have often envied that safety-net and wish that I, too, had a community in which to retreat. One Ojibwa reservation informant told me "a lot of the elders actually moved away to big cities . . . got jobs in factories . . . Now that they're getting older, we do see more coming back. Some of their children are coming with them to be part of the community again. Probably there were big migrations out in the fifties and sixties and now we're seeing migration back" (Chapleski, Sobeck, and Fisher 2003, 384).

Their families do not abandon the Native American elders, generally speaking, and respect for elders is still the ideal, although in reality not as strong as in the past. As one rural Odawa informant said, "It's the norm to take care of family. . . It's not a burden . . . something you know is just part of you" (Chapleski 1997, 385). There's that word again—*burden*—but with a different slant. How comforting it must be to know that your community, your family, does not think in terms of burden but in terms of a natural caring reflex, both expected and welcomed. Sometimes I ponder the direction our country might have taken if the early settlers and leaders had respected the indigenous culture enough to learn from their ideas about spirituality, the environment, materialism, respect for all creatures and especially the wisdom of elders, rather than attempting to eradicate the people and their culture.

Regardless of where one resides, at home or in a nursing facility, whether it is publicly or privately funded, what truly matters is the nature of the caring. Thoughtful protagonists of feminist perspectives are redefining what "caring" might look like in a humane world. Ruth Ray (2008) in *Endnotes,* a book about old age and the end of life, focuses on philosopher Virginia Held's (2006) distinction between "charity" and "caring." A virtuous person is "one who believes in doing good" and a caring person is "one who does good" (Ray 2008, 160). From a caring perspective, "care is always preferable to charity because it allows for expressions of identity and agency on the part of the other; care involves trust and mutuality rather than 'charitable domination'" (Ray 2008, 160). Reading through the LHMH files and the Visitor's notes, we find many examples of charity but few examples of true caring as measured by this standard.

Having just enjoyed another birthday, I continue to read about and explore the terrain of aging, seeking meaning in these years. I am grateful for the opportunity to have become acquainted with the LHMH men and women and their examples of resilience in a difficult time, and to my American Indian friends for their wisdom and resilience across time and for teaching me to *be* as I was attempting to *do*. I see older people who illumine the existence of gerotranscendence, and I know many American Indian women younger than myself who reveal these qualities. With age comes necessary loss, but amidst this loss there is the potential for greater authenticity and growth. There is truth in the poignant question asked by Elisabeth Kubler-Ross (Kubler-Ross and Kessler 2002, 26):

> Are we only able to see who we actually are at life's beginnings and endings? Do only extreme circumstances reveal ordinary truths? Are we otherwise blind to our genuine selves? This is the key lesson of life: *to find our authentic selves, and to see the authenticity in others.*

Perhaps in this process we can free ourselves of the worry of being burdened or becoming a burden. As a society we might learn to embrace aging as an opportunity rather than a burden. Ageist attitudes, ageist behaviors, and ageist policies are the burden, not the aged person.

Notes

1. The New English Bible 1970, 670.
2. National Institute on Aging, Grant (R01-AG11152) (1992-1997)
3. Emphasis added
4. Despite this, what truly took me by surprise in my own research was the resilient spirit of so many elders and their ability to maintain their Native cultures in an un-welcoming urban environment, whether Anishnaabeg (the Native language term for the closely related Ojibway, Odawa and Potawatomie tribes of the region, descended from Algonquian roots) or Lakota or Alaskan villagers. While life conditions in the city led to lower life expectancy, those elders who remained embedded in their culture continued to enjoy the respect of their families and tribes.

References

AARP. 2009. *State by State Long Term Care Costs.* http://www.aarp.org/family /caregiving/articles/state-by-state_longterm.html. Accessed Nov. 10, 2009.

Achenbaum, W. Andrew. 1978. *Old Age in the New Land.* Baltimore: Johns Hopkins University Press.

Board of Trustees. 1930. *The Luella Hannan Memorial Home: A Living Remembrance of William W. and Luella Hannan.* First Annual Report. Detroit, Michigan.

Calasanti, Toni M. and Kathleen Slevin. 2001. *Gender, Social Inequalities and Aging.* Gender Lens Series, CA: Alta Mira Press.

Calasanti, Toni M. and Kathleen Slevin (Eds.) 2006. *Age Matters: Re-Aligning Feminist Thinking.* New York: Routledge.

Calasanti, Toni. 2008. "Gender and Class Relations in the Struggle for Old-Age Security." *Journal of Aging, Humanities and the Arts*, 2, No. 3 and 4: 248-49.

Chapleski, Elizabeth E. 1997. "Long Term Care among American Indians: A Broad Lens Perspective on Service Preference and Use." Pp. 367-94 in *Minorities, Aging and Health*, edited by Kyriakos Markides and Miranda, Manuel. Sage Publications.

Chapleski, Elizabeth E. 2002. "Facing the Future: 2002 City of Detroit Needs Assessment of Older Adults," Wayne State University, Institute of Gerontology.

Chapleski, Elizabeth E., Joanne Sobeck and Charles Fisher. 2003. "Long Term Care Preferences and Attitudes among Great Lakes American Indian Families: Cultural Context Matters." *Journal of Long Term Home Health Care.* 4, No. 2: 94-100.

Crowther; Martha, Michael Parker, W.A. Achenbaum, Walter Larimore, and Harold Koenig. 2002. "Rowe and Kahn's Model of Successful Aging Revisited: Positive Spirituality." *The Gerontologist*, 42, No 5: 613-20.

Detroit: History. 2009. retrieved from http://www.city-data.com/us-cities/The-Midwest/Detroit-History.html (accessed January 12, 2010).

Friedan, Betty. 1963. *The Feminine Mystique.* New York: Dell.

Haber, Carol, 1993. "And the Fear of the Poorhouse: Perceptions of Old Age Impoverishment in Early Twentieth-Century America." *Generations* 17, No. 2: 46-51.

—. 2000. "Historians' Approach to Aging in America." Pp. 25-40 in *Handbook of the Humanities and Aging*, 2nd Edition edited by Thomas Cole, Robert Kastenbaum and Ruth E. Ray. NY: Springer Publishing.

Hall, G. Stanley, 1922. *Senescence: The Last Half of Life.* NY: D. Appleton and Company.

Held, Virginia. 2006. *The Ethics of Care: Personal, Political and Global.* New York: Oxford University Press.

Jackson, Deborah D. and Elizabeth E. Chapleski. 2000. "Not Traditional, Not Assimilated: Elderly American Indians and the Notion of Cohort." *Journal of Cross Cultural Gerontology*, 15 No 3: 229-59.

Katz, Stephen, 1996. *Disciplining Old Age*. Charlottesville and London: University of Virginia Press.

Klingaman, William K. 1989. *1929: The Year of the Great Crash*. New York: Harper and Row.

Kubler-Ross, Elisabeth and David Kessler, 2002. *Life Lessons*. New York: Simon and Schuster.

Luella Hannan Memorial Foundation Collection. Walter Reuther Library of Labor and Urban Affairs. Wayne State University, Detroit, Michigan.

Martin, Lillien J. and Clare deGruchy. 1930. *Salvaging Old Age*. New York: The Macmillan Company.

———. 1979/1933. *Sweeping the Cobwebs*. New York: Arno Press.

Minkler, Meredith and Carroll Estes, eds. 1984. *Readings in the Political Economy of Aging*. Farmingdale, NY: Baywood Publishing.

Moody, Harry R. 2006. *Aging: Concepts and Controversies. 5th Ed.* Thousand Oaks, CA: Pine Forge Press.

———. 2010. *Aging: Concepts and Controversies. 6th Ed.* Thousand Oaks, CA: Pine Forge Press.

New English Bible. 1970. London: Oxford University Press, Cambridge University Press.

Palmore, Erdmore, 1999. *Ageism: Negative and Positive*, 2nd Edition. New York: Springer Publishing Company.

Poole, Mary. 2006. *The Segregated Origins of Social Security: African Americans and the Welfare State*. Chapel Hill, NC: North Carolina Press. Cited in Calasanti, Toni. 2008. "Gender and Class Relations in the Struggle for Old-Age Security." *Journal of Aging, Humanities and the Arts*, 2, No. 3 and 4: 248-49.

Ray, Ruth E. 2006. "The Personal as Political." Chapter 2 in *Age Matters: Realigning Feminist Thinking* edited by Toni Calasanti and Kathleen Slevin. New York: Routledge.

———. 2008. *Endnotes*. New York: Columbia University Press.

Rowe, John W. and Robert L. Kahn. 1998. *Successful Aging*. New York: Pantheon Press.

Tornstam, Lars. 1997. "Gerotranscendence: The Contemplative Dimension of Aging." *Journal of Aging Studies* 11: 143-54.

Tornstam, Lars. 2005. *Gerotranscendence*. New York: Springer Publishing Company.

Chapter 11

The Continuing Struggle for Old-Age Security

Toni Calasanti

July 28, 1931

Mr. and Mrs. Curtis, ages 66 and 68, have lived comfortably all their married life. Mr. Curtis has held middle-management jobs in local companies for many years and at one time supervised forty people. He did contracting work and received both salary and commission. During his later years, he also sold insurance. Mrs. Curtis has never worked outside the home. She gets much enjoyment from her church work and from managing the house.

Mr. and Mrs. Curtis have been referred for assistance by their church. They own their home, but recently took out a mortgage against it to pay back bills. Now the taxes are due, and they cannot afford to pay them. They also have a medical bill they cannot pay. About six years ago, Mr. Curtis suffered a serious illness from which he has never fully recovered; and since that time his personality has changed, and he is difficult to get along with. The couple have been living modestly on their savings, and these are now nearly gone. During the real estate boom four years ago, their house was worth twice what it is worth now. They would like to sell, but cannot find a buyer, even at a greatly lowered price. The house is in need of a few repairs but on the whole has been kept in good condition.

Mr. and Mrs. Curtis live alone, but they have two sons, both of whom are married and who live in the Detroit area, and are trying to buy their own homes. One son, who has a daughter, has worked at the same place for twenty years, but just recently, his hours were cut in half due to the business depression. The second son was out of work for two years, and has just found another job; he has two children. One daughter-in-law will not permit her in-laws to live in her home; the other daughter-in-law might be willing, but it could not be done without great sacrifice, because this family is barely able to make a living without the added responsibilities.

While worthy of aid, the couple is not funded, due to exhaustion of LHMH funds. In December, 1934, they are both admitted to the Detroit Receiving Hospital, Psychopathic clinic. (LHMFC, Case #503)

Introduction

I begin this chapter with Mr. and Mrs. Curtis's case as it contains a number of elements relevant to old people living in the United States in the twenty-first century. Based on the Visitor's notes, this middle-class couple had lived according to the dictates of their society: a gender division of labor, personal responsibility for their futures, hard work, a savings account, and two children raised to independent adulthood. But they had fallen on hard times—precipitated by illnesses that required expensive medical care at the time and from which Mr. Curtis never recovered. Their situation became all the more dire because of the Depression. They had family, but could not rely upon them. Because of the lack of a social safety net beyond private charities or small state programs, they ended up in a state-run mental ward.

Much in this story resonates with the lives of old people in 2010. First, a disruption, such as illness, can impose burdens for which many are unprepared and raise the prospect of economic insecurity, or *risk* (Hacker, 2007). Second, social programs can recognize the shared nature of such risks and thus pool resources to mitigate their effects (for instance, through universal health care or unemployment benefits). Third, ideologies of work and family dictate how citizens' lives should unfold and underlie such policies. This chapter offers a comparative view of old people who applied to the LHMH for aid and old people seeking to minimize risk today by examining how disruptions, support for social insurance, and ideals of the life course interact in shaping the experience of old age.

Risks of later life: How do we handle them?

According to Walker (2009: 596), "Old age was acknowledged collectively as a risk status from the early part of the twentieth century." Western industrial societies such as the U.S. understood that old age raised levels of health and financial insecurity. However, when the Hannan trust was established in 1925, few social programs existed for old people; what we now think of as the welfare state did not come into being until 1935.

The fact that such risks are not equally distributed throughout the population—that is, that some groups, such as women, were more likely to experience these problems in old age—was implicitly acknowledged by the LHMH. Historians Haber and Gratton argue that most of those who were poor in old age were from groups vulnerable throughout their life courses, such as unmarried women, and racial and ethnic minority groups: "Poor in young adulthood and middle age, these aged persons simply arrived at old age with few of the assets obtained by their more successful counterparts" (1994: 172). Indeed, this is the population served by the Scudder trust, such as the clients described in Calasanti and Harrison's chapter, who were working-class members and people of color. Others fell into poverty only in later life. The bulk of the LHMH files tell stories of this group, characterized not by life-long financial struggle but by the onset of poverty in later life, partly as a result of gender relations: women of (previous) means, whose dependence on men (fathers earlier in life, husbands later) presented them with contradictory experiences. They had often lived in comfort if not in luxury, where financial pressures seldom touched them, trading domestic labor, performed directly or in the supervision of others, for financial support. They fell into situations of need dominated by finances over which they had exerted little control and with which they could claim little expertise. Gender relations at that time made women's situations all the more problematic, in that men could (more) easily make decisions about finances over the life course and in old age (over earnings, spending, and investments, pensions where available, and the purchase of life insurance) without their wives' knowledge or consent. Women of means were seldom experienced in such matters.

Today, the ways in which we manage such risk is markedly different. The development of the U.S. welfare state in 1935 marked a turn toward the collective sharing of economic risks in later life. As Walker notes, in the post-World War II era, "the risks associated with later life were accepted as socially legitimate, with few sanctions attached to the welfare responses, unlike those connected with people of working age" (2009: 596). It was acceptable for old people to rely on state support; they were not judged to be morally deficient, as were those collecting other forms of welfare. However, beginning in the 1970s, welfare state expansion halted in light of the rocketing world oil prices and resulting fiscal crisis. Then, in the 1980s, rising neo-liberalism reduced support for public pensions because of the social expenditure they represent (Walker, 2009).

The economic trends of the 1970s and 80s foreshadowed those of today, with globalization on the one hand and the retraction of the welfare state on the other. While some risks have become better controlled by social agencies (such as epidemics), new risks have emerged: of becoming unemployable after age 50 and of insecure work over the life course with little recourse to social protections (Walker, 2009). At the same time, responsibility for such risks is being shifted increasingly to individuals (Marshall, 2009; Walker, 2009; Hacker, 2007). Thus, globalization has increased the number of insecure jobs in the U.S., while at the same times workers are being encouraged to take on the responsibility for funding their own retirement through the use of private pensions, which depend upon the volatile global stock market (Phillipson, 2009). Commenting on the contemporary context in relation to old age, Phillipson and Vincent (2007: 631) note that many of the risks associated with old age, such as the potential for poverty or the possibilities of serious health concerns, have not changed with time. But "[w]hat has changed is that the duty and the necessity to cope with these risks are being transferred to individual families (women carers in particular) and individual older people (notably with respect to financing for old age)."

State versus Family Support

Expecting families to care for their own is not new. The expectation has often been codified; as Jankowski noted in chapter 2, in 1920s Detroit, the MCL (Michigan Compiled Laws) Act 146 of 1925 required that families provide care to their elders (State of Michigan, 1925). Thus, a large part of the Visitors' work in determining client eligibility revolved around discovering what kin were available and might provide care. Often, family members were contacted and asked to demonstrate whether they could care for their elders. If Visitors deemed that any family member could, then the potential client was denied funding.

The development of the Hannan and Scudder trusts, however, and the rapidity with which they were exhausted, provide a graphic example of the problems in expecting families to care for older members. For the hundreds of cases referred to the LHMH for funding, families were either non-existent or unable to help. The case of Mr. and Mrs. Curtis, described at the start of this chapter, was typical. The situation of another LHMH client, Bertram Carruthers, illustrates similar problems in terms of family care. According to the Visitor's notes, Mr. Carruthers, age seventy-nine, was very unhappy living in an old age home when he applied for an LHMH pension in 1931. He had no complaints about the food or the treatment from the staff, but felt "the loss of liberty and home surroundings. Says many people are perfectly content there, but he is too active and restless to endure the life there" (LHMFC, Case #50). With the Visitor's assistance, Mr. Carruthers tried out a couple of boarding homes, but was asked to leave because he was not very clean about himself and left the bathroom dirty. When he was removed from the second boarding home, the Visitor took him to visit his daughter in a rural area of metropolitan Detroit. The Visitor reports that the woman became "almost hysterical at the sight of her father with his belongings" and immediately asked if he expected to stay there. The daughter said that "possibly she might keep him for a few days until arrangements could be made for him," but she did not see how she could take care of him permanently. The Visitor had a long talk with her about the family situation, which she summarizes in her notes:

> Mr. Carruthers does not get along well with [the daughter's] husband; [she says] that she tried for almost a year to live with them both, and that Mr. Carruthers almost caused a divorce between them. . . . States that she is in no situation to take him; that they have just moved into the present home, there are no conveniences, and it is very difficult for her to do the work because of lack of conveniences (LHMFC, Case #50).

The Visitor asked the daughter if she could do anything at all to help Mr. Carruthers. The daughter replied that "she cannot as her husband is not working at this time, and they have practically no income. They have purchased the farm on which they are living, and it appears that they are rather short of funds."

Later, in February of 1932, Mr. Carruthers showed the Visitor a letter he had just received from his other daughter in Phoenix, "telling him how hard pinched they were financially and asking him to loan them $50.00. [He] went on to explain how impossible such a thing would be on his [pension]. It takes very careful planning for him to be able to live on that much himself, let alone loan any to his relatives" (LHMFC, Case #50).

What becomes clear in such stories is that caring for one's parents strained many children, who faced financial difficulties of their own and who suffered the interpersonal challenges of living in multigenerational households. While it is certainly not the case that all such living situations provoked problems—and I will provide more examples of greater success below—the ability to provide for many generations in a household often posed insurmountable challenges.

An older person's reliance on adult children can also negatively affect the elder in terms of life choices. Historians Haber and Gratton (1994) argue that a critical reason that Social Security legislation gained traction was that it would promote a growing middle class by relieving children of the burden of providing financially for their elders. The 1920s had allowed many old people and their children to establish separate households, and they developed expectations that this would continue. However, the Depression made clear the inability of the market to provide long-term economic stability for families, and the government moved to handle the insecurities in a collective manner:

> "The Depression of the 1930s challenged these assumptions [of independent living] and exacerbated many of the unsolved problems of industrial employment. . . . For the poor and working class, the economic crisis challenged the ability of the family fund to meet basic needs. For the middle class, it proved the incapacity of the private market to guarantee autonomy in old age. . . . The Depression . . . struck all classes and forged a coalition that demanded that the government ensure a respectable old age—without a continued reliance on the sacrifices of family members" (Haber and Gratton, 1994: 180).

Historian W. Andrew Achenbaum (1999: 9) concurs: "Legislators . . . felt that people in their prime should not be unduly burdened by caring for dependents at both ends of the life cycle."

The Social Security Act of 1935, which included ten different programs, set up two different kinds of policies (Poole, 2006). The social insurance programs, which included Unemployment Insurance and Old Age Insurance (later renamed Social Security), were based on a recognition of the common risks, such as unemployment, that citizens run and that could result in financial duress. As such, social insurance programs had more universal appeal and enjoyed high levels of public support during the Great Depression. Eligibility was based on membership in the insured group (e.g., a former worker, a retiree), and one could spend the benefits, meager or great, as one chose.

By contrast, social assistance programs, such as Aid for Dependent Children (now named TANF, Temporary Assistance to Needy Families), or what we now call Supplemental Security Income (SSI), were based on need. To receive benefits, one had to demonstrate a lack of means, i.e., poverty. Benefits came with restrictions and also included cash substitutes (such as food stamps) that further constrained how they might be spent.

The Luella Hannan Memorial Home offered a program similar to social assistance, even though the LHMH called their assistance "pensions" or "grants" and even though benefit levels were higher than typical assistance programs because of the desire to help a higher class clientele. The negotiations between visitors and clients described in previous chapters reflect the kinds of oversight that assistance programs can wield and the ways in which recipients respond. We can thus read these stories for lessons about the challenges of retaining identity and dignity in later life when dependent on social assistance programs. Though Social Security maintains much inequality through its benefit formula, it is definitely preferable to a social assistance program.

At the same time, the kinds of power relations that were embedded in the LHMH pensions were also incorporated into the Social Security Act. Northerners who eventually shaped the Act were conscious of race and felt they were shaping a "color blind" policy. But their lack of awareness of their own privileges led them to exclude racial and ethnic minorities, women, and various low-paid workers from coverage in their attempts to protect white, male industrial workers (Poole, 2006). Only paid workers were covered, and occupations that were disproportionately filled by women and racial and ethnic minorities were excluded, as were jobs that did not pay wages high enough to be eligible. Similarly, until the Scudder trust joined the Hannan trust, no people of color or members of the working class were eligible for pensions from the LHMH. The wage issue also reflects the fact that Social Security benefits have been established to pay differing amounts based on earnings and years worked. Those with higher earnings over time collect the highest benefits. The LHMH distributed funds in a similar manner, with those clients of higher status backgrounds receiving higher pensions than those funded by Scudder monies.

The different models of assistance help us to see that the Social Security Act, like the LHMH program before it, set up a bifurcated system for deserving and undeserving old people (Poole 2006) based on the intersections of gender, race and class. As a whole, women and racial and ethnic minority group members were excluded as workers under the Social Security Act and the 1939 amendments, which implicitly recognized women's reproductive labor but only in ways that built upon and reinforced inequalities. Similarly, racial and ethnic minority men and women were excluded as domestic workers and agricultural laborers, occupations in which they predominated but which were not covered by the original legislation. These pieces of legislation established a social insurance program which allowed mostly white men to collect funds for themselves or their wives and their children as survivors of covered workers. Other white women—divorced, deserted, or never married—and their children received much smaller benefits. The failures of their marriages (or lack thereof) were taken to indicate a less worthy status (Rodeheaver, 1987). Women of color or working-class women also were excluded for not fitting the white, middle-class ideal, or for having married men who did not.

Despite these inequities, the importance of Social Security for the well-being of old adults *and* their adult children (and families) today cannot be overemphasized. In 2007, Social Security provided at least half of all income for 53% of old married couples and almost three-fourths (73 percent) of unmarried persons. Even more important, Social Security provides 90 percent or more of income for one-third (35 percent) of married couples and 44 percent of those who are not married. In 2003 (the last year reported), one in five "aged units" (this refers to both married couples and individuals living alone) received all of their income from

Social Security (Social Security Administration, 2005). Even so, according to the official measure, 16.1 percent of old people were either poor or near poor (within 125 percent of the poverty line) (Social Security Administration, 2009a: pp. 7-8). Alternative poverty measures recently put into place double the number of old people below the poverty line. This new measure—which takes medical expenses into account—finds that 18.7 percent or almost 7.1 million of old people are poor, compared to 9.7 percent, or 3.7 million, under the traditional measure (Associated Press, 2010). It is difficult to imagine what a retraction of any part of this critical source of income would do to older people and their families, especially in the present economic climate where unemployment and home foreclosures are critical issues.

Still, as I have noted, today we find ourselves in the midst of what Hacker (2007)—prior to the present recession—called a "Great Risk Shift" wherein families are, once again, being asked to assume increasing shares of the economic risks, including health coverage and retirement benefits, once shouldered by corporations and governments that can more easily spread the risk and burdens. Hacker argues that across the life course we are seeing not only greater economic inequalities, but also "rising insecurity, or the growing risk of slipping from the [economic] ladder itself" (Hacker 2007: 1). And the risk of this happening is unequally distributed along the lines of class, race, ethnicity, and gender (Walker, 2009).

The Social Creation of Dependence: Are Old People a Burden?

Thus far, my discussion has dealt with increased risk across the life course for old people in the 1920s and now. The Social Security data made clear the importance of these benefits for elders' income and quality of life. As a result, it may seem obvious that the answer to the question above is "yes, old people are a burden." Certainly, this is reinforced by the fact that old people comprise the largest group of beneficiaries of social spending (public pensions and health care services) (Walker, 2009).

However, such a conclusion would be incorrect for a number of reasons, only some of which I discuss here. I begin with the social construction of "burden," by which I mean the process of creating a situation of dependence by excluding people from the remuneration of labor and then calling those people "burdens."

First, the dependence of old people on the state is a result of the inability of the economy to provide sufficient, stable income for older people, and for families to be able to provide for all members with what incomes they have. Others (e.g., Phillipson, 1982; Graebner, 1982) have already documented the ways in which retirement was institutionalized in order to regulate labor supply, leaving most old people without incomes. Debates over mandatory retirement demonstrate that demand for the labor of old people varies with commercial needs. Indeed, we see this in our current recession, wherein many older workers (and as young as fifty) are asked to "retire early" to ease layoffs (see, e.g., *Roanoke Times*, March 1, 2010). Those who do, can expect to live for decades without earnings; those who do not, face censure for not stepping aside. Demographic forecasts warn that we will not have enough younger workers in the near future and that society therefore cannot afford the "burden" of supporting so many retirees (King, 2006; Gee, 2000). Thus, we hear calls for "delayed retirement" in the future.

Ageism in the workplace affects this construction of burden, both in the 1920s and today. Within the LHMH case files, we find many examples of older people willing to work but being refused employment on the basis of age. In the case of women, this often related to how they looked; thus we find cases of women trying to "pass" as younger. For instance, the Visitor describes Julie Donnelly, (LHMFC, Case #629), a woman who received a pension from 1929-1942, as having white hair but dyeing it dark brown in order to keep her job as a demonstrator at a local department store. Other notes describe Fanny Reynolds (LHMFC, Case #133) as appearing younger than a woman of seventy-one years and determined to work. However, she was told that she was too old to retain her position at a fudge shop; and indeed, a reference letter from this shop states that Fanny was "hardworking and responsible," and "the only reason we didn't keep her was her age." Such ageism in the workplace not only prevails today (e.g., see studies by McMullin and Berger, 2006; Roscigno, 2010), but is all the more severe in the global economy, given overall job insecurity (Phillipson, 2009; Walker, 2009). In this context, the fact that workers over age fifty have more difficulty finding employment than younger age groups portends even greater insecurity for future cohorts (Walker, 2009).

At the same time, most families cannot financially support older members. In all these scenarios, then, the state has paid the social costs of production. That is, the state has been asked to provide for those whom the economy abandons. Thus, while it might appear that families are to blame for failing to provide, both the Hannan archives and current data show that family wages buy too little. As Haber and Gratton argued, Social Security emerged in an attempt to keep families from having to bear additional costs, above and beyond what they provide for children. Today, many urge us to abandon that attempt, with no alternative plan for provision.

Walker (2009: 597) notes the changing tenor of various national discussions of old age, "in which the previously sacrosanct status of deservingness on the part of this group was replaced by a discourse emphasizing . . . the 'burden' of pensions on the working population." Often this burden has been measured through the use of dependency ratios, in which the working age population (eighteen to sixty-four years) is shown to be steadily shrinking in relation to the growing "dependent" (aged sixty-five and over) population. Such rhetoric has had little impact on the favorable view of Social Security, but in light of such concerns in the 1980s, the U.S. Congress passed legislation that phased in changes to the age of eligibility for full benefits from sixty-five to sixty-seven (these changes took effect in 2000). More recently, however, discourse on dependency ratios has been combined with concerns over the rising costs of providing for an aging population, including potential costs of health and social care services (Walker, 2009: 598). We often see these concerns expressed in the rhetoric of "intergenerational conflict"—in the present instance, an often-contrived characterization that younger and older generations are fighting over social resources and that grasping, "greedy geezers" will drain the public coffers and cause younger people to suffer. Often depicted as wealthy elders vs. increased numbers of poor children, such depictions avoid the real causes of poverty in the global restructuring of a capitalist market for labor.

Dependency ratios, taken to be objective indicators of societal burden, are often used to warn us of threats posed by an aging population and to argue the need for the welfare state to return responsibility and thus risk to individuals and families. However, this presumably objective figure is often a *"crude 'dependency ratio'"* (Walker, 2009: 597; my emphasis), one based on age (and not necessarily actual labor force participation rates) which compares people ages eighteen to sixty-four with those sixty-five and older. By contrast, a *total dependency ratio* includes children (those aged zero to seventeen). Total dependency ratios, when explored over time, give us a clearer statistical picture of the kinds of changes that have occurred in our population and hint at the extent to which we can provide for "dependents." Thus, Social Security Administration (2009b) figures show that the highest total dependency ratio, at .95, occurred in 1965. Projections for the future, using intermediate economic and demographic assumptions, find the total dependency ratio to peak at .82 in 2035-2040 (when all baby boomers will have passed age 67), a substantially smaller ratio than that of 1965.

The difference, of course, is in composition of the so-called dependent population. Apparently, people didn't mind social spending on the young. However, the ageism that serves to characterize the old population as somehow more dependent than children (and which further depends on ignoring the work and care that old people as a group provide) makes it all the more likely that decisions concerning social cutbacks will target the old population.

Debates about the accuracy of dependency ratios and how they construct burden is one issue. As important as it is, however, such analysis can leave intact the faulty assumption that old people make no economic contributions. It thus becomes important to note that many of those over age sixty-five are employed. Data from 2008 indicate that 16.8 percent (6.2 million people) of those over age sixty-five were in the labor force, a full 21.5 percent of men and 13.3 percent of women in that age group. And, contrary to popular opinion, labor force participation rates for those over sixty-five have been rising since 2000 (Administration on Aging, 2010).

Still, employment statistics tell only part of the story—and perhaps not the most significant part. To illustrate, let me draw on another Hannan case file.

As described by her Visitor in 1929, Scudder client Maude Bancroft was born in England and was seventy-four when she applied for a pension, having been referred by the Department of Public Welfare. She lived with her daughter and two grandchildren in a "small cottage" in Ferndale, a small town in greater Detroit. Maude's father had deserted her mother and their eight children. Maude's own husband had deserted *her* after fathering their eight children. Now Maude had four remaining children and was living with her youngest daughter Bessie, whose husband has deserted her and their two children.

Maude had worked hard all her life. She supported herself and the children by taking in sewing; this income was supplemented by the wages earned by the older children. Seven years prior to applying for the pension, Maude had given Bessie $800 for the down payment on the home they were buying in Ferndale. She had been living with her daughter, working as a caretaker, and helping raise her grandchildren since that time.

Maude enjoyed good health for the first three to four years of her pension (at thirty dollars a month). Her health began to decline after that, and the family was beset by financial problems during the Depression. Bessie lost her job as a cashier at Ford's cafeteria, and they lost their home to foreclosure in 1935. By 1937, when Maude was eighty-two, the daughter had become hard to live with (she had "a quick temper" and was "disagreeable," according to the Visitor), and the children were hard to manage in their teenage years. The fourteen-year-old granddaughter would soon be sent to the Methodist Children's Home because her mother couldn't "control her." Maude had gall bladder and heart problems and had suffered a great deal of physical and emotional pain over the last four years. She had often been left alone in the house while her daughter worked or looked for work. She had always been grateful for her small pension (reduced to twenty-five dollars in 1932). She wrote the Visitor in a very shaky hand in February, 1937, begging that she be moved into a convalescent home, as she was no longer able to contribute to the family in the same way. Maude makes her case this way:

> I would not want to leave Bessie but Marjorie is so capable she can cook and make a cake and the washing goes out and Bessie has a whole day on Wednesday to do what she can't do other days. The cooking is too much for me and other jobs Bessie says not to do anything but I can't sit and see things wanted doing so please try to get me somewhere I would even go into the workhouse if ther[e] is no home or take something to end the pain.
>
> I am sure if you knew your dear mother was suffering you would do what you could for her I am ashamed of sitting idle I have always[s] done everything all the washing and work and always the food ready for Bessie and taken care of Marjorie since 3 months old at 68 years of age and bathed both children for years. Please . . . I don't know how to carry on. . . . (LHMFC, Case #92)

She signed the letter, "your suffering friend, Maude Bancroft." In response, the LHMH increased her grant to forty-five dollars and sent her to the Walter Nursing Home, where she died a year later.

This case raises several points that demonstrate how old people who receive pensions are *not* burdens. First, old people are often providing for families, by providing housing, for instance. Maude was not unusual; many other Hannan and Scudder clients owned homes in which their children and grandchildren lived. Similar scenarios play out today. In 2008, almost one million grandparents aged sixty-five or over maintained households in which their grandchildren lived (Administration on Aging, 2009).

Second, contrary to popular notions that only paid work contributes to commerce, productive labor depends upon both paid and unpaid activities. Feminists have shown that caring for young persons or those who are ill, providing domestic labor in one's household, and volunteering services that help better one's community are all unpaid labors that are vital to the maintenance of society and indeed, paid workers. As Brush (1999: 180) notes, unpaid labor both "sustain[s] and add[s] value to individual and community life." Recognition of women's reproductive labor is even incorporated into the Social Security benefit structure, wherein dependent spouses of retirees are entitled to collect benefits (more than 95 per cent of these beneficiaries are women). When we broaden our understanding of productivity to include all economic activities, whether or not they are paid, we see that old people perform a vast amount of such unpaid work (Estes, 1991).

Focusing narrowly on grandparenting, we see that Maude not only furnished housing for her daughter and grandchildren, but she also provided a fair amount of domestic labor and child care. Again, we see this today as well. Data on the amount of care and financial aid that grandparents of all ages supply to younger generations show that elders provide a great deal of family care. These data also reveal the fact that family aid flows from older generations downward toward the young, and not necessarily the other way around. According to the U.S. Census Bureau (2009), in 2007, 40 percent of grandparents whose grandchildren lived with them (a total of 2.5 million grandparents) were responsible for providing most of the basic needs of one or more of these grandchildren. 1.5 million of these grandparents were still working for pay. Nine percent (or 6.6 million) of all children in the U.S. live with their grandparents; of these, the majority (4.4 million) live in their grandparent's home, indicating that in these multigenerational households, it is the grandparents who are providing the support. Finally, grandparents provide regular care for 30 percent of children under age five whose mothers work outside the home.

Further, old people's financial dependence is socially created, insofar as we do not pay for their reproductive labor. If society were to pay family members who care for children, grandparents raising grandchildren would be seen as "productive" members of society and not as burdens. And it is because they receive Social Security benefits that they can continue to take on reproductive labor rather than having to seek employment (in an ageist market place), or their children having to pay for child care. The same case can be made for a wide array of other unpaid, economic activities in which old people engage.

Thus, the construction of old people as burdens can be seen in relation to how population numbers are used, on the one hand, and how the contributions of old people are ignored, on the other. This construction relies, in turn, on ignoring the ways in which commercial activities depend upon unpaid work. This is an argument that feminists have made for some time—that women provide the (unpaid) reproductive labor that is necessary for productive (paid) labor and social survival. In addition, they have also pointed out the contradictions in our ideology along these lines. It is to these contradictions that I next turn.

Contradictory Ideologies: Individualism and Personal Responsibility versus Collective Care

In 1996, Congress passed the Personal Responsibility and Work Opportunity Act, which transformed the original program of the 1930s, Aid to Families with Dependent Children (AFDC), into Temporary Assistance to Needy Families (TANF). Feminist sociologist Sharon Hays (2003) spent three years doing ethnographic research in two different cities, trying to understand the impact of the new program on both social workers and TANF recipients. In her analysis, she found ideological contradictions that are embedded in that legislation and that reflect tensions in relation to policies for old people in the 1920s as well as today.

Hays (2003) lays out the two-pronged (and contradictory) aspects of TANF. On the one hand, there is what she terms the "work plan" that seeks to "rehabilitate" mothers "who would otherwise 'merely' stay at home and care for their children." The goal is to make these mothers self-sufficient and financially independent. On the other hand, there is the "family plan" that "uses work requirements as a way of punishing mothers for their failure to get married and stay married" (p. 19). Not only do these two thrusts push against one another (independence vs. connectedness), but TANF exhibits internal tensions within each of these "plans" as well. Independence and self-sufficiency are contradicted by rules that maintain dependence (such as the dictate that one must take any job available, even if it only provides poverty level wages); "family values" are negated by rules that diminish mothers' control over the care of their children or that strain relations with fathers. More broadly, mothers cannot simply make choices that will help them to be "self-sufficient;" they have children whose welfare they must consider.

While her book focuses on mothers receiving welfare, Hays' notes that all of us face these conflicts in our relations to work and family life. Along these lines, Hays highlights the impossibility of juggling family and work as if they were totally separate across the life course and in old age. They clearly are not separate, and the attempt to live up to the discrepant values of each leads to intense contradictions at best and at worst, a greatly diminished quality of life and poverty. In other words, these problems affect people over the life course in ways that make financial security in old age difficult. For instance, many of the women who were Hannan clients were in need of help in later life because they had lived up to race, class, and gender expectations, taking care of the reproductive labor that helped their husbands obtain wealth (Eisentstein, 1979), while others, such as Hannah Carter, below, were unable to balance the work and family demands.

These contradictory ideologies are also embedded in Social Security, to the detriment of many women and people of color. For example, earlier I pointed to the recognition of reproductive labor in Social Security benefits. However, dependent spouses (almost all women) receive only 50 percent of the retiree's benefit. Thus, reproductive labor is both validated as necessary for production but assessed at only half the value of that of paid work, leaving more women than men destitute in later life. And when families then are also called upon to care for elders in later life it is all the more difficult—for families and for old people.

Such contradictions within the cultural logic of "personal responsibility" and individualism are especially relevant to social policies that govern the lives of old people. As Hays (2003: 216) states, "The notion of personal responsibility denies the embeddedness of all individuals in the wider society and their reliance on it. It is an image of unfettered individualism. . . . This logic most obviously neglects the 'dependency' of children and the fact that no parent is 'unfettered.' It also neglects the importance, the reality, and the necessity of wider social ties and connections. It makes invisible, in other words, our interdependence" and leaves the work of caring for others "hidden, undervalued, and inadequately supported."

This denial of interdependence and the undervaluing of care are apparent in the lives of the men and women in the LHMH case files and today. Again, let me turn to a Hannan case for illustration. Hannah Carter, age sixty-one, and her sister occupied an old seven-room house that was run down inside and out. The rooms were dark, dreary, and damp. The Visitor describes Hannah as follows:

> proud, sensitive, nervous and at the thought of her present condition becomes bewildered and bursts into tears. She appears to have a kind and gracious manner, is straight-forward and frank in all of her statements. She is very ambitious, has worked hard all of her life, and her present state of health is due to a breakdown which she had several years ago on account of over-working. She cared for her mother during her last days and appears to have assumed the family responsibility for many years. She cannot comprehend that her earning powers are exhausted. She still believes that if she can get her health back she would be able to earn a living (LHMFC, Case #401).

Hannah had been employed as a bookkeeper and treasurer for many years in Denver but had returned to Detroit ten years earlier to care for her aging parents, who were in poor health. Her father died soon after and her mother "was a constant care until her death [two years ago]. [Hannah] cared for her mother while her sister worked outside of the home to earn a living." At the time of application, Hannah and her sister had no income and were in "dire need" of assistance.

When read with Maude Bancroft's case in mind, we can see the different ways in which contradictions between work and family, and between personal responsibility and individualism, play out in people's lives. Interdependence—and the undervaluing of care—is the salient issue. Both Maude and Hannah believed in personal responsibility and work—an ideology as important then (Zunz, 1982) as now—and wanted to be "productive" and self-sufficient into old age. At the same time, they were called upon to care for others and saw the value in this activity as well. Maude's inability to work for pay and to care for others caused her pain, and she could not accept that she could not help more; as a result, she felt herself to be a burden and wanted to live out her life in an old age home. Hannah's case points most directly to the contradictory ideologies and how they can play out in the lives of such women; dutifully trying to balance the demands of paid labor and caring for her aging parents, she faced a lack of money and care in her own later life and was "bewildered" by this situation. Today, women of higher classes can sometimes deal with these contradictions by hiring others to take on some of their caring work (Hays, 2003), though they of course still run the risk of appearing to be bad mothers or daughters. But working-class and poor women must live these contradictions, and the result is a decreased quality of life in old age. These are contradictions that families of all statuses face, and with which they grapple with different degrees of success based on social location. Middle-class and well-to-do families, who are more likely to be white than not, have material resources not available to working class families and families of color; they can better afford to supply financial assistance to their elders, or hire others to help provide eldercare.

Discussion

The Luella Hannan Memorial Home came into being before the Depression, when old people without material resources had few alternatives; the economic crisis only exacerbated the situation. Women of means whose husbands died and left them with nothing had no employment experience. Men and women faced ageism in the marketplace, or health issues that made employment difficult, and lacked a social safety net. If families did not exist or could not help, they had no recourse. The pensions that were given by the LHMH were, quite literally, life-saving for those who could get them. Others, as we have seen, ended up in Eloise or charitable institutions.

Phillipson (2009: 620) argues that while old age has become more secure in some ways (e.g, better economic well-being for select groups and greater life expectancy), it has become less so in others, such as job security. This is increasingly true for future generations. And just as the risks associated with aging during the Depression era were unequally distributed across race, ethnicity, class, and gender, the new risks emerging in relation to globalization are borne unequally (Walker, 2009).

The twenty-first century economic context has made the problems of providing care in old age all the more severe. In addition to the strain on public coffers that economic downturns cause, the difficulties of funding Social Security in the future also have grown tremendously as the high unemployment rates decrease SS revenues when the number of workers paying into SS becomes smaller. Such strains on state and federal budgets propel politicians to make choices about where public monies should be spent. We learned from the Reagan years that, in such contexts of "fiscal austerity," old people, and especially those most in need, become targets for spending reductions (Estes, 1982). Public rhetoric has already laid the groundwork for cutting social supports to old people, and the specter of an increasingly old population has been widely characterized as a "burden," despite evidence to the contrary (e.g., Wilson, 2000; Gee, 2000).

Walker (2009: 600) notes that some analysts maintain that welfare states cannot deal with the new kinds of risks that are posed in the present global context. However, he argues that evidence for such assertions is lacking and that, in the context of global changes, pooling risks so as to prevent and respond to them is all the more important.

The problems of the contemporary welfare state in the U.S., and support programs for old people specifically, do not result from an outmoded welfare state that is unable to respond to risks in a globalized economy. Instead, drawing upon and expanding Hays' (2003) analysis, I would argue that problems within the welfare system result not from the pooled-risk approach but from contradictions within the wider cultural logic of personal responsibility that denies the embeddedness of all people in the wider society and their reliance upon each other. The invisibility of our interdependence reinforces our treatment of those who receive welfare—whether single mothers or old people—while also hurting us all as we continue to turn a blind eye to the tensions between the cultural values of individualism and our social commitment to others.

In contemporary discourse and public policy regarding older people, similar contradictions are apparent. Debates on Social Security reform blame old people who need support, impose false conflicts across generations, and ignore both the continued support for the program and the role of class (and race and gender) politics that have caused the fiscal crisis (Walker, 2009; Minkler and Robertson, 1991). Debaters often ignore the realities of intergenerational support in terms of the care being provided by many of those who are old but also the care provided over their life courses, and they deny the structural realities both in later life and across the life course that make it more likely for some old people to need more financial assistance than others.

Because national ideology neither acknowledges interdependence nor values care across the life course, old people are more easily depicted as burdens, and their care work—for communities, children, grandchildren, and each other—goes ignored. Indeed, spouses are the first ones to whom older adults turn for care, providing 25 percent of informal care (Shirey and Summer, 2000); and husbands who engage in spousal care provide the same types and amounts as do wives (Arber and Ginn, 1995). Social institutions also insure that some people are more likely to be "burdens" in old age; for instance, a lack of social policies for childcare provision means that women are penalized in the workplace, especially women of color and working class women. By artificially separating the realm of care from that of work, and not valuing the former, we do not see their interconnection, the reliance of productive labor on reproductive labor, or the work and value of old people.

Hays calls for us to build an ethic of interdependence. She argues that, in addition to making it *possible* for all adults to be financially independent, beginning with the provision of a living wage, we need publicly to support care work, "honoring the work of . . . caring for others, and doing so in a public way that includes financial support as well as lip service . . ." (p. 234). She suggests that this can be accomplished through such things as substantial caregiver tax credits, universally subsidized childcare, and workplace flexibility and policies that accommodate families. In a nutshell, we should address the range of inequalities that influence both work and family, on both structural and cultural levels. What is missing from her discussion, however, is the necessity to do this across the life course.

In addition to understanding the ways in which age and other power relations shape the welfare state and construct old people as dependent, then, we need to understand the contradictions in national ideology concerning personal responsibility and care; we also need to acknowledge the realty of interdependence and the value of care in order to fashion socially just policies. Only when we ignore the realities of care and social embeddeness are we able to divide the population into those who are "burdens" and those who are not. And as happened in the 1930s, the outcry of old people *and* the families charged with their care may be required for policy makers to see the need for change.

References

Achenbaum, W. Andrew. 1999. "In the U.S., We've (Usually) Expected our Elders to Remain Productive." *Public Policy and Aging Report,* 10: 7-10, 13.

Administration on Aging. 2010. "A Profile of Older Americans: 2009." U.S. Department of Health and Human Services. http://www.aoa.gov/AoAroot /Aging_Statistics/Profile/2009/docs/2009profile_508.pdf. Retrieved January 12, 2010.

Arber, Sara and Jay Ginn. 1995. "Gender Differences in Informal Caregiving." *Health and Social Care in the Community,* 3:19-31.

Associated Press. 2010. "Gov't Adopts Formula that Doubles Elderly Poor." March 2. http://www.nytimes.com/aponline/2010/03/02/us/politics/AP-US-Poverty.html?_r=2&scp=2&sq=poverty&st=cse. Retrieved March 2, 2010

Brush, Lisa D. 1999. "Gender, Work, Who Cares?! Production, Reproduction, Deindustrialization, and Business as Usual." Pp. 161-189 in *Revisioning Gender,* edited by Myra Marx Ferree, Judith Lorber, and Beth B. Hess. Thousand Oaks: Sage Publications.

Eisenstein, Zillah R. 1979. *Capitalist patriarchy and the case for socialist feminism.* New York: Monthly Review Press.

Estes, Carroll. 1991. "The New Political Economy of Aging: Introduction and Critique." Pp. 19-30 in *Critical Perspectives on Aging: The Political and Moral Economy of Growing Old,* edited by Meredith Minkler and Carroll Estes. New York: Baywood Publishing Co.

Estes, Carroll. 1982. "Austerity and Aging in the United States: 1980 and Beyond." *International Journal of Health Services,* 12: 573-584.

Gee, Ellen M. 2000. "Population Politics: Voodoo Demography, Population Aging, and Social Policy." In *The Overselling of Population Aging,* edited by Ellen M. Gee and Gloria M. Gutman. New York: Oxford University Press.

Graebner, William. 1980. *A History of Retirement: The Meaning and Function of an American Institution.* New Haven, CT: Yale University Press.

Haber, Carole and Brian Gratton. 1994. *Old Age and the Search for Security.* Bloomington, Indiana: Indiana University Press.

Hacker, Jacob S. 2007. "'The Great Risk Shift': Issues for Aging and Public Policy." *Public Policy & Aging Report,* Vol. 17, No. 2: 1, 3-7. Washington, D.C.: National Academy on and Aging Society.

Hays, Sharon. 2003. *Flat Broke with Children.* New York: Oxford University Press.

King, Neal. 2006. "The Lengthening List of Oppressions: Age Relations and the Feminist Study of Inequality." Pp. 47-74 in *Age Matters: Realigning Fem-*

inist Thinking, edited by Toni M. Calasanti and Kathleen F. Slevin. :NY: Routledge.

Marshall, Victor W. 2009. "Theory Informing Public Policy: The Life Course Perspective as a Policy Tool." Pp. 573-593 in *Handbook of Theories of Aging*, edited by Vern L. Bengtson, Merril Silverstein, Norella M. Putney, and Daphne Gans. NY: Springer.

McMullin, Julie Ann and Ellie D. Berger. 2006. "Gendered Ageism/Age(ed) Sexism: The Case of Unemployed Older Workers." Pp. 201-22 in *Age Matters: Realigning Feminist Thinking,* edited by Toni M. Calasanti and Kathleen F. Slevin. NY: Routledge.

Minkler, Meredith and Ann Robertson. 1991. "The Ideology of 'Age/Race' Wars: Deconstructing a Social Problem." *Ageing and Society*, 11, no. 1: 1-22.

O'Connor, James. 1977. *The Fiscal Crisis of the State*. Boston: Little Brown.

Phillipson, Chris. 1982. *Capitalism and the Construction of Old Age.* London: Macmillan.

Phillipson, Chris. 2009. "Reconstructing Theories of Aging: The Impact of Globalization on Critical Gerontology." Pp. 615-627 in *Handbook of Theories of Aging, e*dited by Vern L. Bengtson, Merril Silverstein, Norella M. Putney, and Daphne Gans. NY: Springer.

Phillipson, Chris and John Vincent. 2007. "Globalisation and ageing" Pp. 630-635 in *Encyclopedia of Gerontology*, edited by James Birrin.

Poole, Mary. 2006. *The Segregated Origins of Social Security: African Americans and the Welfare State*. Chapel Hill, NC: North Carolina Press.

Quadagno, Jill. 2008. *Aging & the Life Course, 4th ed.* Boston: McGraw-Hill.

Rodeheaver, Dean. 1987. "When Old Age Became a Social Problem, women were left behind." *The Gerontologist*, 27: 741-46.

Roscigno, Vincent J. 2010. "Ageism in the American Workplace." *Contexts*, 9, no. 1: 16-21.

Shirey, L. and L. Summer. 2000. "Caregiving: Helping the Elderly with Activity Limitations." *Challenges for the 21st Century: Chronic and Disabling Conditions, No. 7*. Washington, D.C.: National Academy on an Aging Society

Social Security Administration. 2005. "Fast Facts & Figures about Social Security, 2005." http://www.socialsecurity.gov/policy/docs/chartbooks/fast_facts / 2005/fast_facts05.pdf. Retrieved October 4, 2006.

Social Security Administration. 2009a. "Fast Facts & Figures about Social Security. 2009. http://www.socialsecurity.gov/policy/docs/chartbooks/fast_facts /fast_facts09.pdf. Retrieved January 7, 2010.

Social Security Administration. 2009b. OASDI Trustees Report. http://www.socialsecurity.gov /OACT /TR /2009/V_demographic.html#167717. Retrieved February 21, 2010.

State of Michigan. 1925. "Public Act 146." Pp. 188-212 in *Public Acts of the Legislature of the State of Michigan Passed at the Regular Session of 1925*. Lansing, MI: Robert Smith Co.

U.S. Census Bureau. 2009. Facts for Features. http://www.census.gov/Press-Release/www/releases/archives/facts_for_features_special_editions /013971.html Retrieved September 3, 2009.

Walker, Alan. 2009. "Aging and Social Policy: Theorizing the Social." Pp. 595-613 in *Handbook of Theories of Aging*, edited by Vern L. Bengtson, Merril Silverstein, Norella M. Putney, and Daphne Gans. NY: Springer.

Wilson, Gail. 2000. *Understanding Old Age*. Thousand Oaks: Sage.

Zunz, Olivier. 1982. *The Changing Face of Inequality: Urbanization, Industrial Development, and Immigrants in Detroit, 1880-1920*. Chicago: The University of Chicago Press.

Chapter 12

Toward a Future
When We Truly Care for Old People

Ruth E. Ray

"To build a feminist future we need to stretch our imaginations so that we can discover new visions in which caring is a central value and institutions truly facilitate caring."
—Berenice Fisher and Joan Tronto

In previous chapters, authors demonstrated how older people asserted their needs and attempted, with varying degrees of success, to hold onto their autonomy and independence while receiving assistance from a charitable organization during the Great Depression. More broadly speaking, these clients were negotiating the terms of their care in old age. As Tom Jankowski explains in chapter 2 and Toni Calasanti reinforces in chapter 11, such negotiations took place within a larger political economy in which the elder and the family, not the state or the nation, were responsible for care. Local sources of support, such as the Department of Public Welfare, provided only "temporary relief" for elders in the form of food, clothing and shelter. The only long-term care available in 1929 was provided either by charitable organizations in the form of private old-age homes or local government in the form of the county poorhouse, known in the Detroit area as Eloise. As I explain in chapter 3, the Luella Hannan Memorial Home (LHMH), as its name implies, was originally meant to be an old-age home for a specific class of people who had "seen better days." While Eloise housed the indigent, and church-based homes provided care for the members of their congregations, the LHMH was established for elders from the "refined" class—those who, by birth or association, had acquired "culture" over their lifetimes and who had come to need assistance only in later life. Even when the LHMH began to administer Scudder funds, which had been allocated for a broader group of old people without regard to race, class, or background, nearly all of the clients who received pensions were relying on charity for the first time in their lives. Still, they had more social capital—connections to people in positions to assist them, opportunities and experiences in leveraging resources— than other elders living in the city of Detroit and certainly the chronically poor living in Eloise.

While the Great Depression leveled financial differences among elders, social differences prevailed, even within the LHMH, as we can see by comparing the cases of Scudder clients like Mrs. Train (chapter 3), Mrs. Thomas (chapter 5), Mrs. Little and Mr. Burke (chapter 8) with the cases of Hannan clients like Mrs. Landen Nuit and Mrs. Dreyfus (chapter 6). Such differences brought significant material consequences: Hannan clients were generally given bigger pensions and often better health benefits than Scudder clients, presumably because they were accustomed to having more and therefore *expected* more. In this sense, the LHMH served an institutional role in maintaining unequal social relations among older people in the city.

In this final chapter, I consider the moral framework in which such unequal age, gender and class relations were perpetuated during the Great Depression by looking back at LHMH cases through the lens of a feminist ethic of care. I conclude with a discussion of what elder care would look like in a more socially just world where all citizens are considered "equal" in terms of their entitlement to the same level of care. In this world, being old and dependent is not a burden but an opportunity for all members of the community to develop *morally* by acting on their *connectedness* as human beings, rather than their *difference* as social beings. Toni Calasanti (chapter 11) and I come to the same conclusion— the need for an ethic of interdependence—from different directions: she argues for old-age policies based on an understanding of risk and the social responsibility to share that risk; I argue for old-age care based on an understanding of our mutual dependence and the moral duty to provide that care.

A Feminist Ethic of Care

Feminist philosophers, many inspired by the early work of Carol Gilligan, have argued that a just society—one in which all members have equal access to the resources necessary for both survival and well be-ing—is best founded on an ethics of care, rather than an ethics of indi-vidual rights. Gilligan argued that a "justice" approach to decision-making (rational application of universal moral principles) and a "care" approach (rational and emotional consideration of human relations in context) were different but equally important value systems. However, later feminists have argued that they are aspects of the same value sys-tem, with care and caring relations providing the broader moral frame-work under which justice is achieved. Virginia Held (2006), for example, argues that care is the overriding moral value, because humans can live (though not flourish) without justice, but no one can live without care.

A feminist ethics of care focuses on the caring relations that must develop among individuals, groups, cultures and nations for everyone to live a good life. It provides a "way of thinking about and evaluating both the more immediate and the more distant human relations with which to develop morally acceptable societies" (Held 2006, 43). From this pers-pective, Berenice Fisher and Joan Tronto (1991) define "care" as a "spe-cies activity that includes everything that we do to maintain, continue and repair our 'world' so that we can live in it as well as possible. That world includes our bodies, our selves, and our environment, all of which we seek to interweave in a complex, life-sustaining web" (40). In short, caring consists of all the things we do to keep life going, and care—rather than independence, autonomy or individual rights—is at the center of a good life. Such caring is continuous and goes on simultaneously in overlapping spheres, both private and public; the caring done by families sustains and is sustained by the caring done by institutions and organiza-tions (employers, day care centers, health clinics, community groups), which is sustained by the caring done by local, state and national gov-ernments (through laws and social policies that promote healthy and car-ing environments).

Fisher and Tronto identify four phases of caring that exist in all of these spheres and that help us understand not only levels of care but the inequalities in care relations that undermine an ethics of care. The phases include caring about, taking care of, caregiving, and care-receiving. Car-ing about entails attentiveness to the world around us and requires that we know about and take an interest in people and issues. To care about old people, for example, requires that we have some knowledge of their needs and interests, but it does not necessarily mean that we are commit-ted to helping meet those needs. Taking care of requires not only know-ledge but also some commitment to action; we must take responsibility for initiating and maintaining caring programs, including finding the resources needed for the actual care of old people. There is a big leap from caring about to taking care of because "the belief that 'others' matter is the most difficult moral quality to establish in practice" (Tronto 1993, 130). To "feel sorry for" individuals or groups (thinking that others matter) is quite different from working to meet their needs (acting as if others matter). Caregiving involves all the hands-on activities of maintaining and repairing. In the case of elder care, this includes taking people to appointments, preparing meals and helping them pay bills, assisting with medications, talking, comforting, and advising. It also includes the "bed and body work" of tending to more frail and dependent elders. The activities of caregiving are endless, ongoing, and ever-changing, while the activities involved in caring about and caring for are more bounded in terms of the time and resources allocated to them. Care-receiving entails the responsiveness of those receiving care, and it varies depending on the recipients and their capabilities. Care-receivers can give many things to caregivers, including gratitude and appreciation, as well as assistance and encouragement. Care relations also involve tensions and conflicts that must be continually negotiated between caregivers and care-receivers. The caring process is therefore challenging and demanding.

Many of these challenges occur as a result of imbalances, differences and inequalities in the caring process. For example, each phase of the process is a precondition for the next: someone must consider and care about old people before resources will be found to assist them; resources must be found before actual caregiving can occur; and caregiving must occur before old people can respond to it. Imbalances inevitably occur in this process: sometimes there are people who care about, but there is no one to take care of; other times there are people available to take care, but no one to generate the resources they need. Different groups are often involved in each phase of the caring process, and they may have limited knowledge of what is happening in the other phases, resulting in fragmentation. This division of labor is ideological as well as practical. As Fisher and Tronto explain, "many of the features and problems associated with modern caring activities arise from the fact that people engaged in these phases have very different histories and perspectives" (41): they are often of different races, classes, and genders and have different beliefs and values about care. At the social and institutional levels, those who care about and take care of are typically educated, economically advantaged white people (often men) who can generate resources through their social capital. The caregiving phase is gendered, raced and classed, as well (Abel and Nelson, 1991; Tronto, 1993; Walker, 1998; Cancian and Oliker, 2000). People who give care are usually women and minorities with limited options for other types of work. Care-receivers, too, range widely in terms of backgrounds and histories as well as financial resources; some can pay handsomely for high-quality care while others have no money for care and must rely on the generosity of others. Such differences create many complications and difficulties in the caring process.

The Caring Process of the LHMH

If we look at the organization of the LHMH from the perspective of the caring process, we can see how its division of labor created the unequal power relations that clients had to negotiate constantly. At the top of the organizational hierarchy was Luella Hannan, a wealthy white woman, and the Board of Trustees, all professional white men, who cared about old people enough to establish the Hannan trust and who cared for old people by administering and maintaining that trust along with the Scudder fund. The Board itself did not do the work of caregiving. Leon Frost, a professional white man, managed the caring process so that Board members did not have to do the caring labor. Frost read the case files, consulted with Visitors, sometimes negotiated directly with clients, and presented his final recommendations to the Board, assuring that the trustees had very little contact with old people themselves. When a breach of etiquette occurred and a client "stepped out of line" to approach a board member directly, as in the case of Mrs. Drake (chapter 4), Mr. Frost wrote the trustee a letter of apology. The Visitors, all white, middle-class women, directly managed the daily care of clients and provided limited hands-on care themselves. They relied for most of the daily caregiving on a host of other formal and informal providers (almost exclusively women), including family members, friends, landladies, boarding house mothers, and staff members at convalescent and nursing homes. The Visitors found their clients places to live, arranged moves, scheduled appointments, and negotiated for them with Mr. Frost and other authority figures (doctors, lawyers, government bureaucrats). They also provided practical care by taking them to doctors' appointments, shopping for them, and sometimes preparing meals, as well as offering advice, sympathy and companionship. Together, the Visitors and caregivers made it possible for the LHMH Board to continue caring about and caring for old people in the way that it did. This linked set of social relations is what Eva Kittay calls "nested dependencies," and it must be fully acknowledged within an ethic of care.

The Problems with a
Hierarchical Structure of Care

The hierarchical organization of care that we see in the LHMH (and in most social and health-care organizations then and now) is efficient in terms of the division of labor and the allocation of resources. However, it is limited and limiting in terms of achieving social justice through an ethic of care, because much of the caring process is invisible to the people involved. Because the Board did not actually provide care to elder clients, it had little understanding of the care practices it was supporting or how clients received that care. Similarly, clients and those who provided them care had no knowledge of the Board's issues and deliberations and little influence over its allocation of resources; they were largely invisible and powerless within the organization. This division of labor had significant material consequences. As members of the privileged class, Board members were removed from the effects of structural forces (unemployment due to ageism, lack of health care, lack of affordable housing) that directly impacted clients' lives. Yet clients and their caregivers had to deal with the effects of these forces on a regular basis: they had insufficient money for food, rent and heat; they could not find places to live that suited them; they lost the boarders (to unemployment) who had helped them pay their bills; they suffered from chronic diseases (diabetes, high blood pressure) for lack of health monitoring; they could not afford the medicines and special treatments needed to cure their ailments or even relieve their pain. Often LHMH pensioners had to rely on family members who were also suffering the effects of structural forces, including unemployment and under-employment and lack of affordable housing. Thus, we see the kinds of negotiations described in part 3 of this volume: clients appealing to the Board, primarily through the Visitors and Mr. Frost, for more money, better health and dental care, better housing and greater consideration of their own caring responsibilities within the family. These were all situations that the LHMH had not fully anticipated when it established the Hannan trust and which Mr. Frost and the Board sometimes overlooked or resisted in their negotiations with clients.

Clients' race and social class also affected their abilities to negotiate their care needs with the Visitors, Mr. Frost and the Board. As we saw in chapter 6, Madeline Landen Nuit, a formerly wealthy white woman, and Ada Dreyfus, a professional white woman, were effective negotiators, in part because they were social "equals" with the Board of Trustees. As a result, they got better care: more attention to individual needs, permission to use their own doctors, special living arrangements. In contrast, Rachel Little and David Burke, Black clients with limited resources and little social capital within the white community, dared not request anything beyond what was originally allotted them. As receivers of care from an organization that considered them socially "unequal," rather than negotiating for better care, Mrs. Little and Rev. Burke spent their time expressing appreciation and gratitude for what they got.

A hierarchical structure of care not only has material consequences for individual elders and their families, but it also decreases the likelihood of change in the caring process at either the institutional or social level. This is because a hierarchical structure "makes understanding the broader social, moral, and political ramifications of care difficult" (Tronto 1993, 112). For example, because they are not in direct contact with people at all social levels and because they do not actually take care of them, those in positions of power do not understand the labor and costs, especially the human costs, of care. Distanced from caregivers and care-receivers, those in power are more likely to perpetuate inequalities by othering—acting as if people in need are different from and lesser than themselves—and paternalism—acting as if they "know better" and deciding how to meet others' needs for them, rather than trusting them to make their own decisions. Both of these attitudes reflect what Held (2006) calls "benevolent dominance," which is different from care. A third attitude that results from hierarchical caring structures is what Tronto calls privileged irresponsibility, where those in power ignore or deny the needs of others. Such irresponsibility is made possible by privileges of wealth or status that allow some members of society to pay other people to meet their personal needs. Because they do not provide direct care to themselves or their families (cooking, cleaning, doing laundry, taking care of children and elders, etc.), these privileged members of society fail to notice caring labor and become inattentive and unresponsive to the needs of others.

Strong social and psychological forces keep these systems of inequality in place. If the powerful admitted they were part of an interactive web of caregivers and care-receivers and that they, too, were dependent upon others, it would "undermine the legitimacy of the inequitable distribution of power, resources, and privilege" of which the privileged person is the main beneficiary (Tronto, 111). Tronto argues that it is psychologically as well as socially advantageous for privileged groups to maintain the fiction of their independence: "Because neediness is conceived as a threat to autonomy, those who have more needs . . . appear to be less autonomous, and hence less powerful and less capable. The result is that one way in which we socially construct those who need care is to think of them as pitiful because they require help" (Tronto 1993, 120). Within this social construction, "caring about and taking care of are the duties of the powerful. Caregiving and care-receiving are left to the less powerful" (114). Further, the caring needs of some (the privileged who can better negotiate with caregivers) are met more completely than the caring needs of others (the underprivileged who do not have the resources to negotiate), a pattern that parallels the unequal distribution of power in society (Tronto, 146). Hence, the hierarchical structure of care perpetuates an unjust status quo, masking social inequalities and making it difficult for those at the top to recognize and understand the need for change.

We can see the unequal power relations between the LHMH and its clients not only in the case files but also in the organization's public discourse. While the language of Leon Frost, who worked directly with clients, reflects an understanding that elders were individuals with unique needs, the language of the Board, which did not work with clients, more often reflects a generalized and romanticized concept of "old age." Both Frost and the Board, however, use the language of paternalism to describe the work of the organization, characterizing clients as dependent children needing relief from the burdens of old age.

We see Frost's attitude toward elder care in a January 1930 article in the *Detroit Free Press*, as well as in the first annual report of the LHMH, published the same month. In speaking to a reporter for the *Free Press*, Frost emphasized the importance of freedom and independence for LHMH clients: "We want the men and women who have come to our attention to have the maximum of comfort and personal freedom," he said. "We don't want to uproot the lives of these gentle folk, so we consider the requirements of each individual, helping him or her to live in a sensible, wholesome way" (Bower 1930). Frost more fully articulates this philosophy of care in the annual report:

> There is crystallizing, gradually, in America a clean-cut and definite attitude toward old age. The sentimental point of view is being replaced by one which is open-minded and human. The issue has been clouded, perhaps, by the considering of old age as a thing apart and entirely impersonal. If we could but look at the old person as the identical one we had known years before, we would be approaching the problem with a much better chance of understanding. Could we but visualize ourselves

a few years hence, our imagination would tell us what the elderly individual needs and desires (Board of Trustees 1930, n.p.).

Frost goes on to explain that what old people want is to be treated as individuals and "made comfortable among their friends and relatives" in
"the community in which they have been active members." He notes,
however, that "this simple fact seems difficult for public opinion at large
to grasp," mainly because the public assumes that all old people are the
same—infirm and in need of physical care—and that such care is best
provided by institutions. Yet, says Frost, "it is quite possible that as individuals we do not want to be thrown into too close proximity with our
fellow beings, and especially of those not of our choosing. The economic
factor alone is not fundamental in making such a choice, and should not
decide the matter." Frost appeals to a higher social good, arguing that
"one of the fine results of a complex civilization is the real possibility of
flexibility and the ability to develop a highly differentiated individuality.
The thoughtful care of the aged should take into account these possibilities" (LHMH Board of Trustees 1930, n.p). Frost's description reflects
what would have been a progressive attitude toward old-age care in the
1920s and 1930s.

In contrast to Frost's discourse of individualized care, the discourse
of Joseph Vance, president and spokesperson for the Board, generalizes
and sentimentalizes the experience of old age. Vance's foreword to the
annual report reflects this view:

> Twilight is a lonely hour, most of all the twilight of old age. To many it
> brings a time when "life and love have gone away side by side," as old
> age, instead of sitting by a fireside of happy memories, watches the
> ashes go dead and finds "sorrow's crown of sorrow" in the memory of
> happier days. What this hour means, only those know who have come
> to a lonely old age, homeless and poor. To bring some cheer and com-
> fort to men and women in such conditions has been our privilege dur-
> ing the past year as trustees of Mr. and Mrs. Hannan's generosity.
> Where life, by day and night, had become the torture of an anxiety
> which even trust in God did not dispel, the assurance that for the rest of
> life, whether the years were many or few, they would be cared for, has
> taken from them a crushing burden, and brought instead, even in old
> age, almost a return of the radiant, care-free happiness of childhood
> (LHMH Board of Trustees 1930, n.p.).

In this passage, Vance casts old age as a lonely period in which living
and making memories gives way to passive reminiscing. It is a time of

economic and social impoverishment, a "crushing burden" that only kind and generous others (not elders themselves) can relieve.

Later in this report, in a section titled "Now That the Flurry is Over," Leon Frost, too, relies on the language of paternalism, suggesting that, because they are no longer productive (employed) members of society, elders must now depend on others. He describes how industrialization and the speed of life in the "great cities" has made it difficult for old people to keep up. The old person in modern society has become "a child again and the world is big and dark and mysterious." This child needs someone else to "interpret, and lead and provide" (1930, n.p.). The LHMH looms as the parental figure in this narrative. Later in the report, Frost provides brief profiles of selected LHMH clients, whom he refers to as "a few of our family."

Paternal attitudes and the othering of old people were very common in the late nineteenth and early twentieth centuries. Most Americans considered structural poverty inevitable as elders were relegated to the "scrap heap" of industrial society (Haber and Gratton 1994, 10). Old age was a social problem, and old people were separated from other dependent groups by virtue of their age alone. Historians Carole Haber and Brian Gratton explain that "in old-age homes, pension programs, and burgeoning almshouses, advanced years defined the old as unproductive and needy and awarded them distinctive treatment," although this treatment varied depending on their race and gender (15). The first lines of the 1930 *Detroit Free Press* article clearly reflect this general attitude of old-age dependency: "Somewhere in Detroit, in furnished rooms, in boarding homes, in apartments filled with the familiar furniture of home, live 239 men and women, each one a 'little old child whose bed-time is drawing near,' as it was said in 'The Return of Peter Grimm'" (Bower, n.p.).

Although we do know something about society's attitude toward old age during the Great Depression, we know much less about what old people thought and felt. Certainly, their voices are absent from the public discourse of the LHMH, as represented in the annual report, and they are absent from the newspaper articles written about the organization during the early years of its formation. Surely the LHMH clients read the newspaper accounts. What did they think about the reporter's description of them as "little old children"? The fact that the reporter did not interview a single elder for her story reflects the unequal power relations in society at this time. Elders were ignored and their voices silenced as others spoke for them.[1]

A Different Perspective on the Caring Process

If we looked at the caring process from the perspective of old people and their families, rather than from the perspective of old-age institutions and the general public, what else might we see? Feminists ask us to do just this in order to better understand the nature of care and caring relations.

In *Caring: Gender-Sensitive Ethics*, Peta Bowden argues that understanding the myriad practices involved in caregiving and care-receiving is crucial to developing an ethics of care. For Bowden, ethics is "constitutively contextual and based in the actual experiences of actual persons: it is a continuous process of mutual responses and adjustments that recognizes the inherent relationship between the practical details of that process of mutual response and its ethical possibilities" (1997, 4). Progress in ethical thinking therefore requires an understanding of what people must do on a daily basis to live a decent life in the modern world. Bowden calls this the "ethics of everyday life" and notes that without such knowledge, "the important ethical possibilities of practices of care tend largely to be taken for granted, or left out of explicit moral consideration or assimilated to more obvious concerns. Or when they are noticed . . . these possibilities are reduced to their purely instrumental dimensions," and their moral dimensions are lost (6). Gerontologist Martha Holstein (2010) agrees with this view and urges us to turn to the life worlds of old people for the kind of knowledge that would inform an ethics of care. Holstein argues that an important aspect of moral understanding in regard to elder care involves deciding how to distribute caring responsibilities among elders, the family and the public sector. In situations of home care, especially, we can see the effects of structural dependencies and unequal power relations that directly affect the care process and the quality of life for elders and their family members (Holstein 1999).

Understanding family care is especially important because elders have always relied on their families and probably always will. Haber and Gratton (1994) remind us that only 5 percent of America's population aged 65 and over have ever lived in institutions at any one time, and this number was even less in earlier periods (116). During the Great Depression, most elders died at home, attended by unpaid caregivers. In the twenty-first century, far more elders die in nursing homes and hospitals, but family members still take care of them in the months and years before they are transferred to these institutions. In a national survey conducted in 2000, researchers found that more than 25 percent of Americans (over 50 million people, a majority of them women) had provided care for disabled family members in the previous year (President's Council on Bioethics 2005).

In the following section, I tell a story of one family—the elder Mr. Brown, his son James Brown Jr., and his son's wife Mrs. Brown—to describe the experience of family caregiving during the Great Depression. This is an unusual case among the LHMH files. The labor involved in caring for a disabled elder and the emotions evoked in the process are largely missing from the case files, primarily because most clients did not have family members to take care of them, and they were moved to care facilities when they became physically disabled. When they became mentally disabled, they were transferred to Eloise, and their cases were closed. The fact that Mr. Brown was a Scudder client helps us see the inequalities and inconsistencies in the caring process. As Martha Holstein (1999) notes, the home care of old people like Mr. Brown "illuminates the gender and class injustices that are historically endemic to American social welfare policy," because the family caregivers involved are primarily women who cannot relinquish their responsibilities easily and who do not have the resources to pay someone to help them (227).

Caring for Mr. Brown: 1929-1932

Mr. Brown, age sixty-four, had been a sailor, a woodcutter and a salesman earlier in life. When he applied for a pension in May 1929, he had recently suffered a stroke and was no longer able to work. Mr. Brown was referred to the LHMH by the secretary of the First Reformed Church of Detroit, who described him by letter as an "industrious workman and a good provider" who had experienced "domestic troubles" that led to a divorce, after which he "gave his house to his wife" and had "little or nothing left" for himself. Mr. Brown had moved in with his son and daughter-in-law, Mr. and Mrs. James Brown Jr., and their two daughters, who lived in a "middle-class" neighborhood, according to the Visitor's notes. Mr. Brown Sr. said that he felt he was "a burden" to his son and that his presence was a "hardship" on the family (LHMFC, Case #98). The LHMH granted Mr. Brown Sr. a pension of twenty-eight dollars per month from the Scudder fund.

Although Mr. Brown had seven children, only one, James Jr., was willing to take care of him. The lack of filial responsibility in this case was of some concern to Leon Frost. In June, 1930, when Mr. Brown's daughter-in-law asked for two light-weight shirts and undershirts for Mr. Brown (who was still wearing his winter underwear and flannel shirt because he had no summer clothing), the Visitor reports that Mr. Frost advised "that the entire case be more thoroughly investigated and that the six children . . . be interviewed before he will O.K. any more clothing orders."

The Visitor contacted several of Mr. Brown's children in Grand Rapids, Michigan, through the Family Service Association in that city and discovered a great deal of animosity toward Mr. Brown because he had not contributed to the support of his wife after their separation. Following an interview in August 1930 with a second son in Detroit, a laborer at the Ford Motor Co., the Visitor describes this man, too, as "rather antagonistic toward the entire situation":

> He stated that he had always contributed toward the support of his mother and had done what he could for his father . . . [He] stated that whenever he or any of the other children attempted to give [Mr. Brown Sr.] a dollar or two to help him out [the wife of James Jr.] became rather insulting and criticized them severely for not giving more. For this reason, he and the other children ceased to contribute. He rarely sees his brothers and sisters and is not fully informed regarding the economic resources of any of them, although he states that he doubts if any of them have enough money to adequately supply their own needs (LHMFC, Case #98).

The Visitor was unsuccessful in gaining any more assistance for Mr. Brown from the other children, who were all struggling themselves and doing what they could to support their mother.

Meanwhile, Mr. Brown's health continued to deteriorate, and in October 1930 he suffered another stroke. When the Visitor saw him shortly after, he was "sitting in his chair by the window with his head drooping forward and moaning." His tongue was swollen and the muscles of his throat were paralyzed, thus making swallowing almost impossible. The doctor explained that the stroke had affected "his mind and his vocal organs" and that there was little hope of recovery. After this stroke, Mr. Brown was incoherent and confined to bed most of the time. His daughter-in-law fed and cared for him, while his son helped with toileting. The Visitor arranged for a nurse from the Visiting Nurse Association to come once a week to give Mr. Brown a bath.

Within four months, Mr. Brown had lost all control of his bowels, and within eight months he was "having as many as eight involuntary bowel movements per day." Mrs. Brown Jr., who had to keep Mr. Brown clean and wash all his clothing and bedding (without benefit of an electric washer or dryer), was by then "showing signs of fatigue and nervous strain." James Jr. had himself suffered a light stroke and was forced to give up working for several weeks. The doctor informed the family that Mr. Brown might linger in his present condition for several months or pass away at any time.

In October 1931, one year after Mr. Brown Sr. became completely incapacitated, the family was struggling mightily under the stresses of long-term caregiving during the Depression. Mrs. Brown Jr. discussed the situation with the Visitor, who recorded the conversation in her case notes:

> She states that her husband makes only a few dollars a week and some weeks is unable to make any money at all. The doctor has warned her that she must not overwork in caring for [Mr. Brown] or she will not be able to continue doing so . . . . [She] has talked with the family doctor who states that the only other thing he can suggest is that [Mr. Brown] be taken to Eloise. Inasmuch as the family have cared for [Mr. Brown] constantly for the past eleven months, they do not want him to be taken there at this late date and will make any sacrifice necessary in order to keep him with them until the end which cannot be very far distant (LHMFC, Case #98).

In an effort to relieve some of the burden on Mrs. Brown Jr., the Visitor asked for and received permission from Mr. Frost to provide an additional two dollars per week to pay a laundress "insofar as the family have asked no assistance for medical attention for [Mr. Brown] and have apparently been reasonable in their demands and conscientious in the care which they have given [him]." The laundress was of great help to Mrs. Brown, but the family still struggled. The Visitor discovered that they could not afford coal for the winter and were "spending most of their time in the kitchen around a small cook stove in which they burn[ed] coal purchased one bushel at a time." In Mr. Brown's room, they used a small electric heater.

Despite the family's hardship, the following month, when the Visitor asked Mr. Frost for a four dollars petty cash order to reimburse Mrs. Brown Jr. for the laundress, he again expressed reservations about the case. The Visitor reports that she "briefly reviewed the outstanding features of [the case] and called his attention to the fact that seven dollars per week is being paid for [Mr. Brown's] care, that [his son] is without work and has suffered a slight stroke and also an attack of appendicitis recently, and that the family during all of [Mr. Brown's] illness has not called on the John Scudder Foundation for Old People for any assistance in the meeting of necessary doctor bills. In view of these facts Mr. Frost approved of the continuance of this additional allowance for laundry for [Mr. Brown]."

By this time, the family was far behind in paying bills. The rent was six months in arrears, and they had mortgaged the furniture for money to live on. Mrs. Brown Jr. told the Visitor that the family was under a great deal of "nervous strain" and that her husband was "irritable and in poor health as a result of his worry and constant care of his father." She also said that "the other brothers and sisters, although they offer no material assistance, are constantly criticizing [Mr. and Mrs. Brown Jr.] and making things unpleasant for them at every opportunity." Still, the Visitor reports that Mrs. Brown Jr. "desires to keep her father-in-law in the house as long as possible and does not want him to go to Eloise unless there seems to be no other alternative." In January 1932, James Jr. was again out of work and unable to find a job; he was very discouraged because he could not afford to buy coal to heat the house, and his wife reported that he "flies into fits of rage on the least provocation."

Mr. Brown's long-term care required considerable family sacrifice, particularly on the part of Mrs. Brown. In February 1932, the Visitor reported that a "disagreeable odor" was coming from his room, and an open sore was found discharging pus under his paralyzed arm. The arm was rigid and contracted close to his body, making it difficult to wash underneath it. A visiting nurse came to treat the sore, and Mrs. Brown was taught how to bathe and treat the sore every hour for several days.

By May of 1932, the family had not paid rent in over a year, and the landlady was threatening eviction. Mrs. Brown told the Visitor that they would have been evicted during the winter "had it not been for the fact that [Mr. Brown] was in the house bedfast." The family's only income at this time was six dollars a week brought in by one of the daughters, who now worked in a grocery store two days a week, and the seven dollars per week provided by the LHMH. Although the landlady had lowered the rent from thirty-five dollars to twenty-five dollars per month, the Browns still could not pay it. Mrs. Brown offered her twenty dollars a month, which she accepted, and the family struggled through the summer until James Jr. got a job in August driving a bread wagon.

Mr. Brown himself was becoming more difficult and demanding. His daughter-in-law reported that he was "much crosser than before" and that "when no one pays attention, he screams, but stops as soon as [she] enters the room." Still, she did not want to send him to Eloise because "she did not know what she and her husband would do without the income they were deriving from [Mr. Brown's] care. She stated that they used the money to pay their rent, light and gas bills, and that they used what little salary [John Jr.] made to supply them with food and incidentals."

However, Mrs. Brown agreed with the Visitor that Mr. Brown Sr. would not know the difference if he were moved to an institution. The Visitor therefore recommended on November 10, 1932, that the LHMH Board decide whether to rescind his pension, "thereby making it possible for the money expended for [his] care to be used for someone able to derive more benefit from it." Mr. Frost made the case immediately to the Board, which decided to withdraw from the case, continuing Mr. Brown's pension on a day-to-day basis until he could be admitted to Eloise.

Mr. Brown was admitted on November 28, 1932, and the Visitor closed the case. In her final summation, she wrote that Mr. Brown's grant was discontinued, "due to the extreme limitation of the funds of the John Scudder Foundation for Old People." There is no further word in the file about Mr. Brown's family.

Reflections on the Care of Mr. Brown

Political scientist Paul Hoggett argues that "a society which has no sense of tragedy, pain or disappointment is dangerous. Its power is based upon the denial of its relations of interdependence . . . and on a denial of limits, including those provided by nature itself" (2000, 146). Hoggett's point is that human emotion should figure prominently in the development of care policies and practices, because "emotions lie at the heart of the solidarities and divisions which make up group life" (144). Mr. Brown's story evokes feelings of sadness because it is a human tragedy. What makes it tragic is its unavoidability: completely disabled for the last two years of his life, Mr. Brown had no choice but to depend on his son, and his son's family had no choice but to care for him, unless they were willing to release him to the poor house—the ultimate shame for a son who was legally responsible for his father's care and whose family seemed to feel a moral responsibility, as well. The story is also tragic because it is so common: there were many families caring for dependent elders during the Depression, and some did so with no outside assistance at all. Yet the details and sacrifices of this caregiving were (and still are) invisible to the larger society. Even the LHMH Board did not know the financial, physical, emotional and psychological pain suffered by the Brown family during the final three years of Mr. Brown's life.

Based on our knowledge of other LHMH cases, we can guess what happened after Mr. Brown was admitted to Eloise: he died shortly thereafter, and his son's family, which had jeopardized their own welfare to care for him at home, struggled through seven more years of the Depression, their financial and emotional resources depleted. The family continued to suffer the structural disadvantages of their time (limited employment opportunities even for low-paying jobs, no family health insurance), although James Jr. may have received some unemployment benefits under Roosevelt's New Deal policies, and James's mother may have eventually received a state-supported pension (which Michigan passed in 1934), thereby relieving some of the children's responsibility for her care. However, James Brown Jr. and his wife probably struggled for the rest of their lives. James had already suffered one stroke and faced an end similar to that of his father—a disabled old age—if indeed he lived that long after years of wage work and the stresses of the Depression. Mrs. Brown likely took care of her husband in his disabled years, just as she had cared for her father-in-law, and she may well have cared for one or both of her own parents in their old age. After the age of seventy, if she lived that long, Mrs. Brown Jr. herself would have qualified for a pension from the State of Michigan, but it was not enough to live on independently. She therefore faced an end similar to that of her mother-in-law, relying on the support of her children.

The Brown case illustrates the negative consequences of a system that relies heavily on familial care yet supports the individual, rather than the network of caring relations on which the individual relies. The LHMH was very clear in stating that its pensions were for elders only and were not to be used for the support of family members (see chapter 3 for an explanation of this policy, and chapters 4 and 5 for the organization's response to pensioners' breach of it).

The allocation of LHMH resources also reflects inequities in the larger society. Formerly wealthy Hannan clients received bigger pensions than working and middle-class Scudder clients, and the amounts of these pensions were not explained or justified in the case files (or in the minutes of the Board of Trustees meetings, for that matter). There is no explanation for why Mr. Brown (or any other client) received the amount that he did; we do not know how it was determined (or who did so, although it was probably Mr. Frost) that he should receive $28 a month, especially when he had estimated during the intake interview that his monthly expenses were $164.50, presumably the cost of living independently. The LHMH did not pay for Mr. Brown's health care, even though he was disabled and in need of care, and Mr. Frost was reluctant even to pay for his clothing, reasoning that Mr. Brown's many children should have been providing these necessities. Within this individualist approach to care, the structural dependencies that affected all of the Brown siblings and their parents were not taken into account in determining Mr. Brown's pension.

For Mr. Brown to survive (not thrive) on the small amount granted, he had to rely heavily on the uncompensated care of his son and daughter-in-law. While James Brown Jr. provided shelter and food for his father, Mrs. Brown Jr. provided nursing care for over two years, with no (documented) assistance from outside the family besides the services of a laundress and an occasional visiting nurse. It was assumed that she would provide this care freely as part of her familial duties, even though Mr. Brown's care involved demanding bed and body work: feeding, toileting, bathing, and cleaning Mr. Brown's sores several times a day. It also involved meeting Mr. Brown's emotional needs, which he was unable to express other than by screaming when she left the room. Mrs. Brown performed this demanding care work in the context of a family besieged by its own financial worries and the health problems of its breadwinner, as well as the larger context of an anxious city in the throes of the Great Depression. (Recall from chapter 3 that in the summer of 1932, at the same time the Browns were facing eviction, hundreds of other evicted families were living in tents in a city park. As we know from chapter 9, Detroit and its inhabitants, as well as the nation itself, was gripped by fear.) We do not know if Mrs. Brown had friends, her own family members, or a faith community to rely on for emotional support and perhaps respite care, if not financial assistance. If she did, she would not have told the Visitor about them for fear of jeopardizing Mr. Brown's pension. We do know from the Visitor's notes that the family was under considerable "nervous strain," that tensions were high, and in times of desperation, James Jr. flew into fits of rage.

Feminist ethicists argue that the strong ethos of self-care and familism demonstrated by the Browns actually contributes to a lack of caring relations in the larger society. As Martha Holstein (1999) explains, the fear of becoming a burden is closely tied to the ideology of familism—the belief that elders should care for themselves as long as possible and then be cared for by family members. This belief has allowed American society to ignore its moral responsibilities to care for its members by arguing that elders' problems "are their own and of no concern to the rest of us" (Tronto 1999, 273). Because it is based on the assumption that living in a nuclear family is preferable to all other arrangements, familism also limits both the individual and public imaginary by discouraging elders, their family members and society in general from envisioning alternative environments that might actually provide better care. Tronto argues that much of American society has been inattentive to the needs of elders and has indulged in privileged irresponsibility by providing so few affordable options regarding old-age care. While the nuclear family norm is strongest among white, heterosexual Americans, there is more flexibility in living arrangements among African-Americans, Latinos, gays and lesbians (Tronto, 1999). In his research with people "living beyond heteronormative roles," for example, Brian deVries (2010) has found that friendship networks are taking the place of kin-networks in gay and lesbian communities by providing both old-age care and support for caregivers.

Another problem with familism is that it has historically depended on a gendered division of labor and is therefore unjust. Holstein (1999) explains that "familism, reborn in the new rhetoric of family values, not only assumes that someone—most probably the woman—not only *is* at home but *ought to be* there with enough free time to provide a full panoply of services to the person needing them" (237). Women, both elder and younger, have internalized this ideology, feeling that to seek outside help is an admission of weakness and an inability to cope. "Thus, older women simultaneously 'take comfort' in having daughters and recall their own sense of obligation to their mothers in the past, while worrying about the burden they place on these same daughters and feeling shame that they do not exemplify cultural ideals of independence and self-sufficiency" (Holstein 1999, 237). While Mr. Brown, too, expressed concern about being a burden to his son and daughter-in-law, the LHMH and Mrs. Brown following the ideology of familism, assuming that Mrs. Brown would take care of him. The LHMH pension provided food, shelter and clothing for Mr. Brown Sr., but it offered no compensation to Mrs. Brown for her caring labor. Yet she repeatedly resisted the Visitor's suggestion that she place Mr. Brown in the county poor house, because this would have been an admission of the family's (her) inability to care.

For Mr. and Mrs. Brown Jr. to take care of Mr. Brown in their home, they had to rely on assistance from many others in the community. Their landlady let them live in her house for over a year without paying rent and then accepted a reduced monthly payment so that the family would have a home. Local businesses let them buy on credit and loaned them money on their furniture so they could buy food. Periodically, the Department of Public Welfare provided coal to heat their home in the winter. They relied on doctors to make house calls and to treat Mr. Brown for little or no money as a charity case. And they relied on the local grocer to pay their teenage daughter for part-time work, using her wages to help support the family.

Eva Kittay calls these "nested dependencies" and argues that they must be placed at the center of a just and caring society in which "equality" is based on human connection, rather than individual rights and independence. A just society acknowledges that all people depend on others to survive; this dependence entitles them (as human beings) to relationships in which they can care and be cared for, along with the social support necessary to assure that caring relations do not jeopardize anyone's wellbeing. As Kittay explains, connection-based equality is premised on the moral right to have our needs met by others who are genuinely concerned about our wellbeing. It involves reciprocity, but not the exchange reciprocity expected within a framework of individual rights, where "I will care for you, if you will care for me." In a connection-based society, reciprocity is based on the expectations that arise within a chain of obligations that links many people over time. The prevailing attitude is, "I will care for you and, when the time comes, someone will be there to care for me." Within this framework, equality is based on a feeling of human connection across time (past, present and future) and a sense of shared responsibility for all others (not just family members). People who take care of others are therefore entitled to social assistance, and if they do not receive this support, they are being treated unjustly. Within this moral framework, the situation of the Brown family was socially unjust because Mr. and Mrs. Brown had to care for Mr. Brown Sr.—a fate not freely chosen—without full support of the community (in the form of respite care, for example) and without the resources to care properly for either him or themselves.

To assure that such injustices do not arise, Kittay argues that society must operate on a concept of interdependence that recognizes and respects nested dependencies. She calls this the principle of "doulia," after the Greek word for "service," and explains it as follows: "Just as we have required care to survive and thrive, so we need to provide conditions that allow others—including those who do the work of caring—to receive the care they need to survive and thrive" (107). Under this principle, reciprocity—"responsiveness to our dependence on others"—is necessary not only for equal treatment of everyone in the current society but also for justice across generations. As such, "the benefit we bestow on the next generation ought to be the benefit we would have wanted the previous generation to bestow on us" (107). Kittay sums up the ethic of care that underlies a just society: "In order to grow, flourish and survive and endure illness, disability and frailty, each individual requires a caring relationship with significant others who hold that individual's well-being as a primary responsibility and a primary good" (108). The principle of doulia is consistent with the traditional Native American ethic that Chapleski describes in chapter 10, which she explained in terms of a "caring reflex" that is "expected and welcomed" by all members of the community.

In the just society, policies, institutions and community members assist dependency workers in their caring labors; the giving and receiving of care is valued and acknowledged as a public good; and the burdens and costs of caring are shared by all "in a manner that is just to all" (Kittay, 109). In this society, caring labor is de-gendered and de-classed, and it is fully compensated. The state provides universal assistance for dependency work of all kinds—caring for the young, the disabled, the ill and the aged—as a valuable social contribution. In this way, care workers are not disadvantaged by their labors and made "unequal" as participants in the economic, social and political order. They are considered full, contributing members of society in recognition of the fact that good caring relations are the foundation on which "all other civic unions depend" (108). Universal compensation for care work includes unemployment insurance, health care benefits, vacations, "exit options" and retraining when workers' services are no longer needed (143).

The Brown family situation would have been very different if social resources had been allocated in this way and they had not been forced to rely on a charitable organization. Mr. Brown Sr. would have received disability benefits from the state when he suffered the first stroke, and he would not have had to move in with his son. Mr. Brown's ex-wife would have received an old-age pension from the state, and her children would not have had to assume the entire responsibility for supporting her. When Mr. Brown Sr. became disabled by the second stroke, the state would have paid for his long-term care, reimbursing caregivers to assist him at home or in a convalescent center. If they chose to take care of him, Mr. and Mrs. Brown Jr. would have been reimbursed with a living wage, health and unemployment benefits and would have received training in care practices. Other kinds of assistance would be available from community members, including caregivers' support groups and respite care for Mrs. Brown. Many private groups and organizations would also volunteer to help the family, providing meals, doing household chores, tutoring and mentoring the Brown children.[2] Mr. and Mrs. Brown Jr. would not have had to sacrifice their own wellbeing or that of their children to provide care for their father, and they would not have had to rely on the "benevolent dominance" of a charitable organization that could withdraw its assistance at any time.[3]

This kind of universal care would be very expensive, but citizens would help pay for it with tax dollars out of a sense of shared responsibility. Businesses would also support it in the form of paid leaves of absence for family care. In exchange for this financial support, all citizens would feel confident that, when their time came, others would take good care of them, and the community would honor and support these caregivers and their labor. Caring and connection, rather than independence, would be the highest social values. Giving and receiving care would not be a burden but an opportunity to express one's humanity and moral commitment to others. Indeed, the inability to care and be cared for would be considered a moral loss (Tronto 1999). In this system, everyone, regardless of age, gender, race, ethnicity, class, sexual orientation or religion, would enjoy the prospect of a good old age.

Imagining Otherwise: Caring in the Future

In a sermon called "Paul's Letter to American Christians" delivered in 1956, Dr. Martin Luther King observed that through scientific and technological genius, Americans have "made of this world a neighborhood," and yet we have "failed to make of it a brotherhood." This statement is even truer now than it was then. While we may be technologically connected to people around the world, we are not emotionally or ethically connected to the people in our own backyards. Dr. King's point was that ethical communities are connected by a sense of solidarity, mutual respect, and shared responsibility for the wellbeing of everyone. Elders without children, especially, have historically depended on these feelings of social responsibility, as we saw in the cases of many LHMH applicants who had been living on the kindness of landladies and rooming house mothers. But this sense of responsibility is decreasing in non-kin communities. Even in supportive communities of friends and neighbors, the care provided is unstable because participants are often old and in need of care themselves. Recent studies indicate that communal support for older adults varies depending on family situation, gender, and social class. For example, relatively poor support is available to men and women who have been continuously without a partner and are childless, and this is especially true for women over the age of seventy-five. Greater emotional and social support is available to managerial and professional groups than to working class people, particularly when the former live in middle-class neighborhoods conducive to developing informal social contacts (Gray 2009). The message of these studies is clear: people need to develop loving, long-term, intergenerational relationships that will support and sustain them in old age. Such relationships do not take the place of necessary entitlements, such as old-age pensions and health care, but function as one of the many intersecting circles of care required for a good life.

Feminists will most likely lead the reform movement to create a more caring and just society for elders, in conjunction with other groups that work on behalf of dependent people, such as disability activists, and groups which advocate sustainable living, such as ecologists and environmental activists. As Holstein (1999) points out, because the details and costs of caring labor—still considered "women's work"—are often hidden, taken for granted (even by women themselves), and obscured by their "seemingly commonplace nature" (236), feminists will have to attend to these details, inform the public and advance social change. Without feminist critique and advocacy, there will be "little incentive to examine—with intent to modify—the ideological and structural conditions that exacerbate the difficulties implicit in the caregiving experience" (Holstein, 235). Many other activists can assist feminists in advancing this agenda by extending the public understanding of care to include caring for one's friends and neighbors; becoming caring citizens of a city, state and nation; caring for the environment; caring for the planet; and caring for the future by following sustainable lifestyles that will provide a caring environment for many generations to come.

Feminists can also help us imagine a better way to live. As feminist theorist Catriona Mackenzie (2000) explains, oppressive social relationships and institutions restrict people's "imaginative repertoires," and social change depends, in part, on our ability to "imagine ourselves otherwise." Feminists can contribute to a more innovative cultural imaginary by resisting the "dominant cultural metaphors, symbols, images, and representations" that circulate in American society (125). By introducing alternative images and counter-narratives which "trump images that fail to liberate us" (Holstein 2006, 322), feminists can liberate the general public's individual and collective imaginings. Since the imagination has both "affective force and cognitive power," it can dislodge our habitual understandings, loosen the "grip of dominant imagery" and provide a strong incentive for resistance and change (Mackenzie, 143-44). In *Releasing the Imagination*, Maxine Greene confirms this view from the perspective of educational philosophy. She argues that imagination is necessary for individual development, healthy communal life and positive social change, because imagination is what makes empathy possible. Without it, we cannot envision what other people's lives were like in the past or what they will be like in the future. We cannot get beyond the ordinary and familiar days of our own lives to consider a better life for ourselves, much less anyone else.

Fortunately, feminists have already begun to imagine a better old age. They tell us that it begins long before we become old, when we are in the midst of building relationships and caring for others. Robin Fiore (1999) encourages us to "nourish relationships as we move around and work toward a future rendezvous" in later life. We must consider the building of strong relationships with like-minded others as important as the building of strong investment portfolios in our long-range retirement planning. As Fiore notes, unless we want to rely on impersonal, bureaucratically organized care, we all must begin planning early for our social, emotional and financial needs in old age.

Many agree that cooperative living arrangements are the best option for elders in the future, including very frail and disabled elders. These "mini-mutual-aid-societies" will be based on an ethical model of peer care, where peers are friends and neighbors who cooperatively provide physical assistance and moral support (Fiore); they will be integrated by age, race, gender, and socioeconomic level; and they will involve many types of family structures and living arrangements (Tronto 1999). These intentional communities, known variously as "communities of meaning," "communities of resistance," "oppositional communities" and "micro-worlds" (Holstein 2006), will be built around a sense of shared purpose and responsibility for one another, the health of the community and the environment, and the wellbeing of future generations. Residents will support each other in living sustainably, while also meeting their needs for material resources, caring, a sense of purpose and involvement, self-respect, and the respect of others. Tronto (1999) acknowledges that the diversity within such communities will engender conflicts, and Cancian and Oliker (2000) remind us that even voluntary peer care will have to be closely monitored for gender bias and inequalities (such as women doing the invisible labor of hands-on care and men doing the more visible work of fund-raising and advocacy). But these issues will likely be negotiated in good faith because of community members' desire to live the values of a feminist ethic of care. The new communities have the potential to be "fertile sites for cultivating a broader definition of citizenship—one that recognizes the social value of care" and that makes care needs and caring practices more visible and therefore more valued (Cancian and Oliker, p. 141).

Physically, the new communities may resemble the communal or co-housing pioneered in Denmark over 30 years ago: individual housing units built around communal yards, multi-person residences with shared kitchens and living areas, or condominums jointly managed by tenants who look out for each other. Whatever the arrangement, the space will convey the message of "collectively caring for ourselves" (Fiore, 258).

Holstein (1999) offers several guidelines for making such communities "exemplary" in terms of the care they provide to elders. At the very least, they must:

- value old people and promote their self worth;
- provide communal support for individual and collective care-giving;
- encourage caregivers and care receivers to state their needs without guilt or shame and with the expectation that these needs will be met;
- encourage males and females of various ages to take care of elders;
- and reinforce the relational and reciprocal aspects of care, as-sisting elders themselves in caring for others whenever possible.

Such communities will also demonstrate what Mackenzie calls a "robust" understanding of human worth—one that does not depend on a "narrow range of forms of social recognition and that is not overly invested in a narrow range of attributes, capacities, relationships, and so on" (142). People will be expected to give in whatever ways they can, and all contributions will be valued.

These new communities will function, not only for the wellbeing of their members, but also in the service of cultural transformation and policy reform. Holstein suggests, for example, that the communities sponsor public forms to discuss public and policy needs from the perspective of caregivers and care-receivers. She urges that the language of emotion, including compassion, be promoted in these forms. Such language, used to represent lived experience and a passionate advocacy, could "evoke a commitment to action by opening us to the suffering of others and accepting that our reactions to such suffering are fundamentally moral" (1999, 242). In short, the new communities will serve a larger cultural role in demonstrating for others outside the community how to put caring at the center of a moral life.

Nursing home abolitionist William Thomas believes that the baby boom generation, a "potent cultural force," is poised to create the kind of intentional communities in which elders can thrive. Thomas' optimistic word for such a community is "Eldertopia," which he defines as one that improves the quality of life for people of all ages by strengthening and improving the means by which (1) the community protects, sustains, and nurtures its elders, and (2) the elders contribute to the well-being and foresight of the community. An Eldertopia that is blessed with a large number of older people is acknowledged to be 'elder rich' and uses this human capital to the advantage of all (302).

Thomas has two main criteria for building such communities. First, they should be "warm" in terms of human connection: relatively small, non-hierarchical in organization and leadership, and rooted in the shared values of "reciprocal altruism." Second, they should be "smart" in terms of their use of technologies that foster well-being among elders and "green" in the sense that they "rest lightly upon the earth," work to heal the environment, and "honor elderhood's ancient commitment to stewardship" (221). He uses the term "cooperators" rather than "caregivers" to describe the residents of these communities of the future.

One of Thomas' most important points is that elderhood, which involves making peace, giving wisdom, and creating various types of legacies for future generations, is a relational role that exists only through active exchange across generations. Even very frail, disabled and dying elders play an important part in this exchange, showing by example how to "surmount the dizzy bustle that clings to the young—to enter a time and place in which the spiritual and emotional dimensions of human life are wholly precedent over the humdrum workings (and failings) of organs, tissues, and systems." In short, "what the old and frail do is show us the way and provide us with greater insight into and a clearer perspective on the human condition" (281). Thomas' views are consistent with those of feminist ethicists such as Sara Ruddick, who argues that some virtues, though not limited to old people, are more likely to be expressed by those who have experienced multiple losses and whose future is dwindling. Among such virtues are a concern for others, a capacity to forgive and let go, and "wise independence," which entails the acknowledgement of one's limitations and the ability to "accept help in ways that are gratifying to the helper" (1999, 51). Other virtues that Ruddick mentions are the ability to manage pain, to handle increasing disability without bitterness, to mourn, and to prepare one's self and others for death. It is important to note that all of these virtues are relational; they are ongoing efforts involving other people, rather than fixed personality traits. "Being virtuous," says Ruddick, "is something one sometimes does, not something one is" (53). In their intergenerational relations, elders can practice these virtues. In the process, others will benefit and will be moved to become more virtuous themselves.

For all of these reasons, in the imaginative communities of the future, old age will be considered an opportunity for human growth and development, and old people will be a blessing, not be a burden.

Notes

1. There were some counter-narratives, however. See Chapleski, chapter 10, on the work of Lillien Martin and Clare deGruchy, who used focus groups and interviews to learn about the beliefs and mindsets of older people. Martin herself was in her late seventies when she and deGruchy wrote *Salvaging Old Age*, which offers a psychological approach based on mental hygiene to rescuing elders from the "scrap heap" of society. They published a sequel to this book called *Sweeping the Cobwebs* (1933) that provides specific guidelines for the rehabilitation of elders.

2. Abel and Nelson (1991) call these "circles of care" and encourage us to see them as intersecting with, rather than independent of, more formal sources of care (such as convalescent homes).

3. See Sevenhuijsen (1998, 2003) for a fuller discussion of citizenship and the implications for social policy under a feminist ethics of care. See also Bowden's (1997) final chapter in *Caring: Gender-Sensitive Ethics.*

References

Abel, Emily K. 1991. *Who Cares for the Elderly? Public Policy and the Experience of Adult Daughters*. Philadelphia: Temple University Press.

Abel, Emily K. and Margaret K. Nelson, eds. 1991. "Circles of Care: An Introductory Essay." Pp. 4-34 in *Circles of Care: Work and Identity in Women's Lives*, edited by Emily K. Abel and Margaret K. Nelson. New York: State University of New York Press

Board of Trustees. 1930. *The Luella Hannan Memorial Home: A Living Remembrance of William W. and Luella Hannan*. Detroit, Michigan: Luella Hannan Memorial Home.

Bowden, Peta. 1997. *Caring: Gender-Sensitive Ethics*. London: Routledge.

Bower, Helen C. 1930. "239 Live in Comfort under Hannan Will: Clients are Those Who Have Been Accustomed to Higher Standards." *Detroit Free Press*, January 25, Sunday section.

Cancian, Francesca M. and Stacey J. Oliker. 2000. *Caring and Gender*. Walnut Creek, CA: AltaMira Press.

De Vries, Brian. 2010. "The Value and Meaning of Friendship in Later Life." Pp. 141-62 in *A Guide to Humanistic Studies in Aging*, edited by Thomas R. Cole, Ruth E. Ray and Robert Kastenbaum. Baltimore: Johns Hopkins University Press.

Fiore, Robin N. 1999. "Caring for Ourselves: Peer Care in Autonomous Aging." Pp. 245-60 in *Mother Time: Women, Aging, and Ethics*, edited by Margaret Urban Walker. Lanham, MD: Rowman and Littlefield.

Fisher, Berenice and Joan Tronto. 1991. "Toward a Feminist Theory of Caring." Pp. 25-62 in *Circles of Care: Work and Identity in Women's Lives*, edited by Emily K. Abel and Margaret K. Nelson. New York: State University of New York Press.

Gray, Anne. 2009. "The Social Capital of Older People." *Ageing & Society* 29: 5-31.

Greene, Maxine. 1995. *Releasing the Imagination: Essays on Education, the Arts, and Social Change*. San Francisco: Jossey-Bass.

Haber, Carol and Brian Gratton. 1994. *Old Age and the Search for Security: an American Social History*. Bloomington, IN: Indiana University Press.

Held, Virginia. 2006. *The Ethics of Care: Personal, Political and Global*. New York: Oxford University Press.

Hoggett, Paul. 2000. "Social Policy and the Emotions." Pp. 141-55 in *Rethinking Social Policy*, edited by Gail Lewis, Sharon Gewirtz and John Clarke. London: Sage.

Holstein, Martha. 1999. "Home Care, Women, and Aging: A Case Study of Injustice." Pp. 227-44 in *Mother Time: Women, Aging, and Ethics*, edited by Margaret Urban Walker. Lanham, MD: Rowman and Littlefield.

Holstein, Martha. 2006. "On Being an Aging Woman." Pp. 313-34 in *Age Matters: Realigning Feminist Thinking*, edited by Toni M. Calasanti and Kathleen F. Slevin. New York: Routledge.

Holstein, Martha. 2010. "Ethics and Aging: Retrospectively and Prospectively." Pp. 244-68 in *A Guide to Humanistic Studies in Aging*, edited by Thomas R. Cole, Ruth E. Ray and Robert Kastenbaum. Baltimore, MD: Johns Hopkins University Press.

Kittay, Eva. 1999. *Love's Labor: Essays on Women, Equality, and Dependency*. New York: Routledge.

Mackenzie, Catriona. 2000. "Imaging Oneself Otherwise." Pp. 124-50 in *Relational Autonomy: Feminist Perspectives on Autonomy, Agency and the Social Self*, edited by Catriona Mackenzie and Natalie Stoljar. New York: Oxford University Press.

President's Council on Bioethics. 2005. *Taking Care: Ethical Caregiving in Our Aging Society*. Washington, D.C.: President's Council on Bioethics.

Ruddick, Sara. 1999. "Virtues and Age." Pp. 45-60 in *Mother Time: Women, Aging, and Ethics*. Lanham, MD: Rowman and Littlefield.

Sevenhuijsen, Selma. 1998. *Citizenship and the Ethics of Care*. London: Routledge.

Sevenhuijsen, Selma. 2003. "The Place of Care: The Relevance of the Feminist Ethic of Care for Social Policy." *Feminist Theory* 4: 179-197.

Shakespeare, Tom. 2000. "The Social Relations of Care." Pp. 52-65 in *Rethinking Social Policy*, edited by Gail Lewis, Sharon Gewirtz and John Clarke. London: Sage.

Thomas, William H. 2004. *What are Old People for? How Elders Will Save the World*. Acton, Mass: VanderWyk and Burnham.

Tronto, Joan. 1993. *Moral Boundaries: A Political Argument for an Ethic of Care*. New York: Routledge.

Tronto, Joan. 1999. "Age-Segregated Housing as a Moral Problem: An Exercise in Rethinking Ethics." Pp. 261-77 in *Mother Time: Women, Aging, and Ethics*, edited by Margaret Urban Walker. Lanham, MD: Rowman and Littlefield.

Walker, Margaret Urban. 1998. *Moral understandings: A feminist study in ethics*. New York: Oxford University Press.

Afterword

From Charity to Care

Ruth E. Ray

The Luella Hannan Memorial Home (LHMH), which later became the Luella Hannan Memorial Foundation, still exists, although it has changed dramatically over the past eighty years in response to changes in American society and the City of Detroit. Once a charity that offered "limited benevolence" to "worthy" elders, the Foundation now works to enact the values of a broader caring community, assisting a diverse population of older adults in metropolitan Detroit, with particular emphasis on those living in the urban center.

In 1935, due to severe losses in investment income sustained during the Great Depression, the LHMH petitioned the Wayne County Circuit Court for permission to use some of the principle of the Hannan trust to support its pensioners. It was granted this request on the condition that it not accept any more clients until the principle was restored. The LHMH therefore closed its rolls to new clients until 1946, at which time it brought a friendly suit in Chancery Court seeking approval to continue caring for old people in their homes.

The LHMH continued in this way until 1963, when the Attorney General of the State of Michigan, under a recently enacted statue, brought suit against the organization to require construction of a home in compliance with the original intention of the Hannan trust. Although the Board of Trustees argued that elders were better cared for in the community, they were not successful in this petition. The 1946 Chancery Court decision was overturned, and the LHMH was directed to build and operate a home. Consequently, a four-story brick facility called Hannan House was constructed on Woodward Ave. in Detroit, just around the corner from the original LHMH offices at 51 W. Warren. Licensed to accommodate forty-nine residents, Hannan House opened in 1971. This particular site had been selected because of its proximity to Wayne State

University, which proposed to construct a research facility for its Institute of Gerontology on the top floor of the Home (although it never generated enough funds to do so). Also in 1971, the John Scudder Foundation for Old People officially merged with the LHMH. Its funds were kept in a separate account, however, to continue assisting elders in the community through small grants. Today, the Scudder fund assists elders in paying for utility bills, rent, moving expenses, home repairs, and other emergency expenses.

The Hannan House provided residential care until 1993, when, in response to declining occupancy, the Board of Trustees conducted a needs assessment of Detroit's older population. By that time, there were many federally subsidized housing projects in the central city of Detroit, and the Board determined that its old-age home was no longer viable. Through the needs assessment, however, the Board discovered that what elders in the area did need was better knowledge of and access to social services. It therefore decided to convert its forty-five thousand square foot facility to a "multi-tenant nonprofit center." Both the Wayne County Circuit Court and the Michigan Attorney General agreed to this proposal. At that time, the LHMH changed its name to the Luella Hannan Memorial Foundation.

In 2010, the offices of the Hannan Foundation are located in the Hannan House, along with fourteen other non-profit organizations, some of which provide direct services to older adults, including Citizens for Better Care, Operation ABLE of Michigan, and a local office of the American Association of Retired People (AARP), while others, such as Detroiters Working for Environmental Justice and the Center for Community Justice and Advocacy, work to enhance the quality of life for people of all ages. In collaboration with its partners, the Hannan Foundation pursues its mission of "identifying the physical, social and financial unmet needs of senior citizens and maintaining facilities and creating programs that address these needs and preserve their dignity." The Foundation sponsors additional services at the Hannan House, including the University of Detroit Mercy urban law clinic, the MiCafe program to assist seniors in applying for food assistance, and Alzheimer's caregivers' and Parkinson's Disease support groups. Although it no longer provides long-term care, the Foundation collaborates with Presbyterian Village of Michigan, which has experimented with William Thomas' green house concept, to provide assessment and referral services, as well as educational programming, for tenants in residential facilities in Detroit. The Foundation also operates three of its own programs at the Hannan House: the Center for Senior Learning, which provides classes for a nominal fee; the Zena Baum Service Center, which provides direct assistance to seniors through Scudder grants and consultation; and the Ellen Kayrod Gallery, which sponsors art classes and exhibits featuring senior artists.

To oversee these diverse operations, the Board of Trustees has become larger and more diverse, as well. Originally three white professional men who met for many years at the all-male Detroit Club, the Board now consists of twelve ethnically diverse men and women who are professionals in the areas of social work, nursing home administration, senior services, public policy, gerontology, medicine, law, and education. Besides their service on specific committees, most of the Trustees interact directly with elders at the Hannan House through educational programs, special events, and volunteer services.

An Executive Director, three generations removed from Leon Frost, oversees the daily operations of the Foundation with the assistance of three full-time geriatric social workers and a large support staff. In accordance with changing ideas about what constitutes quality care and a good old age, the Foundation operates quite differently from the way it did in 1929, with senior representatives on many committees, focus groups to determine clients' needs and interests, and senior-directed programs and activities. The Foundation emphasizes the civic contributions of seniors through a podcast series featuring elder "Voices of Detroit" and an online archival project with the Wayne State University Honors College called "Living Detroit: Capturing Detroit's History Through Intergenerational Relations."

The dramatic social and economic changes that the City of Detroit has undergone over the past eighty years have required that the LHMH change with the times in order to survive and grow. Its conversion from a residential home to a multi-tenant service center required a major philosophical shift on the part of the Board of Trustees, which had to reimagine for the twenty-first century Luella Hannan's early twentieth century mission to help older people live a better life. As a result, the LHMH was repurposed, and the Hannan House became an example of adaptive reuse for the 1990s and beyond. The Hannan Foundation now has a much broader reach and a potentially greater impact. Between 1929 and 1993, for example, the Foundation served approximately one thousand select clients; it now serves hundreds of Detroit area seniors in a single year. Its current advocacy projects include participating in a Senior Mobility Outreach program to promote better transportation systems in metro Detroit; partnering with Wayne State University's Research and Technology Park to develop a program called "Booming Economy" that assists midlife and older adults in becoming entrepreneurs; and collaborating with the non-profit Corporation for a Skilled Workforce to engage older adults in work and learning opportunities that will help transform the region's economic and social infrastructure.

My participation on the Board of Trustees was one of the driving forces behind this book. In 2005, I learned from Executive Director Timothy Wintermute about the boxes of old case files located in a closet at the Foundation offices, and in 2007, I assisted in transferring these files to the Walter Reuther Library of Labor and Urban Affairs. I also participated in the Trustees' deliberations about making the case files public. We ultimately decided that supporting principled research and advocacy on behalf of older adults today served a greater good than keeping the files private. Mr. Wintermute had been a long-time advocate of scholarly research, recognizing the contemporary as well as historical significance of the Hannan files and encouraging other scholars over the years to study them. He has encouraged and supported the Hannan Archival Research Group in all of our efforts and has shared newspaper clippings, employee records, and the corporate minutes of the Board of Trustees from its inception in 1925. He also made arrangements for Trustee Ruth Dunkle and me to interview Ellen Kayrod, who worked with Anna Wentink and succeeded her as Executive Director, and Margaret Potter, who was secretary for the LHMH for fifty years and knew many of the clients personally. With our book project in mind, Mr. Wintermute recently referred me to the biography of Tracy McGregor, Detroit philanthropist who developed his own charitable fund in 1925, the same year that Luella Hannan established her trust. From this book, I got a better feel for Progressive Era philanthropy and its Christian roots, as well as a better understanding of the political and economic challenges that Detroit charities faced during the Great Depression.

My historical research and my role on the Hannan Board of Trustees have alerted me to the absolute necessity of creating more liveable communities for elders, not just in the city of Detroit but throughout the United States. The Hannan Foundation recognizes the need to advocate for better living conditions and regularly participates in creative problem solving and community-building. In the winter semester of 2007, for example, Hannan social worker Rachel Hewitt and I team-taught a college course that put senior citizens and WSU students in conversation around the theme of making midtown Detroit a "community for all ages." The course involved guest speakers, brainstorming sessions, and projects that addressed issues such as walkability, safety and security, housing and transportation, access to health care, civic participation, commerce, entertainment, and "vital" living. The course ended with a town meeting in which we presented our findings and suggestions to an audience of college students, social service providers, senior citizens, and other interested community members.

Enacting real change in neighborhoods and communities, however, is a slow, complicated, and difficult process that requires constant attention and advocacy. My co-editor Toni Calasanti and I both feel the need to help create better communities that will support others and ourselves in old age. Though our midlife situations are different (she is married with grown children, and I am divorced and childless), we have both experienced the struggles of our elderly parents and feel insecure ourselves when contemplating our later years. This book, therefore, reflects not just the pursuit of academic knowledge but a personal quest on behalf of our generation and future generations. There are thousands of other baby boomers that will soon be looking for sustainable, caring places in which to grow old. We all must participate in building the imaginative, change-oriented communities that will bestow on future generations of elders "the benefit we would have wanted the previous generation to bestow on us" (Kittay 1999, 107).

For Toni Calasanti and me, editing this book has been an act of caring. It is an expression of our concern and our feelings of obligation to create a better old age for ourselves and others. We hope that our efforts have made readers, too, care more deeply about the future of old age.

References

Kittay, Eva Feder. 1999. *Love's Labor: Essays on Women, Equality, and Dependency*. New York: Routledge.

Index

About the Contributors

Chasity Bailey-Fakhoury is a PhD candidate in the Sociology Department at Wayne State University. Her research interests include racial socialization and racial identity development, aging and minority populations, and race/class/gender issues. Currently she is conducting research on the strategies used by suburban African-American mothers to promote a positive racial identity in their young daughters attending predominantly white schools.

Sherylyn Briller is Associate Professor of Anthropology at Wayne State University. As a medical anthropologist, she specializes in the anthropology of aging and end-of-life issues. She has a longstanding interest in cross-cultural gerontology and has examined old age support in the United States and Mongolia. Her research interests include studying what is considered a "good old age" and sensitive and humane end-of-life care in different contexts.

Toni Calasanti, PhD, is a professor of Sociology at Virginia Tech, where she is also a faculty affiliate of both the Center for Gerontology and Women's and Gender Studies. Chosen as the 2008-09 Petersen Visiting Scholar in Gerontology and Family Studies, Oregon State University, she is co-author of *Gender, Social Inequalities, and Aging* and co-editor of *Age Matters: Re-Aligning Feminist Thinking* (both with Kathleen Slevin), and has published in such journals as *Journal of Gerontology: Social Sciences; The Gerontologist; Social Forces; Journal of Aging Studies;* and *Men and Masculinities.* Her recent work focuses on age and gender in relation to spousal carework; aging bodies and the anti-aging industry; middle-aged bodies and doing age.

Elizabeth Edson Chapleski is a graduate of the joint doctoral program in social work and sociology at the University of Michigan-Ann Arbor. She is a retired Associate Professor of Research from the Institute of Gerontology, Wayne State University. Her research has focused on minority elders, specifically older American Indians of the Great Lakes region. She has conducted needs assessments of Michigan's Native American population for the Michigan Department of Public Health (1992) and the Office of Services to the Aging (1989), as well as a four-year Long-Term-Care Study funded by the National Institute on Aging, from 1993-1997. Currently she is working part-time as grant writer and evaluator for the Circles of Care planning project at American Indian Health and Family Services of Southeast Michigan, *Minobaadziwin.*

Shu-hui Sophy Cheng received her PhD from Wayne State University in 2009. She is currently Assistant Professor in the Department of Communication Arts at Chaoyang University Technology in Taiwan. She teaches courses in public relations, and the effects of media on society. Her research interest lies at the intersection of media, communication and aging issues. She focuses on topics such as media portrayals of aging, and health communication in old age.

Heather E. Dillaway is Associate Professor and Director of Graduate Studies in the Sociology Department at Wayne State University. Her research interests lie within the area of women's health and structural inequalities (age, gender, race, class, and sexuality). Her current research projects focus on how women's experiences of menopause, midlife, and aging are shaped by their social locations and contemporary social contexts.

Mary E. Durocher is a PhD candidate and teaches in the Anthropology Department at Wayne State University. Her research interests lie at the intersection of material culture and religious belief systems. She has done fieldwork among the Adja Fon and Yoruba in Benin, West Africa and among practitioners of Santería in Cuba. Her current research focuses on the use of material culture—mainly home altars—among *Mexicano* people in San Antonio, Texas.

Jill Harrison, PhD, is a Post-Doctoral Fellow funded by a National Research Service Award from the National Institutes of Health. Her fellowship is at Brown University's Center for Gerontology and Health Care Research where she works as project director on a study of social networks and advance care planning of women with recurrent cancer. She is currently principal investigator of a cross-national study of social networks, health, and leisure activities among older adults in the United States and Finland. Her other research interests include sociology of culture. She recently co-authored a manuscript on musical tastes and ageing in *Ageing & Society.*

Faith Hopp received her PhD in Sociology and Social Work from The University of Michigan in 1997. Her research focuses on chronic disease and end of life issues among older adults. She is on the faculty at the Wayne State University School of Social Work, serves as the coordinator of the Graduate Certificate in Gerontology at Wayne State Univesity, and is a John A. Hartford Geriatric Social Work Faculty Scholar.

Thomas B. Jankowski is Associate Director for Research at the Institute of Gerontology and the Merrill Palmer Skillman Institute and adjunct assistant professor of gerontology and political science at Wayne State University, where he teaches courses on the public policy of aging and the aged. His research has been published in *The Gerontologist, Journal of Politics, Social Science Quarterly, Political Behavior*, and the *Journal of Aging, Humanities, and the Arts*. He currently directs "Seniors Count!," a funded project to gather, analyze, and publish data on the socioeconomic and health status of the older adult population in metro Detroit.

Janet L. Langlois received her PhD in Folklore Studies from Indiana University and is currently an Associate Professor in the English Department at Wayne State University. Her research interests and publications focus on narrative, especially urban legend, rumor and personal experience narrative analyzed in context. Her current project, "Other Worlds," is an ethnographic study of mystical experiences narrated in hospice and other health-related contexts.

Donyale R. Griffin Padgett holds a PhD in rhetoric and intercultural communication from Howard University and is Assistant Professor in the Department of Communication at Wayne State University in Detroit. Her primary research is concerned with the social dynamics that influence contemporary crisis discourse. She focuses on how people on the margins negotiate within mainstream contexts.

Ruth E. Ray received her Doctor of Arts degree from the University of Michigan and is Professor of English and faculty associate in gerontology at Wayne State University. She has written many articles, chapters and books on feminist gerontology, narrative gerontology and gender and aging, including *Beyond Nostalgia: Aging and Life Story Writing* (2000) and *Endnotes: An Intimate Look at the End of Life* (2008). She is co-editor with Thomas R. Cole and Robert Kastenbaum of the *Handbook of the Humanities and Aging* (2nd ed.) and *A Guide to Humanistic Studies in Aging*.

Nancy Thornton was formerly a PhD student in the School of Social Work at Wayne State University with research interests in elder care and the feminist ethics of care. Prior to her graduate studies at WSU, she was a practicing social worker.